READINGS IN
FAMILY THERAPY

Readings in
FAMILY THERAPY
FROM THEORY TO PRACTICE

JANICE M. RASHEED
Loyola University Chicago

MIKAL N. RASHEED
Chicago State University

JAMES A. MARLEY
Loyola University Chicago

Los Angeles | London | New Delhi
Singapore | Washington DC

For information:

SAGE Publications, Inc.
2455 Teller Road
Thousand Oaks,
   California 91320
E-mail: order@sagepub.com

SAGE Publications India Pvt. Ltd.
B 1/I 1 Mohan Cooperative
   Industrial Area
Mathura Road, New Delhi 110 044
India

SAGE Publications Ltd.
1 Oliver's Yard
55 City Road
London EC1Y 1SP
United Kingdom

SAGE Publications Asia-Pacific Pte. Ltd.
33 Pekin Street #02-01
Far East Square
Singapore 048763

Printed in the United States of America

Library of Congress Cataloging-in-Publication Data

Readings in family therapy: from theory to practice/edited by Janice M. Rasheed, Mikal N. Rasheed, and James A. Marley.
   p. cm.
Includes bibliographical references.
ISBN 978-1-4129-0584-8 (pbk. : acid-free paper)
   1. Family psychotherapy. I. Rasheed, Janice M. (Janice Matthews)
II. Rasheed, Mikal N. (Mikal Nazir) III. Marley, James A.

RC488.5.R39 2010
616.89´156—dc22   2009028027

This book is printed on acid-free paper.

09   10   11   12   13   10   9   8   7   6   5   4   3   2   1

Acquisitions Editor:	Kassie Graves
Editorial Assistant:	Veronica K. Novak
Production Editor:	Carla Freeman
Typesetter:	C&M Digitals (P) Ltd.
Proofreader:	Scott Oney
Cover Designer:	Gail Buschman
Marketing Manager:	Stephanie Adams

Contents

Introduction to the Reader

As instructors of family therapy, one of the major challenges in developing a family therapy course is the need to select auxiliary material that goes beyond the scope of basic textbooks on the subject. This task is a difficult one, in that an increasing wealth of literature has become available in the field. We have responded to this important task in *Readings in Family Therapy: From Theory to Practice*, providing full text articles that illuminate a depth of understanding of family therapy models and related issues.

In the accompanying textbook, *Family Therapy: Models and Techniques*, we have sought to write a volume on family therapy that covers the major models in a comprehensive way—presenting key issues, concepts, theories, and techniques. In addition, our text provides background and important clinical issues central to conducting family therapy. However comprehensive, there is always the need for further elaboration and exploration of content; accordingly, we have included articles in the reader that meet this need. We now discuss each of these articles and how they complement the textbook chapters, and recommend ways to put them to use.

In the first article, "Karl Tomm: His Changing Views on Family Therapy Over 35 Years," Don Collins and Karl Tomm (2009) discuss changing views on family therapy. Tomm is an internationally known family therapist and is well versed in the historical and conceptual influences in the proliferation of the field. This article is actually an interview with Tomm conducted by Don Collins (a social work and family therapy professor at the University of Calgary, in Alberta, Canada). It traces Tomm's 35 years of professional experience and the progression of his conceptual and theoretical orientation in the practice of family therapy. His development as a family therapist parallels the conceptual and theoretical evolution of the field itself, going back to the period in which family therapy emerged as a separate domain of practice. Chapter 1 in our textbook reviews "The History of Family Therapy," and this first article of the reader provides an illustration of the temporal impact on the professional/clinical development of a contemporary family therapist. We hope it will assist readers in deepening their understanding of the historical, conceptual, and theoretical evolution of family therapy as a field of practice.

Chapter 2 in the textbook, "The Ecology of Families," examines the life cycle of the family within the social, economic, and political systems context. The second article in the reader, "Living Arrangements Over the Life Course: Families in the 21st Century," by Regina M. Bures (2009), emphasizes the importance of viewing the family from an ecological life cycle conceptual framework. Families change over time as a result of ecological influences in terms of structure and function. This article examines how ongoing environmental changes impact family structures and roles. Specifically, it provides a discussion on how changes in the contemporary living arrangements of families (e.g., mutigenerational families, divorced and single-parent families, and migrating families) impact family roles and how these roles are shaped by social and cultural factors. Bures discusses the development of specific contemporary family structures and the importance of anticipating the service needs for these families over the life course. Family therapists must assess the "goodness of fit" between the needs and resources of diverse families and the supports offered by their environment. This article emphasizes the importance of anticipating the service needs of diverse family structures over the life course of the family.

Chapter 3 in the textbook, "Ethnicity and Family Life," presents a discussion of culture, race, and ethnicity; how these concepts are defined; and the complexity involved in understanding their part in family characteristics. The cultural backgrounds of families influence any number of important family aspects, including their values, worldviews, family structure, and behavior. The reader article "Understanding Culture and Worldview in Family Systems: Use of the Multicultural Genogram," by Anita Jones Thomas (1998), presents a tool—the multicultural genogram—that assists family therapists in the application of cross-cultural knowledge to clinical practice with families. This tool aids family therapists in examining multigenerational patterns, significant life events, rituals, roles, and family relationships, and generally provides a direction for therapy. Clinical case examples featuring the multicultural genogram illustrate how concepts of race, ethnicity, immigration/acculturation, social class, gender, spirituality/religion, and gender can give guidance to family therapy.

In Chapter 4 of the textbook, "Communications/Humanistic Family Therapy," we present the communication/humanistic family therapy model as articulated by Virginia Satir. This model includes concepts of the influence of the family of origin, families as systems, low self-esteem/self-worth, resources of the whole person, and the person and beliefs of the therapist—all of which formulate the foundation of Satir's therapy approach. At the core of this model of family therapy is the emphasis on the inherent growth potential of the individual, helping people to gain a sense of their wholeness, and a commitment of individual awareness, expression, and self-fulfillment. Central to these principles is Satir's belief that one of the most important functions of the family is the enhancement and facilitation of family members' sense of self-esteem and self-worth.

In the associated reader article, "Maslow Revisited: Constructing a Road Map of Human Nature," Dennis O'Connor and Leodones Yballe (2007) examine Maslow's concepts and philosophy of human nature (i.e., self-awareness and personal growth), which are also articulated in Satir's model of family therapy. The article provides a detailed discussion of Maslow's study of behaviors that lead to internal growth in "self-actualizing." Maslow and Satir share an interest in humanistic psychology relating to the holistic picture of human nature and the resources of the whole person. This article will deepen the reader's understanding and appreciation for Satir's humanistic approach—the individual's potential for growth—in work with families through the implementation of communication/humanistic family therapy.

In her article, "Family-of-Origin Work for Counseling Trainees and Practitioners," Connie M. Kane (1995) explores an important issue discussed in Chapter 5 of the textbook, "Family-of-Origin Family Therapy": the therapist's awareness and understanding of the impact of his or her own family history on the practice of therapy with others. Kane contends that regardless of one's level of self-discipline, training to address one's own family-of-origin issues is uneven at best, and is certainly an ethical dilemma that needs to be addressed. A family therapist's personal reaction to the characteristics of a family being counseled (e.g., style of communication, developmental issues, structure, culture) can present obstacles to objective and effective family therapy. Furthermore, Kane emphasizes the need for more uniform training, since countertransference is an issue for all family therapists— every therapist is part of a family. Transference and countertransference are largely unconscious processes, and therapists typically need to make a special effort to become aware of this interactional process so as not to bring elements of past relationships into others' therapy. This may be a particularly challenging issue in work with families, in that there are simply more people present in session with which to build therapeutic relationships. Kane also points to the added dimension of transference and countertransference of the supervisor—who potentially adds to the process the projection of his or her own issues while training other family therapists. She makes suggestions for various formats and approaches in training to address family-of-origin issues for student trainees, the beginning family therapist, and more advanced therapists in private practice.

Chapter 6 of the textbook presents the *structural family therapy model* (SFT). Minuchin believes that a family's transactional pattern must change and that change cannot take place unless there is underlying change in the family organization or structure. Within this transition, parents must be in charge, in what Minuchin terms the *executive role* or function. The role of the therapist is certainly pivotal to this process; however, he or she does not assume responsibility for change. Rather, the therapist merely *facilitates* change in the family structure, acting as "director." In the related article in the reader, Ryan T. Hammond and Michael P. Nichols (2008) explore the question "How collaborative is structural family therapy?" They assess what makes the style of the therapist collaborative versus aggressive, confrontational, and impositional. This is an important distinction, because the SFT therapist takes on a much more active role in the family interview compared with therapists in other major models (e.g., Bowenian family therapy and Satir's communication/humanistic family therapy). This is often a concern of family therapy trainees, who may be hesitant to take on such involved functions: the roles of *describer* of dysfunctional sequences, *director* of family drama, *expert* in communicating the gravity of the problem, and *educator* providing simple educational instructions. This article serves an important function in helping to explain the therapist's role, and confirming that the SFT therapist does show empathy and that it is an essential part of establishing a collaborative relationship in this mode of family therapy.

Chapter 7 of the textbook describes the *strategic family therapy approach* and the three major related approaches to family therapy: the Mental Health Research Institute interaction model; the strategic model developed by Haley and Madanes; and the model put forth by a group of family therapists in Milan, led by Mara Selvini-Palazzoli. These three approaches view problems as arising from the family's interactional sequences. The family is conceptualized as a "self-regulating system which controls itself and forms rules over a period of time through a process of trial and error" (Selvini-Palazzoli, Boscolo, Cecchin, & Prata, 1978, p. 3). The goal of the strategic therapist is to disrupt dysfunctional family sequences and the ongoing power struggle so as to restore proper authority to the parents and create a clear and stable boundary between parents and their children. In the reader, "For Parents Only: A Strategic Family Therapy Approach in School Counseling," by Judith A. Nelson (2006), describes a strategic family therapy technique based on what Selvini-Palazzoli called the *invariant prescription,* which the Milan group assigned to every family they treated. The article describes the application of this technique by a professional school counselor in a school setting. Nelson's motivation for encouraging this approach is born out of the circumstances of many parents who are frustrated by experiencing chaotic interactions at home with their children but do not have access to counseling/therapy resources. Nelson found that these brief, therapeutic interventions have proven effective and efficient, in that they are time-sensitive and oriented to the present. A case example is given that illustrates the application of this kind of intervention and how it can offer solutions to help parents strengthen their alliances with each other and promote effective ways of managing their children.

The *solution-focused family therapy* approach developed by Steve de Shazer and Insoo Kim Berg and associates is outlined in Chapter 8 of the textbook. The major tenet of this model is that it is a strengths-based approach to family therapy, with theoretical underpinnings in cognitive and behavioral theories. Solution-focused therapy amplifies exceptions to problems—by demonstrating to the family situations in which they have created solutions to the presenting problem—and thus reinforces effective coping behaviors that clients already possess. Solution-focused therapists emphasize collaboration with family members in the construction of solution-oriented possibilities, putting their existing "tools" to use. The effectiveness of the solution-focused family therapy approach is explored in two articles selected for the reader: "The Effectiveness of Solution-Focused Therapy With Children in a School Setting," by Cynthia Franklin, Joan Biever, Kelly Moore, David Clemons, and Monica Scamardo (2001), and "A Helping Hand: Solution-Focused Brief Therapy and Child and Adolescent Mental Health," by John Wheeler (2001). This approach is under such scrutiny in part due to its claim of effectiveness within a short period of time, as well as skepticism toward its techniques—which some feel are formulaic and forced, and question the genuineness of its claim of collaboration. While neither article is conclusive, results do show that the solution-focused family therapy approach is promising but that more research is needed to explore its effectiveness and/or usefulness with an array of problems in diverse settings.

Cognitive-behavioral family therapy (CBFT), described in Chapter 9 of the textbook, is growing in popularity and is beginning to be increasingly embraced by family therapists, as it emphasizes the importance of both cognitive and behavioral traits of family members. The hallmark of this approach is rigorous data-based monitoring of its procedures and a focus on its effectiveness. The article selected for the reader, "The Case of Molly L.: Use of a Family Cognitive-Behavioral Treatment for Childhood Anxiety," by Amy Krain, Jennifer L. Hudson, Meredith Coles, and Philip Kendall (2002), is an extensive case study (not an empirical research study) of the use of family CBFT for childhood anxiety. Literature on CBFT typically is void of clinical case material. To this end, the article describes in great detail not only the procedures used but also the clinical process and issues that arose in the case. The article is also unique in that, based on the featured case study, the authors encourage family therapists to apply therapy manuals in a flexible, rather than mechanical manner—taking time to address issues not directly related to the goals of a particular session. This maneuver may have an overall impact of creating a more positive therapeutic relationship, which may then facilitate therapy goals.

Chapter 10 of the textbook, "Narrative Family Therapy" (NFT), describes a relatively new therapy approach that is still in the early stages of development. This approach is a natural evolution of several family therapy approaches and has generated a great deal of excitement. NFT is quite appealing in its philosophical principles, which emphasize empowerment of the client and cocreating solutions that help clients challenge debilitating self-narratives. However intriguing, many issues need to be considered in this developing family therapy approach. The articles selected for the reader explore two of those issues, ethics and research.

In the first article, "Ethics of Family Narrative Therapy" (2009), Christopher Peyton Miller and Alan W. Forrest explore ethical issues that can be unique to therapy with families. In NFT, there are two types of narratives: the narrative of the family as a whole and the narrative of each individual member. In exploring these narratives, the therapist must be careful not to marginalize or negate the narrative of individuals within the family, especially when they are somehow in conflict with the family narrative. The article explores this kind of ethical dilemma, which is germane to the process of NFT. The second article, "Review of Narrative Therapy: Research and Utility," by Mary Etchison and David M. Kleist (2000), highlights the issue that in light of the growing popularity of this approach, there is limited research on the narrative process. In fact, most of the research on NFT is anecdotal. This article discusses available studies, possible reasons for the scarcity of research on the usefulness of NFT, and implications for practitioners.

Understanding the practical aspects of any form of therapy is an important part of the therapy process. Clinical issues are considered to be another layer of practice in psychotherapy. Chapter 11 of the textbook, "Phases of Family Therapy," outlines important clinical skills that the family therapist must possess. Major models of family therapy largely focus on theory and technique, while paying minimum attention to general clinical issues involved in family practice. Some of these skills are unique to therapy with couples and families, and others go beyond this modality. In the reader article "Basic Principles of Intervention," Mark S. Carich and Karen Spilman (2004) provide 12 basic principles of intervention, which can also facilitate family therapy: respect, rapport, joining, compassion, cooperation, flexibility, utilization principle, safety principle, generative change, metaphoric principle, goal orientation, and multi level communication principle. These can be applied in conjunction with a vast array of techniques derived from various models of family therapy.

Chapter 12 in the textbook, "Families in Transition: Alternative Family Patterns," addresses the complexities of family life—especially in light of diverse family structures in contemporary society (e.g., divorced families, single-parent families, stepfamilies, blended families, extended families, and augmented families), which may include kin as well as non-kin relationships. This chapter also examines the transitions that families make within the family life cycle. The articles selected for the reader reflect important clinical issues facing today's family therapists. The first, "Parental Divorce and Family Functioning: Effects on Differentiation Levels of Young Adults," by Patrick Johnson, Jill M. Thorngren, and Adina J. Smith (2001), explores the impact of divorce on young adults. The second article, "Counseling Gay and Lesbian Families: Theoretical Considerations," by Jennifer L. Adams, Jodi D. Jaques, and Kathleen M. May (2004), presents a discussion of the unique concerns of the families of gay and lesbian couples. The family structures discussed in these articles challenge traditional theoretical constructs and models developed for families that consist of a married heterosexual couple with biological children. Individuals are choosing to organize their family relationships in different ways, and hence family therapy theory must be considered in terms of its relevance to a range of family structures. Both articles challenge family therapists to expand their thinking in the use of traditional theory and to tailor family therapy models to address contemporary situations.

Chapter 13 in the textbook examines the impact of stress, crisis, and trauma on families. External and internal traumatic experiences within the family and the profound disruption of family life are explored—specifically, posttraumatic stress disorder (PTSD), alcoholism/substance abuse, and domestic violence. This chapter presents research that establishes a strong relationship between domestic violence, child abuse, and substance abuse. Research that focuses on traumatic symptoms in children occurring as a result of witnessing domestic violence is sparse, however. The reader article "Trauma Symptoms in Preschool-Age Children Exposed to Domestic Violence," by Alytia A. Levendosky, Alissa C. Huth-Bocks, Michael A. Semel, and Deborah L. Shapiro (2002), features specific research and discussion of PTSD in children exposed to domestic violence. The article gives further insight into the dynamics of this important phenomenon, as well as ideas for the direction of clinical interventions for children.

Chapter 13 also discusses the cycle of domestic abuse and presents guidelines for clinical interventions with couples. Women are more apt to be the victims in domestic violence situations, and most of the literature in this field points out the limits and potential dangers to women of traditional couple therapy in these cases. In the reader article "'It's the Little Things'": Women, Trauma, and Strategies for Healing," Vanja M. K. Stenius and Bonita M. Veysey (2005) explore the treatment of women who have experienced violence. This article also gives insight into the varied ways that women heal from traumatic violent experiences, and provides direction for clinical interventions with women outside of traditional couple therapy.

Our textbook concludes with Chapter 14, "Family Therapy Research: Implications for the Practicing Family Therapist." And the reader concludes with a discussion of ethics, an issue of the utmost importance in the practice of couple and family therapists. Regardless of the setting (agency-based or private practice), many clinical decisions made by therapists carry ethical implications, for example:

- What is the problem, and who will define it?
- What subsystem(s) needs intervention—in other words, where does the problem reside (child, family, conjugal/parental subsystem)?
- What interventive method(s) and therapy approach(s) will be used, and how will they be influenced by cultural aspects of both the therapist and the client (e.g., race, ethnicity, religion, social class, gender, sexual orientation)?
- How will the functionality of a family and/or couple's relationship be determined? (Should they should remain together? Should they even be defined as a "family" or a "couple"?)

In the final article in the reader, "Marriage and Family Counseling: Ethics in Context," Stephen Southern, Robert L. Smith, and Marvarene Oliver (2005) explore the ethics of family therapy/counseling and other related issues. The article ends with the discussion of a case involving several ethical issues arising in the context of community systems.

CONCLUSION

We have included a diverse selection of articles in *Readings in Family Therapy* as an attempt to deepen understanding and highlight important issues in the practice of family therapy. There are myriad issues to consider, and certainly our textbook and this reader do not cover the entire landscape, despite our best efforts. As we look toward the future, we invite family therapy students, trainees, practitioners, instructors, and researchers to share their knowledge with us. This will permit us to continue to compile works generated by those of you involved with the practice of family therapy, and allow us the privilege of learning from each other.

REFERENCE

Selvini-Palazzoli, M., Boscolo, L., Cecchin, G., & Prata, G. (1978). A ritualized prescription in family therapy: Odd days and even days. *Journal of Marriage and Family Counseling, 4,* 3–9.

1

The History of Family Therapy:
Conceptual and Clinical Influences

Karl Tomm:
His Changing Views on
Family Therapy Over 35 Years

Don Collins
University of Calgary, Alberta, Canada

Karl Tomm
Calgary Family Therapy Center, Alberta, Canada

Karl Tomm has been the director of the Family Therapy Program in Calgary for more than 35 years. He has developed an international reputation not only as a family therapist, major innovator, theoretician, and trainer of family therapists but also as a leader in facilitating dialogues among many of the world's family therapists. He started his career applying the problem-solving approach to family therapy developed by Nathan Epstein (Part I). In the 1980s, Karl championed the work of the Milan Group (Part II). More recently, Karl has promoted the work of Michael White and David Epston in narrative therapy (Part III). Don Collins recently had the opportunity and pleasure to interview Karl about the evolution of his thinking and practice over the span of his career.

Keywords: *Karl Tomm; family therapy; history of family therapy; postmodern family therapy*

AUTHORS' NOTE: Correspondence concerning this article should be addressed to Don Collins, Department of Social Work, Southern Alberta Region, University of Calgary, 4401 University Dr., Lethbridge, Alberta TIK 3M4, Canada; e-mail: collinsd@ucalgary.ca.

PART I (1969–1979):
A PROBLEM-CENTERED FOCUS

Collins: What influenced you to become a family therapist?

Tomm: Well, there were many personal influences from my family of origin, but I will talk specifically about professional influences. The professional influences started in my 1st year of psychiatry residency at the University of British Columbia in 1969.

One of my patients was a 14-year-old girl who was admitted because she kept running away from home. I asked her family to come in so I could see what she was running away from. She lived with her two parents and a younger brother, and I was struck by how nice they were, really nice people, all of them. Her brother cared for her a lot and was very worried about her, and both her father and mother were devoted to her; I was bewildered. Why was this happening? Why did she keep running away? I asked my supervisors and they did their best to answer my questions, but I was not satisfied. Around that time, Nathan Epstein from McMaster University visited Vancouver and gave a lecture on family therapy. He seemed to know a lot about families. I talked to him after his lecture and discussed the possibility of learning from him and he was very receptive. So I decided to transfer to McMaster, in Hamilton, Ontario.

After moving to McMaster, I got deeply into family work. My main family therapy supervisor was Sol Levin. He was an early riser and started supervision at 7 in the morning. It was a wonderful experience. Around that time Nate and his colleagues were developing the Family Assessment Measure, the FAM, and the FAD, the Family Assessment Device. Previously, Nate had done a lot of work generating the Family Categories Schema at McGill in Montreal where he had worked with Norm Westley and published the book *The Silent Majority* (Wesley & Epstein, 1969). Nate Epstein had previously been influenced by Nathan Ackerman who founded the Ackerman Institute in New York. Nathan Epstein, Nathan Ackerman, and Sol Levin were all psychiatrists and psychoanalysts as well as systems family therapists.

Collins: What were some of the early concepts influencing your thinking?

Tomm: At that time, the main theoretical concepts that were being used to understand families were Von Bertalanffy's ideas about systems, notions of feedback loops and homeostasis, the whole as greater than the sum of the parts, and change in one part triggering change in all other parts. Those kinds of basic systems ideas were talked about a lot.

Yet it was another client experience at McMaster that influenced me most deeply. She was not my patient, but I got to know about her through discussions in medical rounds while I was working on an adjoining ward at the Hamilton Psychiatric Hospital. She had been admitted after an overdose and she had been in and out of hospital with depression for several years. Her husband was a kind man who was very helpful in the home. So when she was depressed, he would manage the kids and do all the housework and stuff. And of course the more he did, the less she did. Then, an interesting thing happened: The husband was involved in a serious car accident. Because two people were killed in the other car, he was charged with manslaughter. That really sent him for a loop. He got down and began having trouble coping. Interestingly, when he was struggling, his wife seemed to get better. He was heavily preoccupied with the legal issue hanging over his head, and started doing less at home. So she did more. And the more she did, the better she felt about herself, so she could do even more, and he did even less. She became fully functional. Indeed, after a while, it appeared that she had fully recovered from her depression. However, a couple of years later, when the court proceedings about the accident came to a conclusion, he was found "not guilty" because it was a genuine accident. When he received that ruling, he was relieved, became energized, and started doing things again. The more he did, the less she did, and the less she did, the more he did, etc. She became depressed again, felt hopeless, and eventually committed suicide by drinking carbon tetrachloride.

That whole process stuck with me. At the time it was happening, I didn't recognize the pattern of overadequate/inadequate reciprocity between the couple. It became apparent to me in retrospect. I came to recognize the pervasive power of such problematic patterns in family systems. People could get caught in difficult positions in their relationships and sometimes could not get out of them. These interpersonal patterns struck me as having a significant influence on mental health and solidified my commitment to work with families. I thought "if this is happening to some people with mental illness, I want to be able to work with them and their relationship systems" as a way to help them recover.

Collins: Was there a theoretical approach or model you were operating under at McMaster?

Tomm: The approach was very problem centered then. We used the medical model where the therapist would assess the family, determine what the problem was, and then treat it through confrontation. Nathan Epstein was well known for his strength of character and confrontational style. He was a very skilled clinician. He would confront people vigorously and very effectively. His approach was based in part on research he did with a sociologist, Norman Westley, at McGill University where they studied some students at McGill. They made the assumption that students who get into McGill must come from well functioning families because their children were doing so well academically. They examined these families to see what made them tick and found that they were "father-led families." This led Epstein and Westley to believe that families do better when fathers are in charge. In retrospect, what they were studying and reproducing was the dominant culture of patriarchal patterns in families, which they assumed was the basis of good mental health. Epstein took their findings to McMaster and when he saw mothers of problematic children with too much influence, he would "knock down" the mothers and "build up" the fathers to take charge. This approach used lots of confrontation and to get away with it you had to package it with support in what we called "the sandwich technique." You give a bit of support and then you hit them with the "meat" of the intervention and then you give them a bit of support again. For example, "You seem to be an intelligent man, why don't you just stand up to your wife? I know you can do it!" Basically that was the way we would try to treat families at the time.

Collins: Was Epstein influenced by Minuchin at all?

Tomm: No, there was not much influence on each other as far as I am aware. Epstein was more influenced by Ackerman. Nathan Ackerman was very direct and confrontational as well. In retrospect their approach could be seen as "put-the-pants-back-on-father family therapy." While at McMaster, I learned how to confront as well and became quite good at it. However, in retrospect, I am ashamed of the way in which I was so confrontational with families. But that was what we believed in at that time.

After residency I continued on at McMaster for another year as a teaching fellow. During that year I came out to Calgary to visit my father who was ill at the Foothills Hospital. I met Dr. Pearce in the Department of Psychiatry and was promptly offered a job at the University of Calgary. I proposed starting a Family Therapy Program if I moved, and eventually did so in 1972.

Once I left McMaster I was freer to explore other models. I traveled around to see what other people were doing in family therapy. I went to visit Minuchin in Philadelphia, to the MRI (Mental Research Institute) in Palo Alto, and also to the Ackerman Institute in New York. I picked up lots of other ideas and put them together to develop my own blend of family therapy. My understanding was summarized in the "circular pattern diagramming model" that I developed where I tried to integrate psychodynamic ideas, cognitive ideas, and behavioral ideas, by connecting them through a cybernetic feedback loop. My perspective at that time was problem oriented and the therapy focused on solving problems. I was not as aware of alternatives then. I just assumed that was the way you should work with families.

Collins: What ideas did you find particularly useful from visiting Minuchin, the MRI, and Ackerman?

Tomm: I found Minuchin's concepts about boundaries and subsystems very useful. Nate Epstein used those ideas too but not as rigorously as Minuchin did in terms of defining clear intergenerational boundaries and having an executive subsystem and a sibling sub-system. I found that Minuchin was clearer about those ideas and he had specific interventions that he used to push families toward what he felt were healthy or more appropriate boundaries.

At the MRI, I became aware of Bateson's work in cybernetics and the importance of positive feed-back loops and negative feedback loops in family systems. I actually used the cybernetic feedback loop as an organizing principle in my circular pattern diagramming.

The main influence of the Ackerman Institute was in the psychodynamic/psychoanalytic approach to family therapy where one pays attention to the emotional dynamics within family members. Within my circular pattern diagramming I placed emotions within the individual enclosures along with cognitions. But my focus shifted from individual problems toward relationship problems or patterns of interaction that were problematic.

Collins: Could you explain the shift from the McMaster focus on the individual in the family to the patterns of relationships?

Tomm: That was a significant shift; it set me up for further developments. If you think of a family who has a member with a problem and say there are family relationship influences that aggravate or ameliorate the problem, it is still an individual problem. I was moving toward a view where individual family members were quite incidental and the problem was in the pattern of interaction like the overadequate/ inadequate reciprocity between the couple mentioned earlier. It could be that the problem was not within either one of them. The problem was in the organization of their relationship as one of overadequate/inadequate reciprocity. That possibility became more apparent through the "natural experiment" of the car accident, when the positions in the reciprocity reversed but the pattern stayed the same. The husband and wife temporarily occupied different positions in the pattern. It became more apparent to me that the problem was not in either the wife or the husband. It was in the pattern of interaction between the two of them. That is why I was attracted to the cybernetic metaphor of patterns of interaction that was highlighted by the MRI group. However, what I could not get a handle on in those years was the MRI's use of paradoxes. They did not make sense to me at that time, so I did not use paradoxes then.

Collins: How did you see influencing change of the patterns then?

Tomm: The circular diagramming model helped me clarify the problematic pattern, and I could use interventions at different points in the pattern. Depending on the nuances of the family situation and their relationship patterns, I could intervene with the behaviors on the feedback arrows, I could intervene on the emotional dynamics, or I could intervene on the cognitions in terms of how the participants were interpreting the behavior of the others. In other words, I had multiple points of entry to break up the pattern that was problematic. I was less clear about what pattern the family could or should enact, than I was focused on the problematic pattern that I was trying to break up.

Collins: How did you decide which nuances to focus on, whether the feelings, behaviors, or cognition? How did you decide one over the other?

Tomm: I usually decided on the basis of intensity and what emerged most strongly. If there was a particular behavior that was obviously problematic, for example pervasive criticism and persistent dumping on one person, repeated behaviors like that, I would probably focus on that. If the intensity emerged in the emotions like anger, outrage, bitterness, or resentment, I would focus there. If kids were unable to sleep at night because they thought they saw ghosts or monsters, I would focus on that. Or if the pattern was subtle and had to do with ways of thinking or believing, for instance the parents seeing the kids as defiant rather than afraid, I would try to work with the cognitions. It was what jumped out to me as most "obviously out of line."

Collins: When did the concept of first-order and second-order change occur in your thinking?

Tomm: First-order change and second-order change are different than first-order approaches and second-order approaches. First-order change and second-order change are ideas that the MRI developed. By first-order change they meant change analogous to driving in one particular gear and you can speed up or slow down. Second-order change occurs when you change from one gear to another gear: you move into a different frame of reference. Within that new frame of reference, change is again possible, but it is first-order change within that frame. The MRI notion of reframing, where the meaning of a certain behavior is changed, reflects a second-order change.

First-order and second-order approaches refer to a comparison at a different level, namely, the relationships between therapists and families in the therapeutic system. First-order family therapy approaches employ concepts from systems theory and first-order cybernetics, which refers to the cybernetics of control systems or regulation and control in observed relationship systems. If one is engaged in first-order approaches to therapy, then one is interested in these regulatory patterns of control. As an observer, I am outside of the pattern and I am just observing it, analyzing it, and operating upon it.

The second-order approaches include an ongoing awareness and assessment of the therapist's relationship with the family in the therapeutic system and how this is simultaneously influencing interactions within the family system. Second-order approaches are more complex. For instance, they entail a "cybernetics of cybernetics" and imply the domain of understanding in observing systems. The distinction between first-order approaches and second-order approaches didn't come to me until there was a shift in the field, which could be marked around the time the Milan approach emerged in the mid-to late 70s. I think their work had a very significant impact on the understanding and doing of family therapy.

PART II (1979–1989): MILAN WORK: A MOVE AWAY FROM PROBLEM-CENTERED FOCUS

Collins: In the late 1970s you seemed to move away from the problem-centered focus?

Tomm: A major change for me occurred on my first sabbatical of 1978-1979. What led up to that change was very significant. Just before I went on sabbatical I had an experience of a major therapeutic failure. The husband/father in a family I had worked with intensively for 9 months eventually committed suicide. It was a very complex situation (which I wrote about for the book *Failures in Family Therapy,* edited by Sandra Coleman). This failure experience set me up to be more receptive to new ideas because my "good idea" of circular pattern diagramming didn't help. I had worked systematically and thoroughly with a clear problematic pattern between the couple, yet the outcome was tragic. After the suicide I came to realize that, without intending to, I was actually aggravating the problem. In this family there was a recurrent pattern of criticism coupled with distancing between the parents. Each spouse would criticize the other while the other would distance him or herself and vice versa. However,

I ended up criticizing them for criticizing each other, for instance by drawing the pattern on a blackboard and pointing out what they were doing to each other that was problematic. I tried to do so in a supportive and respectful manner but nonetheless it was the same dynamic. I was criticizing them for criticizing each other in a continuing problematic pattern. Without realizing it, I was adding to the problem. This only became apparent to me in retrospect.

I heard about his suicide just before I left on sabbatical to Europe where I encountered the Milan approach through their book *Paradox and Counterparadox* (Selvini, Boscolo, Cecchin, & Prata, 1988). When I first read the book, I could not understand it. This upset me a bit because I thought I was up to date with the family therapy literature. I read it a second time, and a third time. Finally I got up enough courage to write Selvini a letter and ask her whether there was an implicit negative connotation within the positive connotation that accounted for the therapeutic changes. She wrote back saying "very interesting question" and suggested we get together to talk. This was the beginning of my connection with the Milan team and led to a collaborative relationship with Luigi Boscolo and Gianfranco Cecchin that remained quite close for over 10 years. During my work with them a huge shift occurred in me, absolutely huge, it was the biggest single shift I made in my professional thinking and patterns of practice.

Collins: When did the Milan Group influence you?

Tomm: I first met Selvini in Wales in 1979. It was a very exciting meeting for me because I found our discussions very enlivening and energetic. She was a very dynamic woman. One of the things I remember about that conversation was her statement about Bateson claiming that "the mind is social!" That idea really took hold of me and I pondered it for a long time. I made a concerted effort to connect more with her and her colleagues. That year John Burnham and I cosponsored a conference with Boscolo and Cecchin in Birmingham which was the beginning of our clinical collaboration.

I could see that they were onto something quite unique, very different. The possibility of doing something paradoxical had been something I had entertained but never used. For instance, with the family I "failed" by virtue of the father committing suicide, I had considered some paradoxical interventions but had never tried them. I did not have the confidence to do so before connecting with the Milan team. My understanding of the Milan approach at that time was that symptomatic families were regarded as stuck in patterns of interaction that they couldn't get out of. Part of the reason they could not get out of them was because they had certain rigid beliefs and ideas that constrained them. If you use a paradoxical intervention which generated confusion around those firmly held ideas and beliefs, then you loosen the grip of the ideas on the people who hold them. This made it possible for spontaneous change; for family members to entertain different ideas and consequently different patterns of behavior. If these differences made a difference, in allowing the family to move forward, then the paradoxes could be seen as very therapeutic. Thus, I became increasingly interested in what I was doing in the therapeutic relationship to influence the beliefs in the family. I kept asking myself, "What kinds of interventions could I use in terms of ideas and beliefs that could alter the family's ideas and beliefs and secondarily enable change in their behavior patterns with each other?" In retrospect, one of the most useful aspects of the Milan approach was to harness the power of the distinction between good and bad in the so-called "positive connotation" intervention which was highly paradoxical.

A related change occurred in my personal belief system about the nature of knowledge and of therapy. Prior to Milan work, I was trained in a paradigm of empiricism and objectivity, but now I was doing something outside that framework. The domain of constructing alternative knowledges, that are not based on objectivity, led me to explore constructivism, social constructionism, and eventually bringforthism. A whole different way of thinking about reality or "realities" and about myself as a participant in conversations to co-construct realities opened up to me. Indeed, the single most significant change that occurred in my professional development was being able to liberate myself from the empirical paradigm so I could move into a social constructionist or a bringforthist paradigm when I am doing clinical work.

Nowadays, I live and work in both domains. For example, if I am preparing to go flying, I live in the domain of empiricism; I believe the airplane has the objective capability of flying, otherwise I would not board the aircraft. When I am doing therapy, I prefer to live in the domain of social constructionism; I want to be thinking of realities co-constructed in our therapeutic conversation. If you believe in objectivity during therapy and you distinguish something as objectively true, then you are stuck with it and the possibilities for change are reduced. Most schools of family therapy still employ predominantly first-order approaches grounded in empiricism, while the second-order approach of the Milan team was grounded in constructivism. To work in second-order approaches you need to liberate yourself from being stuck in objectivity, and instead entertain alternative ways of thinking, believing, and seeing the world. For me, that was a huge, huge change.

Collins: You also made a shift from circular pattern diagramming to HIPs (healing interaction patterns) and PIPs (pathologizing interaction patterns) in 1991.

Tomm: HIPs and PIPs are components of interpersonal relationships and exist, in my view, in the interpersonal space between people: They are patterns of interaction that are external to the people who engage in them. A circular pattern diagram, on the other hand, incorporates the persons who are interacting; the HIPs and PIPs don't. The PIPs perspective has certain advantages in supporting a social constructionist understanding and in enabling certain initiatives in therapy. If I describe a PIP of criticism coupled with defensiveness, you and I can engage in those behaviors, yet the pattern remains between us, not within us. This view enables therapeutic conversation along the lines of Michael White's way of working and thinking in terms of externalizing problems. HIPs like apologizing coupled with forgiving, on the other hand, begin external to the persons involved, but become more therapeutic as they are internalized. Michael did not talk about internalizing. He mainly talked about externalizing constraints. I suppose you could say that by bringing forth unique outcomes and restorying people's lives, he is engaged in an internalizing process. I have not heard him describe it that way—maybe he does but I never heard it from him.

I talk about both internalizing and externalizing. I sometimes use the metaphor of the immune system of the body as analogous to the work we do in therapy. The immune system of the physical body works at the interface of self and nonself in the physical domain. If some poisons, bacteria, or viruses enter the body, or early cancer cells develop, the immune system identifies these threats as nonself and mounts a response to defend the body and destroy those things, to get rid of them. At the same time the immune system allows nutrients into the body to nourish us and become part of our body, of our self. In other words the immune system operates at the interface of the self and nonself and monitors what comes in and can stay in, and what gets excreted or sent out. Similarly, a good therapeutic conversation operates at the interface of self and nonself, but in the social/psychological domain. If in the course of an argument someone calls you names and says you are arrogant, or you are bossy or inadequate, those descriptions could stick to your identity and if they are "poisonous" you have to do something to get rid of them. A therapeutic conversation could externalize such noxious descriptions of self and get rid of them and instead allow nurturing descriptions about one's identity back in, in other words, about being competent, being capable, being resilient, or being able to survive hardship. Therapeutic conversation, in that sense, also operates at that interface between self and nonself, by monitoring one's psychological self and identity, and by trying to "clean up" the self and get rid of noxious descriptions, which have become stuck to oneself from the words of others.

PART III (1985–PRESENT): SOCIAL CONSTRUCTIONISM AND NARRATIVE FAMILY THERAPY

Collins: The last time we were together, we ended with the influence that the Milan group had on you, and then you introduced meeting Michael White for the first time. Where I'm most interested in starting today is if you could talk about how Michael White influenced your thinking, your theory, and your practice and as well how you think you influenced his theory and practice of family therapy. It was about 20 years ago that you met Michael?

Tomm: I think it was about 1985 or 1986 that we met. Michael influenced my work a lot! I could certainly say that. I'm not sure how much I influenced him; he'd have to speak to that. We did collaborate quite closely for a number of years. One of the first things that attracted me to his work was his process of externalizing and how he engaged in elegant externalizing conversations. That, to me, seemed extremely useful and I think it has been a major contribution to the field. It's a method whereby one can actually implement, in a concrete way, some of the contemporary theory of social constructionism. You can take one conversation about yourself and can separate that conversation out from other conversations about your self, and give priority to one over another to select a preferred identity. The distinctions between self and nonself became highly relevant in the context of therapeutic interviews. So one could bring forth an identity of being a survivor rather than a victim, of having competencies rather than limitations, and move forward in one's life despite past difficulties. One develops a personal story, a narrative of self, and lives out one's story. Through selective conversation and reflection, you bring stories about yourself into focus, carve out parts of the self story that don't fit or you don't want to belong to you anymore and want to get rid of, and start deconstructing them. If it's a certain quality that you don't like, such as being lazy, you might transform the adjective *lazy* into the noun *laziness* and separate it from yourself. For instance, I could shift from thinking "Karl is lazy" to thinking "Karl is under the influence of laziness" and that "laziness has a grip on him" at times. Then you could engage in a conversation or reflection about laziness being a habit or a phenomenon separate from me, and doesn't have to be part of my identity. That way of talking and thinking was such a useful contribution to the field and in developing ideas around therapeutic conversation. So I incorporate it into my practice.

Collins: This is quite a big shift from where the Milan [group] wielded the problem. What was the function of [the] problem, and now you are really shifting into the influence the problem had on you. I think that's a fairly radical shift.

Tomm: Oh yeah. I felt that what Michael was doing in practice, was more compatible with Humberto Maturana's theory of knowledge than what the Milan team were doing (even though I first got involved with Maturana because of my interest in explaining the work of the Milan team). I think I mentioned last time that I abandoned Milan systemic work once I realized that Maturana was challenging functional thinking and used the notion of structure determinism instead. He helped me see how relationship patterns could more usefully be described as mutual invitations.

Collins: Did Maturana influence Michael White's thinking?

Tomm: Well, I don't think Maturana had a lot of influence on Michael, except indirectly through me. Michael and Maturana never really connected, I don't think. I think Michael may have heard him present a few times. I don't know. But Michael would often ask me about Maturana's theory and I did my best to explain it to him several times. Because I felt there was compatibility in the practices that he was developing in his clinical work and the theory that Maturana was espousing, I could see a significant connection there. I still see Maturana as offering the best theoretical foundation that I've come across so far, for the kind of work that I do.

Collins: How do you put Maturana and Michael White's work into that whole circular patterning way of thinking that you have to operate?

Tomm: Well, both helped me shift away from circular pattern diagramming to highlight the mutual invitations of the HIPs and PIPs model which are complementarities that exist in the interpersonal space. With the circular pattern diagramming model, the persons interacting remain part of the description. You represent two people with internal thoughts and feelings in the enclosures, plus the behaviors linking them. With a description using the HIPs and PIPs model, all of the components of the pattern, in my view, remain in the interpersonal space and are external to the people engaged in the pattern.

Collins: Who else has influenced you do you think over the last 15 to 20 years? Were there other major influences in your life, in your family work?

Tomm: Well, there were many, many influences. David Epston clearly was a major influence along with Michael. They're pretty much together in their way of thinking, in narrative therapy. I don't know if I mentioned this to you before or not but at one point they actually invited me to join them in coauthoring their first book on *Narrative Means to Therapeutic Ends* (White & Epston, 1990), for which I wrote a foreword. I didn't join in then because I didn't feel like I was sufficiently into their frame of reference at the time.

Some of the ways in which David has influenced me has been to create unique activities for families, and especially for kids, to enact a process for narrative change. One example could be work with a child who has had a problem with lying and stealing. After we go through an externalizing process, of externalizing "sticky fingers," we set up some "honesty tests" and create conditions for a child to succeed in passing the tests as a counterpoint to being dishonest. The issue of one's "reputation" would also be brought up. Kids who have been lying and stealing often get into trouble in the community and at school because their reputation precedes them. Sometimes these kids are no longer allowed into the stores where they have been caught stealing. Eventually, whenever something goes missing, they get accused, even if they didn't do it. Such accusations are of course problematic for the child because they run them down and they actually become more vulnerable to slip back into old problematic habits of lying and stealing.

One of the things that David might do in situations like that, is to externalize the stealing habit and bring forth the child's desire to be honest and to escape the bad reputation. David might raise questions like, "Can you see how your reputation gets you into trouble? . . . Would you like to change your reputation?" "Yeah, yeah, I'd like to change that." "How would you go about changing it, if you wanted to?" "Don't know." "Well, say you were to pass some honesty tests, and the store knew you were doing that. Do you think that would help?" "Maybe." "What if I asked your mom or your dad to go to the store, before you go to buy some groceries. They could talk to the clerk in advance, and give her an extra dollar and tell her that when you come to buy something, she should give you an extra dollar in change. Now what would you do with that dollar if she give you too much change? If you wanted to develop a reputation for honesty, instead of a reputation for being a thief, what would you do? What would be the smart thing to do?" Well, the kid struggles a bit with this because if one gets too much change back, the child usually thinks the smart thing to do would be to keep it. However, if you want to change your reputation, the new smart thing to do would be to give it back. "If you gave it back to the clerk, what would that do to your reputation in the clerk's mind?" The child really starts thinking about this. David advises the parents (in front of the child) to do this sometime when the child doesn't know it is happening. You don't want him to know when you're doing this. And then the kid is always wondering when this might happen. The kid checks the change and learns to give the extra change back. It's a way to construct real life situations for behavioral change.

David Epston was really good at that. He was really good at developing these kinds of strategies and methods for change, for instance developing fear busting skills, night watching routines, etc. Of course another thing that David did was "therapeutic letter writing." I did a bit of that too.

Collins: So where are you at today? What would you say, if you were to describe your theory and practice today? I'm actually also interested in what you brought from your original family practice, your family-centered practice from Epstein and then of course your Milan influence on you and the narrative influence. If you were to describe your practice today, what did you keep and what has changed?

Tomm: One of the major things that I've retained from the beginning is the very strong focus and commitment to the family as an entity, as a relationship system itself. That has been consistent even though my theoretical frames and patterns of practice have changed. I have continued to focus on the family as a unit. And part of the reason for this is that the intensity of interaction in family relationships is so rich and the conversations are so significant in constructing realities for the members of that family system. There is a phrase that someone wrote about "the family being an epistemological crucible," that is, it is the base out of which epistemology arises, where kids come to know about "reality," and to "know about knowing"— that happens in a family system. Our knowing/knowledge becomes extended of course in school systems and other social systems that we become part of. But the family unit per se remains so crucial because of the richness of interaction that occurs among the members of that system. That focus has been consistent.

At the beginning of my career, I would often insist on seeing the whole family. I was overly rigid about that then and would insist that if they didn't all come, I wouldn't work with them. I've abandoned that practice many years ago because I learned to think in terms of relationship systems. I don't need to see the whole family system in front of me to think in terms of family systems anymore. I'm more grounded now in thinking systemically about relationship and I can hold that perspective even when I'm working with individuals, whereas at the beginning I wasn't able to do that as easily. So while I do work with individuals now or with parts of family systems, such as a parent–child subsystem, a parental subsystem, or sibling subsystem, I still think in terms of whole family system dynamics. This overall systemic commitment informs me in terms of my local therapeutic initiatives, so that has been constant. I think that over time the degree to which I've focused on the co-construction of knowledge and competencies has grown. At the beginning that was very limited. But it's now become more and more part of my way of thinking and practicing. And so I would say that has been a change, but not a complete change, it's a matter of degree.

Collins: So you're much more active with all family members to get them to look at different ways of dealing with things and developing competencies as compared to you pointing them out to people, which was more of an Epstein kind of a model.

Tomm: Yes.

Collins: What about from the Milan group? What have you kind of kept from them that you still use in your practice, some of their thinking or practice?

Tomm: Oh for sure, the notion of circular interviewing and how it is possible through your questions to understand systemic patterns of interaction and relationships so well. That has been a big part of their work that has stayed with me. I still use those kinds of questions a lot. I've extended my thinking to distinguish between circular questions and reflexive questions. But that definitely has its roots in the Milan work. However, I've pretty much abandoned functional hypothesizing, although I employ it somewhat sometimes, but not when I'm thinking clearly. I prefer Maturana's way of conceptualizing. Another thing I still use from the Milan team is the process of creating family rituals.

Actually, I'm working with a family right now where I'm co-constructing a ritual with them that I hope is going to be therapeutic. And it's a family where this couple has three sons, all of whom have autistic spectrum disorder and the boys are all very significantly disabled. This has been a huge trauma, especially for the mother, because her identity as a person is heavily rooted in her motherhood. She feels like she is a profound failure as a mother in bearing these three boys. Every time she sees their limitations, she feels inadequate and struggles with depression. She has been chronically depressed for years. Now, their third son is old enough to go through his bar mitzvah. The mother was dreading this, because for her it's another reminder of how she had failed as a mother. In a conversation with them, I've wondered whether we could modify the bar mitzvah ritual to not only acknowledge the coming of age of the son, but to acknowledge the extraordinary amount of parenting that the mother had provided for him, despite his limitations, to make possible what development he has achieved. I wanted to be sure it was consistent with their culture, and because I'm not Jewish I asked them if they would like me to work with them and their Rabbi to discuss how to do this. The mother's enormous contributions, of putting in far more time and effort than most mothers ever do in helping their children grow, could be acknowledged by the son somehow in the ceremony or by the people that are witness to it. The acknowledgement could be made compatible with the cultural ceremony yet make it a significantly healing event that the mother could remember; that she was indeed "a good mother" by virtue of her incredible contributions. This idea of creating family rituals comes from the Milan team where they have a number of rituals that they often used with different families. I still occasionally use their standard rituals, such as the "odd days and even days" or the "invariant prescription" (of carefully arranged parental "disappearances") but in a more flexible manner. I prefer if possible, to create a specific ritual together with the family that fits their specific situation.

Just recently, I got an e-mail message asking me what I knew about pseudocyesis. It's a subject I actually know next to nothing about. I assumed the person must have read an article that I had written about a family I had worked with many years ago. A female client kept having symptoms of being pregnant when she actually wasn't pregnant. What became apparent was that this might be related to an earlier stillbirth. She had had a couple of daughters who were healthy, and then a son who died in utero. Some time after she delivered the dead fetus she developed pseudocyesis. And so I worked with them as a family to create a ritual where they could symbolically bring the boy into their family, give him a name, and then give him a proper burial. This could then be an opportunity for them to acknowledge the significance of this event as part of their family life and so forth. They actually followed through on this; they went out into the forest and had a private ceremony. The mother made up a little doll to represent the boy, and together the whole family buried it. Immediately afterward the symptoms of pseudocyesis disappeared. It was marvelous.

Collins: I have a tougher question for you. I'm interested in some of the criticisms people have of that systemic form of family therapy. I know you have heard some of them, particularly the people concerned about family violence and people not taking self responsibility for their behaviors. I know you've responded to this in other areas, but I am curious with how you put the whole concept of family violence within your thinking.

Tomm: That's a tough issue. There's a lot of disagreement in the field about how to deal with situations of violence. The systemic approach, generally speaking, is more accepting of what happens, and is less judgmental and less impositional than traditional approaches. For instance, in traditional child welfare, a worker comes in and determines the child is at risk and therefore feels justified in taking the child out of the home or forcing an abusive parent out of the home. If it's spousal abuse, a traditional therapist might insist that the wife go to a shelter, the spouses must separate, or whatever, and refuses to see them together as a couple. In some states there is actual legislation prohibiting marital therapy, or at least it's not funded, when there is spousal violence. The theory is that if conjoint work occurs, there is the implication that somehow "the woman was asking for it" when male to female violence occurs, and therefore men need to be treated alone to take full responsibility for their behavior.

Impositional therapeutic strategies run counter to the systemic position, which is to see the violence as part of the system. That's not to say that the people with less power who were violated are contributing to the violence. But it does imply that there's something that they are doing that is a part of the pattern that includes the violence. I prefer to still work systemically in situations of violence, but there are times when I have to break from that and move into a role of a social control agent. So I've had to certify people at times, or call social welfare. However, I tend to do so in a different way because of my systemic orientation.

Just to give you an example: With an Asian family I was working with, a while back, the father was violent with his daughter, physically violent with her. And from his point of view, it was culturally appropriate: "That's the way things are done in Korea." He believed that she ought to be completely obedient and submit to his authority. When she didn't, he felt justified in beating her. The mother had compassion on the girl and didn't agree with his view and hence the mother insisted on therapy. Now when I heard the story, I said to the father, "Well, this may be compatible with your culture in Korea, I don't know because I'm not knowledgeable about that, but in Canadian culture it is not acceptable. And given that you live in Canada, I need to let you know that I am required by law to inform the authorities. What I'm prepared to do though, is to try to help you to be seen more positively by them and give you an opportunity to report yourself, because if you reported yourself, the authorities are much less likely to be as severe in their intervention with your family than if I had to report you. If I have to report you and you don't want to be reported, then they're going to look at it as a much more dangerous situation. So I'm suggesting that maybe it would be good for you and your family to report yourself." The father retorted, "No God damn way!" So I said to him, "That's fine, I understand that you don't want to do it but I want you to know that I will still give you this opportunity. So I'm not going to call for the next 24 hours. If you change your mind during that time and you want me to help you make the phone call, I am willing to do that." And sure enough, he did call back within 24 hours and he reported himself. In effect, I used the threat of coercive external control as a way to strongly "invite" him into taking some responsibility, which would be quite different from what I would have done before getting into the Milan approach.

Collins: Now if you were to work with that family further, and he's coming back and he's trying to be vigilant to keep family violence out of his life, how would you then look at it with a systemic perspective, further on when you're working with them?

Tomm: Now, after that, what I would do is invite him to learn to "live above suspicion." What he would need to know, given that he now has a record with child protection, is how he can organize his way of being in relation to his daughter such that he is never going to be held suspect with respect to being violent with her, or abusing her again. I asked him, "What would you have to do to live above suspicion? To avoid being held suspect as abusive in the future?" This is particularly useful in situations of sexual abuse or in situations where there are allegations of sexual abuse where you don't know whether it's happened or not. If the person who is considered abusive is invited to recognize how there is now talk in the community and their reputation has been tainted because of the allegations, it would be wise for them to be very careful not to do anything that could feed those suspicions. Therefore they need to live above any suspicions in such a way that they can never be held suspect again. When they really understand that, they usually want to do so because they want to avoid being charged. So I ask, "But how? How could you be sure that this would never arise again, that you'd never be held suspect again?" He might respond, "Well, if somebody else was always there when my daughter and I are together, the other person could vouch for me, even if my daughter did make an accusation. So if there is always a third party present, there would be less risk." "Yeah exactly!" I encourage him to make a personal rule of nonviolence that he lives by and which is supported by "a community of concern," in other words, other people in his social network, both inside and outside the family. That would be one way to work a bit more systemically with violence. I also use their systems of understandings to build new distinctions and behaviors, and work with them to facilitate movement in a preferred direction.

Collins: Let me ask you about another case example, and it was with alcoholism. I remember the old systemic way of sometimes thinking, is to say a person would say that my wife nags me, so I drink. There's at least a subtle part of blaming the other partner for some other behavior and yet we are trying to move very much away from that. What would your thinking be on that and your approach?

Tomm: Well, I like some of the recent work on motivational interviewing which is used with addictions and alcoholism in particular. An effort is made to focus on the internal system of a person and how they organize themselves and their own ideas about themselves and what they want for themselves. Motivational interviewing, in my view, is still in an empirical paradigm in terms of their thinking. They are not in a postmodernist, social constructionist paradigm, at least from what I've seen of Miller's work so far. I like what they do because it's so respectful of clients. They bring forth what they call ambivalence in terms of the person's feelings about themselves drinking; why it's good to drink, why it's not good to drink, and juxtapose the contradictions without putting pressure on them. To me, this is such a useful way to do therapy because you are working with their intrapersonal relationship with their internal systems of meaning, which of course ultimately came from interpersonal relationship dynamics. So I try to do that when I am working with situations of addiction, while at the same time, attending to the interpersonal dynamics that are operating. I try to deconstruct the process that you described of projecting responsibility on the other for the drinking, so it is a combination of bringing forth their internal system of motivation in a direction to be less abusive with drugs and alcohol and live consistently with their preferred way of being, at the same time as creating relationships or interpersonal interactions that are more supportive of that, rather than blocking it. So say there is a partner that is enabling in terms of buying the alcohol, making sure there is a supply of alcohol available, I would certainly work with that person to help them abandon their component of the systemic addiction process.

Collins: Final question on that area, severe mental health issues. Individual ones, what's your thinking on that? I think go back to the old classic issues of schizophrenia, remember the whole original work of the family, schizophrenia, they've changed the thinking out of the individual to the schizophrenic family, and yet there seems to be a shift back to the schizophrenic individual.

Tomm: There's a really interesting story there . . . and it does a disservice to the field of family therapy in a way. After the double bind hypothesis was created at the Mental Research Institute through Bateson's work in distinguishing different levels of meaning and stuff, it was postulated as a psychotogenic dynamic that contributed to schizophrenia. This led to notions of a schizophrenogenic mother, and then a schizophrenogenic father, a schizophrenogenic sister and brother, and so on. Everybody in the family system got painted with the same pejorative stigmatizing brush of mental disorder. The families of persons who were diagnosed as having schizophrenia really got up in arms about this. And they took collective action through NAMI—the National Association for the Mentally Ill in the United States. For a while, NAMI took a very strong stand against family therapy, and gave family therapy a bad name because of the tendency of some therapists to blame families for the mental illness of one of their members.

We've come a long way since then, and NAMI has backed off, partly because of some of the research findings in the expressed emotion (EE) studies. The EE studies came out of England where it was demonstrated empirically that the person diagnosed with schizophrenia was much more likely to require rehospitalization if they lived in families where there were high levels of expressed emotion, high levels of criticism, etc. Those families who participated in psychoeducation and learned to respond to their member with schizophrenia in less emotional ways and more supportively instead, the prognosis was better in terms of staying out of hospital longer. There is more acceptance now about family work even by organizations like NAMI but there is still a sort of hint that family therapy is to blame. What I think is not yet adequately acknowledged is the significance of social dynamics in contributing to psychotic patterns of thought and in ameliorating them as well. The best genetic studies that we have so far, in terms of identical twins, show a 50% concordance rate, i.e., if one identical twin has schizophrenia, 50% of the time the other twin will have it too. How do you account for the other 50% who have the same genetic makeup but do not develop the psychosis? That raises questions about the adequacy of the genetic hypothesis which of course unfolds into brain structures and neurotransmitters, etc. I think there is eventually going to be a drift back to examine what it is in life experiences or relationship patterns that may be psychotogenetic, which promotes psychosis. Murray Bowen came up with a theory for how schizophrenia arises through a series of successive generations of decreasing differentiation of self, which results in people living patterns of weakened "reality testing" in the face of strong demands for familial consensus.

Collins: . . . Includes things like alcoholism passing on from generation to generation too? There's some kind of transmission process there.

Tomm: For sure. Murray Bowen has passed away. But one person carrying forward his ideas and connecting them to the biological domain is David Reese. David has been doing a lot of work in genetics as well as family systems, and has made a distinction between consensus sensitive families and environment sensitive families. Consensus sensitivity is used to describe families in which there is a high need to appear to agree because of the associated emotional dynamics. Thus, people tend to give up their distinctions of their environment or "reality," in favor of a "safer" emotional relationship with the other. Of course in extreme situations a "folie a deux" may arise where people live within the same psychotic belief system. I've had some experience working with families with a member who has been diagnosed with schizophrenia. And I've been able to recognize clear patterns of interaction that appear to be psychotogenic, maybe genic is not the right word, they seem to be psychoto-promoting patterns, they tend to aggravate psychotic process. For instance, patterns of disqualification seem quite pervasive in those family systems and the disqualification can be overt in terms of saying "there are no voices here," that idea is "crazy," or that belief is "stupid" when they suffer from delusion, to quite subtle things of not paying attention to, or ignoring, what the person is saying. One can imply through lack of response that what someone is saying is wrong or irrelevant and is therefore "crazy." I've found that working with these families can be gratifying because you can help family members become more affirming, and less disqualifying, and the family interactions become less psychotogenic. There is a man I worked with off and on for 25 years, who I still see from time to time. I've seen his family for a long time. I still remember one point in the therapy where he abandoned his delusional belief about being a Roman emperor, or being a famous drummer. He developed these beliefs almost as a way to compensate for his profound sense of inadequacy compared to other family members. But at one point in the therapy he said to me,

"I just want to be an ordinary man." It was music to my ears— to hear him say that, when he had been hanging on to these grandiose delusions for so long. It was such a wonderful thing. He's still limited, he's still not working, but he's able to function and help out doing chores for his parents and stuff. Although he's getting into some social relationships, he's still limited in what he can do. He's on medication as well. It's not an either–or, it's a both–and situation. I assume there may be a genetic predisposition and certain life experiences that aggravate one's vulnerability. However, I still see a major role for family therapy in families with members who have serious mental illness.

Collins: I have a final question. I'm interested where you see yourself headed in terms of family therapy, or even like your prediction of where the future of family therapy is, what it may look like, or at least where you're proceeding with it?

Tomm: Well, a number of years ago, I imagined a periodic table of "healing elements of mind," where we as clinicians could understand how we engage in conversations to co-construct certain mental phenomena like hope, responsibility, motivation, acceptance, apology, forgiveness, etc. As we develop more understanding about the kinds of interactions and conversations that allow those phenomena to arise in relationship, and then could be internalized to become part of the self, maybe we can develop the corresponding conversational skills. If we as clinicians could develop a way of outlining an overall structure of meaning systems, and of beliefs and values, and of behaviors that are interconnected, just like the periodic table of elements, then we might see how there are certain patterns of interaction/conversation that create certain phenomena. We could learn to meet people where they are at, tune in to their patterns of interaction and their recurrent conversations, and then open space for them to co-construct with us, and each other, what they need to realize to enact selective conversations for "healthy minds."

Collins: It would be interesting for you to figure that out in the family therapy context of how to help influence hope for people, what do conversations look like to help that happen.

Tomm: I see that as one future possibility. I mean that's a wild fantasy in a way. I also see that there is a lot of potential for using the method that I enjoy in terms of interviewing the "internalized other." When I interview "a significant other" as "part of the self," I bring forth their relationship as it is lived by the person I am speaking to. If this happens in the presence of the actual other, that other person gets to meet their "distributed self," i.e., how they exist in the person I am speaking to. These practices are very rich with possibilities I think.

I also see a future possibility where families will go in to see their "friendly therapist" for an annual family system checkup, to discuss their family relationships and unique patterns and what directions they are evolving or drifting in, and possibly realign their directions. I can see such a tradition as one way toward maximizing mental health and wellness for the future. Every 6 months or year, a family would meet with their friendly therapist, who might not be called a therapist at all; a family coach might be a better term for it, or a family consultant. I do see lots of merit still in the HIPs and PIPs model being extended and elaborated. For instance, I see that the DSM, if it could be expanded, so that every individual diagnosis was sort of connected with a clarifying section to elaborate on common patterns of interaction that contribute to and/or generate the individual phenomenology. For instance, in various types of depression, there could be typical interpersonal patterns that generate such depression which then clinicians can use as ways to understand a particular client's situation more richly and use the knowledge of relationship dynamics to foster change and not just depend on pharmacotherapy. I could see that potentially happening. The DSM is still deeply immersed in assumptions about separate skin-bounded selves; there is lip service to looking at the situation, the context, or stressors, but it's not really incorporated into the theorizing and understanding of the mental phenomena that they are trying to diagnose and treat. So those are some of the things that I see possibly happening in the future.

Collins: Before we end, are there any other questions that you'd like me to ask you?

Tomm: Not really. I enjoyed talking to you; there are many places we still could go.

Collins: Well, we may still. But at the moment this is just a pleasure for me. I'm looking forward to listening to all this. Thank you.

SOURCE: Don Collins and Karl Tomm. (2009). Karl Tomm: His Changing Views on Family Therapy Over 35 Years. *The Family Journal: Counseling and Therapy for Couples and Families, 17,* 106-117. © 2009 SAGE Publications.

REFERENCES

Ackerman, N. (1938). The unity of the family. *Archives of Pediatrics, 55,* 51-62.

Ackerman, N. (1954). Interpersonal disturbances in the family: Some unresolved problems in psychotherapy. *Psychiatry, 17,* 359-368.

Ackerman, N. (1958). *The psychodynamics of family life.* New York: Basic Books.

Ackerman, N. (1966a). Family psychotherapy—Theory and practice. *American Journal of Psychotherapy, 20,* 405-414.

Ackerman, N. (1966b). *Treating the troubled family*. New York: Basic Books.

Bateson, D., Jackson, D., Haley, J., & Weakland, J. (1956). Towards a theory of schizophrenia. *Behavioral Science, 1*, 251-264.

Bateson, G. (1972). *Steps to an ecology of mind*. San Francisco: Chandler.

Bateson, G. (1979). *Mind and nature: A necessary unity*. New York: E. P. Dutton.

Bowen, M. (1978). *Family therapy in clinical practice*. New York: Jason Aronson.

Coleman, H., Collins, D., & Collins, T. (2005). *Family practice: A problem-based learning approach*. Peosta, IA: Eddie Bowers.

Coleman, S. (Ed.). (1985). *Failures in family therapy*. New York: Guilford.

Collins, D., Jordan, C., & Coleman, H. (2007). *An introduction to family social work* (2nd ed.). Belmont, CA: Thomson.

Epstein, N., Baldwin, D., & Bishop, D. (1983). The McMaster family assessment device. *Journal of Marital and Family Therapy, 9*, 171-180.

Epstein, N., & Bishop, D. (1981). Problem-centered systems therapy of the family. In A. Gurman & D. Kniskern (Eds.), *Handbook of family therapy* (pp. 444-482). New York: Brunner/Mazel.

Epstein, N., Bishop, D., & Levin, S. (1978). The McMaster model of family functioning. *Journal of Marriage and Family Counseling, 4*, 19-31.

Epston, D. (1998). *Catching up with David Epston: A collection of narrative practice-based papers published between 1991-1996*. Adelaide, Australia: Dulwich Centre Publications.

Epston, D., & White, M. (1992). *Experience, contradiction, narrative and imagination*. Adelaide, Australia: Dulwich Centre Publications.

Foucault, M. (1978). *Discipline and punish: The birth of the prison*. New York: Pantheon.

Foucault, M. (1980). *Power/knowledge: Selected interviews and other writings, 1972-1977*. New York: Pantheon.

Lee, G., & Barnett, B. (1994). Using reflective questioning to promote collaborative dialogue. *Journal of Staff Development, 15*(1), 75-80.

Maturana, H. (1978). The biology of language: The epistemology of reality. In G. Miller & E. Lenneberg (Eds.), *Psychology and biology of language and thought* (pp. 28-62). New York: Academic Press.

Maturana, H. (1980). *Autopoiesis and cognition: The realization of the living*. Boston: Reidel.

Miller, S., Hubble, M., & Duncan, B. (1995, March-April). No more bells and whistles. *Networker*, pp. 53-63.

Minuchin, S. (1974). *Families and family therapy*. Cambridge, MA: Harvard University Press.

Rossmann, L. C. (2005). What if we asked circular questions to transform controversial issues? Possibilities for the classroom. *Exchanges: The Online Journal of Teaching and Learning in the CSU*, http://www.calstate.edu/itl/exchanges/classroom/1065_Rossmann_pg2.html.

Ryan, D. (2001). A study of the differential effects of Tomm's questioning styles on therapeutic alliance. *Family Process, 40*, 67-77.

Schon, D. (1987). *Educating the reflective practitioner*. San Francisco: Jossey-Bass.

Schon, D. (1995). Reflective inquiry in social work practice. In P. M. Hess & E. J. Mullen (Eds.), *Practitioner-researcher partnerships: Building knowledge from, in, and for practice* (pp. 31-55). Washington, DC: NASW Press.

Selvini, M., Boscolo, L., Cecchin, G., & Prata, G. (1977). Family rituals: A powerful tool in family therapy. *Family Process, 16*(4), 445-453.

Selvini, M., Boscolo, L., Cecchin, G., & Prata, G. (1988). *Paradox and counterparadox*. New York: Jason Aronson.

Selvini-Palazzoli, M., Boscolo, L., Cecchin, G., & Prata, G. (1978). A ritualized prescription in family therapy: Odd days and even days. *Journal of Marriage and Family Therapy, 4*(3), 3-9.

Selvini-Palazzoli, M., Boscolo, L., Cecchin, G., & Prata, G. (1980). Hypothesizing-circularity-neutrality: Guidelines for the conductor of the session. *Family Process, 19*(1), 3-12.

Tomm, K. (1973). A family approach to emotional problems of children. *Canadian Family Physician, 5*, 183-185.

Tomm, K. (1980). Towards a cybernetic-systems approach to family therapy at the University of Calgary. In D. S. Freeman (Ed.), *Perspectives on family therapy* (pp. 3-18). Vancouver, Canada: Butterworths Press.

Tomm, K. (1981). Circularity: A preferred orientation for family assessment. In A. Gurman (Ed.), *Questions and answers in the practice of family therapy* (pp. 84-87). New York: Brunner/Mazel.

Tomm, K. (1982). The Milan approach to family therapy: A tentative report. In D. Freeman & B. Trute (Eds.), *Treating families with special needs* (pp. 1-31). Ottawa: Canadian Association of Social Workers.

Tomm, K. (1984a). One perspective on the Milan systemic approach: Part I. Overview of development, theory and practice. *Journal of Marital and Family Therapy, 10*(2), 113-125.

Tomm, K. (1984b). One perspective on the Milan systemic approach: Part II. Description of session format, interviewing style and interventions. *Journal of Marital and Family Therapy, 10*(3), 253-271.

Tomm, K. (1985). Circular interviewing: A multifaceted clinical tool. In D. Campbell & R. Draper (Eds.), *Applications of systemic family therapy* (pp. 33-45). New York: Academic Press.

Tomm, K. (1987a). Interventive interviewing: Part I. Strategizing as a fourth guideline for the therapist. *Family Process, 26*(2), 3-13.

Tomm, K. (1987b). Interventive interviewing: Part II. Reflexive questioning as a means to enable self-healing. *Family Process, 26*(2), 153-183.

Tomm, K. (1988). Interventive interviewing: Part III. Intending to ask lineal, circular, strategic or reflexive questions? *Family Process, 27*(1), 1-15.

Tomm, K. (1989). Externalizing the problem and internalizing personal agency. *Journal of Strategic and Systematic Therapies, 8*(1), 16-22.

Tomm, K. (1991, Spring). Beginning of a "HIPs and PIPs" approach to psychiatric assessment. *Calgary Participator*, pp. 21-24.

Tomm, K. (1998). A question of perspective. *Journal of Marital and Family Therapy, 24*(4), 409-413.

Tomm, K., Lannamann, J., & McNamee, S. (1983). No interview today: A consultation team intervenes by not intervening. *Journal of Strategic and Systemic Therapies, 2*, 48-61.

Tomm, K., & Wright, L. (1979). Training in family therapy: Perceptual, conceptual, and executive skills. *Family Process, 18*, 227-250.

Von Bertalanffy, L. (1962). General systems theory: A critical review. *General Systems, 7*, 1-20.

Von Bertalanffy, L. (1968). *General system theory*. New York: George Braziller.

Watzlawick, P., Beavin, J., & Jackson, D. (1967). *Pragmatics of human communication*. New York: Norton.

Wesley, W., & Epstein, N. (1969). *The silent majority*. San Francisco: Jossey-Bass.

White, M. (1986). Negative explanation, restraint and double description: A template for family therapy. *Family Process, 25*(2), 169-184.

White, M. (1997). *Narrative of therapists lives*. Adelaide, Australia: Dulwich Centre Publications.

White, M. (2000a). Reflecting-team work as definitional ceremony revisited. In *Reflections on narrative practice: Essays and interviews* (pp. 59-85). Adelaide, Australia: Dulwich Centre Publications.

White, M. (2000b). *Reflections on narrative practice: Essays and interviews*. Adelaide, Australia: Dulwich Centre Publications.

White, M., & Epston, D. (1990). *Narrative means to therapeutic ends*. New York: Norton.

Don Collins, Department of Social Work, Southern Alberta Region, University of Calgary, Calgary, Alberta, Canada.

Karl Tomm, Calgary Family Therapy Center, Calgary, Alberta, Canada.

2

The Ecology of Families:
A Systems-Developmental Perspective

Living Arrangements Over the Life Course

Families in the 21st Century

Regina M. Bures

University of Florida, Gainesville

Living arrangements are influenced by social and demographic trends. Changes in social norms related to marriage, childbearing, educational attainment, and women's employment have reshaped families, making residential family membership much less continuous over the life course. The increasing complexity of family living arrangements makes a life course perspective essential for understanding families. The special issue titled "Living Arrangements Over the Life Course: Families in the 21st Century" addresses several key themes that will characterize families in the 21st century, including gender and the family, union formation and dissolution, living arrangements, and family migration.

Keywords: *cohabitation; divorce; family migration; gender; immigrant families; living arrangements; marriage; union formation*

The fall in household size has had an important effect on the family as a social unit beyond the fertility and "empty nest" effects. . . . Family membership is becoming much less continuous over the life cycle, affecting the relationships between the generations (which are now much less visible to each other) and life cycle patterns of interaction generally.

—*Kobrin, 1976, p. 137*

AUTHOR'S NOTE: I would like to thank Frances Goldscheider for her advice and support during the preparation of this special issue. I also would like to thank the reviewers who contributed their time and effort to this issue and Diane Buehn for her editorial assistance. Please address correspondence to Regina M. Bures, Department of Sociology, University of Florida, P.O. Box 117330, 3219 Turlington Hall, Gainesville, FL 32611-7330; e-mail: rbures@ufl.edu.

The later portion of the 20th century was marked by a number of significant changes in the family. Family researchers documented the consequences of increases in longevity, declines in fertility, increases in cohabitation and marital instability, and changing ages at marriage on the family life cycle (see Glick, 1977, 1988). Implicit in the concept of the family life cycle is that the core functions of the family are to produce and raise children. Yet the timing and meaning of these events have changed for recent cohorts. Family roles and expectations have changed over time. Families have fewer children. Some families have children earlier, some later. Not all families have children. Not all children are raised in nuclear families.

Family scholars increasingly differentiate between events that occur in one's life and the timing of those events over the life course. For example, marital status transitions have become more common throughout the adult life course. Although widowhood has been postponed, the growth of divorce and remarriage has meant that marital status transitions are less concentrated at the beginning and end of adulthood. Changes in marriage and family formation represent a shift in key transitions that can have lasting effects on the trajectories of one's life course.

Furthermore, children often leave the parental home long before they marry. Increased longevity also means that adults are more likely to have surviving parents who may become dependent and need assistance. These changes represent shifts in intergenerational relations. How these intergenerational transitions will affect an individual depends on the characteristics of that individual as well as his or her relationships with other family members, particularly those who reside nearby.

At any given point in time, individuals' family roles are shaped by their ages and the social and cultural factors that have shaped their lives. By examining living arrangements over the life course, we are able to better understand ongoing family transitions and their consequences for individual lives. This special issue focuses on several key themes that will shape families in the 21st century: gender, union formation and dissolution, living arrangements, and family migration.

GENDER AND FAMILY

We now know that the period in the mid-20th century, when the ideal was the breadwinner-homemaker specialization in the home, was the exception to family patterns, not the rule. Increased labor force participation among women, high rates of divorce, child rearing outside of marriage, and an overall decline in marriage and remarriage challenged the dominant paradigm of the nuclear family. Researchers have often focused on the consequences of these changes for women and children, but later in the life course, as family relationships based on marriage and parenthood grow in importance, the consequences of divorce may accumulate for men (Goldscheider, 1990).

Increasingly, not just women, but also men are single parents, both full- and part-time. Single-parent fathers have recently been one of the fastest growing family types. Single fathers are likely to differ from single mothers in the types and amount of resources they provide to their children. In this issue, Ziol-Guest asks whether single fathers invest differently in their children than do other parental types. She finds that the purchasing decisions of single fathers are distinct from those of both married couples and single mothers. Single fathers spend more on food outside the home, alcohol, and tobacco and less on education.

The impacts of fathers' interaction (or lack of interaction) with their children following union dissolution has been an ongoing issue in the literature on child welfare and development. Swiss and Le Bourdais examine the amount of contact between fathers and their children following a union dissolution using data from the Canadian General Social Survey. Their article suggests that father–child relationships are shaped by more than just sociodemographic and attitudinal factors; the dimensions of contact include the costs of maintaining contact, the father's current family situation, and custody arrangements.

A substantial literature documents the intergenerational consequences of divorce (e.g., see Amato & Cheadle, 2005). If divorce puts men at risk of diminished social support later in life, are there early life course trajectories, such as having grown up in a single-parent family, that may make them more likely to create single parent families? In this issue, Goldscheider, Hofferth, Spearin, and Curtin use data from the National Longitudinal Survey of Youth to examine the extent to which childhood family structure influences young men's likelihood of becoming absent fathers instead of resident fathers. Focusing on the key correlates of parental and partner statuses among young men, they examine three contexts that shape young men's family formation: their own family structures, childhood financial well-being, and the time period in which they grew up. Their results are consistent with prior research demonstrating the importance of economic and educational disadvantage. They also document an apparent weakening of the influence of family structure on men's early parental roles.

UNION FORMATION AND DISSOLUTION

Social and economic changes may have contributed to a mismatch between men's and women's preferences and family expectations. Despite the reality that most couples will consist of two earners, a man may prefer the provider role, and a woman may prefer a partner who can provide for her. Similarly, individuals may prefer partners with no prior marital history. Potential partners who are divorced or have children from prior relationships may be less attractive. As marriage markets become increasingly populated with individuals who have been married or have children, it is unclear the extent to which partner expectations have changed with the times. Goldscheider,

Kaufman, and Sassler examine the relationship between attitudes toward partner characteristics and potential union formation. They describe gender differences in partner preferences on several dimensions: Women are significantly more likely to report a willingness to marry someone with children, someone who has been previously married, or someone of a higher status; men are more likely to be willing to marry someone with a lower status.

Other research looks beyond normative commitment-making trajectories. Cohabiting couples may transition into long-term committed relationships outside of marriage. Studying the relationships of long-term gay and lesbian couples, Reczek, Elliot, and Umberson examine how these couples conceptualize commitment formation outside the traditional marriage ceremony. Their findings of the processes by which individuals construct commitments outside of marriage have the potential to contribute to our understanding of alternative forms of union-making among all adults.

Two articles examine the consequences of parental divorce on the union formation patterns of children. Gähler, Hong, and Bernhardt examine the impact of parental divorce on union disruption among young adults in Sweden. Consistent with prior research, they find that young adults with divorced parents are more likely to experience union disruption themselves. However, this effect becomes insignificant once the possible mechanisms associated with divorce are controlled. They discuss these findings in the context of changing perceptions of divorce: One explanation for the weakening of the effect of parental divorce may be that social norms have adjusted to family realities.

Although research has established that parental divorce may be associated with relationship instability among young adults, little work has examined in detail the impact of parents' subsequent unions. Using data from the National Survey of Families and Households, Sassler, Cunningham, and Lichter examine the relationship between parental marital transitions and the union formation patterns of their adult children. Contrasting the effects of specific parental union transitions with those of parents in a stable marriage, they find that parental transitions may indeed influence the union formation patterns of their young adult children. Their article contributes to our knowledge of the relationship between childhood living arrangements and union formation in young adulthood.

LIVING ARRANGEMENTS

Studying contemporary living arrangements can help us better understand ongoing social changes that may be affecting the family. By understanding who lives with whom and the determinants of those patterns, we can better anticipate potential service needs over the life course. Family size is often an important determinant of living arrangements and can reflect the level of social support available to an individual. Individuals who are childless may have fewer familial supports to draw on as they age, but net of marital status, childlessness per se does not appear to have any significant negative consequences on their psychological state, as reported by Bures, Koropeckyj-Cox, and Loree in this issue. Their findings suggest that social networks outside the home as well as coresidential family may play a significant role in well-being.

Patterns of institutionalization may also affect family patterns and living arrangements. A history of incarceration may affect family relationships and contribute to a smaller social support network. London and Parker examine the relationship between duration of incarceration and age at first incarceration on living arrangements. They find that having been previously incarcerated reduces the likelihood that individuals will be married and increases the likelihood of living alone. To the extent that living alone may be associated with lower levels of social integration, these living arrangements may increase the risks that previously incarcerated individuals face for recidivism and/or continued disadvantage.

Placing the family in historical context can help us to understand the changes that have occurred over time. Van Gaalen and van Poppel describe changes in the living arrangements of children in the Netherlands during the period from 1850 to 1985. They find that historically substantial portions of children did not spend significant amounts of time in two-parent households. Despite increases in divorce, children in the 20th century were more likely to have lived with two parents than those in the previous century.

Living arrangements also reflect cultural differences in familial roles and accommodations that families may make to care for their members. In sub-Saharan Africa, both mothers and grandmothers are considered parental figures. Parker and Short find that grandparent-headed households are linked to positive schooling outcomes in sub-Saharan Africa. In particular, grandmothers are associated with increased school enrollment for children, particularly those not living with their mothers. Given the increased absence of mothers due to migration or early death, their findings illustrate the need to consider the complexity of the family context as well as household structure.

FAMILY MIGRATION AND IMMIGRATION

Independence between generations means that the family context often extends beyond a single residence. Family researchers and policy makers are giving increasing attention to the consequences of both migration and immigration for families. Although many studies focus on who lives with whom, researchers acknowledge that the location and proximity of other family members are important considerations as well. Family research needs to explicitly consider the spatial dimensions of families and the consequences of distance between family members. This includes addressing the impact of family context on residential patterns and mobility decisions, patterns of family migration, and the proximity of family members.

Mobility behavior is shaped by the types of family and life course transitions that occur. The family context of mobility across the life course is important for understanding both living arrangements and support networks. Different stages of the family life course are associated with different types of mobility: Local mobility is associated with family transitions; long distance mobility is associated with work and retirement transitions. Bures examines the relationship between the age of the youngest child at home and parental residential change in later midlife. Her findings are consistent with a life course view of family migration behavior that suggests children leaving home may be associated with increased long distance mobility of adults in later midlife. Understanding the relationship between mobility and family change in later midlife will contribute to a better understanding of where aging individuals will reside and with whom they will reside as they age.

International migration affects the lives of family members who migrate as well as those who remain behind and has important consequences for family formation, kinship ties, living arrangements, and children's outcomes. Family scholars need to explicitly address the theoretical and conceptual issues raised by immigration for families, including current patterns of migrant selectivity, appropriate comparison groups for particular immigrant groups, and the long-term impact of immigration on families and family patterns. Clark, Glick, and Bures present a selective review of the literature on immigrant families in the United States as well as suggestions for future research in this increasingly important area of family research and policy.

CONCLUSION

The motivation for this special issue originated with the 2006 conference "Gender and Family: Agendas for the 21st Century," in honor of Professor Frances Goldscheider's career at Brown University. My goal was to bring together a collection of scholarly articles that reflected the breadth of Fran's scholarship and her impact on family demography while at the same time shedding light on current research issues. These articles pose important questions and extend our understanding of current patterns of living arrangements and family processes. Although a substantial body of literature documents current family patterns, one must recognize the ongoing changes that families experience as a consequence of social and demographic change. Given the importance of families for both emotional and instrumental support, we need a more detailed understanding of how living arrangements affect both the current and cumulative lives of individuals and their families.

SOURCE: Regina M. Bures (2009). Living Arrangements Over the Life Course: Families in the 21st Century. *The Family Journal: Counseling and Therapy for Couples and Families, 30,* 579-585. © 2009 SAGE Publications. Originally published online, February 3, 2009, http://jfi.sagepub.com/

REFERENCES

Amato, P. R., & Cheadle, J. (2005). The long reach of divorce: Divorce and child well-being across three generations. *Journal of Marriage and Family, 67,* 191-206.

Glick, P. C. (1977). Updating the life cycle of the family. *Journal of Marriage and the Family, 39,* 5-13.

Glick, P. C. (1988). Fifty years of family demography: A record of social change. *Journal of Marriage and the Family, 50,* 861-873.

Goldscheider, F. K. (1990). The aging of the gender revolution. *Research on Aging, 12,* 531-545.

Kobrin, F. E. (1976). The fall in household size and the rise of the primary individual in the United States. *Demography, 13,* 127-138.

3 Ethnicity and Family Life

Understanding Culture and Worldview in Family Systems

Use of the Multicultural Genogram

Anita Jones Thomas
Northeastern Illinois University

The field of family counseling has recognized the importance of context on individuals' lives. However, few tools for assessing the influence of culture exist. This article describes the multicultural genogram, which assesses both the culture and worldview of family members. The multicultural genogram can be used to assess cultural factors as well as to establish rapport with diverse families. Cultural variables explored in the genogram include race, ethnicity, gender, immigration, social class, and spirituality. Clinical examples are provided.

To be effective, family counselors must be sensitive to the broader ecosystemic context, including cultural factors and worldview, as the context of individual behaviors and functioning often extends beyond the family to culture (Arnold, 1993; Hardy & Laszloffy, 1992; Szapocznik & Kurtines, 1993). Culture has been defined as a set of implicit norms, values, and beliefs that influences the attitudes, behaviors, and customs of a group of individuals (Gushue, 1993). Falicov (1995) defined culture as a set of shared worldviews, meanings, and adaptive behaviors derived from simultaneous membership and participation in a variety of contexts including language, age, gender, race, ethnicity, religion, socioeconomic status, education, and sexual orientation. Both definitions of culture indicate that cultural values define behaviors and therefore establish norms for attitudes and behaviors within families.

Culture influences the behaviors and beliefs of family members and determines expectations for members (Gushue, 1993). The culture of a family affects individual behaviors, child-rearing practices, discipline, and the importance of achievement and education. Culture often determines the form and functioning of families including the type of family, family size, and shape (McGill, 1983; McGoldrick, Giordano, & Pearce, 1996), and culture defines boundaries, rules for interaction, and communication patterns between family members and within the community (Falicov & Brudner-White, 1983; McGill, 1992; McGoldrick et al., 1996; Preli & Bernard, 1993). The roles of family members are determined by cultural factors as well as rules and manifestations of various stages in the family life cycle (McGoldrick et al., 1996; Schwartzman, 1983). Finally, culture defines for families ways of defining problems and outlines specific coping skills (Schwartzman, 1983).

Most of the literature on multicultural issues in family therapy focuses on working with ethnic minorities (Arnold, 1993; Boyd-Franklin, 1989; David & Erickson, 1990; Hightower, Rodriguez, & Adams, 1983; Ho, 1987; McGill, 1983; McGoldrick, 1993; McGoldrick et al., 1996; Pinderhughes, 1995; Saba, Karrer, & Hardy, 1989; Schwartzman, 1983). However, the term *culture* includes more than values and beliefs of a particular racial or ethnic group (Falicov, 1995; Hardy, 1997). The literature on ethnic minorities often serves as a cookbook for counselors working with diverse clients (Speight, Myers, Cox, & Highlen, 1991), and the literature fails to account for intragroup differences or the interaction of various cultural factors. Some family counselors have recognized the interaction of race/ethnicity with other cultural factors (Anderson, 1991; Boyd-Franklin, 1993; McGoldrick et al., 1996; Preli & Bernard, 1993). Ethnicity is affected by the generations that have resided in the United States, immigration patterns, historical and contemporary values, interethnic marriages, socioeconomic status, region, religion, politics, discrimination, language, and unique family experiences (Anderson, 1991; Boyd-Franklin, 1993; McGoldrick et al., 1996; Preli & Bernard, 1993). The culturally sensitive family counselor needs to, therefore, look beyond race and ethnicity to include other cultural factors when working with families. By focusing only on ethnicity, the counselor will fail to understand the richness and complexity of families' cultures and family functioning.

Family counselors also need to be sensitive to differences within various cultural groups, and understanding worldview gives a better indication of lifestyles, beliefs, and value systems as well as individual differences within cultural groups. Worldview is a holistic concept that encompasses belief systems, values, lifestyles, and modes of problem solving for a particular cultural group (Sue & Sue, 1990). There are five dimensions to worldview: view of human nature, relationship to time, social relationships, human activity, and relationship to nature. Montalvo and Gutierrez (1989) suggest that worldview can be inferred in working with families through their orientation and that a basic understanding of cultural issues may give counselors a basis for inferring worldview.

Families serve as the primary agent for transmitting cultural values and worldview to their children (Johnson, 1995), and parents and extended family help children to learn, internalize, and develop understanding of culture through both covert and overt means (Preli & Bernard, 1993). Cultural socialization governs styles of interactions, attitudes, and values (Johnson, 1995). Through cultural socialization, families must teach both positive and negative messages of their particular cultural group as well as other cultures (Preli & Bernard, 1993). Cultural socialization may not be a smooth process. Conflict due to generational differences, levels of acculturation among family members, and differences in racial/ethnic identity may occur as parents attempt to teach or instill culture-of-origin values to their families (Gushue, 1993; Hines, Garcia-Preto, McGoldrick, Almeida, & Weltman, 1992; McGoldrick, Pearce, & Giordano, 1982; Paniagua, 1996). Conflict in families may also result from different gender-role expectations, social class, religious beliefs or spirituality, or sexual orientation. It is imperative then that family counselors understand or be open to understanding the impact of culture and worldview on family functioning and the presenting problem or symptoms and the cultural socialization process in families as well as how culture defines conflict resolution and problem-solving skills.

ASSESSMENT OF CULTURE

Counselors working with culturally diverse families need to assess cultural factors within the early stages of therapy, particularly as they relate to the presenting problem, diagnosis, or functioning of the family. Assessment helps counselors to understand how representative the family is of their cultural group, to determine intragroup differences (Gushue, 1993; Lappin, 1983), and to identify potential resources and family strengths (Anderson, 1991). Assessment of culture is important even if cultural dimensions seem unrelated to the presenting complaint. For example, family members acculturate and assimilate at different rates (Gushue, 1993; Lappin, 1983; Montalvo & Gutierrez, 1989). Members may be at different stage levels of racial or ethnic identity, and the differences in identity and acculturation may lead to various value systems in the family. Finally, assessing the cultural context can help determine the appropriateness of behaviors and whether symptoms are culturally sanctioned.

Many counselors have recognized the importance of assessing cultural variables and worldview when working with families (Canino & Spurlock, 1994; McGoldrick et al., 1982). Family counselors are encouraged to directly ask families to teach them about their culture and acculturation

(Montalvo & Gutierrez, 1983; Paniagua, 1996; Ross & Phipps, 1986) and to ask culturally appropriate questions (Paniagua, 1996). Other family therapists have spoken of the importance of using the genogram or cultural map to assess the impact of cultural factors across multiple generations (Gushue, 1993; Hardy & Laszloffy, 1995; Landau, 1982; Lappin, 1983; McGoldrick, 1993; Preli & Bernard, 1993; Spiegel, 1982). The multicultural genogram should be used to help families explore and clarify worldview. Johnson (1995) suggests that cultural socialization is enhanced through effective communication and that effective communication helps family members to acknowledge feelings and enhances oral traditions, rituals, history, and heritage of culture. The genogram not only enhances communication in families, but also helps families to explore and share cultural backgrounds and traditions. As the multicultural genogram can improve cultural socialization, determine the impact of culture on family roles and functioning, and highlight family differences, it is an important assessment tool for family counselors.

THE MULTICULTURAL GENOGRAM

The genogram is a useful tool for assessing families and determining multigenerational patterns, significant life events, rituals, roles, and the nature of relationships among family members and often provides direction for treatment (McGoldrick & Gerson, 1985). The multicultural genogram provides all the information listed above but includes an assessment of worldview and cultural factors that often influence behaviors of members. Specific questions on cultural factors (race/ethnicity, immigration, gender, socioeconomic status, spirituality) and worldview that can be included in the genogram are discussed in detail below, along with clinical examples. (It should be noted that names and ages have been changed to protect the identity of clients). As cultural factors are complex and often interwoven, family counselors are encouraged to weave all the factors together for families as they tell their cultural stories. It should also be noted that some cultural factors will have more salience to family members, and counselors should allow the family to lead the discussion of cultural factors. Differences in cultural values between family members should also be included, and counselors should facilitate and enhance communication of diverse views and help families find compromise and negotiation of values, if necessary.

Ethnicity

Ethnicity has been defined as an aspect of a person's social identity that is a part of an individual's self-concept that derives from his or her knowledge of membership in a social group together with the value and emotional significance attached to that membership. Ethnicity includes three components: cultural values, attitudes, and behaviors; a subjective sense of group membership; and experiences with minority status (Phinney, 1996). Ethnicity patterns thoughts, feelings, and behaviors including eating habits and patterns, work, relationships, and rituals and traditions (McGoldrick & Giordano, 1996). Individuals also differ in terms of ethnic identity, which includes the sense of membership in the ethnic group and attitudes and feelings about group membership (Phinney, 1996). In families, ethnicity determines family patterns and belief systems (McGoldrick, 1993; McGoldrick et al., 1982), who is included in the family, and the family life-cycle stage issues (Breunlin, Schwartz, & Kune-Karrer, 1992; McGoldrick et al., 1996). Ethnic groups differ in regard to relationships, rules, family and personal dilemmas, and strategies for resolving conflict (Hines et al., 1992). Family members may differ in their stage of ethnic identity (Gushue, 1993), and family members may have conflicts resulting from differences in ethnic identity and values (McGoldrick & Giordano, 1996). Similarly, difficulties may arise in families with interethnic marriages (McGoldrick et al., 1982).

As ethnicity is important to family functioning, counselors should inquire about ethnicity, the ethnic identity of each member, and the extent to which ethnicity affects the family. Exploration of ethnicity may also be useful in establishing or maintaining rituals, tasks, stories, and metaphors and may provide opportunities for change in families (Breunlin et al., 1992). The following questions on ethnicity should be included in the genogram:

1. What is the ethnicity of each family member?

2. What family rules are determined by ethnicity?

3. What roles are assigned due to ethnicity?

4. What is the relationship between ethnicity and worldview?

5. If the ethnicity of members differs, are there similar characteristics across various ethnic groups?

6. How is conflict handled according to ethnic groups?

7. How do family members handle conflicts across ethnicity?

8. What are specific rules for marriage and child rearing according to ethnicity?

Clinical Example

Maria, a 14-year-old biracial adolescent, was referred for treatment by her school due to failing grades, fighting with peers, and difficulty with authority. Maria was in danger of having to repeat the eighth grade for the third time, and her teachers were concerned because Maria threatened to drop out of school if she were retained again. The school was also concerned that Maria may have become involved in gangs. Maria's father, Juan, age 37, is Puerto Rican and left the family when she was 8 years old. Maria has weekend visitations with her father, and when she visits, she spends time with his extended family, including his mother, three brothers, and two aunts. Mary, her mother, is 40 years old and of English descent. Maria has two older half siblings with whom she has no contact. Maria entered treatment with her mother, and both agreed to family therapy. Mary reported concerns about her daughter's future, and both indicated that they have a conflictual relationship. When asked if culture had an impact on the family or family functioning, both seemed to indicate that it did not.

The family agreed to complete a cultural genogram, and the influence of culture both on the family's functioning and presenting problems emerged (see Figure 3.1). Maria's mixed ethnic background seemed to affect her peer relationships, and she reported feeling confused about her ethnicity and racial background. Maria was frequently teased by Latino peers for acting White, and part of her involvement with gang activities was to prove her ethnicity. Maria reported that her mother did not discuss race or ethnicity with her. The family was asked to explore ethnicity, race, and immigration status to improve Maria's understanding of her cultural background, to improve her self-concept, and to foster cohesiveness with both parents. As treatment progressed, Mary became excited about exploring her English background. She learned more about her family's immigration patterns and became reconnected with extended family. Maria also explored her Puerto Rican heritage with her father and was able to express fears that she had of her father returning to Puerto Rico. Eventually, Mary was able to participate in Puerto Rican activities with her daughter, and the two became closer as they cooked traditional meals together.

The discussion of the relationship between ethnicity and worldview exposed differing expectations of interpersonal relationships and coping methods between Maria and Mary. Mary's English background favored individualism and autonomy, and she valued privacy and independence. Juan's family valued collectivism, and the family included not only extended family, but also family friends and important community members such as priests. Maria complained in treatment that she would like to know her mother's family, and as Mary explored her family's history, both developed closer relationships with Mary's family. An exploration of conflict styles according to ethnicity and worldview helped both to understand the patterns of their arguments. Mary was able to gradually increase her conflict tolerance to accommodate Maria's tendency for high verbal expression during arguments, and Maria also learned to try to calmly express her feelings to her mother.

Race

For many families in this country, race may have more salience than ethnicity, and many families may need to explore the importance and impact of racism (Paniagua, 1996). Race is an issue of political oppression in this country (McGoldrick & Giordano, 1996). Because of the history of slavery and oppression, many African Americans view race as inherently more important than ethnicity. Race influences roles, functioning, and belief systems. For example, Boyd-Franklin (1989) discusses the strengths of African American families, including the role of the extended family and the flexibility of family roles. As Asian American and Latino families also value the extended family and greatly respect elders (Sue & Sue, 1990), counselors need to consider the definition of family and functioning when working with these groups.

Racial identity evolves from socialization experiences and psychological and sociopolitical attitudes toward race (Helms, 1995) and includes a sense of group membership to race as well as attitudes toward other races or other groups. Racial identity models postulate that individuals progress through stages of low salience and awareness of race to integration of values and beliefs prescribed by race (Cross, 1995; Helms, 1990). Gushue (1993) indicates that family members may differ in racial identity, leading to conflict within families.

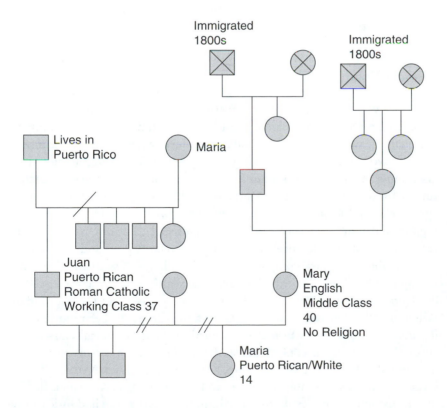

Figure 3.1   Maria's Multicultural Genogram

For African American families, the transmission of values occurs through racial socialization. Racial socialization of African Americans has been defined as the process of helping children integrate a sense of self in a hostile environment or to be physically and emotionally healthy within an environment of extreme stress and occurs through both explicit and implicit methods (Greene, 1992; Stevenson, 1994). As families are primarily responsible for racial socialization and because a positive sense of racial identity is important for self-concept, family counselors should explore the impact of race on family functioning. Breunlin et al. (1992) suggest that family therapists should encourage families to discuss racial oppression and to explore their definition of race. The following questions are suggested to examine racial issues in the family:

1. What is the racial background of family members?

2. Does race differ from ethnicity according to each family member?

3. What roles, rules, or responsibilities are determined by race?

4. What is the relationship between race and worldview?

5. How is conflict resolved according to race?

6. Do racial differences in the family, either current or historical, cause conflict?

Clinical Example

Amber was a 13-year-old African American who was seen in treatment as part of a teenage pregnancy prevention program. At the beginning of treatment, it was believed that Amber may have been pregnant because of sexual involvement with three boys. Amber also was receiving failing grades in a racially mixed school and drug experimentation was suspected. Amber lived with her mother, Marissa, and her younger half brother, Eric, age 6. The multicultural genogram was used with the family to establish rapport in the initial stage of therapy (see Figure 3.2). The discussion of racial issues highlighted differences in attitudes between Amber and her mother. Amber, who has a dark complexion, identified herself as African American as opposed to Black. She explained that she was having difficulty at school due to racial issues. Her African American peers teased her for having dark skin and called her names such as *darky* and *blacky*. Amber reported feeling uncomfortable with White peers, partly because of social class differences. Amber compensated with her African American peers by promoting her sexuality, listening to gangsta rap, and skipping classes. Marissa did not seem to understand Amber's feelings and made many statements reflective of preencounter attitudes (Cross, 1995), indicating that she had little or low salience to race. The family was encouraged to participate in activities that emphasized Afrocentric values and African American heritage to promote

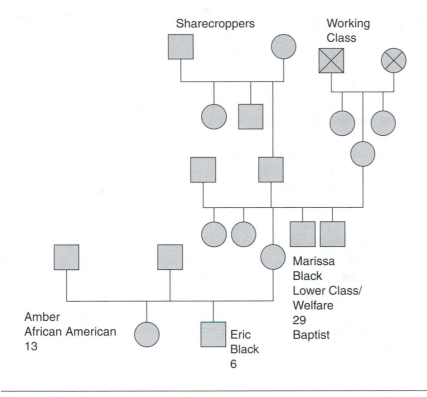

Figure 3.2 Amber's Multicultural Genogram

salience of racial issues for the mother and to provide positive African American images and role models for Amber. The therapist also encouraged discussions on racial issues in the counseling sessions, and the family worked to develop appropriate responses and coping mechanisms for Amber. Amber became more self-confident and comfortable with her racial identity and developed new friendships and a support network. As her self-concept improved, Amber engaged in fewer sexual behaviors.

Marissa also was able to develop a positive racial identity in treatment. She reported that she sometimes felt that her siblings were favored in her family because they had lighter complexions. Marissa coped with her feelings of rejection by not emphasizing the importance of race. The focus on racial issues in treatment helped Marissa to resolve feelings of rejection and hurt from childhood. Additionally, Marissa's gradual willingness to discuss racial issues provided appropriate role modeling for Amber and began the process of racial socialization for the family.

Immigration/Acculturation

Although the process of immigration often brings new opportunities and experiences to families, it can be quite stressful and is often associated with grief and loss issues (Falicov, 1995). Immigration can lead to isolation, enmeshment, and disengagement for families (Landau, 1982), and the impact of immigration often lasts for several generations (McGoldrick et al., 1982). Immigration patterns have an effect on family functioning, family patterns, and reactions to stress (Landau, 1982). The reasons for immigrating to the new setting have an impact on the level of stress experienced by families, as do plans to return to the culture of origin, if they exist (McGoldrick & Giordano, 1996). Parental attitudes on immigration influence child-rearing beliefs and practices including language issues (McGoldrick & Giordano, 1996). Often, family disruptions occur due to the separations and reunions of migration patterns, and parents may be disempowered by raising children in a culture that differs from the culture of origin (Falicov, 1995). Immigration can cause changes in rituals and practices in families, particularly if the socioeconomic status changes.

The process of balancing the values of the host culture with the culture of origin is termed acculturation, and acculturation and the level of stress that families experience is either facilitated or impeded according to the degree of fit or conflict that is experienced in interacting with diverse cultures (Hines et al., 1992). The acculturation process for immigrants differs across generations, with children often having more mainstream values than do parents or grandparents (Gushue, 1993; Lappin, 1983). Acculturation also may be affected by the age of family members at the time of immigration (Canino & Spurlock, 1994). Family members often become split and possibly polarized between dominant values and the values from the culture of origin (Breunlin et al., 1992). Paniagua (1996) indicates that differences in acculturation may cause discrepancies in views, values, lifestyles, and attitudes toward understanding and solving problems within families.

Family counselors should be aware of migration stresses (McGoldrick & Giordano, 1996), and counselors need to explore the impact of immigration on the family and differences that occur due to differing acculturation rates. Lappin (1983) states that examining the migratory history of the family often joins the family with the therapist, allows for assessment of acculturation, and indicates for the therapist the family's capacity for handling stress. This exploration is often helpful in clarifying the nature of conflict in the family (Hines et al., 1992) and determining whether the transition between cultures is related to the presenting problem (Landau, 1982). The family's hopes of returning to the culture of origin should be explored, particularly as this relates to grief and loss issues (McGoldrick & Giordano, 1996). Finally, therapists should explore the availability of resources and social support for immigrant families (Landau, 1982). The following questions on immigration are suggested:

1. What is the family's history of immigration?

2. When did individual members migrate to America and why?

3. Are there plans to return to the country of origin?

4. What difficulties did they face during immigration?

5. Has each member acculturated to the majority culture?

6. Is there conflict between members who retain culture of origin and members who have acculturated?

Clinical Example

Sharla is a 24-year-old second-generation Indian whose parents immigrated to the United States when she was an infant. She presented in treatment with depressive symptoms of depressed mood, irritability, feelings of hopelessness, low self-esteem, and difficulty with concentration. Sharla had just ended her engagement with Mark, who was Italian and Greek, because of tension and conflict from both of their families of origin. Sharla's family had come to the United States in order for the father, Anil, to complete an engineering degree (see Figure 3.3). The family had intended to return to India, but decided to remain in this country after Anil received an excellent job offer. The discussion of immigration during completion of the multicultural genogram revealed differing levels of acculturation. Anil had difficulty initially adjusting to American values and customs and coped with grief and loss issues by immersing himself in his work. He had rigidly adhered to Indian values and tried to raise Sharla to be aware of Indian customs. Sharla reported that her mother, Amina, was more acculturated as she became involved in several community organizations and did volunteer work. She converted to Catholicism and became active in the local parish. Although within the home the family maintained traditional gender roles, Amina was active outside the home and encouraged Sharla to adopt dominant values and beliefs, including academic achievement and independence. The one difference in values that caused conflict in the family was intimate interpersonal relationships. Although Sharla was allowed to date Americans, her father assumed that Sharla would marry an Indian.

Throughout the discussion of immigration and the family's cultural values, Sharla reported that she remembered being confused as a child about value systems. She also indicated that although her mother encouraged her to have dominant values, her mother did not support these ideas in front of her father, leaving Sharla feeling confused and not supported. As the therapy progressed, Sharla was encouraged to continue to develop her identity and to explore and accept her own value systems. After the discussion of cultural values, Sharla was able to discuss grief and loss issues not only from the failed relationship but also from the racism that she felt from her fiancee's family and from the lack of support provided by her mother.

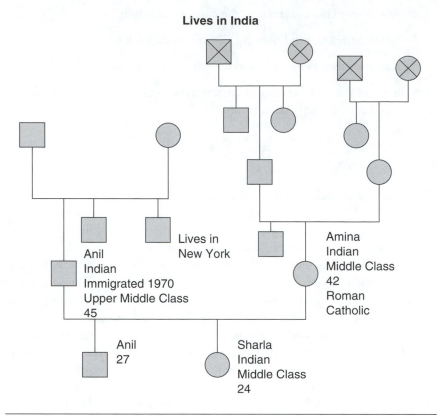

Figure 3.3   Sharla's Multicultural Genogram

Social Class

The social class of families often makes an impact on the way in which families function, and counselors need to assess the role of social class in families' lives as well as the history of social class (Saba & Rodgers, 1989). It is part of the American dream to be financially successful and for each generation to be as successful if not more successful than its predecessors. Many individuals migrate to this country to prosper economically (Breunlin et al., 1992). Intragroup cultural and intergenerational differences are often determined by the family's socioeconomic status (McGoldrick & Giordano, 1996). The upward mobility of families may lead families to dissociate themselves from the culture of origin (McGoldrick et al., 1982) as families may move to dominant-culture neighborhoods to provide opportunities for their children. Similarly, poverty places stress on families and their functioning, and the family's social class may determine treatment strategies selected by therapists (Boyd-Franklin, 1993). For example, counselors may need to work to coordinate services and to empower poor or working class individuals.

Family counselors should assess the socioeconomic status of individuals as well as changes in class structure across generations. Saba and Rodgers (1989) suggest asking families directly about their current job positions and if the wages and salaries are enough to cover current household expenses. It is also important for counselors to assess the impact of socioeconomic status on the presenting problem (Paniagua, 1996). The following questions are recommended for social class:

1. What role/meaning does social class have for members?

2. What is the relationship between social class and worldview?

3. Does social class differ across generations?

4. What resources are available to members due to social class?

5. Has there been a change in current social class?

6. Are there conflicts in the family around finances or social class?

Clinical Example

The Smith family entered treatment on the recommendation of the school because of difficulties with the oldest son, Will, who had been diagnosed with attention deficit hyperactivity disorder since age 8. The family consisted of the father, William, age 45, Sarah, age 42, Will, age 15, and Melissa, age 12. The family had just moved from the East Coast, and the mother, Sarah, reported having difficulty adjusting to the move (see Figure 3.4). Sarah reported that she usually had worked with the school systems to coordinate services for Will but that she was experiencing depression because of the relocation. The family moved because William had completed business school and had secured an executive position. The family's income level had changed dramatically; the family had lived in an urban lower-class community but now lived in an upper-middle-class suburban area. Both Sarah and William had been raised in working-class families, and William regarded the change in social class as positive. With the relocation, the family was separated from the family of origin and extended family members. Sarah had been involved in many community activities before the move and had received social support from community agencies for the children. She found living in the suburban area to be isolating and indicated that she had difficulty making new friends. Because of her depression, Sarah felt that she had not been as attentive to the children and that she was not providing adequate discipline. The therapy focused on helping Will to behave and achieve appropriately in school and on alleviating Sarah's depressive symptoms and helping her to adjust to the social class change. As she became more involved in volunteering and in building social support systems and friendships, her depressive symptoms decreased. Sarah was able to use more appropriate parenting skills and the family's functioning improved.

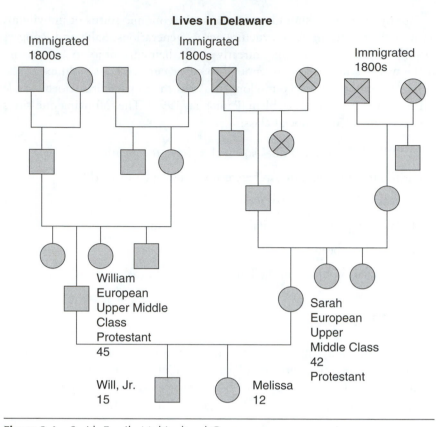

Figure 3.4   Smith Family Multicultural Genogram

Gender

Roles and responsibilities in families are often determined not only by race and ethnicity but also according to gender and members' expectations on gender (Hines et al., 1992). Hardy (1997) states the importance of using race and gender as organizing principles in work with families. Many cultural groups have a clear demarcation of sex-role behavior (Canino & Spurlock, 1994). Comas-Diaz (1994) discusses the complexity of gender for women of color as gender affects attitudes and functioning, including self-esteem and issues of physical beauty. Issues of power and equity are often sources of conflict for family members (Breunlin et al., 1992), particularly if the marital relationship has differing gender expectations. Immigration may also cause a shift in gender roles for families, and differences in gender roles may differ from the culture of origin and the new culture (Canino & Spurlock, 1994). The following questions are recommended to include gender roles and expectations in the genogram:

1. What is the role of gender for each member as defined by ethnicity/ culture of origin?

2. What behaviors, characteristics, beliefs, and values are defined by gender?

3. How are gender roles divided in the family? In the family of origin?

4. How is conflict between gender roles handled?

5. How do beliefs about gender roles influence child-rearing beliefs?

Spirituality/Religion

Spirituality, which includes a notion of transcendence, communal spirit, and a relationship with a higher power, has been used as a source of support and a mechanism for resiliency for many culturally diverse families (Boyd-Franklin, 1993; Johnson, 1995). According to Johnson, spirituality connects people with each other, nature, the spirit world, and Mother Earth; prescribes moral and ethical behaviors; and provides supportive guidelines for dealing with grief and loss. Spiritual beliefs are related to the development of self, and spirituality is associated with being balanced and psychologically healthy (Comas-Diaz, 1994). Breunlin et al. (1992) also indicate that spirituality often serves as an interpretation of behaviors for culturally diverse families. Spiritual beliefs are used as a source of coping and serve as personal strengths in times of crisis (Comas-Diaz, 1994). Because spirituality has an impact on behaviors and family rules, spirituality and religious practices can be assessed in the genogram through the following questions:

1. What is the spiritual or religious history of the family?

2. What characteristics, values, and beliefs are influenced by spirituality or religion?

3. What is the relationship between spirituality and worldview?

4. If members differ in religious or spiritual beliefs, what are the similarities in values?

5. What are the differences in values and beliefs according to spirituality?

6. How are conflicts due to different religious values resolved?

Clinical Example

Sasha, 15 years old, presented in treatment due to extreme phobia of walking, especially walking to school, which developed after she had been hit by a snow plow on the way home from school. Sasha's family had immigrated to this country from Czechoslovakia when she was 10 and indicated their willingness to participate in Sasha's treatment despite their limited English skills. The family had completed an extensive intake assessment that included cultural issues and had indicated that they practiced a form of Eastern religion and that they would like to have spiritual issues included in the therapy. Systematic desensitization was used to help with anxiety, and the parents were taught the hierarchy and relaxation techniques to use at home. During one of the sessions, Sasha's mother eagerly told of a religious practice that the family had used before immigrating. In the practice, the family would light incense and then engage in relaxation techniques. Each person would then use visual imagery and focus on a bright light that represents the life force and imagine that the light envelopes and cleanses them, bringing them closer to the higher power. The family decided to use a variation of the meditation and systematic desensitization, having Sasha imagine being enveloped by the light and surrendering her fears to the light and the life force. Blending the cultural and spiritual ritual with a traditional psychotherapy technique used family strengths and cultural resources. Sasha was able to more quickly resolve her fear.

CONCLUSION

Because of the increase in culturally diverse families that family counselors will treat, it is imperative that family counselors are sensitive to cultural issues. Culture and worldview should be examined in connection to family functioning, roles, rules, responsibilities, expectations, the presenting problem, and problem-solving methods and traditional healing practices. Family counselors are encouraged to use the multicultural genogram to assess worldview, ethnicity, race, immigration, social class, gender, and spirituality of family members. Other areas of concern that could be included in the multicultural genogram include majority/minority status, sexual orientation, regional background, and physical disabilities (Breunlin et al., 1992). Questions on culture and worldview should include identification, expectations, the relationship to the presenting problem or conflict, and conflict resolution styles. The multicultural genogram is suggested to help family counselors to collect information on cultural issues from families in a systematic manner and to enhance the therapeutic process. The genogram serves as a tool for examining all cultural factors that have salience or meaning for families, and family counselors are encouraged to use the genogram to help families tell their cultural stories.

SOURCE: Anita Jones Thomas (1998). Understanding Culture and Worldview in Family Systems: Use of the Multicultural Genogram. *The Family Journal: Counseling and Therapy for Couples and Families, 6,* 24-32. © 1998 SAGE Publications.

REFERENCES

Anderson, J. D. (1991). Group work with families: A multicultural perspective. *Social Work With Groups, 13*(4), 85-101.

Arnold, M. S. (1993). Ethnicity and training in marital and family therapists. *Counselor Education and Supervision, 33,* 139-147.

Boyd-Franklin, N. (1989). *Black families in therapy A multi-system approach.* New York: Guilford.

Boyd-Franklin, N. (1993). Race, class, and poverty. In F. Walsh (Ed.), *Normal family processes* (pp. 361-376). New York: Guilford.

Breunlin, D. C., Schwartz, R. C., & Kune-Karrer, B. M. (1992). *Metaframeworks: Transcending the models of family therapy.* San Francisco: Jossey-Bass.

Canino, I. A., & Spurlock, J. (1994). *Culturally diverse children and adolescents: Assessment, diagnosis, and treatment.* New York: Guildford.

Comas-Diaz, L. (1994). An integrative approach. In L. Comas-Diaz & B. Green (Eds.), *Women of color: Integrating ethnic and gender identities in psychotherapy* (pp. 287-318). New York: Guilford.

Cross, W. E., Jr. (1995). The psychology of nigrescence: Revising the Cross model. In J. G. Ponterotto, J. M. Casas, L. A. Suzuki, & C. M. Alexander (Eds.), *Handbook of multicultural counseling* (pp. 93-122). Newbury Park, CA: Sage.

David, A. B., & Erickson, C. A. (1990). Ethnicity and the therapist's use of self. *Family Therapy, 27*(3), 211-216.

Falicov, C. J. (1995). Training to think culturally: A multidimensional comparative framework. *Family Process, 34,* 373-388.

Falicov, C. J., & Brudner-White, L. (1983). Shifting the family triangle: The issue of cultural and contextual relativity. In J. C. Hansen & C. J. Falicov (Eds.), *Cultural perspectives in family therapy: The family therapy collections* (pp. 51-67). Rockville, MD: Aspen.

Greene, B. A. (1992). Racial socialization as a tool in psychotherapy with African American children. In L. A. Vargas & J. D. Koss-Chioino (Eds.), *Working with culture: Psychotherapeutic strategies with ethnic minority children and adolescents* (pp. 63-81). San Francisco: Jossey-Bass.

Gushue, G. V. (1993). Cultural-identity development and family assessment: An interaction model. *The Counseling Psychologist, 21,* 487-513.

Hardy, K. V. (1997). Steps toward becoming culturally competent. *Family Therapy News, 28*(2), 13, 19.

Hardy, K. V., & Laszloffy, T. A. (1992). Training racially sensitive family therapists: Context, content, and contact. *Families in Society: The Journal of Contemporary Human Services, 73*(6), 364-370.

Hardy, K. V., & Laszloffy, T. A. (1995). The cultural genogram: Key to training culturally competent family therapists. *Journal of Marital and Family Therapy, 21,* 227-237.

Helms, J. E. (1990). *Black and White racial identity: Theory, research, and practice.* New York: Greenwood.

Helms, J. E. (1995). An update of Helm's White and people of color racial identity models. In J. G. Ponterotto, J. M. Casas, L. A. Suzuki, & C. M. Alexander, (Eds.),

Handbook of multicultural counseling (pp. 181-198). Thousand Oaks, CA: Sage.

Hightower, N. A., Rodriguez, S., & Adams, J. (1983). Ethnically mixed co-therapy with families. *Family Therapy, 10*(2), 105-110.

Hines, P., Garcia-Preto, N., McGoldrick, M., Almeida, R., & Weltman, S. (1992). Intergenerational relationships across cultures. *Families in Society, 73*(6), 323-338.

Ho, M. K. (1987). *Family therapy with ethnic minorities.* Newbury Park, CA: Sage.

Ibrahim, F. (1985). Effective cross-cultural counseling and psychotherapy: A framework. *The Counseling Psychologist, 13,* 625-638.

Johnson, A. C. (1995). Resiliency mechanisms in culturally diverse families. *The Family Journal: Counseling and Therapy for Couples and Families, 3,* 316-324.

Landau, J. (1982). Therapy with families in cultural transition. In M. McGoldrick, J. K. Pearce, & J. Giordano (Eds.), *Ethnicity in family therapy* (pp. 552-572). New York: Guilford.

Lappin, J. (1983). On becoming a culturally conscious family therapist. In J. C. Hansen & C. J. Falicov (Eds.), *Cultural perspectives in family therapy: The family therapy collections* (pp. 122-135). Rockville, MD: Aspen.

McGill, D. W. (1983). Cultural concepts for family therapy. In J. C. Hansen & C. J. Falicov (Eds.), *Cultural perspectives in family therapy: The family therapy collections* (pp. 108-121). Rockville, MD: Aspen.

McGill, D. W. (1992). The cultural story in multicultural family therapy. *Families in Society, 73*(6), 339-349.

McGoldrick, M. (1993). Ethnicity, cultural diversity, and normality. In F. Walsh (Ed.), *Normal family process* (2nd ed., pp. 331-360). New York: Guilford.

McGoldrick, M., & Gerson, R. (1985). *Genograms in family assessment.* New York: W. W. Norton.

McGoldrick, M., & Giordano, J. (1996). Overview: Ethnicity and family therapy. In M. McGoldrick, J. Giordano, & J. K. Pearce (Eds.), *Ethnicity and family therapy* (2nd ed., pp. 1-27). New York: Guilford.

McGoldrick, M., Giordano, J., & Pearce, J. K. (Eds.). (1996). *Ethnicity and family therapy* (2nd ed.). New York: Guilford.

McGoldrick, M., Pearce, J., & Giordano, J. K. (Eds.). (1982). *Ethnicity and family therapy.* New York: Guilford.

Montalvo, B., & Gutierrez, M. J. (1983). A perspective for the use of the cultural dimension in family therapy. In J. C. Hansen & C. J. Falicov (Eds.), *Cultural perspectives in family therapy: The family therapy collections* (pp. 15-32). Rockville, MD: Aspen.

Montalvo, B., & Gutierrez, M. J. (1989). Nine assumptions for working with ethnic minority families. In G. W. Saba, B. M. Karrer, & K. V. Hardy (Eds.), *Minorities and family therapy.* New York: Haworth Press.

Paniagua, F. A. (1996). Cross-cultural guidelines in family therapy. *The Family Journal: Counseling and Therapy for Couples and Families, 4*(2), 127-138.

Phinney, J. S. (1996). When we talk about American ethnic groups, what do we mean? *American Psychologist, 51,* 918-927.

Pinderhughes, E. (1995). Empowering diverse populations: Family practice in the 21st century. *Families in Society: The Journal of Contemporary Human Services, 76,* 131-140.

Preli, R., & Bernard, J. M. (1993). Making multiculturalism relevant for majority culture graduate students. *Journal of Marital and Family Therapy, 19*(1), 5-16.

Ross, J. L., & Phipps, E. J. (1986). Understanding the family in multiple cultural contexts: Avoiding therapeutic traps. *Contemporary Family Therapy, 8,* 255-263.

Saba, G. W., Karrer, B. M., & Hardy, K. V. (1989). *Minorities and family therapy.* New York: Haworth.

Saba, G. W., & Rodgers, D. V. (1989). Discrimination in urban family practice: Lessons from minority poor families. In G. W. Saba, B. M. Karrer, & K. V. Hardy (Eds.), *Minorities and family therapy.* New York: Haworth.

Schwartzman, J. (1983). Family ethnography: A tool for clinicians. In J. C. Hansen & C. J. Falicov (Eds.), *Cultural perspectives in family therapy: The family therapy collections* (pp. 122-135). Rockville, MD: Aspen.

Speight, S. L., Myers, L. J., Cox, C. I., & Highlen, P. S. (1991). A redefinition of multicultural counseling. *Journal of Counseling and Development, 70,* 29-36.

Spiegel, J. (1982). An ecological model of ethnic families. In M. McGoldrick, J. K. Pearce, & J. Giordano (Eds.), *Ethnicity in family therapy* (pp. 31-51). New York: Guilford.

Stevenson, H. C. (1994). Validation of the Scale of Racial Socialization for African American adolescents: Steps toward multidimensionality. *Journal of Black Psychology, 20,* 445-468.

Sue, D. W., & Sue, D. (1990). *Counseling the culturally different: Theory and practice* (2nd ed.). New York: John Wiley.

Szapocznik, J., & Kurtines, N. M. (1993). Family psychology and cultural diversity. *American Psychologist, 48*(4), 400-407.

Anita Jones Thomas is assistant professor in counselor education at Northeastern Illinois University, 5500 N. St. Louis Avenue, Chicago, IL 60625. Dr. Thomas is a member of the IAMFC Ethics Committee. Electronic mail may be sent to a-thomas7@neiu.edu.

4 Communications/ Humanistic Family Therapy

Maslow Revisited

Constructing a Road Map of Human Nature

Dennis O'Connor
Le Moyne College

Leodones Yballe
Nazareth College of Rochester

Given the scope and intent of Maslow's work, the current textbook treatment is wanting. Therefore, an inductive exercise has been created and is offered here to build "the road map of human nature." This age-old, philosophic focus on our true nature has been a way to successfully engage and inspire both our students and our pedagogy. In the spirit of Maslow, the meaning of self-actualization is explored, and the understanding and managing of motivation is embedded into the larger context of leadership, for example, quality, spirituality, ethics, self-awareness, and personal growth.

Keywords: *Maslow; self-actualization; leadership; pedagogy; hierarchy of needs*

AUTHORS' NOTE: Please address correspondence to Dennis O'Connor, Management and Leadership, 1419 Salt Sprints Road, Le Moyne College, Syracuse, NY 13214; e-mail: oconnor@lemoyne.edu.

A few years ago, we began to reexamine Maslow's works with an appreciative eye: What was the best in his work? What was his vision of human nature? What did he hope to accomplish? How can Maslow help our students in their personal development, and as future managers and leaders? Visiting original sources, scholarly common sense often forgotten (Patzig & Zimmerman, 1985), led to an eye-opening experience. Long overlooked and forgotten in Maslow's writings, we found a more holistic picture of human nature and a deeper purpose for management and leadership. Our growing excitement was tempered by the limited, and partially inaccurate, portrayal that we saw in current textbooks. This article explains our disappointment and describes an exercise to alternatively convey a richer, more interconnected, and inspiring picture of Maslow's work. We offer tips to debrief the activity, to connect to organizations and leadership, and to guide our pedagogy.

CURRENT TREATMENT

All Organizational Behavior (OB) textbooks have a motivation chapter that includes a brief section on Maslow's hierarchy of needs, a chart depicting the upward progression of those needs, and a useful set of tips for motivating employees. Two early classics in management writing provided a solid launching point for this wide usage. Douglas McGregor (1960) drew upon Maslow's positive conceptions of human potential and the hierarchy of needs in his management classic, *The Human Side of Enterprise*. His premise, similar to Schein's (2004) metaphor of culture as an iceberg, was that fundamental, and often unexamined, beliefs and assumptions about human nature lurked below the surface of management practice. McGregor's Theory Y, the set of positive beliefs that people have a range of needs and prefer to grow up and contribute, is basic to all modern innovation in leadership and management. Maslow (1965) also took a keen interest in the application of humanistic psychology beyond one-on-one therapy to larger endeavors (organizations and education) where greater numbers of people could be positively affected.

In spite of the hierarchy's good pedigree and wide recognition, we believe that current textbook treatment suffers in three ways: (a) Maslow is misreported and misunderstood, (b) the positive message is undercut by references to nonvalidating research, and (c) the hierarchy of needs is taken out of context and offered in a too narrow perspective, thereby losing its original intent and spirit.

In 1985, Patzig and Zimmerman pointed out three glaring inaccuracies in standard texts. The leading OB texts reported that Maslow had found in American society that 85% of physiological needs were met, 70% of security, 50% of social needs, and ego and self-actualization needs were 40% and 10% satisfied, respectively.

The actual passage from Maslow (1943) quoted in their critique stated,

> So far, our theoretical discussion may have given the impression that these
> five sets of needs are somehow in a stepwise, all-or-none relationship to
> each other. We have spoken in such terms as the following: "If one need
> is satisfied, then another emerges." This statement might give the false
> impression that a need must be 100% satisfied before the next need
> emerges. In actual fact, most members of society who are normal are
> partially satisfied in all their basic needs and partially dissatisfied in all
> their basic needs at the same time. A more realistic description of the
> hierarchy would be in terms of decreasing percentages of satisfaction as
> we go up the hierarchy of prepotency. For instance, if I may assign
> arbitrary figures for the sake of illustration, it is as if the average citizen
> is satisfied 85%. (pp. 388-389)

It is clear that these figures were generated by Maslow to simply illustrate
a key point, but unfortunately, this error still shows up. Several current texts
report these numbers, and one added that "many critics disagree with these
figures however, particularly the 10% figure for self actualization" (Ivancevich
& Matteson, 2002, p. 152). It would seem that textbooks are prone to
"viruses" that slip in, promulgate, mutate, and become common knowledge as
textbook authors draw upon each other and cross-check their chapters.

The passage just listed also supports our second concern: Maslow's positive message is being unfairly undercut. The textbook presentation of
Maslow's hierarchy is typically followed by the caveat that even though
many managers still find it intuitively useful, his model is not supported by
research. Specifically, research has failed to find evidence that individuals
rigidly progress through the hierarchy, that is, that a lower level need must
be totally satisfied before the next level can begin to provide motivational
force. As one textbook stated, "Scholars have mostly dismissed Maslow's
theory . . . because it is much too rigid to explain the dynamic and unstable
characteristics of employee needs" (McShane & Von Glinow, 2005, p. 140).
Many textbooks add that Alderfer's ERG theory was developed to overcome these problems with Maslow's theory, because it states that more
than one need may be activated at the same time. Evidence for this more
flexible approach is seen as "encouraging."

Although it is important for students to realize the role of research in providing reliable knowledge, these criticisms are invalidated by the previous
quote. The reason that Maslow originally offered the hypothetical example
was to illustrate the point that his model is a simplification (as all theories are)
and that in ordinary life, behavior is often multiply determined, that is, several
needs can and do operate at once. To quote Maslow (1943) again, "Most
members of society are partially satisfied in *all* their basic needs at the same
time." Later, he adds, "any motivated behavior . . . is a channel through

which many basic needs may be simultaneously expressed or satisfied. Typically, an act has more than one motivator" (p. 370).

Maslow understood that there is a very fluid emergence and combination of needs and activity in the rhythm of day-to-day life. The human group survived by bonding together (social needs) to meet the challenges of food and shelter. In fact, right now you, the reader, may have several needs operating simultaneously as you read this (e.g., curiosity, thirst for knowledge, and hunger). It turns out that researchers were right: There is no evidence of a rigid progression through the hierarchy or that the completion of one level ensures the emergence of the next, but these were never Maslow's theory.

A third major concern about current coverage is the "tool" perspective from which the model is offered. Randolph New, in a conversation with four leading textbook authors (Cameron, Lussier, Ireland, New, & Robbins, 2003), concluded that all four write their books to support a managerial ideology. Robbins, who represented the majority of mainstream OB textbook authors, is of particular interest here.

> OB texts . . . support a managerial perspective. This reflects the market—business schools. We need to genuflect to the Gods of productivity, efficiency, goals, etc. This strongly influences the dependent variables the researchers choose and the ones that textbook authors use. So we reflect business school values. (p. 714)

As Joan Gallos (1996) noted, "Strong beliefs in technical rationality . . . keep us locked into teaching methods and course formats that convey empirically based management truths" (p. 295). Although conveying information, skills, and tips in managing others is important, it begs the bigger questions of values, meaning, and leadership, with which Maslow was deeply concerned. Surgically removing the hierarchy, and adding tips for managing others, violates the larger spirit of Maslow's work. Living systems have integrity. "Dividing an elephant in half does not produce two small elephants" (Senge, 1990, p. 66).

Lacking a larger context, the management approach can play into a manipulative mind-set that many students already bring to the topic of motivation. How do you get people to do what you want? In a carrot-and-stick Theory X approach, you give them something. In the hierarchy context, you provide ways for them to get their needs met. That is, of course, part of the answer, but there is much more to it. We need to transcend the limited "tool" perspective of managing others to the larger context of leadership. Both Maslow (1965) and seasoned management educators have taken deep interest in leadership in all its varied dimensions: values and ethics (Lund Dean & Beggs, 2006), spirituality and meaning (Neal, 1997), emotional intelligence (Brown, 2003), systems thinking and sustainability (Bardoel & Haslett, 2006; Bradbury, 2003), and self-awareness and personal growth (Bilimoria, 2000a, 2000b; Hunt & Weintraub, 2004; Schmidt-Wilk, Heaton, &

Steingard, 2000). We can richly connect motivation to these important dimensions of leadership by understanding and teaching Maslow well.

WHAT DID HE ACTUALLY SAY?

Maslow played a key early role in the humanistic psychology movement, sometimes known as the "third force" in psychology. He felt stifled in an American psychology dominated by behaviorism. He strongly believed that humans are more than billiard balls on the pool table of life. Maslow (1943) begins with a statement that the *integrated wholeness of the organism* must be one of the foundation stones of motivation theory, that is, motivation (and all other OB topics) cannot be studied only in isolation. Motivation must be seen in the context of the whole being and in connection with other key focuses. Based on his clinical psychology experience, he inductively constructed a rich model of the forces and needs that move us to action.

Over the next several decades, Maslow became increasingly intrigued by what he eventually labeled the "farther reaches of human nature" (Maslow, 1971). He sought to build an appreciative understanding of human beings at their best. In contrast with the preoccupation of Freudian psychopathology, this "psychology of the higher life" was to attend to the question "of what the human being should grow *toward*" (Maslow, 1964, p. 7). He interviewed folks who had been identified as great people and found that they had somehow become themselves more fully. He began to spell out in more detail the processes and character of self-actualization.

In Maslow's view, self-actualization is not an endpoint, but rather an ongoing process that involves dozens of little growth choices that entail risk and require courage. He noted that it was a difficult path to take and often puts us at odds with surrounding people and norms. He also found that self-actualizing people were deeply committed in action to core values that look very similar to those put forward in all major religious traditions. These "being-values" are simple yet difficult to fully embody in the everyday challenges of life—for example, truth, justice, goodness, beauty, order, simplicity, and meaning or purposefulness.

He observed that self-actualizers were attuned to their own unique biological nature (talents, likes, tastes, etc.) and had a unique, intangible spiritual nature, an interconnected combination of being-values and purpose. He saw these values as "meta-motivators." For example, individuals might be moved to seek justice in the world, as well as do justice to their own inner voice or truth. In general, they seek to put things right and to do it the right way. To a person, the self-actualizers were deeply engaged with their immediate worlds. They also were much more likely to report peak, transcendent experiences that helped them see beyond the immediate and develop a spiritual focus. They were "called" to act, and they responded.

We see that there are several identifiable and distinct dimensions to self-actualization in Maslow's writings: the unique self, peak experience and transcendence, spirituality and meaning, and the aesthetic–creative element. Although these dimensions were never fully sorted out, Maslow had begun to posit self-transcendence as the highest need (Koltko-Rivera, 2006.) He helped begin what some have called the "fourth force": exploring the role of transcendence of self and spirituality in personal psychology. We agree that we need to find our unique true self *and* to discover that is part of a greater whole still. Many joined him in this quest, and in 1969, he helped to establish the *Journal of Transpersonal Psychology*. Others have since taken up this challenging work in the organizational realm by clarifying the critical role of spirituality and meaning in the workplace and leadership. Like Jung, the sheer breadth and significance of the connections Maslow made were an important launching point for thinkers of all types.

Finally, Maslow (1965) was also one of a small group of groundbreakers who connected a positive psychology of people to the practical challenge of management and productivity. He saw management and education as potential arenas to reach more people than the one-on-one approach of traditional therapy. He struggled to understand humanity at its best and sought to create a positive psychology and a positive vision for both the individual and the leader. His broad conception of leadership and collaboration is the place to situate our understanding of motivation.

In the context of OB pedagogy, as we continue to seek newer heights of teaching excellence in the service of developing the whole person (Bowen, 1980; Boyatzis & McLeod, 2001; International Commission on the Apostolate of Jesuit Education, 1986), we are convinced that Maslow has much to offer beyond a simple tool. We need to explore what his work can tell us about one's inner desire and hunger for peak performance, creativity, ethics, values, and meaning, and the interconnections of all these processes in the context of management and leadership. We have created an exercise that we believe helps us get to the deeper values and hopes that we see in Maslow's writings.

AN EXERCISE TO INDUCTIVELY CONSTRUCT A ROAD MAP OF HUMAN NATURE

Introduction. Much pedagogy is dominated by a deductive approach to knowledge. In the interests of efficiency, key findings and models are presented in neat packages. When this approach is paired with exams, "Tell me what's important" becomes a common refrain from students. In contrast, this exercise uses an inductive, discovery method, which parallels Maslow's original approach, and grounds the inquiry into motivation in the students' own experiences. Although some students prefer a compact presentation of models, the intrinsic interest of certain questions will slowly hook most others: What is human nature? What moves you to act? What do you really need? What do you want? Why do you want? What is missing for you? What is already in you?

Priming the pump. The topic is motivation, and a key question is what moves us to act. We wonder out loud about why people are really here, right now, in this room. What was the *motive* force that brought you here? We ask them to rate from 1 to 10 their levels of energy, satisfaction, and productivity over the last week. We also ask them to recall two moments of best performance and two experiences of real satisfaction in the last couple of weeks. This brief appreciative exercise (Yballe & O'Connor, 2000) helps to give depth to the session and to weight the focus toward the best of what we can be, consistent with the spirit of Maslow. After we share a brief definition of needs as the tension we experience that drives us to act, we suggest it might be quite useful to have the complete, everything-you-wanted-to-know "road map" of human needs and motivations. We further submit that this big picture would not only be great to grasp the complex dynamics at work, but also a tremendous aid to better understand our own experience and all our day-to-day interpersonal and group situations.

Small-group brainstorm. After offering a couple examples of needs, we begin the work of constructing a "road map of human nature." We have found that reframing motivation in this larger and more meaningful context tends to hook both the students' and the instructor's imagination and hence result in more enthusiasm and creativity. We ask our newly formed class-project teams to take a crack at brainstorming a written list of needs. "We want any and all that you've ever experienced, seen, or heard about!"

Brainstorming is fun work, and a list of needs is an easy success for groups in an early stage of development. It is also more engaging for them to get in touch with their own life experience than listening to a description of *the* list of five human needs, à la the Maslow chart. Right in the room, there are hundreds of years of human experience to draw upon in building a rich, experientially grounded map! *In fact,* we have found that students are usually able to generate 90% of almost any topic that we've asked them to brainstorm, for example, management skills, qualities of an ideal, effective group, sources of differing perception, sources of stress, and so on. As they work, we go around to interact with the groups, giving a nudge or two, and reminding them that brainstorming that produces nothing funny or truly dumb is not good brainstorming! "Put down everything, and anything. Censor later." (Another variation that takes slightly longer is to ask small groups to create collages of images from old magazines that reveal the driving forces that they feel in themselves or that "catch their eye" as something important about human nature and motivation.)

Reporting and debriefing. After a short time, we title the board "THE ROAD MAP OF HUMAN NATURE" and ask small groups to report out. As we begin to "simply record" three or four items per group, we unobtrusively organize the data higher and lower on the board without letting on that we are following Maslow's hierarchy. There is usually a dazzling array of needs. Many items, such as education or a new car, could go in several places, so we ask for an explanation of why that is a need. Some items we put to the left of the board to deal with later (money, sex) and others in a "not sure" area to the right. After they exhaust their lists, we ask if any other ideas have come to mind. Finally, we conclude, "So, this is it, the total range of human needs? Everything you've always wanted to know? . . . Is there anything else, in any time or place that anyone might have needed?"

In this process of generating and reporting ideas, group members learn to appreciate and trust their own and others' resources while we are free to function as a resource in helping to label and organize the output, and then to link and integrate it to other course topics and themes. They feel competent, and we look smart.

With so much material to work through, the options and order are really a matter of course goals, personal preferences, and spur-of-the-moment insights. We start by marveling at the richness of expression, noting the dozens of items that comprise our road map. We then draw some lines to separate the items according to the levels in Maslow's model and inquire if anyone noticed that his or her responses had been mapped into Maslow's hierarchy.

We briefly describe the biological and emotional forces that make the lower needs prepotent. If you are running out of air, all other concerns are quickly forgotten! As we find ways to handle the physiological needs, they lose their intensity, and attention can turn to other concerns, such as the safety and security needs. We all need some order and stability in our lives: Will I eat tomorrow? Am I safe from physical danger? Will I be OK? Such needs can also become very intense and drive out other concerns for the time being. With the third level, social needs, we point out that we are, in our deepest roots, social beings. It was the tribe that survived. Everyone in the room is and always has been complexly interconnected with others. We are a physical being first, but as infants, we soon begin bonding, and our social nature becomes quite apparent. We bond with others throughout life, and we need friends, family, inclusion, acceptance, and unconditional love.

The fourth level focuses on the need for self-esteem. Our basic nature is also individual. With language, we begin to form a personal identity, which is always rooted in a social matrix of a particular time and place. We are separate from others and existentially alone. As we feel secure and confident in our group memberships, our attention can turn to standing out from the group. We need inclusion, but we also seek to stand apart and influence others. Good self-esteem is "soundly based on real capacity, achievement, and respect from others. . . . Satisfaction of self esteem needs leads to feelings of self confidence, worth, strength, capability, and adequacy of being useful and necessary in the world" (Maslow, 1943, p. 382).

Listing esteem needs as "higher" has caused a certain amount of cross-cultural debate. The word *higher* tends to connote better, but we have not found any evidence that Maslow judged someone motivated predominantly by self-esteem needs (preferred by individualistic cultures) as better than someone at the social need level (preferred by cultures that favor collectivism). He simply saw "social needs" as more basic, or prepotent. Life is a constant unveiling of self. Certain aspects of our nature come forward first, and others are brought to play later. Furthermore, every culture shapes both social and individual nature together. Relative to their differing circumstances and history, each develops unique configurations of behavior and values that shape the expression of needs and puts different emphasis and accent on each of the basic needs. Hofstede (1977) found that American society overemphasizes individualism. Is this a better, purer, higher, more effective motivation than a collective emphasis? Maslow would conclude that functioning chiefly at either the social or self-esteem levels is dangerously incomplete and unhealthy. For an extended psychodynamic treatment of each need level as an organizing, but incomplete psychology of work, see Schwartz (1983).

At this point, we pause and revisit our initial musing about why people are here. We try to place the reasons in the hierarchy and speculate as to the power of various motivations to bring about excellent performance at school and work. We demonstrate that it is possible to use this model to reflect on and analyze one's performance and suggest that more data be gathered by examining what other needs have come into play during the last week. What need-satisfying behavior has been in the service of your goals? What has been distracting? How might a diary or journal be helpful in building deeper awareness? We give small groups a few minutes to share some examples of good performance and to make their best guess at the underlying motivations. We point out that there is a story or pattern that underlies most of our best performances. It is worth clarifying and developing this storyline in contrast to the ones associated with mediocre performance (Adams, 1986).

Two items, money and sex, are usually of great interest and central to understanding motivation. We sometimes play devil's advocate to those who argue money is the most powerful and effective motivator. How effective is money for you? Would a promise of $100 at the end of the semester help you study today and tomorrow? How so? Data on happiness tell us that families who make $100,000 are no happier than those who make $50,000. Can this be true?

"Sex" is perhaps most amusing, when the class fails to mention it. We announce, "We have exciting news, our road map is incomplete, and you have something really good to look forward to!" This can lead nicely into discussion about what is our "true" nature. Can all motivation be reduced to the biological drives of sex and aggression, à la Freud? Or do we have a spiritual nature (as intangible as love or ego) that is just as real in its effects and that "pulls" us to act (à la Jung, Maslow, and all major religions)? What is the relationship between these two realities, biological and spiritual? Are they necessarily opposed and in conflict? Can we celebrate both together?

MASLOW, THE SELF, AND OTHERS: A LECTURETTE ON SELF-ACTUALIZING

The question of our intangible nature leads us to look at "self-actualization," and we need to do some digging to establish what this really means. Generally, only a few of the reported needs (e.g., spiritual, religion, meaning, challenge) qualify for this category. The road map needs more work; it is still fuzzy and incomplete. We ask how many have heard the term *self-actualization* and how many can define it. Although some have heard this term, rarely are students able to expound on its meaning. Making your self "actual" is the most basic meaning. Although it sounds simple enough, it is not easy according to Maslow. "We must be very careful to imply only that the higher life is in principle possible, and never that it is probable, or likely, or easy to attain" (Maslow, 1965, p. 314). So how do we become more real? We offer a few of Maslow's suggestions for behaviors leading to self-actualization:

Self-actualizing and self. Maslow provides some ideas on how one can focus on internal growth.

1. **See life as a series of choices.** "Making the growth choice, rather than the fear choice a dozen times a day is to move a dozen times a day to self-actualization" (Maslow, 1971, p. 44). Life is precious. Become curious and fascinated with choice and outcome. Experiment, reflect, refine.

2. **Be honest with yourself, take responsibility, be fair, and be true to one's inner voice** are powerful strategies. "What tastes good to you, what do you believe is right?" These simple behaviors slowly root one in the solid foundation of one's own unique nature. They eventually provide the courage to be different, to stand up for the self and for one's convictions, and to sustain a difficult mission in the face of external pressure for conformity and personal needs for safety, acceptance, and status.

3. **Have "something to admire, to sacrifice" oneself for, "to surrender to, to die for"** (Maslow, 1964, p. 42). You are on solid ground in the self-actualizing journey when searching for something greater than the limited, individualized self. The journey progresses more deeply when you put yourself in the service of that which is greater than yourself—such as country, faith, or human dignity.

4. **Be open to the eternal, the divine, the noble, the sacred, and the poetic.** Revisit your religious tradition with a new eye; try meditation (Alexander, Rainforth, & Gelderloos, 1991); notice your peak experiences. The artist's route is to open the self and allow the larger "force" to express itself, thus transcending the narrow limits of a small conscious mind directing all activity and greatly expanding creative power. Maslow saw the transcendent aspect of peak experiences as an important element in learning to appreciate the eternal and the sacred. Developing and clarifying our spiritual side and identifying with a greater purpose extends and strengthens the self in a turbulent world (Schmidt-Wilk et al., 2000). We could think of these activities as disciplines to build "spiritual intelligence." Become a spiritual being on a human journey.

Self-actualizing and others. Maslow also has advice for self-actualizing when being with others.

1. **Be honest with others, be not afraid of the truth.** Truthfulness often requires courage, enhances integrity, and buttresses credibility. The honest person is in a greater position to effectively serve others—to coach and mentor, to provide fraternal correction, to provide feedback that the other can hear and use, or to provide solace and comfort to those who are confused or distressed. "All profoundly serious, ultimately concerned people of good will can travel together for a very long distance" (Maslow, 1964, p. 54).

2. **Profess your values before others.** "Trying to be value-free, trying to be purely technological (means without ends) . . . all these are value confusions, philosophical and axiological failures. . . . And inevitably, they breed all the value pathologies" (Maslow, 1964, p. 51).

3. **Help others to be self-actualizers and develop their capacity for peak experiences.** It is best to assume that "non-peakers" are really "weak" peakers rather than people who lack the capacity all together (Maslow, 1964, p. 86). As others begin to see themselves as having had peak experiences, it is possible for them to understand and identify with the great "peakers."

Finding and becoming one's self is critical work, but the idea has been coopted and misinterpreted by ubiquitous marketers (e.g., "It's all about me!"). We pointedly note that Maslow found that self-actualizers are not self-centered, but are quite the opposite. To a person, self-actualizers possess a contributory mind-set as opposed to a comparative (what-do-I-get) approach. These individuals extended themselves and sought to improve the well-being of their groups and community. They looked inward and outward. Their choices in what to do and how to do it were guided by their understanding of their own unique talents, preferences, values, and meaning. Their experience of self is extended to include the wider world.

To further deepen the understanding of the values dimension of self-actualization, we ask groups to take a few minutes to list some of the core values they endorse or identified as important in religious training. Classes are quite amazed when we compare their lists to the being-values that were integral in the lives of those identified as self-actualizing: honesty, truth, beauty, justice, goodness, wholeness, simplicity, meaning, and so on (Maslow, 1965, chap. 23). We ask, "Don't we need these? Why aren't they on the map?! (They seldom are, by the way.) Can you imagine a world (or an organization) without such qualities, where everything is gray, tarnished, and ugly?"

Maslow (1971) argued that a spiritual sickness, an anomie, results when these intangible being-values are not present in one's life or in one's community. Our spiritual nature has its own set of unique requirements. It is as fundamental and real as our biological nature. How much energy do we invest in creating beauty, truth, goodness, dignity, meaning, and justice on a day-to-day basis? Why not imagine our lives with more of these qualities in place?

We believe that there is a cascade of positive consequences in the self-actualization process that are antidotes to the powerful forces of pop culture and bureaucratic life that keep so many of us operating in a deficiency mode. Young people, at any particular moment, find themselves in a vast sea of images and stories of deficit, weakness, separation, and vulnerability, seemingly best resolved through greed, consumption, and cheap thrills (Vaill, 1989). In such a "pursuit of happiness," the bulk of conscious attention and action becomes overfocused on security, social, and ego needs and is fundamentally unsustainable.

Of course, self-actualizers also have basic needs. They eat and will be hungry again tomorrow. They need security and love and esteem like everyone else. That is our collective human nature. The difference is that the pursuit of their basic needs is organized, aligned, elevated, and sublimated by meaning and purpose, which are rooted in a truer sense of one's values, inclinations, and talents, as well as experience with and connection to the "greater self." Such perspective helps to moderate the immediacy and discomfort of lower order deprivations. The self-actualizer is more inner directed, delaying gratification until the right moment. Through experiment and reflection, satisfying basic needs becomes an integrated, consciously managed aspect of a whole life and is not compulsive or desperate, or dominating of all other concerns. A paradigm shift takes place: You become a person who has needs, not a needy person.

The individual, like a culture, must solve the challenges of external adaptation and internal integration. Only the individual is equipped to meet his or her challenges in an optimum way. We use the concept of sustainable development (Bradbury, 2003) to suggest that the process of self-actualization is the core of sustainable happiness: to uncover one's unique self as a foundation to take charge of one's own growth, to struggle with the meaning of existence, and to reintegrate one's various talents, natures, and values. This, we believe, is also the path of leadership.

EXTENDING MASLOW TO ORGANIZATIONS AND LEADERSHIP

Maslow and self-actualization speak directly to critical clusters of topics in current leadership writing and pedagogy: knowing oneself, personal mastery, and emotional intelligence (Bennis, 1989; Boyatzis, 1994; Drucker, 1999; Dupree, 1990; Goleman, 1997; Senge, 1990); values, meaning, spirituality, and ethics (Bolman & Deal, 2001; Daniels, Franz, & Wong, 2000; Ethics Education Task Force, 2004; Ferris, 2002; Tischler, 2000; Vaill, 1989); and quality and peak performance (Deming, 2000; Walton, 1988). Similar to the way that the overarching process of self-actualization reshapes and guides the meeting of lower order needs, the wider context of leadership helps us better understand motivation and use the tools of management. "Good teachers . . . are able to weave a complex web of connections among themselves, the subject, and the student" (Palmer, 1998, p. 11). There are endless ways to make these connections. We offer a few examples and thoughts, but it is ultimately up to each professor to find personally meaningful ways to illuminate the rich connections to leadership.

We usually begin the final discussion by rhetorically asking what the road map of human nature means for leadership. We begin discussion with a need that we save for the end: QUALITY. Quality, the key focus of the biggest management trend ever, has yet to turn up in any group's brainstorm! This is particularly ironic with MBA students, because many have been exposed to Total Quality Management programs. Do we have a need for quality? Do others? What is the basis of our need for quality? How close to the surface is it? How do leaders make it a key concern for all? To build "quality" into your life, what steps would you need to take specifically? What systems of management, what culture, what leadership will result in quality?

Japanese organizations transcended the false dichotomy of increased costs versus quality, by taking a longer term view. They discovered that an intense focus on quality eventually led to innovations in the processes of work. Costs decreased and quality rose. They demonstrated that quality is a product of a connected, integrated work culture that strives to constantly improve, rather than a series of quick fixes. In a similar way, when trying to reconcile the needs of the individual and the needs of the organization, Maslow (1965) argued that the ultimate goals of the organization, the individual, and the society are not at odds but actually coincide in the long term. The best leaders see the interconnections, transcend the seeming dilemmas, and seek to create a synergy and alignment between the needs and goals of all three. This isn't easy, of course. It requires, among other things, a deep understanding of the full road map and the farther reaches of human nature.

Maslow (1965) firmly believed that leadership should be in the service of the being-values: putting things right, deepening purpose, making things truer, more beautiful, and so on. The good leader provides purposes and goals that are worth caring about and works to craft a spiritual foundation of meaning (Bolman & Deal, 2001). He or she can appreciate and work with others' religious and spiritual practices (Pielstick, 2005).

With rising expectations for ethical conduct and education, Maslow allows—no, requires—us to raise questions of values. Lund Dean and Beggs (2006) found that most business faculty believe "ethics is a values-driven and internal construct, but teach using compliance-driven and external methods" (p. 40). Maslow's positive vision of the role of the being-values in leadership provides an internal context to situate these compliance and critical analysis approaches. This positive vision helps practitioners and students shore up ethical goals that are too often subject to erosion in competing with the short-term bottom line (Bardoel & Haslett, 2006), particularly when students perceive a double corporate standard (Rynes, Quinn Trank, Lawson, & Ilies, 2003).

We must challenge the assumption that good ethics costs the company money (Jackson, 2006). Similar to a long-term focus on quality, a being-values focus is an effective leadership strategy. It provides the leader with the ability to more easily identify with wider concerns. He or she is better able to find common ground with others to build interdependence and generate creative dialogue, rather than fighting over a fixed sum, and mired in life-is-a-jungle, and your-loss-is-my-gain.

Influence, power, creative ideas, and love are not fixed quantities. Unlike fixed tangible resources on which so much business logic and procedure are based, we can generate *more* of these critical but intangible qualities through our interactions and leadership. We can negate each other's influence so none exists, or we can extend a powerful joint influence on unfolding events. If I share an idea with the group, I still have my idea, and together we can build even more. Such synergy is more holistic and based in mutual interdependence. It transcends the selfish–unselfish dichotomy. It is "an actual perception of a higher truth" (Maslow, 1965, p. 97) and the best bet to energize sustainable high performance.

It is clear that leadership, even on the small scale of student group projects, is a challenging endeavor. The student must go beyond managing others to also managing oneself in the process of leadership (O'Connor & Yballe, 2007). It should come as no surprise that sustainable leadership requires reflection, self-confrontation, and learning. Self-actualization is essential to strengthen and deepen the internal anchors needed to persevere in the face of unprecedented turbulence and uncertainty. We explore this connection of self-actualization and leadership to conclude the exercise but also throughout the course.

One last caveat: Management professors are continually faced with difficult decisions of breadth versus depth. We believe the wholeness of the road map and the rich connections of Maslow to leadership provide a memorable and sufficient framework to address other theories and models of motivation that the reader finds important. The road map activity allows the professor to weave in other views on the spot or provide foreshadowing for following sessions.

CONCLUSION: WHAT WOULD MASLOW HAVE US DO?

The road map exercise clearly brings to light the multiple dimensions of our nature: physical, social, individual, and spiritual. At any moment, and across a lifetime, we are driven and pulled by many different and interconnected needs. Each of these dimensions is real, is essential, and requires attention for health and wholeness. Maslow offers a rich scheme for understanding ourselves, others, and the leadership situation (see Table 4.1).

Table 4.1 Benefits and Challenges in the Road Map of Human Nature

People	Benefits	Challenges
Students	Richer, multidimensional model of human nature	Take self-actualization seriously.
	Exposure to positive vision of personal growth and leadership	Get on the path of leadership.
		Examine and expand own performance and motivation.
	Connections to a wide range of leadership focuses: values, spirituality, ethics, emotional intelligence, sustainability	Commit to difficult but satisfying work of finding self, finding calling, and finding purpose.
	Frame to understand current experience at work and in relationship	
	Tips to pursue self-actualization	
	Experience with inductive theory building	
	Experience with Appreciative Inquiry (bring out and build on the best)	
Professors	All the above	All the above
	Put the care of the individual student and personal growth front and center.	Create the context of values and leadership, and make the rich interconnections between topics, particularly when not established in the supporting texts.
	Practice with facilitative role as resource in inductive and appreciative processes.	Create assignments and activities that focus on integration of theory, self, and action.
	Enrich our task and supports deeper, more satisfying meaning for our work.	Educate for personal growth.
		Revisit purpose of course, design of sessions.
		Clarify role of teaching in the context of one's own purpose and growth.

Maslow (1965) realized that we need theories of leadership and motivation adequate to the tasks of modern organizations. His thinking has provided a firm foundation not only for many modern leadership theorists, but also for broad cross-fertilizations of philosophy, systems thinking, and humanistic psychology, for example, Transpersonal and Integral Psychology (Wilber, 1996). Maslow (1971) railed against the "influence and ubiquity of stupidly limited theories of motivation all over the world" (p. 310), for example, cause–effect behaviorism, Freudian reductionism of human life to only biological drives, blank-slate sociological models, and the materialistic, rational-economic models that underlie so much of business education. "We must say harshly of the 'science' of economics that it is generally the skilled, technological application of a totally false theory of human needs and values, a theory which recognizes only the existence of lower or material needs" (p. 310).

Our current textbooks acknowledge that employees are valuable assets in a globally competitive environment, but this is not enough. They are not employees or assets; they are people (Drucker, 2002). The people "problem" in organizations is unstructured and fraught with uncertainty. The more structured and tangible technical considerations of business, because they are more concrete and readily accessible, will seem more compelling and draw the most energy and resources. The technical system is, in a sense, prepotent. Too often the "valuable assets" or the social system is an afterthought to which "programs" are applied.

A subtler difficulty with the utilitarian, valuable asset approach is illustrated by the fate of the retired racehorse. The sticky problem of "what have you done for me lately" arises. What happens when I become less "valuable" and who is to say when I'm no longer valuable? The social glue of commitment is eventually weakened.

The mind-sets and methods appropriate to the accounting and managing of assets and numbers fall pitifully short, when we need people and teams to operate at their creative best at a world-class level. It's not enough to provide only tools to manage others as assets. Although it is important to understand our place in a turbulent world and the skills needed to thrive (O'Connor, 2001), Maslow would also have us (as pedagogical leaders) set students on the path of leadership, for example, increasing self-awareness and the capacity for self-discovery (O'Neil & Hopkins, 2002), deepening one's knowledge and curiosity about human nature, and seeking and connecting to the broader purposes and goals of life and work (Bolman & Deal, 2001). For all topics in OB, Maslow requires us to establish an explicit background of values and leadership. The path of leadership becomes the evolving, lifelong context for the collecting and using of management tools, and the basis for joining with others in collaborative activity at the highest levels of performance and creativity.

As professors, we have a role as coaches (O'Neil & Hopkins, 2002) in our students' being and becoming: extending a hand at the elbow, providing an imperceptible nudge, creating a climate of freedom and dignity, asking deep questions, challenging values, and calling for reflection. And our pedagogy must be appreciative (Yballe & O'Connor, 2004), helping our students to be aware of their peak experiences and best moments. "There is a kind of I-thou communication of intimates, of friends . . . which then enables others to see and appreciate the great artists and the great leaders" (Maslow, 1964, p. 87). Our task is to help students become aware that they can have experiences of self-actualizing and build on those experiences as a basis for a satisfying life and good leadership. We want students to better use the knowledge and tools they gain, and so we must also provide a positive and sustainable vision of leadership and life: the challenge and joy of the trip, collaborative working as if the future mattered, commitment to core values, dedication to a higher purpose. It's "the heart's longing to be connected to the largeness of life" (Palmer, 1998, p. 5).

Finally, the OB professor must also take his or her own development as seriously as that of others (Bilimoria, 2000c). As Palmer (1998) cogently argued, we teach who we are, "knowing my students and my subject depends heavily on self-knowledge" (p. 2). This is particularly true for OB and leadership. Venturing onto the path of leadership and self-discovery more intimately acquaints us with the theories, skills, and values that we teach. We believe a deeper understanding of Maslow will motivate and inspire the OB professor to find ways to explore and clarify his or her value foundation for leadership and teaching.

On a basic level, Maslow's work challenges us to reflect on our course objectives, the overall course design and choice of pedagogy, and ultimately the underlying values that we embrace and that guide our choices. Personal growth always involves self-confrontation. Am I going beyond a neutral, detached provider of theory and tools for managers to gain results? Am I helping students along a path of self-discovery and providing them positive visions and models of leadership? Is each and every topic and activity an opportunity to explore leadership and meaning? Where am I going through this class, through this course, through my teaching? Am I a real person involved in finding myself and humbly seeking deeper insights in every class? We need to continually seek opportunities for reflection and feedback to take better aim at the "inner target" of who we are (Herrigel, 1978).

In the long term, Maslow also challenges us to consider the wholeness of our lives, the contribution of our work, and the overall meaning of who we are. This self-confrontation puts us on the path of leadership by involving us in a slow, and sometimes painful, process of crafting pedagogical choices and action that align with and clarify our values and unique talents.

SOURCE: Dennis O'Connor & Leodones Yballe. (2007). Maslow Revisited: Constructing a Road Map of Human Nature. *Journal of Management Education, 31*, 738-756. © 2007 SAGE Publications.

REFERENCES

Adams, J. D. (1986). Achieving and maintaining personal peak performance. In *Transforming leadership: From vision to results*. Alexandria, VA: Miles River Press.

Alexander, C. N., Rainforth, M. V., & Gelderloos, P. (1991). Transcendental Meditation, self-actualization, and psychological health: A conceptual overview and statistical meta–analysis. *Journal of Social Behavior and Personality, 6,* 189-247.

Bardoel, E. A., & Haslett, T. (2006). Exploring ethical dilemmas using the "drifting goals" archetype. *Journal of Management Education, 30,* 134-148.

Bennis, W. (1989). *On becoming a leader.* New York: Addison-Wesley.

Bilimoria, D. (2000a). Management education's commitments to students. *Journal of Management Education, 24,* 422-423.

Bilimoria, D. (2000b). Redoing management education's mission and methods. *Journal of Management Education, 24,* 161-166.

Bilimoria, D. (2000c). Teachers as learners: Whither our own development? *Journal of Management Education, 24,* 302-303.

Bolman, L. G., & Deal, T. E. (2001). *Leading with soul.* San Francisco: Jossey-Bass.

Bowen, D. D. (1980). Experiential and traditional teaching of OB: A dubious distinction. *Exchange: The Organizational Behavior Teaching Journal, 5,* 7-12.

Boyatzis, R. E. (1994). Stimulating self-directed learning through the managerial assessment and development course. *Journal of Management Education, 18,* 304-323.

Boyatzis, R. E., & McLeod, P. L. (2001). Our educational bottom line: Developing the whole person. *Journal of Management Education, 25,* 118-123.

Bradbury, H. (2003). Sustaining inner and outer worlds: A whole-systems approach to developing sustainable business practices in management. *Journal of Management Education, 27,* 172-187.

Brown, R. B. (2003). Emotions and behavior: Exercises in emotional intelligence. *Journal of Management Education, 27,* 122-134.

Cameron, K. S., Lussier, R. D., Ireland, R. N., New, R. J., & Robbins, S. P. (2003). Management textbooks as propaganda. *Journal of Management Education, 27,* 711-729.

Daniels, D., Franz, R. S., & Wong, K. (2000). A classroom with a worldview: Making spiritual assumptions explicit in management education. *Journal of Management Education, 24,* 540-561.

Deming, W. E. (2000). *Out of the crisis.* Cambridge, MA: MIT Press.

Drucker, P. F. (1999). Managing oneself. *Harvard Business Review, 77,* 64-74.

Drucker, P. F. (2002). They're not employees, they're people. *Harvard Business Review, 80,* 70-77.

Dupree, M. (1990). *Leadership is an art.* New York: Random House.

Ethics Education Task Force. (2004). *Ethics education in business schools: Report of the Ethics Education Task Force to AACSB International's board of directors.* Retrieved January 8, 2007, from http://www.aacsb.edu/Resource_Centers/EthicsEdu/EETF-report-6-25-04.pdf

Ferris, W. P. (2002). Gifting the organization. *Journal of Management Education, 26,* 717-731.

Gallos, J. V. (1996). On teaching and educating professionals. *Journal of Management Education, 20,* 294-297.

Goleman, D. (1997). *Emotional intelligence: Why it can matter more that IQ.* New York: Bantam.

Herrigel, E. (1978). *Zen and the art of archery.* New York: Random House.

Hofstede, G. (1977). *Culture's consequences: International differences in work-related values.* Beverly Hills, CA: Sage.

Hunt, J. M., & Weintraub, J. R. (2004). Learning developmental coaching. *Journal of Management Education, 28,* 39-61.

International Commission on the Apostolate of Jesuit Education. (1986, December 8). *The characteristics of Jesuit education.* Retrieved January 8, 2007, from the Jesuit Education Web site: http://www.sjweb.info/education/doclist.cfm

Ivancevich, J., & Matteson, M. (2002). *Organizational behavior and management* (6th ed.). New York: McGraw-Hill/Irwin.

Jackson, K. T. (2006). Breaking down the barriers: Bringing initiatives and reality into business ethics education. *Journal of Management Education, 30,* 65-89.

Koltko-Rivera, M. E. (2006). Rediscovering the later version of Maslow's hierarchy of needs: Self-transcendence and opportunities for theory, research, and unification. *Review of General Psychology, 10,* 302-317.

Lund Dean, K., & Beggs, J. M. (2006). University professors and teaching ethics: Conceptualizations and expectations. *Journal of Management Education, 30,* 15-44.

Maslow, A. H. (1943). A theory of motivation. *Psychological Review, 50,* 370-396.

Maslow, A. H. (1964). *Religions, values, and peak-experiences.* Columbus: The Ohio State University Press.

Maslow, A. H. (1965). *Eupsychian management: A journal.* Homewood, IL: Dorsey.

Maslow, A. H. (1971). *The farther reaches of human nature.* New York: Viking.

McGregor, D. (1960). *The human side of enterprise.* New York: McGraw-Hill.

McShane, S., & Von Glinow, M. (2005). *Organizational behavior: Emerging realities for the workplace revolution* (3rd ed.). New York: McGraw-Hill/Irwin.

Neal, J. A. (1997). Spirituality in management education: A guide to resources. *Journal of Management Education, 27,* 121-139.

O'Connor, D. J. (2001). The organizational behavior future search. *Journal of Management Education, 25,* 101-112.

O'Connor, D. J., & Yballe, L. D. (2007). Team leadership: Critical steps to great projects. *Journal of Management Education, 31,* 292-312.

O'Neil, D. A., & Hopkins, M. M. (2002). The teacher as coach approach: Pedagogical choices for management educators. *Journal of Management Education, 26,* 402-414.

Palmer, P. (1998). *The courage to teach.* San Francisco: Jossey-Bass.

Patzig, W. D., & Zimmerman, D. K. (1985). Accuracy in management texts: Examples in reporting the works of Maslow, Taylor, and McGregor. *The Organizational Behavior Teaching Review, 10,* 1985-1986.

Pielstick, C. D. (2005). Teaching spiritual synchronicity in a business leadership class. *Journal of Management Education, 29,* 153-168.

Rynes, S. L., Quinn Trank, C., Lawson, A. M., & Ilies, R. (2003). Behavioral coursework in business education: Growing evidence of a legitimacy crisis. *Academy of Management Learning and Education, 2,* 269-283.

Schein, E. H. (2004). *Organizational culture and leadership.* San Francisco: Jossey-Bass.

Schmidt-Wilk, J., Heaton, D. P., & Steingard, D. (2000). Higher education for higher consciousness: Maharishi University of Management as a model for spirituality in management education. *Journal of Management Education, 24,* 580-611.

Schwartz, H. S. (1983). Maslow and the hierarchical enactment of organizational reality. *Human Relations, 36,* 933-956.

Senge, P. M. (1990). *The fifth discipline: The art and practice of the learning organization.* New York: Currency Doubleday.

Tischler, L. (2000). The growing interest in spirituality in business: A long-term socio-economic explanation. In G. Biberman & M. Whitty (Eds.), *Work and spirit: A reader of new spiritual paradigms for organizations*. Scranton, PA: University of Scranton Press.

Vaill, P. (1989). *Managing as a performing art*. San Francisco: Jossey-Bass.

Walton, M. (1988). *The Deming management method: The complete guide to quality management*. New York: Perigree.

Wilber, K. (1996). *Up from Eden*. Adyar, India: Theosophical Publishing.

Yballe, L. D., & O'Connor, D. J. (2000). Appreciative pedagogy: Constructing positive models for learning. *Journal of Management Education, 24,* 474-483.

Yballe, L. D., & O'Connor, D. J. (2004). Toward a pedagogy of appreciation. In D. Cooperrider & M. Avital (Eds.), *Advances in appreciative inquiry: Constructive discourse and human organization* (pp. 171-192). New York: Elsevier Science.

5 Family-of-Origin Family Therapy

Family-of-Origin Work for Counseling Trainees and Practitioners

Connie M. Kane
California State University, Stanislaus

Marital and family therapy training programs typically include work on the students' own family of origin (Smith, 1993) as preparation for their work with client families. In contrast, counselor education programs may recommend or even require that students participate in individual or group therapy (Corey, 1991) but do not give a clear focus on family of origin for that work. Yet graduates of these programs also are likely to become involved in marriage and family counseling (Horne, Dagley, & Webster, 1993). Although some elements of marriage and family therapy training are being incorporated into counselor education programs, the attention to trainees' families of origin is generally not one of them (Horne et al., 1993). Counselor education programs could better prepare their trainees by including family of origin work in the curriculum, and practitioners whose training did not include family-of-origin work may need to pursue it independently.

With the goal that counselor trainees form therapeutic relationships characterized by congruence, genuineness, and immediacy, qualities that should be offered in a manner guided by the needs of the client rather than by countertransference, most training programs include some attempt to develop the person of the therapist (Aponte, 1994; Corey, 1991; Smith, 1993). Trainers in multicultural counseling have suggested the need for trainees to study their own cultural heritage (Arnold, 1993; Preli & Bernard, 1993), and marital and family therapy training programs are requiring family-of-origin work (Nichols, 1993). Because the initial experiences of self, culture, and relationships usually happen within one's family of origin, the work on family-of-origin issues currently being done in marriage and family therapy programs may be equally applicable to individual

85

and group therapy trainees and to practitioners whose training did not include it. There is a need to consider the rationale behind family-of-origin work in marital and family therapy training programs and supervision settings, the models currently used, and the ethical implications. Subsequently, there is a need to develop models that provide the necessary opportunites, for both trainees and practitioners, without the ethical complication of dual relationships.

RATIONALE

The belief that there is a natural tendency for people, including counselors, to repeat interactional patterns throughout adulthood that were learned in childhood has its roots in the work of Sigmund Freud, who proposed that people continue to seek gratification from childhood relationships by internalizing the parent and then relating to others as if they were that parent. This notion was the basis for the development of object relations theory (Hamilton, 1989), which holds that the resolution of current relationship difficulties requires an examination of internalized object relationships based on early interactions between parents and children.

According to object relations theory, the healthy development of infants is a movement from autism, or psychological isolation, through stages of differentiation (recognition of the mother and the other as separate with properties of their own), practicing (moving about and exploring their world), and rapprochement (recognition of their own vulnerability and periodically returning to mother for reassurance) to the stage of object relations constancy (Mahler, Pine, & Bergman, 1975). At this point, the child, who is probably 2 to 3 years old, realizes that he or she is separated but related to his or her parents and that these relationships are primarily good even though they may have some undesirable qualities. Additionally, the child develops the capacity to recognize his or her own impulses, whether positive or negative, without projecting them onto others, thereby achieving whole object relatedness (Hamilton, 1989).

In transference, a person brings elements of a past relationship, particularly internalized objects, into a current relationship in the form of expectations. That is, he or she expects the current other to relate according to the patterns experienced with the primary figures in his or her past. Countertransference is the reciprocal response to transference, through which the other acts out intrapsychic images. The result is that each person is relating to the other according to internalized object relations patterns from former relationships for the sake of gratification in the current relationship (Becvar & Becvar, 1993).

Because both transference and countertransference are unconscious processes, they are not subject to conscious control. It is only when they are brought to light, usually through the interpretation of an objective observer in therapy or supervision, that the actor is invited to explore the internal objects being projected. Through family-of-origin work, however, counselors and trainees may uncover the significant aspects of their relationships with their parents that they have internalized before they bring the resulting expectations into client relationships, thereby forestalling potentially damaging countertransference before it occurs and increasing their ability to respond to clients with objectivity.

Transgenerational approaches to family therapy have in common the conceptualization of emotional pain as "arising out of interactional, human systems, primarily families of origin" (Nelson, Heilbrun, & Figley, 1993, p. 254) as well as the belief that unless there is intervention to resolve dysfunctional patterns, the effects of these patterns will be transmitted from one generation to the next.

Consistent with object relations theory, these approaches also emphasize the importance of self-differentiation in the therapist (Bowen, 1978), which is defined as "the separation of one's intellectual and emotional functioning; the greater the distinction, the better one is able to resist being overwhelmed by the emotional reactivity of his or her family (or client), and is thus less prone to dysfunction" (Goldenberg & Goldenberg, 1991, p. 322). Finally, transgenerational theorists have suggested that such differentiation can be facilitated through family-of-origin work in training (Aponte, 1994; Boszormenyi-Nagy, 1987; Bowen, 1978; Framo, 1976; McDaniel & Landau-Stanton, 1991).

CURRENT APPROACHES TO FAMILY-OF-ORIGIN WORK

One way to categorize current approaches to family-of-origin work in marital and family therapy training and postdegree supervision is according to the context of the work: (a) prior to and apart from clinical experience or (b) simultaneously and in conjunction with clinical experience as part of supervision. A second distinction is whether the supervisee's family meets with the supervisee and his or her therapist or supervisor.

McDaniel and Landau-Stanton (1991) have described in detail the format of their Family of Origin Seminar, an elective course that is separate from clinical experience. Besides reading and discussing the work of primary authors on family of origin, trainees have three opportunites to present a description of their own families that is based on their own perceptions as well as material gleaned from talking with their family members. They also write a paper summarizing their findings. If family therapy seems warranted for some trainees, seminar leaders recommend it; sometimes trainees pursue therapy on their own initiative.

According to McDaniel and Landau-Stanton (1991), the Family of Origin Seminar helps to "humanize the experience of family therapy and family therapy training; . . . further the development of self of the trainee; and . . . emphasize the inherent richness, strength, and diversity in families" (p. 465).

Aponte (1994) and McDaniel and Landau-Stanton (1991) offered two different approaches to family-of-origin work in the context of clinical supervision. Aponte has supervisees work in groups of approximately 12 with two trainers, meeting monthly for 2 days at a time. Supervisees take turns presenting their material, using 1 hour to discuss personal issues or clinical material and 2-hour periods for live interviews with client families or with their own family members. McDaniel and Landau-Stanton (1991) asked supervisees to give 45- to 60-minute presentations on their families of origin during the beginning phase of their live supervision groups. Supervisees are asked to develop their own genograms (McGoldrick & Gerson, 1985) to use as tools for examining transgenerational patterns, current themes, and the possible impact of any of these issues on their roles as therapists. The supervisor uses this information to be more attuned to possible countertransference triggers for each supervisee. Again, if therapy seems warranted for a particular supervisee, it is recommended but not undertaken by the supervisor.

ETHICAL CONSIDERATIONS

The ethical dilemma posed by incorporating family-of-origin work into counselor training and supervision is that of the possible dual relationship. On the one hand, supervisors are entering into very personal territory with supervisees, territory that often includes some unresolved issues and pain. Such an encounter demands a therapeutic response. On the other hand, supervisors must also give an evaluative response to supervisees, that is, they must give a grade or an evaluation for licensure or certification.

McDaniel and Landau-Stanton (1991) suggested that an evaluation of pass-fail that is based only on whether a trainee completes the required elements minimizes the evaluative role of the trainer. Aponte (1994) argued that there is a need to distinguish between the letter of the law and the spirit of the law regarding dual relationships and that there is a difference between dual relationships and relationships with dual components. The spirit of the ethical principle forbidding dual relationships, Aponte has suggested, is to avoid exploitation of clients and supervisees. The fact that counselor educators know of trainees' personal issues and then must grade or supervise them does not imply exploitation; neither does it constitute a dual relationship but rather a relationship with dual qualities.

What is not addressed by any of these authors is the question of whether the educator-supervisor's objectivity may be compromised in some way by his or her knowledge of the supervisee's personal issues. A second concern is whether supervisees are truly free to be honest about their issues or to limit their disclosures when they know that their supervisor must submit an evaluation that could affect their professional lives.

CASE OF BILL

Bill is a community counseling intern who generally demonstrates relationship, conceptualization, and intervention skills quite advanced for his stage of training. However, when faced with a female client who dared to question his suggestion that she needed to be more supportive of her husband, he suddenly shut down, offering minimal responses to the client's attempt to continue, and then closed the session early. He came out of the therapy room angry, describing the client as rigid and difficult to work with and expressing a conviction that there was no point in wasting time with her.

With the help of his supervisor, who reviewed a videotape of the session with him, Bill was able to acknowledge that his emotional response to the client's behavior seemed disproportionate and biased, a countertransference reaction rather than a therapeutic response. Further exploration for the possible roots of such countertransference led to Bill's eventual disclosure that his own parents had divorced when he was 5 years old and that, at some level, he still believed it was because his mother expected too much from his father. He said that all he could remember about his parents' relationship was that his mother was "always mad at" his father. After his parents' divorce, Bill quickly lost contact with his father, and his mother never spoke of him. Bill had never reexamined his parents' relationship from an adult vantage point. Neither had he ever talked with his mother about his sense of loss over his father's disappearance and his fear that if she ever became sufficiently angry with him, she would expel him too. At the recommendation of his supervisor, Bill began working on reexamining his relationship with his parents, with the help of a therapist.

RECOMMENDATIONS

Although there is ample reason to believe that family-of-origin work is a valuable component of training, not only for marital and family therapists but also for school and mental health counselors, there remains a need to develop formats for family-of-origin work that clearly protect the boundaries between therapeutic and evaluative roles. One possibility might be to use therapists in private practice or at the university counseling center whose only involvement in the training program would be the family-of-origin component and whose only report on a trainee's participation would be a certificate of completion. It would, of course, be critical that the therapists who are used have the appropriate training in family systems and therapy. If private practitioners are used, payment might either be covered directly by the trainees or by the university as a seminar fee included in the students' tuition.

Practitioners who did not have the opportunity to explore family-of-origin dynamics as part of their training might do so later in a number of ways. They might avail themselves of a graduate counseling course, such as that described by McDaniel and Landau-Stanton (1991), or a therapeutic relationship with someone whose theoretical orientation includes an appreciation and knowledge of family-of-origin work. Keeping in mind that issues uncovered in supervision may need to be addressed in therapy, the trainee may choose to enter into supervision with someone who has expertise in family-of-origin work as a preliminary step. Equally preliminary might be some independent study that begins with a reading list of primary sources, such as Bowen (1978), Framo (1972), and Boszormenyi-Nagy (1987). This could be followed by interviews with family members, as suggested by Hawkins and Killorin (1979), and development of a family genogram (McGoldrick & Gerson, 1985). Again, the further development of this work my require participation in therapy or at least a group seminar.

SOURCE: Connie M. Kane. (1995). Family-of-Origin Work for Counseling Trainees and Practitioners.*The Family Journal: Counseling and Therapy for Couples and Families, 3*, 245-248. © 1995 SAGE Publications.

REFERENCES

Aponte, H. J. (1994). How personal can training get? *Journal of Marital and Family Therapy, 20*, 3-15.

Arnold, M. S. (1993). Ethnicity and training marital and family therapists. *Counselor Education and Supervision, 33*, 139-147.

Becvar, D. S., & Becvar, R. J. (1993). *Family therapy: A systemic integration.* Needham Heights, MA: Allyn & Bacon.

Boszormenyi-Nagy, I. (1987). *Foundations of contextual therapy: Collected papers of Ivan Boszormenyi-Nagy.* New York: Brunner/Mazel.

Bowen, M. (1978). *Family therapy in clinical practice.* New York: Aronson.

Corey, G. (1991). *Theory and practice of counseling and psychotherapy* (4th ed.). Pacific Grove, CA: Brooks/Cole.

Framo, J. (1972). *Family interaction: A dialogue between family researchers and family therapists.* New York: Springer.

Framo, J. L. (1976). Family of origin as a therapeutic resource for adults in marital and family therapy: You can and should go home again. *Family Process, 15*, 193-210.

Goldenberg, I., & Goldenberg, H. (1991). *Family therapy: An overview* (3rd ed.). Pacific Grove, CA: Brooks/Cole.

Hamilton, N. G. (1989). A critical review of object relations theory. *American Journal of Psychiatry, 146*, 1552-1560.

Hawkins, J. L., & Killorin, E. A. (1979). Family of origin: An experiential workshop. *American Journal of Family Therapy, 7*(4), 5-17.

Horne, A. M., Dagley, J. C., & Webster, C. B. (1993). Strategies for implementing marriage and family counselor training in counselor training programs. *Counselor Education and Supervision, 33*, 102-115.

Mahler, M. S., Pine, F., & Bergman, A. (1975). *The psychological birth of the human infant*. New York: Basic Books.

McDaniel, S. H., & Landau-Stanton, J. L. (1991). Family-of-origin work and family therapy skills training: Both-and. *Family Process, 30*, 459-471.

McGoldrick, M., & Gerson, R. (1985). *Genograms in family assessment*. New York: Norton.

Nelson, T. S., Heilbrun, G., & Figley, C. R. (1993). Basic family therapy skills: IV. Transgenerational theories of family therapy. *Journal of Marital and Family Therapy, 19*, 253-266.

Nichols, W. C. (1993). Critical issues in marital and family therapy education: Introduction. *Contemporary Family Therapy, 15*, 3-8.

Preli, R., & Bernard, J. M. (1993). Making multiculturalism relevant for majority culture graduate students. *Journal of Marital and Family Therapy, 19*, 5-16.

Smith, R. L. (1993). Training in marriage and family counseling and therapy: Current status and challenges. *Counselor Education and Supervision, 33*, 89-101.

Connie M. Kane *is a faculty member in the Department of Advanced Studies in Education, California State University, Stanislaus, California.*

6 Structural Family Therapy

How Collaborative Is Structural Family Therapy?

Ryan T. Hammond

*Central Texas Veterans Administration Hospital,
Temple, Texas*

Michael P. Nichols

College of William & Mary

In response to the charge by "collaborative" therapies, such as solution focused and narrative, that structural family therapy is an aggressive, confrontational, and impositional approach, this investigation examines the role of therapist empathy in creating a collaborative partnership in structural family therapy. Twenty-four videotaped therapy sessions were used to correlate therapists' empathic response to family members and in-session change in the family's core problem dynamic. Findings suggest that empathy is not only evident in structural family therapy, but may be an essential ingredient in establishing a collaborative relationship and facilitating within-session change.

Keywords: *structural family therapy; empathy; collaborative therapy*

Structural family therapy offers (a) a theoretical framework for describing family organization (Minuchin, 1974) and (b) a set of techniques for restructuring problematic patterns (Minuchin & Fishman, 1981). The theoretical framework, with its concepts of subsystems, boundaries, and

AUTHORS' NOTE: Please address correspondence to Michael P. Nichols, Psychology Department, College of William & Mary, Williamsburg, VA 23187-8795; e-mail: mpnich@wm.edu coalitions, has proven useful enough to become part of the everyday vocabulary of family therapy (Goldenberg & Goldenberg, 2004), but the restructuring techniques, with their emphasis on active therapist direction (Colapinto, 1991), have proven more controversial. Leading practitioners of structural therapy call it an "interventive approach" and emphasize the need for "intensity" to challenge clients to change (Minuchin & Nichols, 1993), and critics (e.g., Anderson & Goolishian, 1988; Luepnitz, 1988) have described this model as aggressively confrontational and have called for more collaborative approaches.

Structural family therapy has been around long enough to have accumulated substantial empirical support for its effectiveness (cf. Pinsof & Wynne, 1995; Rowe, Gomez, & Liddle, 2006). In addition, a series of recent studies have established that the active interventionist use of enactments, challenging dysfunctional structures, and intervening with intensity are correlated with the model's effectiveness (Favero, 2002; Fellenberg, 2003; Miles, 2004; Nichols & Fellenberg, 2000). Thus, structural family therapy, with its liberal use of confrontation, appears to be out of step with family therapy's contemporary emphasis on collaborative partnership with clients (Anderson, 1993; Nichols & Schwartz, 2008). But is a therapy that challenges family members aggressively necessarily incompatible with a collaborative approach?

All forms of family therapy consist of two elements: (a) listening to what clients have to say about their problems and (b) intervening to help them deal more effectively with those problems. Narrative therapists, for example, speak of mapping the influence of the problem or getting the family's "problem-saturated story" before beginning to transform these stories using externalization and searching for unique outcomes (White & Epston, 1990). Similarly, structural therapists begin by "joining"—accepting the family's presentation of their problems and themselves—and "tracking" their story of the problem before shifting to the more active, interventionist techniques of "boundary making" and "unbalancing" (Minuchin & Fishman, 1981). Although the second part of this process, the techniques of change, gets a lot of attention, the first step, acknowledging clients' accounts of their difficulties, does not always get much emphasis.

Critics of the newer technique-driven approaches have taken them to task for failing to listen to clients and make them feel understood before introducing interventions to alter their experience. Some commentators have used the phrase *solution-forced therapy* to suggest that by doggedly focusing on positives, solution-focused therapists have a tendency to silence their clients' doubts and fears (Efran & Schenker, 1993; Miller, 1994; Wylie, 1990). Narrative therapists have been accused of ignoring family conflict in the process of redefining problems as alien entities (Held, 1995; Minuchin, 1998). Nor has structural family therapy been immune to the charge of not spending enough time listening to clients before trying to change them. Although joining is described as an essential first step in this approach (Minuchin & Fishman, 1981), critics have pointed out that joining often consists of little more than a brief paraphrase of clients' opening statements as a ploy to circumvent resistance (Nichols, 1987).

In fact, what we call the first step in family therapy, listening to what clients have to say, is related to empathy, long considered one of the core ingredients of psychotherapy. Carl Rogers made empathy the centerpiece of his whole approach to treatment (Rogers, 1951), and empathy is often cited as one of the common factors in all forms of therapy (Asay & Lambert, 1999; Blow & Sprenkle, 2001; Hubble, Duncan, & Miller, 1999).

Heinz Kohut (1971, 1977) defined empathy as "sustained immersion in the experience of another person" and emphasized its role in healthy development and psychotherapeutic treatment. Although they are related, joining and empathy are two different things. Joining is an operation consisting of eliciting and acknowledging clients' opinions, and it can be used with genuine concern or merely as a device to prepare them for the challenges to follow. A collaborative, empathic approach, on the other hand, cannot be just a technique or a ploy. Empathy means understanding the inner experience of another person (Schafer, 1959), and it requires a receptive openness that would seem to contraindicate a confrontational approach to treatment such as structural family therapy. But let us restate the question we asked earlier: Is a therapy that challenges family members aggressively necessarily incompatible with a collaborative, empathic stance?

This study was designed to explore the role of empathy in creating a collaborative relationship in structural family therapy. Specifically, we hypothesized that therapists who established a bond of sympathetic understanding and maintained it throughout the session would be more effective in getting family members to cooperate in restructuring their interactions in those sessions.

METHOD

Sample Description

This investigation included videotaped family therapy sessions from 24 different families. To represent a broad range of therapist experience, the tapes included 12 sessions conducted by experienced therapists and 12 sessions conducted by inexperienced therapists. A total of 6 therapists made up the sample, 2 of whom were Caucasian men; 2, Caucasian women; 1, a Hispanic man; and 1, a Hispanic woman. The experienced therapists were leading practitioners of the structural approach (with at least 15 years of experience), and the inexperienced therapists were graduate students (with 2 years of supervised training in structural family therapy).

The videotaped sessions included both couples and families with children, resulting in a mean family size of three. The majority of clients in the sessions were White, three included African American clients, and one included Latin American clients. The clients represented a range of socioeconomic statuses and presented with a wide variety of problems, although none was psychotic.

Undergraduate psychology students were recruited and trained to rate within-session change. Nine student raters were selected to attend five 90-minute training sessions. The investigators reviewed the students' ratings after each training session to assess interrater agreement. The undergraduates' ratings were compared with a benchmark predetermined by an experienced structural family therapist and two doctoral students. Six undergraduates whose ratings most closely agreed with the benchmark ratings were selected as the primary raters. Three undergraduates whose ratings fell within 1 or 2 points of the benchmark were used as alternates to replace raters who might drop out.

Two groups of three students were used to make ratings on the Change in the Core Problem Dynamic Scale; the remaining three served as alternates. To maximize the number of sessions rated and minimize the number of hours raters were required to put into the study, each of the two groups rated half of the tapes in the sample. Ratings were made independently and privately.

Clinician judges rated therapist collaborative empathy. The clinician judges consisted of two clinical psychology doctoral students and one clinical psychologist experienced in structural family therapy. To ensure adequate interrater reliability, before rating tapes in the study sample the clinician judges practiced rating therapist collaborative empathy on a set of tapes not used in the study until 100% agreement was reached.

Measures

Although there are already several measures of empathy in the literature (Greenberg, Watson, Elliot, & Bohart, 2001), most of these rely on responses from clients and therapists, and unfortunately, such responses were not available in this study. Therefore, we developed the Therapist Collaborative Empathy Scale, which relies on observer ratings to measure the extent to which a therapist demonstrates an effort to elicit and accept a client's perspective and to maintain a collaborative relationship. Ratings are made on a Likert-type scale ranging from 1 (*extremely unempathic*) to 7 (*extremely empathic*). To aid in making these ratings, qualitative descriptions are provided for each point on the scale. For example, a rating of 1 includes the description "Therapist actively ignores or cuts client off," whereas a rating of 7 includes the description "Therapist makes an extended effort to elicit and accept the client's feelings in a very sympathetic manner."

The Change in the Core Problem Dynamic Scale (Miles, 2004) measures the degree to which clients demonstrate significant in-session change in the defined problem dynamic. This scale is also a 7-point Likert-type scale with descriptions assigned to each numerical value. For example, a rating of 1 (*significant negative change*) includes the description "a destructive session which may threaten either the continuation of treatment or family relationship or both." A rating of 7 (*significant and manifest change*) includes the description "Client understands and accepts the therapist's interpretations and begins to make clear behavioral changes in the session; client accepts his or her own role in problems and begins to interact more effectively in the session."

In previous studies, we found that trained undergraduate raters were able to assess in-session change on this instrument because the observations called for are based on concrete, observable behaviors.

Procedures

Before rating the tapes included in the study sample, the clinician judges provided the undergraduates with a written description of the core problem dynamic in each session and the kind of interactions that would characterize positive change. The problem dynamic for each session was reliably defined in previous studies (Fellenberg, 2003; Miles, 2004). The undergraduate raters submitted ratings weekly to Ryan T. Hammond on completion. In addition to providing numerical ratings of change based on the Change in the Core Problem Dynamic Scale, raters documented their rationale for their ratings and recorded any questions or concerns that occurred during the rating process. Raters attended three booster sessions to address questions, undergo reliability checks, and receive further training as necessary. The clinician judges used the Therapist Collaborative Empathy Scale to rate therapist collaborative empathy after viewing each session. Booster sessions were used to obtain interrater reliability checks and address questions and concerns.

Data Analysis

Cronbach's alpha was used to assess interrater reliability for undergraduate raters' and clinician judges' ratings. In addition, percentage of agreement among undergraduate raters' and clinician judges' ratings were assessed during training and data collection. A Pearson product-moment correlation was used to assess the relationship between therapist collaborative empathy and within-session change. An independent *t* test was used to assess the difference between experienced and inexperienced therapists with respect to therapist collaborative empathy.

RESULTS

The mean within-session change for the entire sample was 4.10. The mean therapist collaborative empathy rating for all sessions was 4.79. The mean, standard deviation, skewness, kurtosis, and minimum and maximum of therapist collaborative empathy and within-session change ratings are presented in Table 6.1.

Table 6.1 Descriptive Statistics for Collaborative Empathy and Within-Session Change Ratings

Variable	M	SD	Skewness	Kurtosis	Minimum	Maximum
Therapist empathy	4.79	1.10	−0.08	−0.82	2.67	7.00
Within-session change	4.10	0.86	0.65	−0.30	3.00	6.00

NOTE: $N = 56$.

Undergraduate Raters' Within-Session Change Ratings During Training

Nine undergraduates participated in more than 15 hours of training in which they were familiarized with structural family theory, viewed five videotaped sessions of structural family therapy in their entirety, and rated the degree of clients' within-session change. On completion of the training phase, the researcher selected six undergraduates to provide ratings on the sample used in the current study. Selection was based on those who obtained the highest percentage agreement with a predetermined benchmark on within-session change. Table 6.2 provides a summary of instances when

Table 6.2 Percentage Agreement Among Undergraduate Raters During Training

	Point Discrepancy and Percentage of Occurrence					
Rater	0	%	1	%	2	%
A	6	67	4	33	0	0
B	7	58	5	42	0	0
C	9	75	3	25	0	0
D	10	83	2	17	0	0
E	8	67	4	33	0	0
F	4	33	8	67	0	0
G	7	58	5	42	0	0
H	7	58	3	25	2	17
I	9	75	3	25	0	0

undergraduates' ratings were in complete agreement with or fell within 1 or 2 points of the predetermined benchmark.

Undergraduate Raters' Within-Session Change Ratings

Both groups of undergraduate raters rated 12 videotaped sessions, 6 conducted by experienced therapists and 6 conducted by inexperienced therapists. Before viewing the sessions, raters were given a description of the core problem dynamic. Similar to the sessions used during the training phase of the study, the core problem dynamic of each session was defined by clinician judges in previous studies (Miles, 2004). After watching a session in its entirety, raters used the Change in the Core Problem Dynamic Scale to independently rate each client in the session. The mean of the three ratings was used to obtain the final within-session change rating for each client. The mean within-session change for the entire sample was 4.10. The minimum within-session change rating was 3, and the maximum was 6.

Percentage of agreement for undergraduates' ratings was used to determine interrater reliability. Table 6.3 provides a summary of percentage of agreement among undergraduates' ratings.

Because sessions varied with respect to the number of clients, there was a slight variation between the number of individuals rated by Groups 1 and 2. Cronbach's alpha was used to measure the degree of homogeneity of responses among each group's ratings of within-session change. Results from this analysis show interrater consistency to be high for both Group 1 (.93) and Group 2 (.86).

Table 6.3 Within-Session Change Percentage of Agreement Among Undergraduate Raters

	Point Discrepancy and Percentage of Occurrence					
Group	0	%	1	%	2	%
1	9	38	11	46	4	17
2	17	53	15	47	0	0

Clinician Judges' Collaborative Empathy Ratings

After viewing each videotaped session in its entirety, clinician judges independently rated collaborative empathy using the Therapist Collaborative Empathy Scale. Therapists' responses to each family member were rated. The mean of the clinician judges' ratings provided the final rating for each client. The mean collaborative empathy rating for all sessions was 4.79. The minimum collaborative empathy rating was 2.67, and the maximum was 7.

Percentage of agreement of clinician judges' ratings was used to measure interrater reliability. Clinician judges were in complete agreement 34% of the time, differed by 1 point 57% of the time, and differed by 2 points 9% of the time. Table 6.4 provides a summary of the percentage of agreement among clinician judges' ratings. A Cronbach's alpha of .92 shows an acceptable degree of homogeneity among clinician judges' ratings of therapist empathy.

Table 6.4   Percentage of Agreement of Collaborative Empathy Among Clinician Judges

	Point Discrepancy and Percentage of Occurrence					
Variable	*0*	*%*	*1*	*%*	*2*	*%*
Therapist empathy	19	34	32	57	5	9

Collaborative Empathy and Within-Session Change

The means of undergraduate raters' and clinician judges' ratings were used to explore the relationship between collaborative empathy and within-session change. A Pearson product-moment correlation yielded a significant positive relationship between collaborative empathy and within-session change, $r(54) = .54, p < .01$.

The more therapists demonstrated an effort to listen to and understand clients' feelings, the more likely clients were to explore new ways of interacting. What follows is an example of an empathic success that appeared to be positively related to within-session change.

In Session 3, an experienced therapist met with a couple to explore their demand–withdraw relationship. The wife felt that her husband did not spend enough time with her; as a result, she became angry, and in response, her husband withdrew further. For within-session change to occur the wife needed to express her feelings to her husband without attacking and the husband needed to listen without withdrawing.

As the wife explained her frustration with her husband's tendency to interrogate her about what she was feeling when she got upset, the therapist said, "I don't quite understand; tell me more about that." After she elaborated, the therapist said, "I see. You wish he would just hold you?" The wife started crying and said, "Yes."

In addition to listening to the wife without interrupting, the therapist asked questions to draw out the wife's feelings, which paved the way for him to empathize with her. This continued throughout the session. The therapist was given a mean rating of 6 for his extended efforts to elicit and acknowledge the wife's feelings. The wife was given a mean rating of 5 for her subsequent ability to express her feelings calmly to her husband toward the end of the session.

The following is an example of a collaborative failure that appeared to be negatively related to within-session change. In Session 4, an experienced male therapist met for a consultation with a married couple in their 40s to explore their relationship problems. The husband felt that his wife was not affectionate and did not spend enough time with him. The wife complained that her husband wanted too much attention and affection, and so she withdrew. For within-session change to occur, the wife needed to speak up forcefully and express her point of view, and the husband needed to listen to and acknowledge what she said.

Throughout the session, the husband and wife argued. Almost all of the therapist's comments to the husband encouraged him to try harder to listen to his wife. For example, when the couple was arguing, the therapist said to the husband, "You win if she gets her point of view across and feels that you hear her." At one point, when the wife was explaining her view of their situation, the husband said, "Do I get a turn now?" The therapist responded, "Can you convince her that if she hears you, then you will listen to her?" This was an attempt to alter the couple's problem dynamic, but it was considered a collaborative failure because although the therapist kept telling the husband to listen to his wife, he made no attempt to acknowledge the husband's position. The husband ignored the comment and repeated that his wife never listens to him.

The therapist was given a mean rating of 4.67 because although he listened to the husband without arguing or cutting him off, he made only minimal effort to accept his feelings and often criticized his behavior. The husband was given a mean rating of 3 because he spent most of the session defending himself and criticizing his wife. Perhaps the husband might have been more willing to listen to his wife if he had been given a hearing for his own point of view. This case suggests that challenging clients without first empathizing with them is a tactical error, especially with high-conflict couples, because clients get caught up in quarreling and making themselves heard rather than working on changing the problem dynamic.

Experienced Versus Inexperienced Therapists

A significant difference was found between experienced and inexperienced therapists with respect to collaborative empathy. Specifically, experienced therapists were significantly more collaborative ($M = 5.16$) than inexperienced therapists ($M = 4.38$), $t(54) = -2.79$, $p < .01$ (see Table 6.5).

Table 6.5   Inexperienced Versus Experienced Therapists on Collaborative Empathy

Variable	Inexperienced Therapists		Experienced Therapists		
	M	SD	M	SD	t(54)
Therapist empathy	4.38	0.96	5.16	1.12	−2.79*

*p < .01.

DISCUSSION

Before considering the clinical implications of our findings, it is important to remember that this study was done with a small sample of families (24) and only 6 therapists. The correlations between collaborative empathy and within-session change were based only on observer-rated scales and did not include the important perspectives of the therapists or clients. Finally, the significant positive correlation found between collaborative empathy and in-session change demonstrates a relationship between the factors but does not establish a causal connection. These methodological limitations mean that the following clinical implications should be taken as tentative hypotheses at this point, and perhaps as subjects for further study.

Although structural family therapy is well known for its forceful interventions, such as boundary making and unbalancing, the results of this study suggest that a collaborative partnership may be a prerequisite for making these interventions effective. Therapists were seen to be most effective when they made a conscientious effort to elicit and accept family members' points of view before challenging them to restructure their interactions. It may also be necessary to reestablish a collaborative relationship if a client seems to resent a challenging intervention. In other words, a collaborative partnership is not something you can establish and then forget about; it may take work to reestablish if restructuring interventions provoke resentment. Moreover, experienced therapists were found to be significantly more empathic than inexperienced therapists. Combined with results from previous studies showing that focusing on structural problems, intervening with intensity, and challenging clients directly led to positive in-session change (Miles, 2004; Nichols & Fellenberg, 2000), these findings suggest that structural family therapists are most effective when they make active efforts to understand family members' motives for acting as they do and then challenging them to change their role in dysfunctional structures.

Our operational definition of a collaborative partnership rested heavily on therapists' empathic efforts to elicit and accept family members' points of view. When Anderson and Goolishian (1988) introduced the notion of a collaborative relationship, they emphasized more what collaborative therapists do not do. They do not adopt the role of expert, they do not assume that they know how families should change, and they do not push them in any particular direction. Thus, Anderson and Goolishian emphasized the role of egalitarian partnership in the collaborative model. An aspect of structural family therapy that might seem to involve an authoritarian rather than a collaborative relationship is the way structural therapists challenge family members' overinvolvement (enmeshment) and underinvolvement (disengagement). Does taking this critical position negate a collaborative partnership? We do not think so.

What we observed in this study was that the challenges made by experienced structural therapists amounted to pointing out what the family members were doing and its consequences. Therapists who had established a collaborative partnership with their clients were able to make these observations without undermining that partnership. What the therapists did was point out what people were doing, not what they should be doing. This point was amplified in the most recent statement of the structural model (Minuchin, Nichols, & Lee, 2007), in which the authors made clear that although a therapist may take the lead in pointing out what's keeping a family stuck, in discussions of how the family might change, the family should take the lead.

> Without this step, which turns the process of assessment from an operation performed on families into an operation performed with them, therapy often becomes a process of pushing people where they see no reason to go. No wonder they resist. (Minuchin et al., 2007, p. 11)

Thus, a collaborative relationship is not one in which therapists abdicate leadership, but rather one in which clients and therapists work together as respectful partners. Specifically, this means that therapists must explore and respect family members' points of view, and although they may point out unwanted consequences of what family members are doing, they should not dictate who needs to change or how. In this study, we observed experienced therapists asking clients, "What can you do to make this better?" and "How can you two work together to make you both happier?" not telling them what they should do.

Qualitative analyses showed that it was not necessary for therapists to avoid confronting family members to be seen as collaborative. In fact, clients appeared quite receptive to forceful criticism—but only after the therapist had first listened to and acknowledged their point of view. In cases in which therapists challenged clients before showing empathy for their perspective, the clients resisted the therapist's efforts, and little therapeutic change was seen in those sessions.

Although it was not part of our formal hypothesis, we suspected that inexperienced therapists might show more empathy and relate in a more respectful way to clients than their more experienced colleagues. We had learned from previous studies, as well as our own experience as supervisors, that experienced therapists tend to zero in on structural problems and intervene more forcefully in challenging family members to alter their roles in dysfunctional structures. We were therefore surprised to discover that experienced therapists related in a significantly more collaborative manner with client families. What we observed when we reviewed the sessions in our sample was that inexperienced therapists tended to begin sessions with transparent attempts at joining. They complimented family members on their appearance, asked children questions about sports heroes, and said things like "I know how you feel" in response to family members' statements. Otherwise, they tended to listen passively as though just hearing clients talk about their experience might be helpful. Listening with a passive show of interest is not the same as actively eliciting and respecting clients' points of view.

In some instances, we observed inexperienced therapists making what appeared to be half-hearted efforts to sympathize with certain difficult family members. Joining by pretending to sympathize apparently does not fool anyone. Patronizing responses do not fool family members, and they certainly did not fool our student raters, who gave such responses low scores on the collaborative empathy scale. Responding with "I understand how you feel" to a bullying family member's complaints is phony. A more genuine response might be "I don't understand your position; can you explain it to me?"

Although the experienced therapists in this study tended to be more genuinely collaborative and to intervene more forcefully, we observed several examples of experienced therapists challenging family members to change their interactions before hearing out their feelings. Although these therapists appeared to be concerned about helping family members interact more effectively, our observations suggest that a therapist who pushes people to change before he or she has understood and affirmed them is indistinguishable from a destructive parent who criticizes and rejects them.

Our observations suggest that constructive change occurs in structural family therapy when family members develop new perspectives that lead them to new actions. Because it is difficult for people to see their own role in destructive interactions, therapists must be adept at identifying problematic structures and in intervening forcefully to encourage clients to risk exploring new alternatives. However, to be effective therapists must reach and motivate family members to accept responsibility for changing their behavior. For this to happen, therapists must make active efforts to elicit and acknowledge what their clients think and feel—and to work as respectful partners—before challenging them to change. Moreover, how family members should change must emerge in a mutual, give-and-take discussion between therapists and family members if therapy is to remain a collaborative enterprise.

Establishing a collaborative relationship in family therapy does not require a radical change in strategy. It means working a little harder to understand people before challenging them to change. Simple empathic comments convey understanding and can be used to draw out what is incompletely expressed. Thus, empathy helps break down resentments that often keep family members at odds. Brooding is unnecessary if there is someone to hear and accept those feelings. The empathic therapist can be that someone.

However, a genuinely collaborative relationship requires more than just empathic comments. It requires sustained respect for clients and working in active partnership with them. What this study supports is that such a partnership can be maintained even in an interventive approach like structural family therapy.

SOURCE: Ryan T. Hammond and Michael P. Nichols (2008). How Collaborative Is Structural Family Therapy? *The Family Journal: Counseling and Therapy for Couples and Families, 16,* 118-124. © 2008 SAGE Publications.

REFERENCES

Anderson, H. (1993). On a roller coaster: A collaborative language systems approach to therapy. In S. Friedman (Ed.), *The new language of change: Constructive collaboration in psychotherapy* (pp. 323-344). New York: Guilford Press.

Anderson, H., & Goolishian, H. A. (1988). Human systems as linguistic systems. *Family Process, 27,* 371-393.

Asay, T. P., & Lambert, M. J. (1999). The empirical case for the common factors in therapy: Qualitative findings. In M. A. Hubble, B. L. Duncan, & S. D. Miller (Eds.), *The heart and soul of change: What works in therapy* (pp. 33-56). Washington, DC: American Psychological Association.

Blow, A. J., & Sprenkle, D. H. (2001). Common factors across theories of marriage and family therapy: A modified Delphi study. *Journal of Marital and Family Therapy, 27,* 385-401.

Colapinto, J. (1991). Structural family therapy. In A. S. Gurman & D. P. Kniskern (Eds.), *Handbook of family therapy* (Vol. 2, pp. 417-433). New York: Brunner/Mazel.

Efran, J., & Schenker, M. (1993). A potpourri of solutions: How new and different is solution-focused therapy? *Family Therapy Networker, 17,* 71-74.

Favero, D. (2002). *Structural enactments as methods of change in family therapy.* Unpublished doctoral dissertation, Virginia Consortium Program in Clinical Psychology, Virginia Beach.

Fellenberg, S. (2003). *The contribution of enactments to structural family therapy: A process study.* Unpublished doctoral dissertation, Virginia Consortium Program in Clinical Psychology, Virginia Beach.

Goldenberg, I., & Goldenberg, H. (2004). *Family therapy: An overview.* Pacific Grove, CA: Brooks/Cole.

Greenberg, L. S., Watson, J. C., Elliot, R., & Bohard, A. C. (2001). Empathy. *Psychotherapy: Theory, Research, Practice, Training, 38*, 380-384.

Held, B. (1995). *Back to reality: A critique of postmodern theory in psychotherapy.* New York: Norton.

Hubble, M. A., Duncan, B. L., & Miller, S. D. (Eds.). (1999). *The heart and soul of change: What works in therapy.* Washington, DC: American Psychological Association.

Kohut, H. (1971). *The analysis of the self.* New York: International Universities Press.

Kohut, H. (1977). *The restoration of the self.* New York: International Universities.

Luepnitz, D. A. (1988). *The family interpreted.* New York: Basic Books.

Miles, D. (2004). *The effectiveness of therapist interventions in structural family therapy: A process study.* Unpublished doctoral dissertation, Virginia Consortium Program in Clinical Psychology, Virginia Beach.

Miller, S. (1994). The solution-conspiracy: A mystery in three installments. *Journal of Systemic Therapies, 13*, 18-37.

Minuchin, S. (1974). *Families and family therapy.* Cambridge, MA: Harvard University Press.

Minuchin, S. (1998). Where is the family in narrative family therapy? *Journal of Marital and Family Therapy, 24*, 397-403.

Minuchin, S., & Fishman, C. (1981). *Family therapy techniques.* Cambridge, MA: Harvard University Press.

Minuchin, S., & Nichols, M. P. (1993). *Family healing: Tales of hope and renewal from family therapy.* New York: Free Press.

Minuchin, S., Nichols, M. P., & Lee, W.-Y. (2007). *Assessing families and couples: From symptom to system.* Boston: Allyn & Bacon.

Nichols, M. P. (1987). *The self in the system.* New York: Brunner/Mazel.

Nichols, M. P., & Fellenberg, S. (2000). The effective use of enactments in family therapy: A discovery-oriented process study. *Journal of Marital and Family Therapy, 26*, 143-152.

Nichols, M. P., & Schwartz, R. C. (2008). *Family therapy: Concepts and methods* (8th ed.). Boston: Allyn & Bacon.

Pinsof, W. M., & Wynne, L. C. (1995). The efficacy of marital and family therapy: An empirical overview, conclusions, and recommendations. *Journal of Marital and Family Therapy, 21*, 585-614.

Rogers, C. R. (1951). *Client-centered therapy.* Boston: Houghton Mifflin.

Rowe, C. L., Gomez, L. C., & Liddle, H. A. (2006). Family therapy research: Empirical foundations and practice implications. In M. P. Nichols & R. S. Schwartz, *Family therapy: Concepts and methods* (7th ed., pp. 399-440). Boston: Allyn & Bacon.

Schafer, R. (1959). Generative empathy in the treatment situation. *Psychoanalytic Quarterly, 28*, 342-373.

White, M., & Epston, D. (1990). *Narrative means to therapeutic ends.* New York: Norton.

Wylie, M. S. (1990). Brief therapy on the couch. *Family Therapy Networker, 14*, 26-34, 66.

Ryan T. Hammond, PsyD, is a staff psychologist at the Central Texas Veterans Hospital in Temple, Texas. His clinical interests include couples therapy and post-traumatic stress disorder.

Michael P. Nichols, PhD, is professor of psychology at the College of William & Mary. His research program is focused on exploring the active therapeutic ingredients in family therapy.

7 Strategic Family Therapy

For Parents Only

A Strategic Family Therapy Approach in School Counseling

Judith A. Nelson

Sam Houston State University

Schools are excellent resources for families whose children are experiencing behavioral problems at home and at school. School counselors who have training in systems theory are situated to help families make lasting positive changes in family structure and to avoid costly interventions that may or may not be helpful. According to Selvini-Palazzoli (1986), the problems between parents and children can be addressed using a universal set of directives that immediately restore the proper authority to the parents so that the parents can, in effect, help the child give up the symptomatic behavior. This article presents a technique based on Selvini-Palazzoli's "invariable prescription" (p. 342) for professional school counselors working with families and their acting-out children.

Keywords: *parents; children; family therapy; school counseling; therapeutic interventions; systems theory*

Professional school counselors, unlike other mental health professionals, focus primarily on interventions that promote student achievement. The service delivery of this focus falls into four categories: guidance curriculum, responsive services, individual planning, and system support (Gysbers & Henderson, 2006). Parent consultation is included in responsive services.

There are compelling arguments for the use of systems-based interventions in the school setting in responding to families (Hinkle, 1993; Nicoll, 1992; Stone & Peeks, 1986). Often families with young children do not have the means to access private practitioners or social service agencies. Some families may feel that they have exhausted all of these types of resources and are frustrated because their children continue to have difficulty in school. These families may rely on school personnel to assist them with their children's medical, social, academic, emotional, and developmental issues. School counselors typically do not take on cases that require long-term psychotherapy because of large caseloads and other noncounseling duties; and yet most readers would agree that school counseling interventions must be therapeutic and effective to keep students on track for learning. Involving parents in brief, therapeutic interventions has proven effective in the school setting, particularly when the child exhibits problematic behaviors that interfere with learning.

In my school counseling experience, parents of misbehaving children often are referred to the school counselor by the teachers, principal, or other school officials. Sometimes parents refer themselves in hopes that the school counselor can offer suggestions for improvement of their child's behavior at home and at school. When the presenting problem is the child's misbehavior, couples often report that there is constant bickering about parenting strategies between the parents as well as a feeling of being "held hostage" in one's own home by a demanding and unyielding child. Some parents describe chaotic interactions over relatively simple tasks such as bathing, eating, getting to bed, and choosing what to wear to school. In addition, parents often report their frustrations with each other and their disagreements about how to get their child to behave. When parents seek help with child management issues, professional school counselors trained in systems theory and techniques have a unique perspective at their disposal to assist with improving family functioning.

SCHOOL COUNSELORS AND THE "INVARIABLE PRESCRIPTION"

The approach described in this article is based on strategic family therapy (Madanes, 1981) and, more specifically, the later therapeutic views of Mara Selvini-Palazzoli (1986). A strategic focus lends itself to working with clients in the school setting. Strategic models are time-sensitive and oriented to the present. The history or etiology of the problem is not the focus of counseling. The strategic therapist takes a nonblaming stance and avoids pathological labeling. The focus is on the symptom and how it relates to the family interactional sequences. When the problematic behavior has been alleviated, therapy is over. Most strategic therapists work by giving directives to be completed in the time between sessions. These directives do not include rationales or lengthy explanations but, rather, are the therapist's attempt to interrupt the interactional patterns that maintain the presenting problem.

In her break with the original Milan group, Mara Selvini-Palazzoli's (Diller, 2000) *invariable prescription* of the 1980s was a return to some of her strategic ways of working with families. This universal directive was designed to interrupt the "family games" of psychotic families by creating a boundary between generations, a boundary that strengthened the parental alliance (Selvini-Palazzoli, 1986). Like Selvini-Palazzoli's invariable prescription, which was designed to work universally in families and to loosen the grip of the collusive parent-child relationship, school counselors have helped parents strengthen the parental alliance in a relatively short time period using a similar, brief intervention.

Selvini-Palazzoli's (1986) directives to parents included sessions with the parents alone in which they were instructed to keep everything about the sessions a secret; to go out in the evenings without explaining their absence to the child(ren); and to keep a notebook, separately, describing the behaviors of the family members. The results were astonishing. The family games were broken up and symptomatic children improved dramatically.

Using a slightly more tentative approach, school counselors can accomplish the same results. When parents are asked whether they would be willing to try an "experiment" to help their problematic child, most of them are happy for any suggestion. The school counselor cannot tell the parents to go away on outings but can certainly suggest that they keep adult conversations private and choose a walk-in closet or bathroom in which they will always go together to discuss "child" issues. They must not emerge until they have agreed on a plan of action or a consequence for misbehavior, and they cannot give any explanation for their behavior. The only words they can say in the way of an explanation to the child are "This is what Mom and Dad have decided." Most often this statement would follow a directive or consequence on which the parents have previously agreed.

The intervention is brief and solution-focused. In the first meeting, the school counselor works together with the parents to identify the problem situation and to begin to formulate a picture of what the solution will look like. The counselor enlists the parents as change agents for their child's behavior problems by asking them to participate in an experiment. The experiment is described in detail so that the parents know exactly what to do and how to respond to the child's misbehavior at home. First, they are to choose a private place in which to retreat when their child's behavior is inappropriate, and they must agree that they will use this approach for any misbehavior. Furthermore, they must agree to calmly discuss the consequences or outcomes for the misbehavior while they are in their retreat. The parents come out of the retreat together and announce their decision calmly to the child. Any attempt by the child to undermine the parents' strategy must be met with a firm but loving commitment to remain steadfast in their position. They must not engage in arguments or pleading but should respond with the words "This is what Mom and Dad have decided." The experiment itself is preplanned during the session with the parents, and the counselor can role-play some possible scenarios before ending the session. During the follow-up sessions, the counselor has an opportunity to support any success the parents have had as well as discussing the challenges. The parents may need a great deal of encouragement if their child has reacted negatively to the experiment. Looking for the exceptions—the small successes—will help the parents remain steadfast in their new behaviors until they see more improvement in their child's behavior.

CASE EXAMPLE

The following case study illustrates the use and effectiveness of this universal intervention in the school setting. Again, the approach described here is based on the invariable prescription (Selvini-Palazzoli, 1986).

Jeff and Ann were the parents of Elaine, a fourth grader who was placed in an alternative school for persistent misbehavior at her home campus. Her behaviors in school included talking back to teachers when she was corrected, refusing to follow simple directions, arguing with authority figures, and being generally noncompliant. Elaine's parents referred themselves to the professional school counselor at the alternative school for help with Elaine's behavior in school and at home. They admitted that they had similar problems at home with Elaine, described her as "spoiled," and stated that they had let her behavior "get out of control." They also said that she was prone to dramatized outbursts and often made up elaborate stories to try to get out of trouble. When asked about Elaine's strengths, the parents both agreed that she was very creative and intelligent, loved to draw, was fond of animals, and could be very loving and affectionate. Elaine was the youngest of two daughters but, at this point, was being raised as an only child because the older daughter was an adult and living on her own.

The family's pediatrician had referred the family to a psychiatrist who saw Elaine individually about six times the previous school year. No family therapy had been considered at that time. The psychiatrist diagnosed Elaine with a conduct disorder and bipolar disorder. Several different medications were prescribed during a 1-year period, and Elaine was referred to a psychologist for therapy. Jeff, in particular, did not see enough improvement in his daughter's behavior to warrant continuing the sessions with the psychologist or the medication that had been prescribed by the psychiatrist. The parents were, as Jeff said, "at their wit's end."

The school counselor wanted to know how the parents handled Elaine's behavior at home. Ann offered this explanation: "Elaine is a master at getting us upset one way or another. It usually starts with some annoyance behavior designed to get our attention, like refusing to follow a direction or being too rough with one of the animals." Ann went on to describe how she usually just asks Elaine to stop, but the child rarely complies. Then Jeff yells and threatens, and Elaine becomes very disrespectful and argumentative. Elaine screams at her parents that she always gets in trouble, that life is not fair, and that she would be better off with another family. Refusing to follow the simplest requests, she resorts to crying, screaming, and throwing herself on the floor, all the while claiming that her parents' directions or requests are "too hard," "boring," or "ridiculous." Then Ann continued to describe how she usually tries to rationalize with Elaine and often offers bribes to get her to follow the rules. Sometimes Ann admitted that she even consoles the misbehaving child by promising treats or special privileges if Elaine would simply comply. By this time, Jeff is totally exasperated and begins yelling at Ann about her ineffective parenting techniques and how he is always put in the position of being the "bad guy." According to Jeff, "After that, it's just chaos." In the end, Elaine receives no consequences for her poor behavior, and her parents are furious with each other. The counselor agreed that Elaine did seem to be smart and "masterful" in many ways: getting the parents' attention, diverting dad's anger toward mom instead of herself, and keeping the family "on edge."

Then the counselor asked the parents whether they would be willing to try an "experiment" at home for the next 2 weeks. Jeff and Ann figured that they had nothing to lose. The counselor instructed the parents to be very secretive at home regarding their visit to the school. If Elaine pressed them for information, they were to simply say that it was "none of her concern" and that it was "for parents only." In addition, the counselor prescribed a series of directives for the parents to follow each and every time Elaine was misbehaving.

First of all, they were to choose a place in the home in which they could retreat to discuss their strategy; it could be a walk-in closet or bathroom. A room with a lock on the door would be most appropriate. Jeff and Ann said they had a small bathroom in the laundry area right off the kitchen that would work. They agreed that as soon as Elaine became argumentative about following a direction, they would walk hand in hand into their retreat and discuss the issues quietly. Second, they had to agree on some consequences for the offending behaviors. Both parents felt that taking away television privileges and time on the computer would be the most effective consequences. They also considered taking away access to the family pets and assigning work duty, like cleaning the bathroom or kitchen. Third, they had to be totally discreet about their new form of discipline, not offering any explanations, rationales, or lectures. The one sentence they could say in response to any protest would be "This is what Mom and Dad have decided." The counselor stressed to Ann and Jeff that this was of the utmost importance. Engaging in Elaine's arguments, pleading, and manipulations would only keep them from reaching their goal of teaching their child to follow the requests of adult authority figures. Armed with their new plan of action, Jeff and Ann made an appointment for a follow-up visit with the counselor in 2 weeks.

During the next 2 weeks, the counselor noticed that Elaine had very few discipline infractions at school. The structure of the alternative school appeared to agree with her. Elaine was completing her work, making good grades, and, in general, getting along with teachers and peers. The school counselor saw Elaine only for the routine classroom guidance lessons and group counseling sessions that all students in the school received. Elaine was not referred to the counselor or the assistant principal for crisis intervention or behavioral issues a single time during her placement at the alternative school.

When her parents returned for their second appointment, they also had good news to report. Ann described what had happened at home. "At first, we felt ridiculous walking into the bathroom to discuss our parenting issues, and Elaine definitely didn't like it." Ann went on to say that Elaine basically "threw a fit" the first time they tried their new approach. She yelled and screamed for them to come out of the bathroom. She banged on the door and tried to force it open. It eventually became clear to her that they were not going to respond to her demands, so she just lay on the floor and cried. Her parents did not respond in any way to Elaine at this time. When Jeff and Ann came out to give Elaine her consequence for refusing to clean up her room, she argued that she would do it later. The parents persisted, using the prescribed statement that this is what "Mom and Dad had decided." Eventually, Elaine went upstairs to her room and didn't come out until it was picked up. The parents reported that it was almost 2 hours before this was accomplished, but they were patient. By dinner time, the room was clean, and Elaine was ready to join the family again. She was exceptionally pleasant at dinner even though she had lost her television privileges for the night, and her parents had plenty of opportunity to praise her for appropriate behaviors, including cleaning her room. During the following days, there were other opportunities for the parents to experiment further with their new parenting techniques. They were obviously pleased with the results, and, as they so aptly put it, they felt that they had "reclaimed their home."

The counselor asked the parents to enlighten her. How did they manage to transform their quality of family life so dramatically in so short a time? Ann said that they were absolutely "mystified" at how such a simple experiment could make such a difference when they had literally spent thousands of dollars on doctors' visits and medication the previous school year. However, the couple did have a theory. Ann believed that because she and Jeff knew exactly what they were going to do and say each time Elaine misbehaved, they were less likely to argue with each other, and they were working more like a "team." She saw the retreat into the tiny enclave as a kind of symbol to Elaine that "this is for parents only." When they came out to give her their decision about what the consequence would be, they felt "empowered by each other."

CONCLUSION

Diller (2000) reframed the acting-out child's "repetitive unconscious behavioral attempt" as a question that asks the parents, "Are you steady and strong enough to take care of me?" (p. 59). Perhaps Elaine experienced her parents' disagreements and hesitation to give her a consequence for poor behavior as parental weakness. Having a weak captain at the helm of the ship would be frightening for anyone but particularly so for a young child. These fears could certainly exacerbate the poor behavior which, in turn, would frustrate the parents even more, causing them more uncertainty and disagreements. Ann's attempts to rescue Elaine resulted in triangulation that proved to be too much stress on the family system. The parents' power was subjugated, and the symptoms of the child were maintained. In a strategic sense, the school counselor was able to interrupt the cycle of interaction that was maintaining the symptomatic behaviors by helping the parents create a clear and stable boundary between themselves and their child. There is no doubt that the theoretical perspective of Selvini-Palazzoli's (1986) invariable prescription is much more complex than the intervention itself. The nature of a strategic approach is that the complexity of it is lost in its simplicity. The counselor sees the interactional patterns (games) of the family members but does not find it necessary to point them out to the family. These observations are simply used in designing the intervention. Professional school counselors who understand this concept and work within a systems perspective are poised to assist large numbers of families who are struggling with children who do not follow rules, do not accept consequences, and, in general, appear to be noncompliant.

In my work with families with children who were placed in Discipline Alternative Education Programs for misbehavior at their home campuses, this particular intervention has been effective with some of the toughest cases I have seen in school counseling. In case after case of acting-out students, the parents disagreed in general about how to manage the child or had polarized styles of parenting. One parent often placed blame on the other and frequently critiqued the other's parenting abilities during heated arguments about a particular course of action regarding their child. In most cases, the child was present during the arguments and was aware of the disagreement that the offending behavior was creating. Some parents feared that they would divorce over their parental dichotomy, even when they reported to me that they had high levels of satisfaction with other marital issues. They simply had difficulty parenting together. The intervention was useful in individual consultations with parents as well as a technique shared with parents during parent education classes. The careful alignment of the parental unit seemed to always improve the child's behavior, even in cases in which the child met the criteria for attention deficit disorder, conduct disorder, or bipolar disorder. The intervention was used with families of varied ethnicity, in a variety of developmental stages, and in a range of socioeconomic circumstances.

It is not a new idea that good parenting skills are effective in managing children's behavior, yet parents often seem unwilling or unable to take a stand on discipline issues or to work together to manage their children's behaviors in effective ways. School counselors who use interventions based on systems theory can offer powerful solutions for helping parents strengthen their alliance with each other and promoting effective ways of managing children.

SOURCE: Judith A. Nelson. (2006). For Parents Only: A Strategic Family Therapy Approach in School Counseling. *The Family Journal: Counseling and Therapy for Couples and Families,14,* 180-183. © 2006 SAGE Publications.

REFERENCES

Diller, L. (2000). The invariant prescription redux. *The Family Therapy Networker,* 24(6), 55-62.

Gysbers, N., & Henderson, P. (2006). *Developing and managing your school guidance program* (4th ed.). Alexandria, VA: American Counseling Association.

Hinkle, J. S. (1993). Training school counselors to do family counseling. *Elementary School Guidance and Counseling, 27,* 252-257.

Madanes, C. (1981). *Strategic family therapy.* San Francisco: Jossey-Bass.

Nicoll, W. G. (1992). A family counseling and consultation model for school counselors. *The School Counselor, 39,* 351-361.

Selvini-Palazzoli, M. (1986). Towards a general model of psychotic family games. *Journal of Marital and Family Therapy, 12,* 339-349.

Stone, G., & Peeks, B. (1986). The use of strategic family therapy in the school setting: A case study. *Journal of Counseling and Development, 65,* 200-203.

Judith A. Nelson, PhD, is an assistant professor of counselor education at Sam Houston State University.

8 Solution-Focused Family Therapy

The Effectiveness of Solution-Focused Therapy With Children in a School Setting

Cynthia Franklin
University of Texas at Austin

Joan Biever
Our Lady of the Lake University

Kelly Moore
University of Texas at Austin

David Clemons
Our Lady of the Lake University

Monica Scamardo
Our Lady of the Lake University

Objective: This study examined the effectiveness of solution-focused therapy with children in a school setting using AB single-case designs. *Method:* The research team provided 5 to 10 sessions of solution-focused therapy services to seven children who were referred with learning disabilities and classroom behavioral problems. Data from Conners Teacher Rating Scales were analyzed using visual analysis of the data in relationship to clinical change scores, effect sizes, and improved percentage scores. *Results:* Results indicate that solution-focused therapy was followed by positive changes on a range of behavioral problems. *Conclusions:* Solution-focused therapy shows promise for helping special education students with their academic difficulties and classroom behaviors.

AUTHORS' NOTE: Correspondence may be addressed to Cynthia S. Franklin, School of Social Work, University of Texas, 1925 San Jacinto Blvd., Austin, TX 78712-1203.

Solution-focused therapy is a strengths-based therapy model developed at the Brief Family Therapy Center in Milwaukee, Wisconsin, by Steve de Shazer (de Shazer, 1985, 1988, 1991, 1994; de Shazer et al., 1986) and Insoo Kim Berg (Berg, 1994; Berg & DeJong, 1996; Berg & Miller, 1992) and associates (e.g., Miller, Hubble, & Duncan, 1996; Walter & Peller, 1992) over the past 15 years. Solution-focused therapists use a set of behaviorally and cognitively oriented therapy techniques to amplify positive behaviors and reinforce the use of effective coping strategies. Solution-focused therapy is different from other prescriptive approaches because of its emphasis on process and its focus on changing future behaviors to help clients accomplish their goals. Focusing on the future causes solution-focused therapists to spend little time exploring problems and instead work with the client to construct a set of behavioral tasks that lead to a rapid solution.

Solution-focused therapy was developed by clinical practitioners in clinic settings using idiographic, case study analysis. Because there is often a wide gap between clinical researchers and practitioners, the effectiveness of the model has not been established using experimental methods. Practitioners, however, have found solution-focused therapy to be a useful model that has led to its wide usage in clinical practice. Currently, solution-focused therapy is being applied to diverse clinical problems and fields of practice, such as child welfare and family-based services (Berg, 1994), inpatient psychiatric disorders (Webster, Vaughn, & Martinez, 1994), alcohol abuse (Berg & Miller, 1992), crisis-oriented youth services (Franklin, Corcoran, Nowicki, & Streeter, 1997; Franklin, Nowicki, Trapp, Schwab, & Petersen, 1993), sexual abuse (Dolan, 1991), spouse abuse (Sirles, Lipchik, & Kowalski, 1993), and school-related behavior problems (e.g., Kral, 1995; Metcalf, 1995; Murphy, 1994a, 1994b).

Applications of solution-focused therapy in school settings are growing, and the model seems to offer an appropriate set of interventions for work with children, teachers, and parents in schools (Kral, 1995; Metcalf, 1995; Murphy, 1994a, 1994b; Selekman, 1997). The major tasks of the solution-focused therapist in school settings have been described by Kral (1995), who discusses a five-dimensional model: The therapist is to help the client develop an image of a realistic solution; discover how and in what ways the solution is already occurring in the client's life; determine small, measurable steps (goals) towards the solution; describe those thoughts, actions, and feelings that can be utilized in obtaining the goals; and do something to make a difference. Overall, the solution-focused therapist helps clients think of ways already in clients' repertoires of skills to approach the problem differently. Franklin and Moore (1999) provide a comprehensive overview of solution-focused therapy methods. Practitioners who use the therapy have clearly defined and illustrated the processes, methods, and procedures that are used in solution-focused therapy practice, which makes the therapy viable for research studies.

At present, however, few outcome studies have been conducted on solution-focused therapy. The ones that have been completed show the model as a promising approach that deserves further evaluation (DeJong & Hopwood, 1996; Kiser, 1988; Kiser & Nunnally, 1990). Early studies on the model are limited by their research designs. Most studies did not use standardized outcome measures, adequate baselines, control groups, or other experimental procedures (for reviews, see Berg & DeJong, 1996; McKeel, 1996). Only recently have practitioners and researchers worked together to evaluate the effectiveness of solution-focused therapy using a variety of quasi-experimental research designs (e.g., Franklin et al., 1993, 1997; Lee, 1997; Lindforss & Magnusson, 1997; Macdonald, 1997; Schindler, Zimmerman, Prest, & Wetzel, 1997). Franklin and colleagues (1993, 1997) and Murphy (1992) evaluated the effectiveness of solution-focused therapy using single-case experimental designs. Single-case designs appear to serve as a useful approach for providing a beginning empirical basis for the therapy.

PURPOSE OF THE STUDY

The purpose of this study is to examine the effectiveness of solution-focused therapy with children in a school setting. This study investigates the effectiveness of solution-focused therapy with children who have been labeled learning disabled by their school and have also been identified as needing help in solving school-related behavior problems. Using clinical case studies, Metcalf (1995) and Kral (1995) described the usefulness of solution-focused therapy with school-related behavior problems, but no outcome measures were used to support their claims. Murphy (1992) further provided a single-case study using a repeated measures design and permanent products to evaluate brief therapy (including some solution-focused strategies) for school problems. This research builds on the existing case studies in this area. Results from seven single-case experiments are reported.

METHOD

The study began in January 1997 with a completion date of May 1997. The two principal investigators and two therapists delivering the therapy services were trained by the developers of solution-focused therapy at the Brief Family Therapy Center in Milwaukee. The principal investigators were a clinical social worker and a counseling psychologist. Both principal investigators were licensed mental health professionals and had several years of experience working in schools and with children and family services. Therapists in the study were advanced doctoral students: one male therapist with a master's degree in psychology and one female therapist with a master's degree in social work. Each therapist had at least 3 years of experience in clinical practice.

Solution-Focused Therapy Interventions

Each student was provided 5 to 10 sessions of 30 to 45 minutes of solution-focused therapy. Therapists also spoke with teachers about the progress of the cases and provided teacher consultations for the cases. The teacher consultations, however, were minimal, lasting only 10 to 20 minutes a week for most cases. However, some teachers were provided more consultations than others, contingent on the teacher's investment in participating and the needs of the case. A treatment protocol was followed as a guide for implementing the solution-focused therapy model with children in the school (Franklin & Biever, 1996). The use of at least three main process sequences in a session is necessary for a therapy to be considered solution-focused (Berg & de Shazer, personal communication, January 2, 1997). These three sequences are that the therapist asked the "miracle question," used scaling questions, and gave clients compliments, sometimes followed by homework tasks at the end of the session. The miracle question is a way of helping clients envision solutions to a problem. The therapist asks something like, "Let's suppose that overnight a miracle happened and the problem you are having with your teacher disappeared. But you were sleeping and did not know it. When you came to school the next day what would be the first thing that you would notice?" Scaling questions ask clients to rate their problems on a scale of 1 to 10 and project their future progress (see Franklin & Moore, 1999, for a more detailed explanation of therapeutic questioning techniques associated with solution-focused therapy).

Solution-focused therapy methods such as the miracle question emphasize the co-construction of solutions from conversations between a therapist and a client (Berg & DeJong, 1996). Co-construction emerges as a result of the practitioner's carefully and skillfully using Socratic questioning to facilitate recognition of prior successes and solutions (i.e., exceptions to the problem) and visualizations of future solutions (i.e., miracle questions). However, sequences of the therapy may not be serial in that therapists sometimes change the order of the questions asked. For example, the miracle question may be asked before scaling questions in some cases. Because a main focus of solution-focused therapy is to be flexible and idiographic using what works in an individual case, a set of steps for the process of the therapy and techniques employed were identified in the treatment protocol. Every session therefore followed the same process and used the same questioning techniques.

Ensuring Treatment Integrity

The methods specified in the treatment protocol are the ones followed most closely by the developers of solution-focused therapy, Insoo Kim Berg and Steve de Shazer at the Brief Family Therapy Center in Milwaukee. Berg examined the therapy protocol for the study and gave her approval that the methods specified constituted solution-focused therapy. Berg also trained each member of the therapy team during a 4-day training in Milwaukee. Both principal investigators also served as clinical supervisors for the cases. Each session was videotaped, and the principal investigators watched the sessions to determine if the two therapists were closely following the treatment protocol and to provide guidance on how to improve the therapists' treatment strategy.

Procedures

Solution-focused therapy took place in the Dobie Intermediate School (5th and 6th grades) in the Schertz Cibolo Universal Unified Independent School District in Cibolo, Texas. Cibolo, Texas, is a rural community now transitioning to a suburban, bedroom community of San Antonio, Texas.

Participating students were enrolled in the special education program at Dobie Intermediate School. Participants were purposively selected by a school diagnostician in consultation with classroom teachers. Students selected for the study had been labeled learning disabled and had received more than one behavioral referral from classroom teachers that warranted attention from a school psychologist or another mental health professional. Students were excluded from the study if they were diagnosed with a learning disorder and a major mental disorder such as childhood schizophrenia or bipolar disorder or were known to be at risk for suicide. Dual diagnoses of learning disorder and other psychiatric disorders such as conduct disorder, oppositional defiant disorder, attention-deficit/hyperactivity disorder, and anxiety disorder were accepted into the study when the main presenting problem was the resolution of behavioral and academic difficulties in the classroom. Because Dobie Intermediate School does not have adequate services making counseling available for behavioral referrals, the research project was seen as a service-related benefit to the children and the school. The study met full internal review board approval, and assent from a child and written consents from parents were obtained before a child was accepted into the study.

The research team provided 5 to 10 sessions of solution-focused therapy services to 19 children who were referred with the above profile in exchange for the opportunity to conduct single-case experiments on some of the cases. Examination of baseline data from the cases indicated that several of the children did not have problems that were extreme enough to meet the clinical significance criterion on the Conners Teacher Rating Scale (Conners, 1990). The researchers decided to include only cases considered clinically significant ($M > 69$ with 50% or more of the observations in the baseline phase falling above 70) on one or more of the subscales of the Conners Teacher Rating scale. Based on this criterion, 7 of the 19 children referred were selected for conducting single-case studies. All children referred, however, were offered the counseling services in accordance with the research team's agreement with the school.

Measures

Two standardized measures were used to evaluate outcomes, the Conners Teacher Rating Scale–39 (Conners, 1990) and the Feelings, Attitudes and Behavior Scale for Children (FAB–C) (Beitchman, 1996). Although administered to the children, the FAB–C was not used in the study because none of the students' self-reported scores fell into the clinical range on that measure. We therefore eliminated the FAB–C as an outcome measure. In addition, individualized rating scales were used as a part of the scaling technique to measure clinical progress toward goals to resolve problem behaviors; however, due to space limitations and concerns about the validity and reliability of these measures, discussion of them is not included in this article.

Conners Teacher Rating Scale–39 (CTRS–39). The CTRS–39 is the original 39-item behavioral rating scale developed for teachers which characterizes patterns of behavior in children 3 to 12 years old. The measure includes seven subscales: Hyperactivity (17 items), Conduct Problem (13 items), Emotional Indulgent (8 items), Anxious Passive (6 items), Asocial (5 items), Daydream-Attention Problem (3 items), and Hyperactivity Index (10 items derived from a composite score of items measured). Note that some items are used in more than one subscale. According to the manual, it takes approximately 15 minutes to fill out the measure. Responses are marked 0 (*not at all*), 1 (*just a little*), 2 (*pretty much*), or 3 (*very much*). The psychometric properties of the CTRS–39 are good for a clinical rating scale, and the measure has been used widely in hundreds of efficacy and effectiveness studies. The CTRS–39 is the best researched of the Conners Rating Scales and has the largest norm group. The predictive, concurrent, and construct validity of the CTRS–39 has been examined in several studies (e.g., Beck, Collins, Overholser, & Terry, 1985; Conners, 1969; DeHaas, 1986; Sandoval, 1981; Taylor & Sandberg, 1984; Trites, Blouin, & Laprade, 1982). Reliability studies indicate that the CTRS–39 is an internally consistent measure with acceptable temporal stability and excellent interrater reliability. Edelbrock, Greenbaum, and Conover (1985) report an average internal consistency reliability of .94 for the various scales. Test-retest reliability is reported to be fairly high for one month, ranging from .72 to .91.

Research Design

Research participants were evaluated using AB single-case designs. The basic design consisted of a single case with $n_A = 6$ to 8 observations made during a baseline phase and $n_B = 5$ to 10 observations made during an intervention phase on the Conners Teacher Rating Scales. The observations for the baseline were made approximately twice a week for 4 weeks, and the observations in the intervention phase were made approximately once a week for the duration of the therapy. In addition, one follow-up observation was made approximately 1 month after the last intervention period. There are variations in the numbers of baseline and intervention points for individual cases because it was not possible to get measures at each time-point on every student.

Although there are numerous limitations and threats to internal validity in using AB designs to study therapy effectiveness, given the setting and the service-related nature of the project, it was not possible to employ a more rigorous single-case design. Multiple replications ($N = 7$) were used to strengthen internal validity of the AB single-case experiments. We believe that the multiple replications of the AB design in this study may serve as an appropriate approach for developing a beginning empirical basis for the effectiveness of the solution-focused therapy model in a school setting.

Data Analysis

Data analysis was conducted using visual analysis of observed changes on clinical cutting scores. For the CTRS–39, the clinical range is 70 and above. Cases with subscales averaging 69 or higher with 50% or more of the observations greater than 70 in the baseline phase were analyzed to see if the data would support clinical success. Clinical success was determined by scores subsequently moving into the nonsignificant clinical range (below 70) during the intervention phase. Effect sizes and improved percentage scores were also calculated to corroborate the magnitude of changes observed in the visual analysis. Effect size calculations for those cases were determined to be clinically significant when they reached 0.50, and the intervention phase score had a lower percentage of subsequent observations below 70 and a mean score below 70. Follow-up scores were used to assess whether clinically significant improvements were maintained for one month following termination.

RESULTS

Case 1

RS was a 13-year-old sixth grader of mixed ethnicity (Latino and Anglo) who lived with both parents. He had been diagnosed with attention-deficit/ hyperactivity disorder and Tourette's syndrome. He was referred to the project due to his inability to make decisions for himself and his passive behavior in class (e.g., not turning in his work). RS was taking Ritalin throughout the study, but this medication did not appear to alleviate his behavioral and academic problems completely. One year earlier, he was found to demonstrate a significant academic deficit in math calculation and a significant behavioral deficit in peer relationships. RS was seen for eight 30- to 45-minute sessions. His interest in video games was seen as an area of strength that the therapist built upon in framing interventions.

Teacher 1. On the Emotional Indulgence subscale, Teacher 1 recorded 63% of the observations in the baseline over 70 for a mean score of 73. During the intervention phase, Teacher 1 recorded 0% of observations over 70, resulting in a mean score of 65. The effect size was calculated to be −1.39 for an improvement of 42%. The 1-month follow-up data was at 70, indicating a postintervention decline back into the clinical range.

On the Hyperactivity Index subscale, Teacher 1 recorded 100% of the observations in the baseline over 70 for a mean score of 82. During the intervention phase, Teacher 1 recorded 89% of observations over 70, resulting in a mean score of 75. The effect size was calculated to be −0.92 for an improvement of 32%. These changes are clinically relevant in that they indicate a trend toward clinical improvement, although they are not clinically significant in that they did not move out of the clinical range. The 1-month follow-up data was above 70 (final score 85), indicating that the case continued to have clinically significant problems. (See Figure 8.1.)

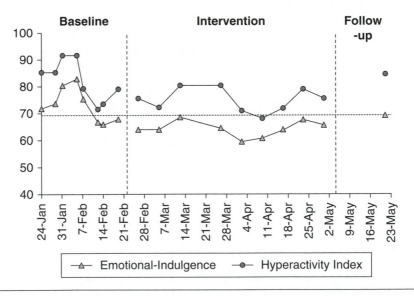

Figure 8.1   Case 1, Teacher 1

Teacher 2. On the Hyperactivity subscale, Teacher 2 recorded 50% of the observations in the baseline over 70 for a mean score of 69. During the intervention phase, Teacher 2 recorded 0% of observations over 70, resulting in a mean score of 66. The effect size was calculated to be –1.39 for an improvement of 42%. The 1-month follow-up data was below 70 (final score 66), indicating a sustained postintervention effect.

On the Conduct Problem subscale, Teacher 2 recorded 50% of the observations in the baseline over 70 for a mean score of 69. During the intervention phase, Teacher 2 recorded 0% of observations over 70, resulting in a mean score of 62. The effect size was calculated to be –2.47 for an improvement of 49%. The 1-month follow-up score for Teacher 2 was below 70 (final score 61), indicating a sustained postintervention effect.

On the Hyperactivity Index subscale, Teacher 2 recorded 100% of the observations in the baseline over 70 for a mean score of 90. During the intervention phase, Teacher 2 recorded 100% of observations over 70, resulting in a mean score of 84. The effect size was calculated to be –1.76, which indicated a 46% improvement. These scores indicate a trend toward improvement, but the changes were not clinically significant because the scores did not move out of the clinical range. The 1-month follow-up score was above 70 (final score 83), indicating that the student continued to have clinically significant problems in this area. (See Figure 8.2.)

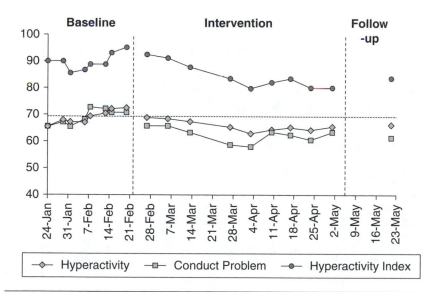

Figure 8.2 Case 1, Teacher 2

Case 2

ER was a 10-year-old Anglo fifth grader who lived with her recently divorced mother and two older brothers. ER was referred to the project due to withdrawal from peers and difficulties getting along in the classroom. She was classified by the school as learning disabled and was placed in regular classrooms with resource room assistance for dyslexia. The school had found her to demonstrate significant academic deficits in basic reading skills, reading comprehension, and spelling, with no significant behavioral deficits. School records revealed no significant mental health problems or occurrences; however, she was diagnosed with ulcers in the past. ER was seen for five sessions. She was absent from school on three occasions during the course of treatment due to illness. ER made rapid changes in her behavior by becoming more active and initiating interactions with her peers. Her teachers told the therapist that she had made significant changes.

On the Asocial subscale, one teacher rated 71% of the observations in the baseline over 70 for a mean score of 73. During the intervention phase, the teacher recorded 0% of observations over 70, resulting in a mean score of 55. The effect size was calculated to be –1.24 for an improvement of 39%. There was, however, a strong trend in the baseline toward improvement and a regression at the beginning of the treatment that make it extremely difficult to conclude that the changes observed during treatment were due to the effect of the therapy. The 1-month follow-up was below 70 (final score 43) indicating a sustained postintervention effect. (See Figure 8.3.)

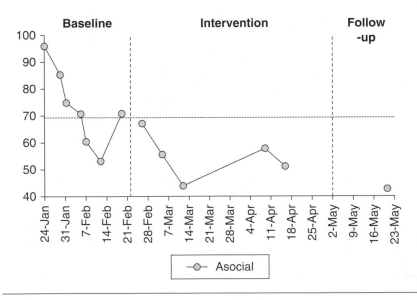

Figure 8.3   Case 2

Case 3

LA was an 11-year-old Latina sixth grader. LA's parents were divorced, and she lived with her mother, stepfather, and three younger brothers. She had not had contact with her father for several years. LA was referred to the project due to poor organizational skills and not completing work on time. Concerns were also expressed regarding her choice of friends and her behavior within this peer group. LA had been classified by the school as learning disabled and emotionally handicapped. She had more recently been diagnosed with generalized anxiety disorder with characteristics of oppositional defiant disorder and reading disorder. LA was seen for six 30- to 45-minute sessions. The therapist believed that progress was made on her goal of becoming more organized and handing in her work. Her overall behavior in the classroom was also believed to be improved.

On the Conduct Problem subscale, one teacher recorded 88% of the observations in the baseline over 70 for a mean score of 77. During the intervention phase, the teacher recorded 0% of observations over 70, resulting in a mean score of 50. The effect size was −5.69 for an improvement of 50%. The 1-month follow-up score was below 70 (final score 47), indicating a sustained postintervention effect.

Case 4

TP was an 11-year-old Anglo sixth grader. TP was an only child who lived with both of her biological parents. TP was referred to the project because of difficulty with peer relationships. For example, she was frequently teased by her peers, and she would overreact and begin screaming. She had most recently been found to demonstrate significant academic deficits in math, spelling, and written language and significant behavioral deficits in distractibility and hyperactivity. Her mother reported that TP had a history of allergies and took Ritalin to reduce hyperactivity. TP was seen for six 30- to 45-minute sessions. The therapist believed that she made rapid and sustained progress in her ability to control her temper when teased by peers. She made new friends and reported that she was talking to her parents more easily. Teachers confirmed these changes when asked. (See Figure 8.4.)

Teacher 1. On the Emotional Indulgence subscale, Teacher 1 recorded 75% of the observations in the baseline over 70 for a mean score of 74. During the intervention phase, Teacher 1 recorded 0% of observations over 70, resulting in a mean score of 59. The effect size was −2.86 for an improvement of 50%. The 1-month follow-up data was below 70 (final score 59), indicating a sustained postintervention effect.

On the Asocial subscale, Teacher 1 recorded 88% of the observations in the baseline over 70 for a mean score of 75. During the intervention phase,

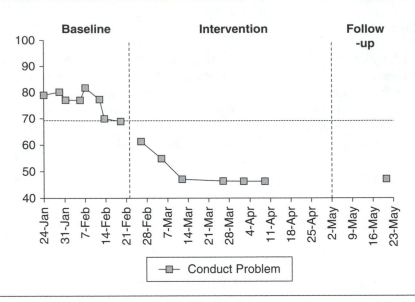

Figure 8.4 Case 3

Teacher 1 recorded 43% of observations over 70, resulting in a mean score of 64. The effect size was calculated to be –2.41 for an improvement of 49%. The 1-month follow-up score was below 70 (final score 65), indicating a sustained postintervention effect.

On the Hyperactivity Index subscale, Teacher 1 recorded 100% of the observations in the baseline over 70 for a mean score of 97. During the intervention phase, Teacher 1 recorded 86% of observations over 70, resulting in a mean score of 80. The effect size was calculated to be –3.76 for an improvement of 50%. Although this improvement was not clinically significant in that the scores did not move out of the clinical range, it did show a clinical trend toward improvement. The 1-month follow-up score was above 70 (final score 86), indicating the case continued to show clinically significant problems in this area. (See Figure 8.5.)

Teacher 2. On the Hyperactivity Index subscale, Teacher 2 recorded 63% of the observations in the baseline over 70 for a mean score of 77. During the intervention phase, Teacher 2 recorded 43% of observations over 70, resulting in a mean score of 67. The effect size was calculated to be –0.52, which indicated a slight improvement of 20%. There was, however, a trend in the baseline toward improvement, making it difficult to conclude that the changes observed during treatment were due to the effect of the therapy. In addition, the cyclical nature of the problem ratings indicates extreme variation in responding with a tendency to improve and regress. There is some

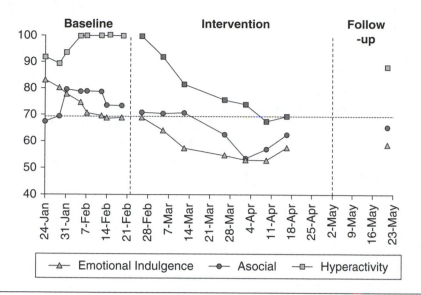

Figure 8.5   Case 4, Teacher 1

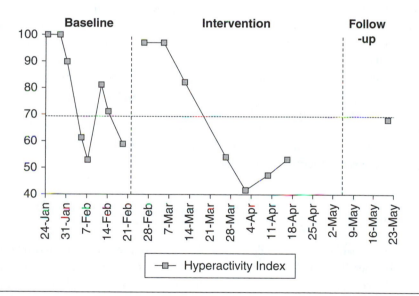

Figure 8.6   Case 4, Teacher 2

indication that this pattern may continue in the intervention phase, although it does appear that the improvement periods are increasing. The 1-month follow-up score was below 70 (final score 68), indicating that the teacher viewed the student as having moved outside the clinical range for that problem. (See Figure 8.6.)

Case 5

CF was a 12-year-old Latino sixth grader who lived with his divorced mother. CF was referred to the project due to lack of organizational skills and difficulty in remembering to do his homework. His most recent evaluation, conducted when he was in second grade, determined that he met the eligibility criteria for the handicapping condition of learning disability. School records revealed that he had a history of head trauma. He was taking stimulant medication for attention deficit disorder. He was diagnosed by a neurologist as having myotonic dystrophy when he was 7 years old. CF was seen in seven 30- to 45-minute sessions, and the therapist consulted with his teacher on two occasions. Initially, CF was uninterested in therapy and unable to identify goals. He had made progress, however, toward the referral goal of completing his work between the time of the referral and the initiation of therapy. In accordance with solution-focused therapy this was interpreted to be pretreatment change. Consultation with one of CF's teachers yielded the goal of improving peer relationships. Solution-focused techniques, such as the miracle question and relationship questions, were not effective until the therapist took a paradoxical stance by betting CF that no change would occur. Following this intervention, CF began reporting exceptions to the problems of his peer relationships and was able to use solution-focused techniques to enhance the changes.

On the Asocial subscale, one teacher recorded 63% of the observations in the baseline over 70 for a mean score of 71. During the intervention phase, the teacher recorded 0% of observations over 70, resulting in a mean score of 54. The effect size was calculated to be –4.63 for an improvement of 50%. The 1-month follow-up score was below 70 (final score 56), indicating a sustained postintervention effect. (See Figure 8.7.)

Case 6

MJ was an 11-year-old Anglo fifth grader who lived with her parents and one older brother. The family had one pet, a dog that was very important to MJ. MJ was referred to the project due to social difficulties with peers and teachers. MJ was most recently determined to meet the eligibility criteria for being speech handicapped. School records revealed no significant health problems. MJ was seen for eight 30- to 45-minute sessions. The therapist believed that MJ made steady progress toward her miracle of talking more in class. MJ also noted an improved relationship with one of her teachers and with her mom.

Teacher 1. On the Asocial subscale, Teacher 1 rated 75% of the observations in the baseline over 70 for a mean score of 76. During the

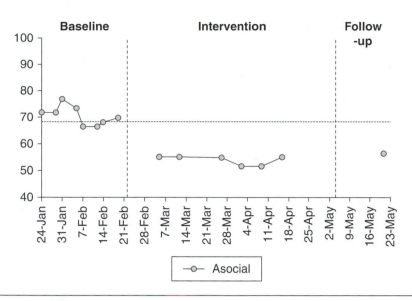

Figure 8.7   Case 5

intervention phase, Teacher 1 rated 0% of observations over 70, resulting in a mean score of 52. The effect size was calculated to be –4.85 for an improvement of 50%. The 1-month follow-up score was below 70 (final score 45), indicating a sustained postintervention effect. (See Figure 8.8.)

Teacher 2. On the Emotional Indulgence subscale, Teacher 2 recorded 88% of the observations in the baseline over 70 for a mean score of 77. During the intervention phase, Teacher 2 recorded 89% of observations over 70, resulting in a mean score of 76. The effect size was calculated to be –0.24 for an improvement of 9%, indicating that this case did not change on this subscale. The 1-month follow-up score was above 70 (final score 95), indicating that the student remained in the clinical range for that problem.

On the Anxious-Passive subscale, Teacher 2 recorded 63% of the observations in the baseline over 70 for a mean score of 73. During the intervention phase, Teacher 2 recorded 22% of observations over 70, resulting in a mean score of 68. The effect size was calculated to be –0.48, for a small improvement of 18%. There was, however, a trend in the baseline toward improvement, making it difficult to conclude that the minimal changes observed during treatment on this subscale were due to the effect of the therapy. The 1-month follow-up score was below 70 (final score 56), indicating a sustained postintervention effect.

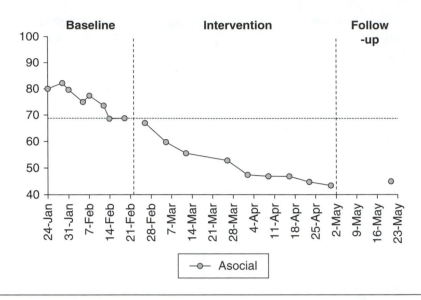

Figure 8.8   Case 6, Teacher 1

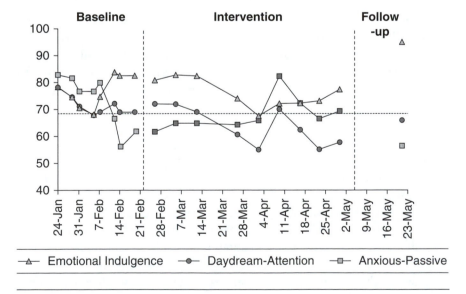

Figure 8.9   Case 6, Teacher 2

On the Daydream-Attention subscale, Teacher 2 recorded 50% of the observations in the baseline over 70 for a mean score of 71. During the intervention phase, Teacher 1 rated 33% of observations over 70, resulting in a mean score of 64. The effect size was calculated to be –2.18 for an improvement of 49%. There was, however, a trend in the baseline toward improvements, making it difficult to conclude that the changes observed during treatment on this subscale were due to the effect of the therapy. In addition, the lag in changes observed at the beginning of the intervention phase proposes additional difficulties in concluding that the therapy was responsible for the observed changes. The 1-month follow-up score for Teacher 2 on the Daydream-Attention subscale was below 70 (final score 66), indicating that the case maintained gains out of the clinical range. (See Figure 8.9.)

Case 7

JR was a 10-year-old fifth grader of mixed ethnicity (Latino and Anglo). JR lived with his parents and younger brother. His two older brothers lived outside of the home. JR was referred to the project due to talking out of turn in class and distractibility during reading. His most recent evaluation, conducted when he was in the second grade, found significant academic deficits in math, spelling, basic reading skills, math reasoning, math calculation, reading comprehension, and listening. He demonstrated no significant behavioral deficits. It was determined that he met the eligibility criteria for the handicapping condition of learning disability. School records revealed no significant health problems or occurrences. JR was seen for seven 30- to 45-minute sessions. He began changing his behavior during the baseline collection period and built on these changes over the course of therapy. His changes during the baseline were attributed by his teacher to two weekly meetings with the therapist even though no actual therapy had taken place except the scaling question and completion of a standardized measure. In accordance with the solution-focused therapy model, the therapist interpreted these changes as pretreatment changes and sought to build on these exceptions to the problem when the therapy began. In addition to meeting his goal of participating more in class, JR reported that his teachers noticed the changes in him and reported the changes to his parents.

Teacher 1. On the Anxious-Passive subscale, Teacher 1 recorded 50% of the observations in the baseline over 70 for a mean score of 72. During the intervention phase, Teacher 1 recorded 50% of observations over 70, resulting in a mean score of 69. The effect size was –0.42 for an improvement of 16%, but these changes were not clinically significant. The 1-month follow-up score was below 70 (final score 60), indicating that the teacher viewed the student as out of the clinical range for that problem.

Teacher 2. On the Anxious-Passive subscale, Teacher 2 recorded 63% of the observations in the baseline over 70 for a mean score of 71. During the intervention phase, Teacher 2 rated 0% of observations over 70, resulting in a mean score of 58. The effect size was −1.86 for an improvement of 47%. There was, however, a trend in the baseline toward improvement, making it difficult to conclude that the changes observed during treatment were due to the effect of the therapy. The 1-month follow-up score was below 70 (final score 60), indicating a sustained postintervention effect.

DISCUSSION

The overall findings of the single-case studies indicate that solution-focused therapy is a promising model for working with learning disabled students in a school setting. Although not all findings from the case studies supported the success of solution-focused therapy, there were clear, observable, positive changes in five of the cases (Cases 1, 3, 4, 5, and 6). That is, in these cases, at least one teacher indicated improvement on one or more subscales of the CTRS–39, and this improvement did not include positive trends in the baseline or other questionable effects. Positive clinical changes in these cases are supported by the visual changes, movement out of the clinical range, and effects sizes calculated on the different subscales. Changes observed by teachers were also generally maintained at follow-up with the exception of Case 1, Teacher 1, which did relapse into the clinical range.

Four of the seven cases (Cases 1, 4, 6, and 7) had two different teachers rating problem behaviors. It is predictable that two teachers keeping the ratings on the CTRS–39 will not always agree on the observed problems, and even when they do agree on the problems they may not agree on the outcomes. This resulted in mixed findings across four of the cases. For example, in Case 6 teachers did not agree on any of the problem behaviors observed, resulting in a completely different set of findings across teachers for that case. In Case 1 teachers agreed on the subscale, Hyperactivity Index, but both teachers saw additional problems and rated their progress differentially. In Case 4 the two teachers agreed on one subscale, Hyperactivity Index, as being a problem, but in addition one of the teachers rated the student as having other problems on additional subscales. The other problems rated—Emotional Indulgence and Asocial—further showed clinically significant changes whereas the Hyperactivity Index subscale on which the two teachers agreed did not change that much. In Case 7, the two teachers agreed on the problem Anxious-Passive subscale but did not see the same outcome, as one teacher rated more change than did the other.

One explanation for differences in observed problems is that students may demonstrate different behaviors across various classroom settings and

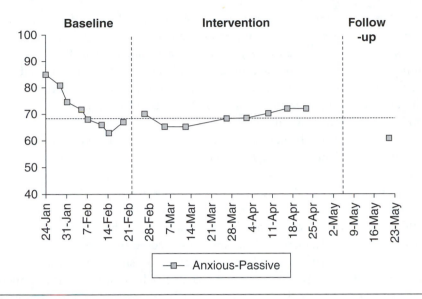

Figure 8.10   Case 7, Teacher 1

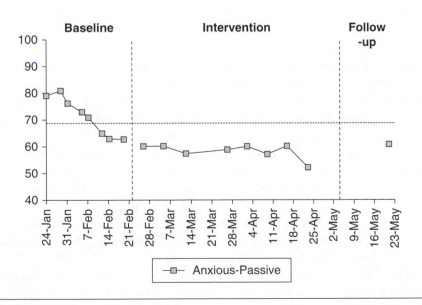

Figure 8.11   Case 7, Teacher 2

under differing contingency conditions. We do not believe, however, that having only one teacher see progress or that not achieving positive effects across all subscales negates the positive clinical findings that did occur. It is important in practice to make progress with individual problems that one teacher can observe. Still, mixed findings raise questions in relation to the clinical effectiveness of the therapy and make the overall effects of case studies more difficult to interpret.

Two clinical explanations are offered to explain the discrepancies encountered in findings across teachers. First, as noted, all teachers did not observe the same behavioral problems for students, which might mean that some problems got addressed in the therapy whereas others did not. Because the therapy was short-term, solutions were not likely to be developed for all behavioral deficits confronting these children in the classroom. Thus, problems were partialized and certain goals focused on whereas others were not given as much attention. The clinical case files suggest that this was the case. Second, it is also possible that not all teachers observed the changes because the therapists did not focus on enough work with some teachers. Teacher consultations were minimal due to the limited time of the therapists and teachers involved in the study, but when they took place they were reported to be helpful. Cases in which teachers observed more progress were also the cases in which the individual teachers reporting the progress had several therapist contacts, for example.

Positive trends in the baseline toward improvement proved to be a challenge for interpretation of some cases. A positive trend in the baseline means that the case begins to change in a positive way before the introduction of the intervention. Cases 2, 4, 6, and 7 showed some positive trends in the baseline toward improvement for at least one subcale rated by one of the teachers. Case 6 showed some trends across two teachers but on different subscales, and Case 7 showed a clear positive trend in the baseline across two teachers for the same subscale. Solution-focused therapists view people as always being in a state of change and believe that this change also means that there are times of improvement even when problems exist. From this viewpoint, positive trends in the baseline would be interpreted as exceptions to the problem and as examples of pretreatment change. Solution-focused therapists seek to build on pretreatment changes as an intervention method for amplifying positive behaviors. According to the solution-focused therapy model, it is possible to amplify pretreament change in a manner that produces more and more positive changes that may have a lasting effect. Theoretically, this assumption may hold true for some of the cases but presents a challenge for data interpretation using single-case designs.

From the viewpoint of single-case designs, however, a positive trend in the baseline is a threat to internal validity and makes the interpetation of the data extremely difficult in that the data fail to show that the change coexisted with the introduction of the intervention. Thus, the researcher cannot clearly demonstrate that the intervention was what produced the change. This also negates the claim that the intervention caused the client's change. On selective subscales across Cases 2, 4, 6, and 7, for example, changes are clearly evident, but it is not possible due to the positive trend in the baseline to conclude that it was the intervention making the changes.

It is plausible that the reactivity produced by the researchers being on the school campus and by administration of the measurement instruments may have produced these positive effects in the baseline. It is notable that there is a strong positive, sequential trend in the baseline in most cases and that this trend did not diminish across weeks. Even though the researchers set aside 4 weeks to collect the baseline data, this did not appear to be enough time to mitigate the reactivity effects. Prior to the beginning of this study, teachers were counseled not to feel pressure to see the student change because of the study but to offer their observations in accordance with what they saw in the student's behavior. In the future, it may be necessary to confront reactivity more directly by providing more training for teachers on the measurement instruments.

CONCLUSION

Although not conclusive, enough positive findings exist from this study to warrant further investigation of solution-focused therapy with children in schools. Overall, the results of the seven single-case studies support the previously reported clinical findings of Kral (1995), Metcalf (1995), and Murphy (1994a) concerning the outcomes of this therapy with children in a school setting. Results indicate that children receiving solution-focused therapy made positive changes on a range of behavioral problems. This therapy appears to show promise for helping special education students with their academic difficulties and classroom behaviors. In future work in schools, more emphasis should be placed on teacher consultations in every case. This work would undoubtedly increase teacher effectiveness with individual students. The research team agreed that it would be important for all teachers to be trained in the solution-focused therapy model.

SOURCE: Cynthia Franklin, Joan Biever, Kelly Moore, David Clemons, and Monica Scamardo (2001). The Effectiveness of Solution-Focused Therapy With Children in a School Setting. *Research on Social Work Practice, 11*, 411-434. © 2001 SAGE Publications.

REFERENCES

Beck, S., Collins, L., Overholser, J., & Terry, K. (1985). A cross-sectional assessment of the relationship of social competence measures to peer friendship and likability in elementary age children. *Genetic Psychology Monographs, 111*, 41-63.

Beitchman, J. H. (1996). *FAB-C: Feelings, Attitudes, and Behavior Scale for Children*. Toronto: Multi-Health Systems, Inc.

Berg, I. K. (1994). *Family based services: A solution-focused approach*. New York: Norton.

Berg, I. K., & DeJong, P. (1996). Solution-building conversations: Co-constructing a sense of competence with clients. *Families in Society, 77*, 376-390.

Berg, I. K., & Miller, S. D. (1992). *Working with the problem drinker: A solution-focused approach*. New York: Norton.

Bloom, M., Fischer, J., & Orme, J. (1995). *Evaluating practice: Guidelines for the accountable professional*. Englewood Cliffs, NJ: Prentice Hall.

Conners, C. K. (1969). A teacher rating scale for use in drug studies in children. *American Journal of Psychiatry, 126*, 884-888.

Conners, C. K. (1990). *Conners Rating Scales Manuals*. Toronto: Multi-Health Systems, Inc.

DeHaas, P. A. (1986). Attention styles and peer relationships of hyperactive and normal boys and girls. *Journal of Abnormal Child Psychology, 14*(3), 457-467.

DeJong, P., & Hopwood, L. E. (1996). Outcome research on treatment conducted at the Brief Family Therapy Center. In S. D. Miller, M. A. Hubble, & B. L. Duncan (Eds.), *Handbook of solution-focused brief therapy* (pp. 272-298). San Francisco: Jossey-Bass.

de Shazer, S. (1985). *Keys to solution in brief therapy*. New York: Norton.

de Shazer, S. (1988). *Clues: Investigating solutions in brief therapy*. New York: Norton.

de Shazer, S. (1991). *Putting differences to work*. New York: Norton.

de Shazer, S. (1994). *Words were originally magic*. New York: Norton.

de Shazer, S., Berg, I., Lipchik, N. E., Molnar, A., Gingerich, W., & Weiner-Davis, M. (1986). Brief therapy: Focused solution development. *Family Process, 25*, 207-222.

Dolan, Y. M. (1991). *Resolving sexual abuse: Solution-focused therapy and Ericksonian hypnosis for adult survivors*. New York: Norton.

Edelbrock, C. S., Greenbaum, R., & Conover, N. C. (1985). Reliability and concurrent relations between the teacher version of the Child Behavior Profile and Connors Revised Teacher Rating Scale. *Journal of Abnormal Child Psychology, 13*, 295-303.

Fischer, J., & Corcoran, K. (1994). *Measures for clinical practice* (2nd ed.). New York: Free Press.

Franklin, C., & Biever, J. (1996). *Treatment manual and research protocol for solution-focused therapy with learning-challenged students in schools*. Unpublished manuscript, University of Texas at Austin.

Franklin, C., Corcoran, J., Nowicki, J., & Streeter, C. L. (1997). Using client individualized rating scales to measure outcomes in solution-focused therapy. *Journal of Systemic Therapies, 16*(3), 246-265.

Franklin, C., & Moore, K. C. (1999). Solution-focused brief family therapy. In C. Franklin & C. Jordan (Eds.), *Family practice: Brief systems methods for social work* (pp. 105-141). Pacific Grove, CA: Brooks/Cole.

Franklin, C., Nowicki, J., Trapp, J., Schwab, A. J., & Petersen, J. (1993). A computerized assessment system for brief, crisis oriented youth services. *Families in Society, 74*(10), 602-616.

Jordan, C., & Franklin, C. (1995). *Clinical assessment for social workers: Quantitative and qualitative methods.* Chicago: Lyceum Press.

Kiser, D. (1988). *A follow-up study conducted at the Brief Family Therapy Center.* Unpublished manuscript.

Kiser, D., & Nunnally, E. (1990). *The relationship between treatment length and goal achievement in solution-focused therapy.* Unpublished manuscript.

Kral, R. (1995). *Strategies that work: Techniques for solutions in schools.* Milwaukee, WI: Brief Family Therapy Press.

Lee, M. (1997). A study of solution-focused brief family therapy: Outcomes and issues. *The American Journal of Family Therapy, 25,* 3-17.

Lindforss, L., & Magnusson, D. (1997). Solution-focused therapy in prison. *Contemporary Family Therapy, 19,* 89-104.

Macdonald, A. J. (1997). Brief therapy in adult psychiatry: Further outcomes. *Journal of Family Therapy, 19,* 213-222.

McKeel, A. J. (1996). A clinician's guide to research on solution-focused brief therapy. In S. D. Miller, M. A. Hubble, & B. L. Duncan (Eds.), *Handbook of solution-focused brief therapy* (pp. 251-271). San Francisco: Jossey-Bass.

Metcalf, L. (1995). *Counseling toward solutions: A practical solution-focused program for working with students, teachers, and parents.* New York: Simon & Schuster.

Miller, S. D., Hubble, M. A., & Duncan, B. S. (Eds.). (1996). *Handbook of solution-focused brief therapy.* San Francisco: Jossey-Bass.

Murphy, J. J. (1992). Brief strategic family intervention for school-related problems. *Family Therapy Case Studies, 7,* 59-71.

Murphy, J. J. (1994a). Working with what works: A solution-focused approach to school behavior problems. *The School Counselor, 42,* 59-65.

Murphy, J. J. (1994b). Brief therapy for school problems. *School Psychology International, 15,* 115-131.

Sandoval, J. (1981). Format effects on two teacher rating scales of hyperactivity. *Journal of Abnormal Child Psychology, 9,* 203-218.

Schindler, K., Zimmerman, T. S., Prest, L. A., & Wetzel, B. E. (1997). Solution-focused couple therapy groups: An empirical study. *Journal of Family Therapy, 19,* 125-144.

Selekman, M. D. (1997). *Solution-focused therapy with children.* New York: Guilford.

Sirles, E. A., Lipchik, E., & Kowalski, K. (1993). A consumer's perspective on domestic violence interventions. *Journal of Family Violence, 8,* 267-276.

Taylor, E., & Sandberg, S. (1984). Hyperactive behavior in English school children: A questionnaire survey. *Journal of Abnormal Child Psychology, 12,* 143-155.

Trites, R. L., Blouin, A. G., & Laprade, K. (1982). Factor analysis of the Conners Teacher Rating Scale based on a large normative sample. *Journal of Consulting & Clinical Psychology, 50,* 615-623.

Walter, J. L., & Peller, J. E. (1992). *Becoming solution-focused in brief therapy.* New York: Brunner-Mazel.

Webster, D. C., Vaughn, K., & Martinez, R. (1994). Introducing solution-focused approaches to staff in inpatient psychiatric settings. *Archives of Psychiatric Nursing, 8,* 251-261.

A Helping Hand

Solution-Focused Brief Therapy and Child and Adolescent Mental Health

John Wheeler

Child & Family Unit, Queen Elizabeth Hospital, Gateshead, UK

Abstract: Solution-focused brief therapy is a relatively new approach for Child and Adolescent Mental Health Services in the UK. While the approach lacks the support of outcome studies compared with more conventional approaches, it is argued that the model does offer some specific advantages, and relates well to the range of problems which present and the manner in which many clients use the service. An outline of the approach is provided, along with an overview of research and comments on contraindications. A variety of clinical

ACKNOWLEDGMENTS: Thanks to the many clients who have allowed me to test the possibilities of solution-focused brief therapy and inspired me by their responses. I also wish to thank my wife Marie and our children for tolerating my passion, my son Matthew for the figures and the uncanny likeness in the Cycle of Blame diagram, and my colleagues David Bone and Jill Smith who have supported the development of my practice.

CONTACT: Child and Family Unit, Queen Elizabeth Hospital, Sheriff Hill, Gateshead NE9 6SX, UK.

examples is used to illustrate how the approach works in practice. Concluding comments question the manner in which new approaches gain acceptance.

Keywords: *Child and Adolescent Mental Health Services, clinical practice, research, solution-focused brief therapy*

Solution-focused brief therapy (SFBT) has been promoted in the UK for around 10 years, with clinicians from a variety of settings adapting the approach to their practice. As a social worker in an outpatient child and adolescent mental health service (CAMHS), I have been impressed by the contribution this approach can make to my service. After outlining the approach, its current research credentials, and contraindications, I illustrate a number of areas of potential relevance.

ORIGINS OF SFBT

The most specific crystallization of SFBT can be attributed to Steve de Shazer and Insoo Kim Berg. Along with colleagues, in 1978, they established the Brief Therapy Centre in Milwaukee, USA, planning at the time to set up "The MRI of the Mid-West" (Nunnally, de Shazer, Lipchik, & Berg, 1986, p. 77), inspired by the brief family therapy model developed by Weakland, Fisch, Watzlawick, and Bodin (1974). From the outset they committed themselves to a trilogy of therapy, training and research. By 1984 their articles spoke of a shift away from Weakland et al.'s model, emphasizing a solution- rather than problem-focused approach, and a recognition that clients could often create their own strategies for change (de Shazer & Molnar, 1984). Several techniques were found to operate like skeleton keys (de Shazer, 1985), able to unlock a process of problem resolution without having to be tailored to the problem in question. Gradually, de Shazer and colleagues articulated a set of assumptions and techniques named as SFBT. In practice these two aspects, assumptions and techniques, link to each other in a recursive manner. The techniques without the assumptions often fail to be of benefit, whereas the assumptions can be seen as propositions which can be tested out by using the techniques.

SFBT ASSUMPTIONS

- Presenting problems are seldom static—they usually vary in frequency and intensity.

- Clients often have resources to deal with their difficulties.
- Small steps can change a vicious cycle of problem maintenance to a virtuous cycle of problem resolution.
- The clinician's responsibility is not to offer the client solutions but to help them find their own.
- Problems fluctuate in their severity and exceptions are waiting to be found.

SFBT TECHNIQUES

Problem-Free Talk

Once it is respectful and sensitive to do so, clients are invited to talk about aspects of their life other than their problems. They might be asked about how they cope, or about their work, or other aspects of their life in which they enjoy more success. As well as providing important information about family resources, this can also remind parents and children of abilities they may have forgotten, raising morale in the process.

In one family in which the teenage son was refusing to go to school the father had appeared ineffective in sessions. When asked about his work it emerged that he was a ticket collector with a fearsome reputation. Suddenly, he became a potential source of authority in the family, and a significant resource for securing the boy's return to school.

Goal Clarification

Clients are invited to define their preferred outcomes in specific, concrete and measurable terms. In most cases, goals are used as the primary target for change. When parents are overwhelmed by concern goals are often stated vaguely and/or as an absence of the presenting problem, such as "he'll stop being naughty." A detailed description of the preferred behaviour also allows the clinician to ask if any of this has happened before. One parent, when asked what her 7-year-old son would be doing when he behaved better, identified occupying himself in play. When the family were asked if this had happened yet, the boy's sisters commented that it had, and gave examples.

Compliments

At the end of a session, and often throughout, clinicians comment on abilities and resources they have noticed both in parents and children. This again can alert clients to resources they may have lost sight of. A teenage boy who had unwillingly attended for help with soiling had told his mother that he was not going to say anything. He was complimented on his ability to stick to his plans, an important ability when dealing with soiling. He subsequently returned for individual sessions during which he devised effective strategies for gaining control of his soiling.

Pre-Session Change

Weiner-Davis, de Shazer, and Gingerich (1987) found that two-thirds of people attending for first appointments were reporting either progress or times when the presenting problem was not happening. When parents are able to report this, the clinician has a useful opportunity to explore how this may have come about. Sometimes parents or children then identify strategies which, if continued, can resolve the presenting problem. In a family in which a teenage girl had been over-defiant it emerged that the mother had instituted a reward system the night before the appointment. In subsequent work the parent was able to build on this useful beginning.

Scaling Questions

Scaling questions can be used to check for pre-session change, evaluate how much progress is needed and identify what would constitute one step forward. A mother attending with a teenage girl who had been running away from home, identified her anxiety as 10 on a scale of 0 to 10 at the time of referral, and 7 at the first appointment. It was judged that 3 would be good enough, and 6 would be achieved by the girl letting her mother know her whereabouts. For this family an improvement in communication was the main goal for change. When the family returned six weeks later the girl had continued to avoid running away, and the mother reckoned that they were at 3 on the scale due to improvements in communication.

Exceptions

Often parents can report times when the presenting problem does not happen, or happens in a different way. A mother who thought she always gave in when her daughter cried, spoke of taking her daughter to buy a new bed, the daughter crying when she didn't like her mother's choice, and of not giving in because she couldn't afford her daughter's preference. When the parents returned for the next appointment the mother proudly announced that she had consciously ignored her daughter's crying on one occasion, there turning out to be two on further discussion. Once confident that change was possible the couple continued to build on this ostensibly small step.

The Miracle Question

This particular question can help to clarify goals, identify existing progress, clarify options for action and act as a catalyst for change. Typically the question is worded as "Imagine as you sleep tonight a miracle happens and the problems go away, but because you are asleep you don't know it's happened. When you wake in the morning, what would be a sign to you that the miracle has happened?" The mother of a strong-willed 4-year-old boy spoke of waking to find that he'd slept all night in his own bed. She then gave a rich description of how the rest of the day would be as a consequence. On their way home the boy told his mother that he was going to sleep in his own bed as he was "a big boy now." The boy was true to his word. The mother was so encouraged by this that she visited her parents the same day to insist that they stop undermining her authority. She also decided that two appointments were sufficient and after seven years has not been re-referred.

RESEARCH

When practitioners in a CAMHS turn to research on a particular therapeutic model they typically ask two questions. Is there evidence that the model makes a significant difference to presenting problems, and is there evidence that these improvements last?

Client satisfaction surveys were used from early on by de Shazer and colleagues as an intrinsic part of SFBT, clients typically being contacted six, 12 and 18 months after treatment. The first study (de Shazer, 1985) reported an 82% success rate in a six-month follow-up of 28 clients; success being defined by clients reporting that they had met their goals for therapy or felt that significant progress had been made. A later study (de Shazer et al., 1986) reported a 72% success rate, at six months, with a 25% sample of 1600 cases. Studies by Kiser in 1988, and Kiser and Nunnally in 1990 (cited in deShazer, 1991) reported an 80.4% success rate which had risen to 86% when clients were re-contacted at 18 months. DeJong and Hopwood (1996) contacted 141 cases eight months after discharge. Goals were achieved by 45% and 32% had made some progress towards their goals. The studies were based on a mental health population, of which, in the DeJong and Hopwood study, 50% were aged under 19 years. George, Iveson, and Ratner (1990) reported a good outcome with 66% of a child and adult mental health population of 62 who were contacted six months after treatment. A caseload outcome analysis by Wheeler (1995a) offered tentative support for the usefulness of SFBT in a CAMHS.

In 1999 Gingerich and Eisengart presented a review of outcome research on SFBT to the International Family Therapy Association in the U.S. They listed 15 controlled studies, all carried out by investigators outside the original Milwaukee group (Cockburn, Thomas, & Cockburn, 1997; Eakes, Walsh, Markowski, Cain, & Swanson, 1997; Franklin, Corcoran, Nowicki, & Streeter, 1997; Geil, 1998; LaFountain & Garner, 1996; Lambert, Okiishi, Finch, & Johnson, 1998; Lindforss & Magnusson, 1997; Littrell, Malia, & Vanderwood, 1995; Polk, 1996; Seagram, 1997; Sundmann, 1997; Sundstrom, 1993; Triantafillou, 1997; Zimmerman, Jacobsen, MacIntyre, & Watson, 1996; Zimmerman, Prest, & Wetzel, 1997). The studies researched the following populations, respectively: depression in a university population; academic and personal concerns in a high school; unspecified problems in a high school; problem drinking in an employee assistance program; parent–child conflict in a university clinic; orthopaedic injury in occupational rehabilitation; schizophrenia in outpatient mental health; parent–child conflict in outpatient family counselling; drugs and discipline problems in a prison; adolescent offending in secure custody; child welfare in public social services; depression, hyperactivity and oppositional behaviour in a residential setting; marital difficulties in a university clinic; behaviour problems in an elementary school; depression, substance abuse and anxiety in private practice. Of these, 13 reported improved client outcomes, and of 11 which compared the approach against standard treatments, seven reported that SFBT was as effective or more effective.

Zimmerman and colleagues (1996) explored the impact of a solution-focused approach with parents attending five parenting groups, using parents on a waiting list as a comparison. A standardized measurement tool was used to evaluate change, the researchers concluding that the study provided empirical support for the efficacy of a solution-focused approach to parenting.

Triantafillou (1997) studied the impact of staff using solution-focused techniques to deal with suicidality, anxiety and arousal disorders, motivational issues, anger management and crisis intervention in a residential setting for boys aged between 10 and 14 years. Contrasts were drawn between a treatment group of six boys and a control group of seven, using frequency of serious incidents and use of psychotropic medication as outcome measures. After a 16-week period, the number of serious incidents had reduced by 65.5% in the experimental group compared with 10% in the control group. In addition, two of the experimental group had stopped using medication, while use had increased in the control group by 60%. This was taken to be evidence of the approach having a positive impact on client outcomes, as measured.

Macdonald, as research coordinator for the European Brief Therapy Association, has also reviewed a variety of studies on SFBT (Macdonald, 2000). Burr (1993) followed up 55 children and young people seen at a children's clinic, six to twelve months after treatment. Of the 34 who were traced, 77% reported improvements. Macdonald, in a contribution to a forthcoming handbook on SFBT, also refers to process studies which have explored the impact of focusing on pre-session change and exceptions, and the use of the miracle question, compliments and scaling questions. (For example, Allgood, Parham, Salts, & Smith, 1995; Johnson, Nelson, & Allgood, 1998; Metcalf, Thomas, Duncan, Miller, & Hubble, 1996.) Macdonald takes the view that "Solution Focused Brief Therapy process research is beginning to show us which elements of therapy are effective and for which clients. The outline which emerges is similar to that now being discerned in studies of other psychotherapies. The important difference for Solution Focused Brief Therapy is that many non-essential elements within therapy have already been discarded" (Macdonald, personal communication, 2000).

To date then, whereas SFBT has been supported by client satisfaction surveys and process research, more work remains to be done to clarify whether controlled studies offer as much encouragement, especially with regard to the durability of the improvements which come about. Macdonald (1999), hoping to rectify this deficit, is currently co-ordinating a multi-site study into the effectiveness of SFBT.

CONTRAINDICATIONS

Research studies, to date, demonstrate the wide variety of client populations with which SFBT is being used. In time, studies might identify particular problems for which the approach is most effective. For the time being contraindications tend to draw more on general issues. Talmon (1996), for example, advised that SFBT should not be used with clients who have specifically asked for something different, or in situations in which the clinician feels too scared to be able to trust the client.

In a CAMHS, parents do make specific requests on occasion, such as for diagnosis. Successful engagement often depends on meeting parents at the point at which they have arrived through their own thinking. When working with parents who suspected that there was something odd about their son, the results of assessments were shared along with a list of the diagnostic criteria for Asperger's syndrome. They returned with a conclusion that he had sufficient features for them to use books written by parents of children with the condition, although they had decided that he did not completely fit the diagnosis. Through sharing the process of diagnosis it was possible to respect the expert knowledge they had of their son. The way was then clear to discuss how best to deal with his behaviour and liaise with his school.

Given that SFBT is essentially a conversational approach, there does need to be some scope for conversation to happen. It is unlikely, for example, that the approach could be used successfully with a client whose thinking is wildly irrational, or with a family that is too chaotic or conflictual.

In some situations other steps have to be taken first before SFBT can be tried. A mother and father were referred because of their difficulty in working together. In the first interview there appeared to be no room for manoeuvre. For the second interview they were seen separately, and when asked about each other's qualities were better able to say something constructive. The second appointment ended with a sharing of these discoveries, much to each party's surprise and pleasure. This small area of mutual appreciation provided a basis for further joint work in which significant progress was made in reducing the arguing.

RELEVANCE TO CAMHS

In adapting SFBT to my practice in a CAMHS I find the approach to be relevant in a number of regards:

- reduction of problem saturation;
- appropriate to patterns of involvement;
- relevant to the variety of situations which present;
- a safeguard against cycles of blame;
- the enhancement of binocular vision.

Problem Saturation

Parents are often preoccupied with concerns about their children when they present to a CAMHS. Many feel they that have run out of effective strategies. Many conclude that there is something "wrong" with their child. Where the child clearly does have intrinsic difficulties, parents have often lost hope that they can make any difference to the child's future. White (1995) has referred to this type of thinking as "problem saturation." Problem thinking has become so pervasive that the parent forgets past successes and views the future with despondency. Frequently, the child thinks in a similar way. Picking up on the parent's negativity, their self-esteem and sense of self-efficacy are low, and they have little motivation to do anything different. As Street (1994) pointed out, negativity in a parent–child relationship frequently damages the attachment, and damaged attachment breeds negativity. SFBT can be particularly helpful in loosening the parent's despondency, enabling them to realize that their situation might not be as bad as they feared. For example, parents of a teenage girl with an eating disorder were reassured to realize that their daughter had already stopped using laxatives, as a step towards regaining her health. A clear statement of the parent's preferred future can also often be reassuring for children. A parent who had complained of her son's behaviour explained that she was aiming for a future in which she and her son had fun again. This was very different from the complaints he was more used to hearing.

Patterns of Involvement

Talmon's book on single session therapy (1990) was sub-titled "max-imising the effect of the first, and often only, therapeutic encounter." Talmon researched 30 mental health professionals, finding their modal number of sessions to be one, regardless of profession or therapeutic orien-tation. Talmon then contacted 200 patients seen by himself for only one appointment. Seventy-eight percent reported improvements, as did 79% of 60 clients contacted a year later.

After using SFBT for a while, I also analysed how often I was seeing people, and also found my modal number of sessions to be one: most clients being seen for six sessions or fewer. Interestingly, when I then analysed the distribution of involvements prior to my use of SFBT, there was little dif-ference. This appeared to say more about how people used my service rather than the model I chose to use.

Beer (1992) reported on a pre-school child mental health service in which 70% of the cases were seen for three sessions or fewer. The audit of CAMHS in Scotland (Hoare, Norton, Chisholm, & Parry-Jones, 1996) reported that 61% of clients were seen for fewer than three appointments. Stallard and Sayers (1998), who offered the "two plus one" model (Barkham & Shapiro, 1989) to 36 people who opted into a CAMHS, found that three sessions were sufficient for most, and that 16 of these were seen only once.

Taken together, these findings suggest that many clients need less from a CAMHS than might be imagined. SFBT, by concentrating on what needs to change, what might bring about change, and what parents and children might contribute to this, matches well with the time commitment which many parents are likely to make to being involved with the service.

The Variety of Situations Which Present

Children referred to a CAMHS can be considered to fall into the fol-lowing five groupings, as outlined in Table 8.1.

1. Child is normal but is misperceived by carers and/or teachers to be abnormal.

2. Child presents with abnormal behaviour as an unintentional result of parents and/or teachers using ineffective strategies.

3. Child is reacting to other issues in the family which are masked by the child's behaviour.

4. Child has intrinsic difficulties.

5. Child responding to stresses outside family.

Arguably, these situations range from being entirely resolvable with family resources to depending, to some extent, on resources external to the

Table 8.1   Potential Consequences of Using Solution-Focused and Problem-Focused Approaches in Child Mental Health

Type of Problem	Solution-Focused Approach	Problem-Focused Approach
Child normal. Parents/others misperceiving behaviour as abnormal.	Parents' perception shifts. "Problem" evaporates.	Risk of reinforcing parents' misperception, and arguments over child's normality. Risk of premature discharge.
Child's symptomatic behaviour is unintentionally maintained by ineffective strategies.	Parents adopt more useful solutions. Problem disappears.	Risk of parents feeling criticized and arguments over solutions. Risk of premature discharge.
Child's symptomatic behaviour is a reaction to other issues in family.	Parents shift focus from child to other issues, with confidence that these can be tackled.	Risk of reinforcing parents' labelling of child, and arguments over aetiology. Risk of premature discharge.
Child has intrinsic difficulties.	Parents and child produce their optimum efforts in collaboration with other services.	Risk of explaining everything in terms of intrinsic difficulties. Risk of over-dependency on services.
Child responding to stresses outside of family.	Parents and child produce their optimum efforts in collaboration with other services.	Risk of explaining everything in terms of external stresses. Risk of over-dependency on services.

family. As outlined in Table 8.1, the consequences for the family can be significantly different, depending on whether the clinician's approach is mainly solution focused or problem focused.

One parent saw her daughter as having an eating disorder following the daughter's decision to lose weight. The girl had been overweight, her brothers and father still were, and the girl had become concerned about her health. When the mother was asked for signs of a good outcome, she clarified that she needed evidence that her daughter was taking care of her health and had enough self-control to prevent her weight plummeting. Armed with this information, the girl was able to demonstrate that she had learnt a lot about healthy lifestyles and was able to be sufficiently self-controlled to reassure her mother about her immediate future. Had we concentrated on the mother's fears about an eating disorder, we might either have demoralized the daughter or ended up arguing with the mother about her misperception.

In a family in which the parents were dealing with their daughter's tendency to cry excessively, they had for many years adopted a strategy of avoidance, to minimize their daughter's distress. In a second session the parents were asked what ideas they had about the daughter's behaviour. The father said he was wondering if the crying might be temper tantrums. On further discussion it was agreed that this fitted the facts well. When asked what ideas they had about dealing with temper tantrums they explained that they knew about setting limits and not giving into crying, although the mother thought this might be impossible for her. By the next appointment the mother had already surprised herself by not reacting when her daughter cried. Had we concentrated on deficits we may well have drawn attention to the parents' actions and appeared critical of parents who had been acting in good faith. They might have stopped attending, taking the view that they sought help for their daughter and were told it was their fault.

In a family in which an 8-year-old girl had become withdrawn and insecure, the mother's reply to the miracle question was that the family would be peaceful and relaxed in the morning. Further questioning revealed that this depended on the step-father controlling his temper more successfully and the mother being confident that he was committed to doing so. It emerged that the step-father suffered from a post-traumatic stress disorder relating to an experience in the armed services. An involvement with the adult mental health services was helping him to maintain self-control and subsequent appointments were attended by the couple to maintain their relationship. While a problem-focused assessment might have revealed the same information, the step-father may have felt that he was seen to be the cause of the girl's difficulties. A solution-focused approach ensured that the family maintained ownership of the assessment process, and were thus more committed to subsequent targeting of the intervention.

A mother was seen with a 3-year-old who was very defiant and had not started to talk. While speech and language assessment was organized, the mother was asked to say what her ambitions for her son were and what she had been doing to realize these. It emerged that she had developed an impressive variety of strategies and looked forward to hearing him call her "Mam." Had a deficit-focused approach been used, her fragile morale could have been undermined, and an already complicated attachment might have been further weakened by feelings of futility. During subsequent appointments solution-focused questions continued to help direct attention to the boy's growing abilities and the strategies the mother was using to encourage them.

A family sought help with their second son who was becoming delinquent, the eldest son having already acquired a criminal record. The father had become despondent over the increase in delinquency on the housing estate where they had lived for many years, and listed many sources of distress including damage to their garden and the poisoning of their dog. After further discussion it was agreed that, while they couldn't control what happened outside their front door, they might be able to do something about what happened behind it. When the family were asked for examples of something different, the boy referred to a time when the mother hired a video which they watched and laughed at together as a family. Extra services were used to divert the boy away from delinquency while the parents did what they could to influence him at home. Had the conversations focused entirely on the difficulties, the parents' despondency may have prevailed and potentially undermined the impact of the diversionary activities.

Cycle of Blame

Figure 8.12 outlines how a problem-focused assessment can perpetuate a negative cycle of interaction between clinician and family in a CAMHS outpatient involvement.

Parents often blame the child, while suspecting they may be at fault and open to blame by the clinician. Children often assume the fault is theirs, know of their parents' disappointment in them and expect to be reprimanded by the clinician. The clinician in turn is open to blame if the involvement is not effective. This risk has been further explored by Wolpert (2000), who analysed the extent to which blame and exoneration occurred with a sample of 10 families. She concluded that it may be useful for clinicians to "hone their sensitivity to issues of blame and exoneration" and saw this as "an important factor that may contribute to premature termination of treatment" (p. 128).

As Figure 8.12 shows, the moment the clinician chooses what to focus on when meeting a family may influence the subsequent involvement. It is at this point that SFBT can be particularly beneficial in establishing a more collaborative and constructive involvement.

A 10-year-old boy had been brought back to the department by his mother, aunt and grandfather, following a serious worsening of his challenging behaviour to his mother. He was asked what he had been doing to stop the deterioration, when he'd heard that he was coming back to the department. Without prompting, he identified all significant areas of concern along with steps he was taking and planning to take. As the family left, the aunt, who had previously viewed the boy very critically, said how reassured she was to know that the boy took their concerns seriously, and how much more hopeful she subsequently felt.

Binocular Vision

When professionals become involved in other people's lives, it is important to maintain a balanced view of the people they are encountering. This

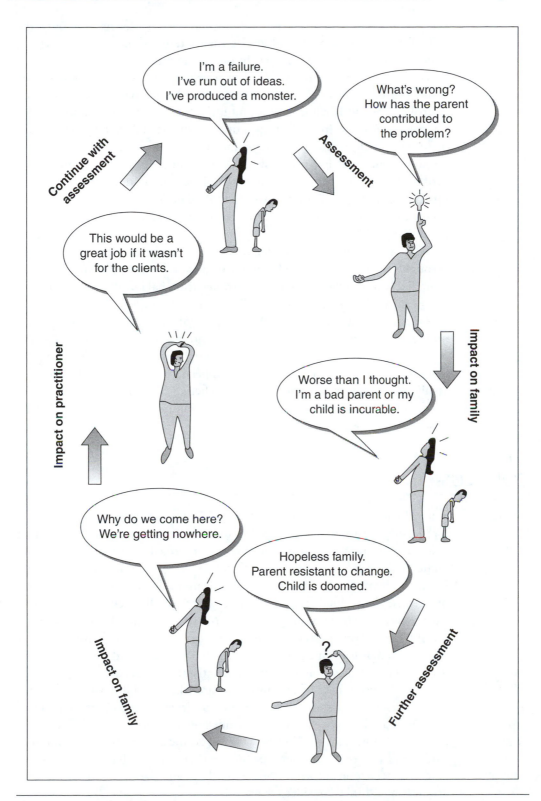

Figure 8.12 Cycle of Blame

can be thought of as a form of binocular vision—seeing not only the difficulties people come with, but also their strengths and resources, which may play a crucial part in the resolution of the difficulties.

Tollinton (1999), a retired clinical psychologist, was surprised by the behaviour of the professionals she encountered when her husband suffered a stroke. She and her husband found little "natural kindness and psychological sensitivity" (p. 21). They noticed how feelings of "disempowerment, loss of any sense of efficacy, (and) feelings of worthlessness" (p. 23) were engendered by professionals who adopted expert positions. Professionals who behaved differently played an important part in her husband's recovery. Tollinton found that "Focusing on the solutions we sought and on small steps towards the goals we aimed towards was immensely helpful" (p. 22).

SFBT can easily be misunderstood as a device for seeing the world through rose-tinted glasses. In practice those who use this approach are more likely to use the techniques to established a balanced view, one that is less negative than might otherwise have come about.

An account has been given (Wheeler, 1995b) of a first interview with a mother with a fractious toddler. Commenting on the mother's strengths helped put her at ease. She then demonstrated more of her positive interactions with the child than might have happened had she felt criticized as a result of the conversation focusing on deficits. The child also settled, and was able to demonstrate more of his endearing qualities than might otherwise have been evident.

CONCLUSION

Since SFBT was first introduced into the UK there has been a growing interest in using the approach in CAMHS. SFBT has, understandably, generated a degree of scepticism and concern that the approach is not sufficiently adequate to the needs of those who present to the service. It is also probably too early to know whether the approach is useful because of its techniques, or because the techniques enhance the extent to which clinicians relate to clients in ways which existing studies show to be useful. Outcome research for SFBT based on random control studies is at a relatively early stage compared with that for some approaches which have been used for much longer in CAMHS. Studies drawing on client satisfaction speak more encouragingly of the usefulness of the approach and the durability of the changes which clients have reported. In the UK the drive towards a greater use of evidence-based practice is directing clinicians to treatments which are supported by "gold standard" studies. However, the government is also urging clinicians to listen to the views of service users. Arguably, if clinicians can place confidence in the views of clients they will already be on fairly safe ground should they consider trying SFBT.

It is also worth considering that, from a historical point of view, therapeutic approaches have usually found a place in services before scientifically rigorous studies have confirmed their value. Therapeutic approaches have often been a matter of clinician preference. Miller (1994), an enthusiastic proponent of solution-focused brief therapy, reviewed the literature hoping to find that his preference for the approach was supported by outcome studies. While he found studies which suggested that SFBT was as useful as other therapeutic approaches, he found no evidence that it was a best choice. He was left with the conclusion that his preference was due mainly to personal enjoyment and client satisfaction. Perhaps these are stronger influences on clinician preference than we might otherwise suspect. Roth and Fonagy (1996, pp. 376–377) were of the view that "On the whole, research has only limited impact on services," going on to comment that "Clinicians are experts in their field, and on many issues may be ahead of empirically generated research findings . . ." Target and Fonagy (1996), having reviewed outcome studies relating to child and adolescent mental health, recommended that "it is important that a variety of treatment approaches be maintained at an adequate level, so that clinicians have a choice in relation to a particular child's needs and family's circumstances. It is certainly not enough to provide simply the treatment that has come out best in research studies of non-referred children with a single difficulty" (p. 319).

To use a developmental metaphor, even established therapeutic approaches were young once. At one time SFBT may have been small enough to ignore. Over time, clinicians interested in the approach have adapted and developed SFBT to a stage of development which might now be looking like maturity. Suppose a miracle happened and a majority of clinicians considered SFBT to be a significantly useful contribution to a CAMHS. What would clinicians have noticed?

Further studies, in particular those coordinated by the European Brief Therapy Association, may, in time, provide one sign of this. Until then the responsibility will rest with us as clinicians to continue exploring how the approach may contribute to our work. For my own part, I already judge the model to be a useful asset as I endeavour to offer a helping hand to those who turn to me for help.

SOURCE: John Wheeler. (2001). A Helping Hand: Solution-Focused Brief Therapy and Child and Adolescent Mental Health. *Clinical Child Psychology and Psychiatry, 6*, 293-306. © 2001 SAGE Publications.

REFERENCES

Allgood, S. M., Parham, K. B., Salts, C. J., & Smith, T. A. (1995). The association between pretreatment change and unplanned termination in family therapy. *American Journal of Family Therapy, 23*, 195-202.

Barkham, M., & Shapiro, A. (1989). Exploratory therapy in two-plus one sessions: Rationale for a brief therapy model. *British Journal of Psychotherapy, 6*, 79-86.

Beer, R. (1992). A preschool child psychiatric service: Predictors of post-assessment default. *Child: Care, Health & Development, 18*, 1-13.

Burr, W. (1993). Evaluation der Anwendung losungsorientierter Kurztherapie in einer kinder- und jugendpsychiartischen Praxis [Evaluation of the use of brief therapy in a practice for children and adolescents]. *Familiendynamik, 18*, 11-21.

Cockburn, J. T., Thomas, F. N., & Cockburn, O. J. (1997). Solution-focused therapy and psychosocial adjustment to orthopaedic rehabilitation in a work hardening program. *Journal of Occupational Rehabilitation, 7*(2), 97-106.

DeJong, P., & Hopwood, L. E. (1996). Outcome research on treatment conducted at the Brief Family Therapy Centre 1992–1993. In S. D. Miller, M. A. Hubble, & B. L. Duncan (Eds.), *Handbook of solution-focused brief therapy* (pp. 272-298). San Francisco: Jossey-Bass.

de Shazer, S. (1985). *Keys to solution in brief therapy*. New York: Norton.

de Shazer, S. (1991). *Putting difference to work*. New York: Norton.

de Shazer, S., Berg, I. K., Lipchik, E., Nunnally, E., Molnar, A., Gingerich, W., & Weiner-Davis, M. (1986). Brief therapy: Focused solution development. *Family Process, 25*, 207-222.

de Shazer, S., & Molnar, A. (1984). Four useful interventions in brief therapy. *Journal of Marital and Family Therapy, 10*(3), 297-304.

Eakes, G., Walsh, S., Markowksi, M., Cain, H., & Swanson, M. (1997). Family centred brief solution-focused therapy with chronic schizophrenia: A pilot study. *Journal of Family Therapy, 19*(2), 145-158.

Franklin, C., Corcoran, J., Nowicki, J., & Streeter, C. (1997). Using client self-anchored scales to measure outcomes in solution-focused therapy. *Journal of Systemic Therapies, 16*(3), 246-265.

Geil, M. (1998). *Solution focused consultation: An alternative consultation model to manage student behaviour and improve classroom environment*. Unpublished doctoral dissertation, University of Northern Colorado, Greeley, CO.

George, E., Iveson, C., & Ratner, H. (1990). *Problem to solution: Brief therapy with individuals and families*. London: Brief Therapy Press.

Gingerich, W. J., & Eisengart, S. (1999, April 1). *Solution-focused brief therapy: A review of the outcome research*. Paper presented at the International Family Therapy Association, Akron, OH.

Hoare, P., Norton, B., Chisholm, D., & Parry-Jones, W. (1996). An audit of 7,000 successive child and adolescent psychiatry referrals in Scotland. *Clinical Child Psychology & Psychiatry, 1*(2), 229-249.

Johnson, L. N., Nelson, T. S., & Allgood, S. M. (1998). Noticing pretreatment change and therapeutic outcome: An initial study. *American Journal of Family Therapy, 26*, 159-168.

LaFountain, R. M., & Garner, N. E. (1996). Solution-focused counselling groups: The results are in. *Journal for Specialists in Group Work, 21*(2), 128-143.

Lambert, M. J., Okiishi, J. C., Finch, A. E., & Johnson, L. D. (1998). Outcome assessment: From conceptualisation to implementation. *Professional Psychology: Research and Practice, 29*(1), 63-70.

Lindforss, L., & Magnusson, D. (1997). Solution-focused therapy in prison. *Contemporary Family Therapy, 19*(1), 89-103.

Littrell, J. M., Malia, J. A., & Vanderwood, M. (1995). Single-session brief counselling in a high school. *Journal of Counselling and Development, 73*(4), 451-458.

Macdonald, A. (1999). *Proposed research protocol*. Presented at the European Brief Therapy Association Conference, Carlisle, UK.

Macdonald, A. (2000). European Brief Therapy Association website: http://www .ebta.nu

Metcalf, L., Thomas, F. N., Duncan, B. L., Miller, S. D., & Hubble, M. A. (1996). What works in solution-focused brief therapy. In S. D. Miller, M. A. Hubble, & B. L. Duncan (Eds.), *Handbook of solution-focused brief therapy* (pp. 335-349). San Francisco: Jossey-Bass.

Miller, S. (1994). The solution conspiracy: A mystery in three instalments. *Journal of Systemic Therapies, 13*(1), 18-37.

Nunnally, E., de Shazer, S., Lipchik, E., & Berg, I. K. (1986). A study of change: Therapeutic theory in process. In D. Efron (Ed.), *Journeys: Expansion of the strategic and systemic therapies* (pp. 77-96). New York: Brunner/Mazel.

Polk, G. W. (1996). Treatment of problem drinking behaviour using solution-focused therapy: A single subject design. *Crisis Intervention, 3*(1), 13-24.

Roth, A., & Fonagy, P. (1996). *What works for whom?* London: Guilford Press.

Seagram, B. C. (1997). *The efficacy of solution-focused therapy with young offenders*. Unpublished doctoral dissertation, York University, New York, Ontario.

Stallard, P., & Sayers, J. (1998). An opt-in appointment system and brief therapy: Perspectives on a waiting list initiative. *Clinical Child Psychology & Psychiatry, 3*(2), 199-212.

Street, E. (1994). A family systems approach to child–parent separation: "Developmental closure." *Journal of Family Therapy, 16*(4), 347-365.

Sundmann, P. (1997). Solution focused ideas in social work. *Journal of Family Therapy, 19*, 159-172.

Sundstrom, S. M. (1993). *Single-session psychotherapy for depression: Is it better to focus on problems or solutions?* Unpublished doctoral dissertation, Iowa State University, Ames, IA.

Talmon, M. (1990). *Single session therapy*. San Fransisco: Jossey-Bass.

Talmon, M. (1996). *Single session therapy*. Workshop. London.

Target, M., & Fonagy, P. (1996). The psychological treatment of child and adolescent psychiatric disorders. In A. Roth & P. Fonagy (Eds.), *What works for whom?* (pp. 263-320). London: Guilford Press.

Tollinton, G. (1999, September). Helping and hindering stroke recovery. *Clinical Psychology Forum, 131*, 21-23.

Triantafillou, N. (1997). A solution-focused approach to mental health supervision. *Journal of Systemic Therapies, 16*(4), 305-328.

Weakland, J. H., Fisch, R., Watzlawick, P., & Bodin, A. M. (1974). Brief therapy: Focused problem resolution. *Family Process, 13*(2), 141-168.

Weiner-Davis, M., de Shazer, S., & Gingerich, W. J. (1987). Building on pretreatment change to construct the therapeutic solution. *Journal of Marital and Family Therapy, 13*, 359-363.

Wheeler, J. (1995a). Believing in miracles: The implications and possibilities of using solution focused therapy in a child mental health setting. *Association for Child Psychology and Psychiatry Review and Newsletter, 17*(5), 255-261.

Wheeler, J. (1995b). Supporting self-growth: The solution focused approach. *Mental Health Nursing, 15*(2), 24-25.

White, M. (1995). *Re-authoring lives: Interviews and essays.* Adelaide: Dulwich Centre Publications.

Wolpert, M. (2000). Is anyone to blame? Whom families and their therapists blame for the presenting problem. *Clinical Child Psychology & Psychiatry, 5*(1), 115-131.

Zimmerman, T. S., Jacobsen, R. B., MacIntyre, M., & Watson, C. (1996). Solution-focused parenting groups: An empirical study. *Journal of Systemic Therapies, 15*(4), 12-25.

Zimmerman, T. S., Prest, L. A., & Wetzel, B. E. (1997). Solution-focused couples therapy groups: An empirical study. *Journal of Family Therapy, 19*(2), 125-144.

John Wheeler gained a first degree at Lancaster University and qualified as a social worker at Newcastle-upon-Tyne Polytechnic. He subsequently gained an MA in Systemic Practice at the University of Northumbria at Newcastle, where he is currently studying for a Diploma in Systemic Teaching, Training, and Supervision and registration with the UKCP as a family therapy supervisor.

9

Cognitive-Behavioral Family Therapy

The Case of Molly L.

Use of a Family Cognitive-Behavioral Treatment for Childhood Anxiety

Amy Krain
Jennifer L. Hudson
Meredith Coles
Philip Kendall
Temple University

Abstract: The present case study illustrates how a family cognitive-behavioral therapy (FCBT) was used to treat a 9-year-old girl diagnosed with separation anxiety disorder and agoraphobia without panic. The first half of treatment focused on teaching specific coping skills, whereas the second half consisted of exposure tasks that provided opportunities for Molly to practice what she had learned. The therapy also addressed issues of family communication and emotional expression. Through flexible application of the manual, the therapist helped Molly's parents recognize how their expectations affected their daughter's behavior and helped Molly with her own self-image and expectations for coping. Following treatment, Molly and her parents reported that her anxiety had decreased and that her coping skills had improved. Overall, this case illustrates the successful application of FCBT and highlights the importance of applying a treatment manual flexibly to address client needs.

Keywords: child, anxiety, family, cognitive-behavioral treatment.

1. THEORETICAL AND RESEARCH BASIS

An accumulating body of evidence supports the efficacy of cognitive-behavioral treatment (CBT) for childhood anxiety disorders (see Kazdin & Weisz, 1998; Ollendick & King, 1998). Independently and conducted in different countries, several randomized clinical trials have shown that individual cognitive behavior therapy produces significant improvements in self-reported, parent-reported, and clinician-rated measures from pretreatment to posttreatment (Barrett, Dadds, & Rapee, 1996; Kendall, 1994; Kendall et al., 1997; Silverman et al., 1999; Spence, Donovan, & Brechman-Toussaint, 2000). These improvements have been shown to be maintained at 1-, 3-, and 6-year follow-ups (Barrett, Duffy, Dadds, & Rapee, 2001; Kendall & Southam-Gerow, 1996), and some studies have found added benefits associated with including a family component in the child-focused treatment. These "family" effects have been strongest for younger children, girls, and children with parents scoring high on anxiety (Barrett et al., 1996; Cobham, Dadds, & Spence, 1998).

Consistent with these promising findings, Howard and Kendall (1996) designed a 16- to 20-session family CBT (FCBT) treatment based on the original individual CBT program. Although the program is manual based, each session is designed to be implemented in a flexible manner (Kendall, Chu, Gifford, Hayes, & Nauta, 1998) and to be tailored to the individual needs of the child/family. An early version of the FCBT was evaluated (Howard & Kendall, 1996) using a multiple-baseline design across cases with 6 anxiety-disordered children (ages 9 to 13). Significant improvement was reported at posttreatment for 4 out of the 6 children. An updated version of FCBT is currently being evaluated as part of a randomized clinical trial.

An assumption underlying the family treatment program is that the parents or family are involved in the development and/or maintenance of the child's anxiety. Although research is sparse and somewhat unclear as to the precise role of the family in childhood anxiety disorders, several studies reveal potential influences. For example, Barrett et al. (1996) showed that anxious children were more likely to report avoidant responses to a hypothetical situation of ambiguous threat following a discussion of the situation with their parents. In contrast, nonclinical children (and oppositional defiant children) showed a decrease in avoidant responding following a family discussion. Further analysis of the family discussion revealed that parents of anxious children encouraged and supported the child's suggestions of avoidant behavior. Other observational studies have shown that parents of anxious children are less granting of autonomy than parents of nonclinical children (Hudson & Rapee, 2001; Siqueland, Kendall, & Steinberg, 1996). These findings in combination with the promising results of family involvement in treatment (e.g., Barrett et al., 1996; Howard & Kendall, 1996) provide support for the decision to involve the parents in the treatment program.

RATIONALE BEHIND CBT FOR CHILDHOOD ANXIETY

According to a cognitive-behavioral perspective, there are three factors central to a child's experience of anxiety. The first is the child's physiological response to the feared situation. This response may include diffuse abdominal pain, increased heart rate, increased breathing, sweating, blushing, or trembling (Beidel, Christ, & Long, 1991). These reactions are frequently distressing to an anxious child. The second factor relates to the child's threat-related cognition. Anxious children are more likely than nonclinical children to interpret an ambiguous situation as threatening (Barrett et al., 1996). Anxious children typically perceive and then focus on threat in their environment and overestimate the likelihood of negative consequences. It is this threat-related cognition that contributes to the experience of anxiety. Third, the anxious child's behavioral response is generally avoidant. These children typically avoid situations they interpret as threatening (Kendall, 1992). In avoiding anxiety-provoking situations, the child fails to learn that he or she can cope and that the negative outcome is not likely to happen.

The family treatment (FCBT), too, focuses on all three aspects of anxiety: physiological, cognitive, and behavioral. During the first 8 weeks, as in child-focused CBT, the therapist teaches the child and parents, using the acronym FEAR, several skills to deal more effectively with anxiety. The child learns to recognize when he or she is "*F*eeling frightened." The child learns to identify somatic symptoms associated with anxiety and learns relaxation techniques to cope with them (see King, Hamilton, & Ollendick, 1988). Second, the child learns to examine his or her anxious cognition (self-talk) and to recognize that feeling anxious is associated with "*E*xpecting bad things to happen." Using cognitive restructuring techniques, the child learns not only to identify his or her self-talk but also to challenge anxious thoughts and develop coping thoughts. Third, using problem-solving techniques, the child learns to develop "*A*ctions and attitudes" that will help him or her to feel less anxious and to approach rather than avoid feared situations. The final step involves "*R*esults and rewards." The child learns to evaluate and reward both effort and performance. Additional techniques, including emotion recognition and family communication skills, are also covered in the first 8 weeks. Weekly homework assignments, "Show that I can" (STIC) tasks, are assigned to both parents and child (Hudson & Kendall, 2001). The STIC tasks relate to the material covered in the session. The child is rewarded for completing the STIC tasks with stickers (or points for older children). Stickers are also given to the child if the parent(s) completes their STIC tasks. The stickers/points are redeemed throughout the program for more substantial rewards (e.g., CDs, games).

Two additional sessions are scheduled for the therapist to meet with the child alone and with the parents alone. The aim of these sessions, in addition to building individual rapport, is to create an opportunity for the therapist to address parenting behavior that may be helping to maintain the child's anxiety. For example, the parents may be supporting the child's avoidance of anxious situations. The therapist addresses these issues with the parents and discusses more effective ways for the parents to manage their child's anxiety.

In the second half of the program, the child learns to use the FEAR plan to face situations in which he or she feels unwanted anxious distress. Using both imaginal and in vivo exposure tasks, the child, parents, and therapist plan out situations for the child to practice. The child has to practice facing situations repetitively with the knowledge that the more the child practices, the less anxious the child will become. During this part of the program, parents may also practice the FEAR steps in situations they find anxiety provoking. At the end of the program, the therapist and family discuss relapse-prevention strategies for the future. The final session of the program involves the family developing a commercial (a video) that outlines what they have learned. The aim of the commercial is for the family to demonstrate the learned skills in an effort to help other children with anxiety problems. In so doing, they organize what they have learned in their own language—a task hat helps to consolidate the various parts of CBT.

2. CASE STUDY

In this article, we present a case that demonstrates the use of the manualized FCBT with a 9-year-old girl.[1] Molly and her parents came to the Child and Adolescent Anxiety Disorders Clinic at Temple University seeking help for Molly's excessive anxiety, which had been worsening over the past 3 years. Previous treatment with supportive and behavioral psychotherapies had been unsuccessful, and Molly was currently taking antidepressant medication, which was having limited effect. Her parents, Mr. and Mrs. L., were extremely concerned because Molly's anxiety had recently worsened and was making it difficult for Molly to attend school. Although the school year had ended, Molly's parents were worried that she would be unable to attend school in the fall. Following a comprehensive assessment of Molly's anxiety, including semistructured diagnostic interviews with Molly and her parents, self-report questionnaires, and teacher reports, Molly received diagnoses of separation anxiety disorder, agoraphobia without panic disorder, and generalized anxiety disorder.

Throughout the assessment process, it became clear that Molly's family played a significant role in her anxiety. First, several of her fears involved separation from her mother, and as a result, Mrs. L. had restricted her own activities to accommodate her daughter. Second, Molly's anxiety surrounding long car trips made travel difficult for the entire family. Third, Molly's parents were becoming frustrated because they felt helpless and unable to help their daughter when she was anxious. The family-based approach seemed appropriate.

Molly and her parents agreed to participate in our 18-week FCBT. As outlined earlier, the primary goal of therapy was to improve Molly's coping skills and to reduce her anxiety in difficult situations. To achieve this goal, the therapist taught Molly and her parents a number of coping skills, including early identification of anxious feelings, identification of anxious thoughts, the use of alternative coping thoughts and actions, and self-rating and reward. Molly and her parents responded well to the structure of the FEAR plan, and it became an effective tool during the exposure tasks in the second half of treatment. A secondary goal of therapy was to improve communication among family members. The therapist stressed the importance of expressing one's feelings and encouraged discussion within the therapy sessions and as homework assignments. By the end of treatment, Molly had successfully coped with all of the items on her hierarchy in session and at home and had even attempted situations that were not on the list (i.e., taking the bus). Overall, the FCBT was effective at reducing Molly's anxiety and helping her parents feel more effective when helping her in difficult situations.

As therapy progressed, a number of critical issues arose that were ultimately integral to the success of Molly's treatment. First, Molly's anxiety was a source of significant anger, frustration, and guilt for Molly and her parents. These emotional responses needed to be addressed directly in therapy. Second, Molly felt that her anxiety was "abnormal" and that she did not deserve praise for her accomplishments because they were simply what "normal" children do. Third, it became clear that the entire family system was affected by changes in Molly's behavior and that this often led to misunderstandings and feelings of confusion. For example, Molly's parents became frustrated when she was unable to cope effectively with a situation that she had successfully coped with a few days earlier. In addition, Molly often became distressed when her parents assumed that she was afraid when she was not. The therapist encouraged the family to discuss these issues and helped them to understand the dramatic impact that Molly's improvement had on the whole family. Finally, Molly was feeling misunderstood, particularly when her parents failed to recognize her efforts when she was attempting to cope with difficult situations.

3. PRESENTING COMPLAINTS

Molly's mother first contacted the clinic reporting that her daughter had been experiencing "severe anxiety." Furthermore, she reported that Molly often vomited as a result of her anxiety and that she had recently started to refuse attending school. Mrs. L. reported that the anxiety was particularly severe when riding in the car and when Molly was separated from her (the mother, e.g., at school).

4. HISTORY

At the time of initial contact, Molly was 9 years old and in the third grade. She lived with her parents, both college graduates. Both parents were employed, with the mother working 15 hours a week outside of the home and the father working 40 to 50 hours a week outside of the home. The father had one previous marriage. Molly had two siblings, a monozygotic twin sister and an older sister (age 10).

At the time of initial contact, Molly had a previous course of therapy and was currently enrolled in a second course of therapy. She worked with the first therapist for a period of about 6 months and the second for about a year. According to her parents' report, these therapies were "behavioral," and they did not see improvements from them. At the time of intake, Molly was also taking 100 mg of Zoloft once a day and had been taking that medication for 2 years. Mr. and Mrs. L. reported that Molly's twin sister experienced similar traveling anxiety and that she was also in therapy but that her anxiety was not as severe as Molly's.

5. ASSESSMENT

The Child and Adolescent Anxiety Disorders Clinic uses a multimethod procedure to assess childhood anxiety (Kendall & Ronan, 1990). The initial evaluation and follow-up assessments include independent diagnostic interviews of the child and his or her parents using the Anxiety Disorders Interview Schedule for the *Diagnostic and Statistical Manual of Mental Disorders* (4th ed.) Child Version and Parent Version (ADIS-C/P) (Silverman & Albano, 1997). These companion interviews assess the symptomatology, course, and severity of anxiety, mood, and behavior disorders. For each diagnosis assigned, the interviewee (i.e., parent/child) is asked to rate the general interference of the child's symptoms (Global Interference Rating). In addition, based on this information, the clinician assigns a clinician severity rating. Both ratings are made on a scale from 0 to 8, with higher scores indicating greater severity and scores equal to or above 4 indicating symptoms of a clinical level. Two diagnostic profiles are formulated and then subsequently combined using specified criteria to yield a composite diagnostic profile that is reflective of both parent and child interviews. The ADIS-C/P interviews have been shown to have favorable psychometric properties (March & Albano, 1998). Based on the information acquired during these interviews, the clinicians assign a rating of general functioning using the Children's Global Assessment Scale (CGAS) (Shaffer et al., 1983). The CGAS is appropriate for children between the ages of 4 and 16 and uses a scale from 1 to 100 to reflect the level of the child's functioning. Higher scores indicate better functioning.

In addition to the structured interviews, the child, his or her parents, and the child's teacher complete a number of questionnaires that assess the child's behavioral and emotional functioning and family functioning. The child's anxiety and depression are assessed using four self-report measures. The Revised Children's Manifest Anxiety Scale (RCMAS) (Reynolds & Richmond, 1978) is a 37-item questionnaire that assesses anxiety across three domains: physical, worry/oversensitivity, and social concerns/concentration. The RCMAS has been shown to possess good reliability and validity (Reynolds, 1982; Reynolds & Paget, 1983). The Multidimensional Anxiety Scale for Children (MASC) (March, Parker, Sullivan, Stallings, & Connors, 1997) is a 39-item self-report inventory containing four major factors: Physical Symptoms, Social Anxiety, Harm Avoidance, and Separation Anxiety. Retest reliability has been shown to be excellent over periods of 3 weeks and 3 months (mean intraclass correlation = .93 and .78, respectively), and there is support for the convergent and discriminant validity of the scale (March & Albano, 1998; March et al., 1997). The Coping Questionnaire (CQ) assesses children's ability to cope with anxious distress in challenging situations via both child report and parent report. The child identifies the three most anxiety-provoking situations, and then the child's ability to cope in each of these situations is rated from 1 "not at all able to help myself feel less upset" to 7 "completely able to help myself feel less upset." Both forms of the CQ have been shown to have adequate internal consistency, strong retest reliability, and to be sensitive to treatment gains (Kendall & Marrs-Garcia, 1999). The Children's Depression Inventory (CDI) (Kovacs, 1981) is a 27-item self-report inventory that assesses cognitive, affective, and behavioral symptoms of depression. The CDI has been shown to have high internal consistency, moderate retest reliability, and strong convergent validity (Kazdin, French, Unis, Esveldt-Dawson, & Sherick, 1983; Kovacs, 1981).

The child's parents and his or her teacher also complete questionnaires that assess the child's anxiety and other mood and behavioral symptoms. As indicated earlier, the child's parents complete the CQ, rating the child's ability to help himself or herself feel less anxious in situations that the child has chosen. Parents are also asked to complete the Child Behavior Checklist (CBCL) (Achenbach, 1991a), which assesses behavioral problems across eight domains. Compared to normative data, behavioral problems of clinical significance can be identified by T scores of 70 (or 65) or greater. Similarly, the child's teacher completes the CBCL–Teacher's Report Form (CBCL-TRF) (Achenbach, 1991b).

The child and his or her parents also complete measures of family functioning, including the Family Assessment Device (FAD), which measures six dimensions of family functioning (e.g., communication, behavior control, etc.) based on the McMaster model of family functioning (Epstein, Baldwin, & Bishop, 1983). Higher scale scores are indicative of unhealthy family functioning. The 60-item FAD has been shown to have good internal consistency and factorial validity and to differentiate clinical, nonclinical, and medical samples (Kabacoff, Miller, Bishop, Epstein, & Keitner, 1990).

MOLLY L.'S PRETREATMENT ASSESSMENT

During the interviews, it became clear that Molly experiences severe anxiety in a number of situations, particularly separating from her mother. Consistent with this, Molly became visibly upset when asked to separate from her parents for the diagnostic interview. However, with some reassurance that she could ask to see her parents at any time during the interview, she was able to accompany the diagnostician to a nearby room. Regarding these separation fears, Molly's parents reported that she often expresses concern about getting lost and not being able to find her parents. They further indicated that Molly worries about who would take care of her if her mother was not around (i.e., if she were hurt or killed). Molly expressed similar worries in her interview and reported that this is why she is so afraid that her mother will be hurt. Molly indicated that she constantly feels "queasy" when not with her mother and that this makes it difficult for her to go to school or to sleepovers. When asked how a magic wand could make things better for her, Molly responded that she would want to know where her mother is at all times. Mr. and Mrs. L. indicated that Molly's separation anxiety has a significant impact on the family's functioning. For example, when they plan to go somewhere without her, she often runs to the car and begs them to stay home. Furthermore, both Molly and her parents reported that her anxiety is not reduced when she is left with other adults such as her grandparents or a baby sitter. As a result of this, Mr. and Mrs. L. indicated that they rarely go out without their daughter.

Molly's parents also reported that she experiences intense anxiety about traveling (e.g., riding in cars, trains, planes, etc.) and other situations that may result in her vomiting. They reported that Molly refuses to ride in a car unless one of her parents or a specific family friend is driving. Even when she is driving with her parents, Molly is reported to become very distressed when traveling outside of her "safety zone," an area of a few miles around the family home. Furthermore, Molly reported avoiding places and settings where she has vomited before. For example, she reported that she no longer takes the school bus and that she feels unable to ride in the backseat of cars, both places where she has vomited before. Molly reported that her anxiety builds to the point of vomiting and that this happens about once or twice a day. Molly's family members have also changed their behavior to accommodate her fears. For example, Mrs. L. reported that she keeps plastic bags and water in the car, in case Molly needs to vomit. Furthermore, Molly's older sister is consistently asked to sit in the backseat of the car, which is often a subject of much contention. Molly's fears have also limited the family's travel plans and have caused Molly to miss events that she would have liked to attend (e.g., school trips). When asked if she would be willing to ride in the backseat of a car for a longer time to go to a "cool" place (e.g., the beach, an amusement park, etc.), Molly responded that she would rather not go.

Mr. and Mrs. L. described their daughter as a worrier. They reported that she anticipates events for days and sometimes weeks ahead. They indicated that Molly worries excessively about getting good grades, staying healthy, the health of friends and family members, and family affairs such as finances. For example, they reported that even though she just completed the third grade, she is already worried about starting school in the fall and whether she will like her teachers. They reported that Molly's excessive worry often causes sleep difficulties (both falling and staying asleep) and leads to nausea and vomiting. This, in turn, leads Molly to worry that she will get sick the next time she becomes anxious.

Finally, Molly's parents reported that their daughter had been feeling sad more days than not over the past 2 years. They reported that she often apologizes for her anxiety and feels guilty because she believes that her problems have created a burden for others. Mr. and Mrs. L. reported that she expresses hopelessness via statements such as "I can't be fixed." Despite Molly's low mood, they reported that she continues to be very active on a regular basis. During the child interview, Molly denied feelings of sadness.

In sum, composite diagnoses (based on information from both the parent and child interviews; see Table 9.1) resulted in a primary diagnosis of separation anxiety disorder. Additional clinical diagnoses of agoraphobia (without a history of panic) and generalized anxiety disorder were also assigned. In addition, based on parent and child reports, school refusal[2] was assigned (as was a specific phobia of thunderstorms as a subclinical diagnosis) (see also Table 9.1). Based only on the parents' report, the diagnostician assigned a subclinical diagnosis of dysthymia. However, because the child failed to endorse any mood symptoms, the final composite did not include a dysthymia diagnosis. Finally, Molly was assigned a CGAS of 54, representing variable functioning with sporadic difficulties or symptoms in several areas but not all social areas. This level of disturbance would be apparent to those who encounter the child in a dysfunctional setting or time but not those who encounter the child in other settings.

As can be seen in Table 9.2, Molly and her parents also endorsed very severe levels of anxiety on questionnaire measures. On the RCMAS, her total score and all three scale scores were above the 90th percentile for girls her age (for normative data, see Reynolds & Richmond, 1985). On the MASC, all four subscale scores and her total score were well in the clinical range based on comparison to her same-age peers (see March & Parker, 1999, for normative data). Ratings on the CQ revealed that Molly and her parents rated a low coping ability. On average, they rated Molly's ability to cope between a 2 and a 3 on the scale from 1 to 7. This indicates that they believed her ability to cope fell between "not at all able to help myself/ herself cope" (1) and only "somewhat able to help myself/herself cope" (4). In addition to severe symptoms of anxiety, Molly's self-report on the CDI also indicated a disturbance of her mood. Her CDI score of 11 is higher than that of 73% of all girls ages 7 to 12 and is consistent with that found in a

Table 9.1   Molly's Composite Diagnostic Profile and Clinician Ratings Before and After Treatment

| | Before Treatment | | After Treatment | |
	GIR	CSR	GIR	CSR
Separation anxiety disorder	8	6	4	5
Agoraphobia without history of panic	8	5	6	4
Generalized anxiety disorder	6	5	5	5
Specific phobia–natural environment type	4	3	—	—
School refusal	8	3	—	—
Children's Global Assessment Scale		54		62

NOTE: GIR = global interference rating as assigned by interviewee; CSR = clinician severity rating as assigned by diagnostician. CSR ratings ≥ 4 indicate clinical severity and those < 4 indicate subclinical diagnoses. Dashes indicate that the diagnosis was not given at that time point.

Table 9.2   Questionnaire Measures of Molly's Symptom Levels Before and After Treatment

| | Child Report[a] | | Mother Report | | Father Report | |
	Before	After	Before	After	Before	After
RCMAS						
Physical	9 (96)	2 (13)				
Worry/ oversensitivity	11 (99)	0 (4)				
Social concerns/ concentration	6 (93)	0 (7)				
Total	26 (99)	2 (3)				
MASC						
Physical symptoms	24	5				
Social anxiety	17	5				
Separation anxiety	20	8				
Harm avoidance	23	21				
Total	84	39				
CDI total	11	1				

	Child Report[a]		Mother Report		Father Report	
	Before	After	Before	After	Before	After
Coping Questionnaire						
Situation 1	2	4	3	3	2	3
Situation 2	1	3	1	3	2	3
Situation 3	5	5	4	5	3	5
Average coping rating	2.67	4.00	2.67	3.67	2.33	3.67
CBCL-TRF						
Internalizing T scores	53	37	78	71	—	65
Externalizing T scores	42	42	48	53	—	48
Anxiety raw scores	6	0	29	18	—	12

NOTE: RCMAS = Revised Children's Manifest Anxiety Scale; MASC = Multidimensional Anxiety Scale for Children; CDI = Children's Depression Inventory; CBCL-TRF = Child Behavior Checklist–Teacher's Report Form. For the RCMAS, numbers outside of the parentheses are raw scores, and those inside parentheses are percentiles for females age 3 = at school during thunderstorm, with higher scores indicating better ability to help self cope. For the CBCL-TRF, T scores ≥ 70 indicate the clinical range. Dashes indicate missing data at first assessment.

a. For the CBCL-TRF, this is a teacher report rather than child report.

sample of children with dysthymic disorder (CDI mean = 11.7, SD = 6.7; Kovacs, 1985). Information from the CBCL mother report revealed clinically significant internalizing distress, including symptoms of anxiety and depression, and somatic complaints. The teacher's report did not indicate any scales within the clinical range. The father did not complete a CBCL before treatment.

The 60-item FAD was used to assess family functioning before treatment. FAD scores according to child, mother, and father report indicated levels of family functioning typically seen in clinic families (Sawyer, Sarris, Cross, & Kalucy, 1988) (see Table 9.3). Furthermore, these scores represent patterns of family functioning that are less healthy than found in community families (Sawyer et al., 1988).

6. CASE CONCEPTUALIZATION

Molly experienced severe anxiety when she was separated from her parents or when she anticipated separation. A "hot" feeling, stomach pain/queasiness leading to vomiting, chattering of teeth, and crying evidenced the physical manifestation of her anxiety. The threat-related cognitions associated with these physical symptoms included the following: "Something bad will

Table 9.3 Family Functioning Before and After Treatment

	Child Report		Mother Report		Father Report	
	Before	After	Before	After	Before	After
Family Assessment Device						
Problem solving	12	9	11	12	11	10
Communication	17	15	16	13	17	13
Roles	17	17	23	22	20	16
Affective responsiveness	12	13	11	12	12	11
Affective involvement	18	16	16	16	16	12
Behavior control	16	19	17	17	14	12
General functioning	27	21	28	26	28	21

NOTE: High scores suggest unhealthy family functioning.

happen to Mom when I leave"; "I must know where Mom is at all times"; "If something happens to Mom or Dad, I don't know who will look after me"; and "If I am on my own, I will get lost and I won't be able to find my parents." As a result, Molly avoided situations involving separation such as school, sleepovers, and staying at her grandparents. Based on a cognitive-behavioral conceptualization, Molly's avoidance of separation from her parents was maintaining her negative expectations: Without experiences of separation/reunion and successful coping, the belief that "something bad will happen" and her inability to cope persisted.

Molly worried excessively about getting good grades, staying healthy, family finances, and the health of family and friends. The physical symptoms associated with the worry were nausea and stomach distress leading to vomiting. The threat-related cognitions accompanying these physical symptoms were "I am going to fail," "I will get sick," "My sister will get sick," and "We won't have enough money." As a result, Molly had difficulty falling and staying asleep at night. She anticipated events weeks in advance and spent a lot of time thinking about the "What ifs?" of a situation. Further maintaining the anxiety was the fact that Molly worried that her worrying would cause her to vomit.

In addition, Molly was apprehensive in and avoidant of situations in which she might experience anxiety-related stomach distress and vomiting.

Molly avoided traveling on the school bus, going on long trips in the car, and visiting shopping malls. When riding in the car, she would only sit in the front seat and carried plastic bags and water at all times. In addition, she would not ride in the car outside her safety zone. When visiting new places or the mall, Molly had to determine where the bathrooms are located. She felt queasy whenever she was faced with these situations. The cognitive component to these fears consisted of thoughts such as "I will get sick"; "If I get sick, I won't be able to escape from the car"; "If I get sick, I won't be able to find the bathrooms"; and "If I get sick, I won't be able to find help." The physical symptoms of stomach distress associated with Molly's separation anxiety and generalized anxiety further maintained Molly's agoraphobia: Her anxiety increased the likelihood of stomach distress and subsequent vomiting.

Prior to treatment, Molly's anxiety was being maintained by her parents' response to her behavior. Molly's parents supported her avoidant behavior by giving in to the tantrums that occurred in response to the feared situations. In addition, the result of their giving in reinforced her tantrums and increased their likelihood. Molly's parents had reorganized their schedules around Molly's fears and avoided traveling on long trips or leaving her on her own. Molly's parents felt guilty when they gave in to her but felt that they had no other alternatives. Molly's parents were frustrated by her behavior and felt helpless and hopeless. These feelings were further exacerbated by the failure of previous psychological and psychopharmacological treatments. In addition, Molly's parents held the belief that Molly should be able to cope with these situations. They pressured Molly to cope in these situations and became frustrated with her lack of coping. Molly felt pressured by her parents and held the beliefs that she could not cope, that her parents did not understand her, and that she could not be fixed. These thoughts were accompanied by feelings of sadness. Overall, these feelings of helplessness, frustration, guilt, and tension and the limited family activity were draining the family's resources and further contributed to their perceived inability to cope with the situation.

7. COURSE OF TREATMENT AND ASSESSMENT OF PROGRESS

Molly and her parents attended their first therapy session in July, following completion of the clinic's diagnostic assessment procedures outlined earlier. During this first session, Molly's parents reported that Molly's difficulties had started 2 or 3 years previously and had progressively worsened. They indicated that they had sought psychological and pharmacological treatment but were not satisfied with Molly's progress. Molly remained quiet throughout most of the discussion and often allowed her parents to respond for her. However, when asked what she worries about when she is away from her mother, Molly indicated that she believes that "something's going to happen to her [mother] . . . she might not come back." Following this, the therapist explained the course of therapy to the family, outlining the importance of maintaining a weekly appointment for the duration of the 18-week treatment. In addition, it was explained that they would be asked to complete homework assignments, or STIC tasks, which would serve as opportunities to practice what was learned in session. The reward system was also explained at this time: Molly would receive individual rewards and the family would receive a family reward for weekly completion of the STIC tasks.

Molly seemed more comfortable during the second session and participated in a discussion of treatment goals. She stated that she would know that the treatment was successful "if I get invited to go somewhere . . . I can go without being afraid." Her parents expressed that their goals for treatment were for Molly to be able to enjoy herself more and for her to travel without significant distress. Most of this session focused on normalizing anxiety and introducing the FEAR plan. First, the therapist reminded Molly and her parents that everybody feels nervous at times and therefore Molly should not view herself as "abnormal" for being worried or afraid. The therapist went on to explain that most people have at least a little difficulty controlling their worry and that this too can be seen as normal. Molly expressed that she becomes embarrassed when her mother congratulates her for coping successfully with a difficult situation. She reported that it is difficult to be proud of these accomplishments because she feels that she is simply "being normal." The therapist tried to help Molly to understand that by coping successfully with her anxiety, she was achieving something that she had not done before or that others may not be able to do and that this should make her feel proud. This topic was revisited in later sessions.

Later in the session, the first step, Feeling frightened, was explained and discussed, and the therapist helped Molly to identify her somatic responses to anxiety and to understand the physical expression of different emotions. She indicated that when she is anxious, she gets a "hot feeling," her stomach hurts, her teeth chatter, she may cry, she may throw up, and her thoughts race. The therapist helped Molly to design a rating scale that she would use to rate her anxiety in different situations throughout the rest of treatment. The scale ranged from 1 to 5 and was based on the severity of Molly's somatic responses. For example, a 1 indicated no anxiety and feeling relaxed, and a 5 indicated severe anxiety with racing thoughts, teeth chattering, crying, and vomiting. She used this scale throughout the rest of treatment, in her homework tasks and in session, to quantify her anxious responses.

Molly and her mother attended the third session alone (Molly's father was unable to attend due to his work schedule). During an initial discussion of the week's events, Molly and her mother recounted a recent incident when Molly was so anxious about an upcoming trip to the beach that she felt very unhappy and became sick and vomited. As a result of her distress, the trip was cancelled for the entire family. Molly and her mother were both very upset by this. Mrs. L. discussed her frustration with missing an opportunity to go to the beach and her feelings of helplessness when Molly becomes upset. She indicated that she often feels like "we give in and that we're avoiding something . . . you don't want to give in to that avoidance behavior." However, she has not found any alternatives to help alleviate Molly's distress. Molly reported that she felt happy that they did not go to the beach, but she also felt guilty for letting her family down. It became clear to the therapist that these feelings of anger, frustration, and guilt served to exacerbate an already difficult situation and that this pattern of emotional responses was common in this family. Therefore, to treat Molly's anxiety, these emotions too would be a part of the focus of therapy. Due to the length of this discussion, the therapist was unable to complete Session 3 exactly according to the manual. The discussion shifted to the communication of emotions and the need to initiate a fun activity to help Molly and her mother to learn more about which feelings they express to others and which they choose to keep to themselves. It was agreed that these issues would be explored further during the following session when Mr. L. was able to attend.

The fourth session was divided into three parts: 30 minutes with the whole family to complete material from Session 3, 20 minutes with Mr. and Mrs. L. alone, and 20 minutes with Molly alone. Following from the previous session, the therapist further explored the expression of emotions and differences among family members in the feelings they choose to express to others. She outlined a number of effective communication and listening skills and encouraged the family to use them during structured conversational tasks during the session and during the week for their STIC tasks. Mr. L. indicated that he does not often share his feelings with others. He reported that he carefully chooses what he shares with Molly because he does not want to upset her or provoke her feelings of guilt. He also indicated that he likes to be "well-prepared" and that this is what often makes Molly's anxiety attacks difficult for him; they cannot be planned for and do not seem to follow any consistent sequence. Another prominent theme in this session was Molly's return into school in 3 weeks. During their time alone with the therapist, Mr. and Mrs. L. discussed their concern, given Molly's previous difficulties with going to school and particularly with taking the bus. Again, they expressed their ambivalence about responding to Molly's anxiety: giving in versus discouraging avoidance. They indicated that they were unsure how much to push Molly to face her anxiety and that they felt they were contributing to her pattern of avoidance. The therapist helped them to understand that forcing Molly into anxiety-provoking situations before she had the appropriate coping skills could increase her anxiety and promote feelings of helplessness. The topic of returning to school was also addressed in Molly's session alone with the therapist. Molly indicated that she was afraid of starting school because she did not know the teacher. Although the therapist had not formally introduced coping skills yet, she encouraged Molly to make a list of strategies to help herself feel better about school. Molly and her mother had already planned to visit the teacher prior to starting school, so the therapist helped Molly to think of questions and encouraged her to think about what she would like the new teacher to know about her.

The primary goal of Sessions 5 through 8 was to introduce the remaining three steps of the FEAR plan and to gain additional information about Molly's fears to establish a hierarchy of anxiety-provoking situations that would be used during the second half of treatment. During Session 5, the family discussed their STIC tasks that asked them to discuss their feelings with each other and other family members. They had some difficulty with this, and they were reminded of the importance of effective listening skills and of sharing their emotions verbally rather than allowing others to guess what they are feeling. In the second half of the session, the therapist taught Molly progressive muscle relaxation according to Ollendick and Cerny (1981). These skills, particularly the deep breathing, would later become an integral part of Molly's coping strategy. Molly was then asked to teach these skills to her parents so that they may help her to practice them at home. Session 6 focused primarily on teaching Molly and her parents the "E" step of the FEAR plan (Expecting bad things to happen) by helping them to identify anxious thoughts using cartoons with thought bubbles. As an example, the therapist asked Molly to think of the anxious thoughts she might have when she visits her school 2 days before the 1st day of school. (The family had already planned to do this, hoping it would help Molly feel more comfortable on the 1st day of classes.) Molly indicated that she might think, "What will it be like when we do it for real?" and "What if someone stops me, like while I'm up there. . . . What if someone stops me and asks me what I am doing, what should I say?" The therapist then briefly introduced the next step and asked Molly to suggest coping thoughts that would help to ameliorate her anxiety. Molly's coping thoughts included "It will be fun to see my friends" and "Maybe my teacher will be nice."

Following this discussion, Molly initiated an important conversation about a recent incident in which she felt angry with her parents because they had planned to go out and had not told her until that day. The therapist encouraged the family to focus on the first two FEAR steps and to explore their thoughts and feelings around this situation. Molly's anger stemmed from her belief that her parents had "tricked her" when they left her at her grandparent's house while they went out for the evening. She also indicated that she felt guilty when she became upset in front of her grandparents because she believed that she had hurt their feelings. Mr. and Mrs. L. expressed feelings of frustration because they had no intention of tricking their daughter; rather, they had thought that they would limit her distress throughout the week. Molly agreed that she would have felt bad if she had known ahead of time but that she was still angry. Molly's interpretation of her parents' report was that they were mad at her and frustrated with her: "They tell me they're tired of me." In response to this, Mrs. L. told her daughter, "We are frustrated, but not with you. . . . It's that I can't help you." It became clear that Mrs. L. felt frustrated that she could not help her daughter and felt unable to fix these situations. The therapist explained to her that she cannot always help her daughter and that it is not even her responsibility to do so. She reminded the family that the goal of therapy was to teach Molly ways to cope more effectively with her anxiety and to help her parents learn how to encourage their daughter's progress. The therapist also sought to point out the importance of discussing feelings of anger, guilt, and frustration and the accompanying thoughts so that they can be better understood and will not be misinterpreted.

At the seventh session, Molly and her parents reported that she successfully returned to school. She had slightly more difficulty the 2nd day of school than the 1st, but she was able to attend and remain in school for the full day. Although Molly had successfully attended school, it had been an extremely stressful situation for her. This became apparent when she had significant difficulty on the following Saturday when her mother went out to see a friend 2 hours away. Molly was so anxious about this that she wet the bed in the morning and became extremely upset as her mother was leaving. According to Mrs. L., her daughter was inconsolable, and this made Saturday morning very stressful for everyone in the family. Again, Mrs. L. reported feeling very frustrated because she did not know how to soothe Molly and was unsure whether to continue with her plans or to stay at home. She indicated that they tried unsuccessfully to use the relaxation tape. Finally, Molly's father convinced Mrs. L. that she needed to keep her plans and that Molly would be fine at home. The therapist used this situation to introduce the third FEAR step (Actions and attitudes that can help) by teaching Molly and her parents the steps of problem solving new coping strategies to help Molly when she is feeling anxious. Using the Saturday morning incident as an example, the therapist asked Molly about her anxious thoughts. Molly indicated that she was thinking, "What if something bad happens?" and "What if I really need her, she'll be 2 hours away." The therapist then encouraged Molly to think of coping thoughts that may have helped her to relax. She offered, "She [Mom] will be fine" and "My dad is here if I need something." As another example, the therapist asked Molly what "actions and attitudes" might she use to help herself if she feels anxious about school. Molly and her mother provided a list of 20 strategies, including doing relaxation exercises, lying on the couch, talking to her sister about her worries, and thinking about the fun activities at school. The therapist encouraged Molly to remember this list over the next week so that she could try these strategies if she felt nervous about attending school.

Molly and her mother arrived at the eighth session with positive reports of the previous week. When asked what was different about this week, Molly responded that she "just felt brave." The therapist encouraged her to remember that feeling so that she could tap into it in the future. There were two main goals of this session: first, to explain the final FEAR step and to practice using the complete FEAR plan and, second, to begin constructing a hierarchy of anxiety-producing situations to be used during the exposure phase of treatment. The therapist introduced the final FEAR step (Results and rewards) and encouraged Molly to rate her own coping skills and reward herself for her efforts. Molly helped to design a rating scale to measure her "coping efforts" and came up with a list of rewards, such as a can of soda and time to bake cookies with her mother. At the end of the session, as a review, the therapist helped Molly and her parents to design a FEAR plan for a common anxiety-provoking situation (see Figure 9.1).

The therapist helped Molly and her mother to construct a hierarchy of anxiety-provoking situations that Molly would experience throughout the second half of treatment (see Figure 9.2). Molly became upset when discussing higher level exposure tasks such as getting dropped off alone. The therapist reassured her that this situation might seem scary now but that it was likely that it may no longer seem difficult in 6 weeks, after she had a lot of practice using her new coping skills. It is common for children to become upset during this discussion because it reminds them that they will be asked to face challenging situations.

During the ninth session, the therapist again met separately with Molly and with her parents. Molly's comfort with the clinic and increased ability

Situation: Parents are going out to dinner while Molly stays at a neighbor's house	
Feeling frightened:	A little nervous, butterflies in the stomach, head feels hot, loss of appetite
Expecting bad things to happen:	"What time are they coming home?" "Is the neighbor going to stay home the whole time?" "Will we have to run errands with her?" "Does my mother have her cellular phone?" "If my brother and sister get nervous, I will get nervous too."
Actions and attitudes that can help:	Actions: Ask her mother to take her cellular phone with her; lie down, watch television, get toys and activities together to bring to the neighbor's house; try to eat dinner Attitudes: "I already asked the neighbor if she will be staying home"; "I know that my mother will come home"; "If my brother and sister get nervous, I may get nervous, but I may not"
Results and rewards:	Bring a can of soda to the neighbor's house if Molly tries hard to cope and/or copes effectively

Figure 9.1   Example of a FEAR Plan

1. Leaving her mother to:

   > Go to school (2)
   > Go to the neighbors' house (3)
   > Go to a friend's house (3)
   > Go to another floor in the psychology building (3)
   > Leave the psychology building to walk around (4)

2. Mrs. L. leaving Molly to:

   > Go outside of the house (1 during the day; 2 at night)
   > Go shopping (2 if Molly is left at home; 4 if Molly is left with a neighbor)
   > Go somewhere unknown to Molly (3 if Molly is left at home; 5 if Molly is left with neighbor)
   > Leave the psychology building (3 if Molly is with therapist; 5 if Molly is left alone)

3. Mrs. L. dropping Molly off at the front of the psychology building for her appointment (5)

4. Taking a new route in the car (4)

5. Going to a new place that is approximately 30 minutes away (5)

6. Taking the school bus (8)

Figure 9.2   Molly's Hierarchy of Anxiety-Provoking Situations With Subjective Units of Distress Scale Ratings

NOTE: Molly was asked to rate each situation on a 0–8 scale (0 = *no anxiety*, 4 = *some anxiety*, 8 = *extreme anxiety*).

to cope was clear when she sat easily in the waiting room while her parents met with the therapist. This was in stark contrast to the previous divided session when she only felt comfortable sitting directly outside the therapy room door. Mr. and Mrs. L. reported several improvements in Molly's anxiety. For example, she was now able to stay home alone with her father, and she had not vomited in more than a month. Mrs. L. informed the therapist about an upcoming school trip that she would like Molly to attend. Interestingly, they had not asked Molly about her feelings and thoughts concerning taking the bus. The therapist suggested that they discuss the issue with Molly to find out the nature of her fears so that they could be addressed directly. She also reminded Mr. and Mrs. L. about the importance of taking small steps so that Molly is ensured success and is less likely to fail to cope. Mr. and Mrs. L. were encouraged to keep their goals realistic and to remember that Molly's anxiety had been developing for 3 years, and therefore, it was not likely that it would disappear within a couple of months. During her time alone with Molly, the therapist focused on furthering the therapeutic relationship by engaging Molly in an art project. She also encouraged Molly to talk about any issues that she was reluctant to speak about in front of her parents. Molly declined and instead talked to the therapist about her school-work, friends, and sister.

A number of issues arose during the second half of treatment—addressing these issues illustrates the flexibility in the application of the treatment manual. First, the distress that Molly experienced in Session 8 during a discussion of the exposures worsened when she was expected to put herself in anxiety-provoking situations. During several of the sessions, Molly became extremely upset and oppositional when the therapist started to discuss the exposure tasks. At times, this behavior allowed her to avoid these tasks because of time constraints. Despite these incidents, Molly's ability to cope with her anxiety significantly improved throughout the second half of treatment. Interestingly, these positive behavioral changes had a dramatic impact on her self-image and on her role within the family. As Molly's anxiety decreased, she became confused about her emotional responses in situations that had previously been anxiety provoking. She was also frustrated by the expectations placed on her by herself and her family. The therapist helped her to explore these emotions and addressed several important issues, including Molly's feelings toward her anxiety, Mr. and Mrs. L.'s feelings toward her progress in therapy, and how Molly's parents could effectively help her to cope with anxiety-provoking situations.

Session 10 began with a discussion of the week's STIC tasks. First, Molly and her parents reported two successful exposure situations. Molly rode in her neighbor's car during a thunderstorm, which is something she was not able to do the previous year. In addition, she had walked home from school several times. The therapist praised Molly for continuing to challenge herself and for her successful coping. Second, Molly and her mother discussed their attempt to complete the second half of the STIC task, which was to discuss the upcoming exposure situations. Mrs. L. explained that Molly had become upset the previous evening when they were completing this homework. There was obvious disagreement as to the cause of Molly's distress. Mrs. L. believed that Molly had become upset because of the topic of the discussion; Molly indicated that she had become upset because her mother "was being a pain" when she left in the middle of their discussion. A disagreement ensued between Molly and her mother about the events of the previous evening, and Molly became extremely upset. When asked to write her feelings on the board, Molly wrote, "Not scared—nobody understands me." She indicated that she felt angry and frustrated because her mother had assumed she was scared the night before and had told this to her father without asking Molly how she was feeling. She believed that it was not fair that everyone was playing a "guessing game" with how she was feeling when she did not know she was even playing. When asked by the therapist how they felt when they heard this, Mr. L. reported that he felt confused and frustrated, and Mrs. L. reported feeling bad that her daughter was upset. Through this discussion, it became clear that Molly's new ability to cope with her anxiety was affecting the entire family system, including her interactions with her parents. In addition, Molly was becoming confused about her own emotional responses and about the expectations placed on her to cope effectively. The therapist attempted to help Molly cope with her emotions during the session by suggesting that she slow her breathing in order to calm herself. The therapist also reminded the family of the importance of sharing their emotions and helped to facilitate a discussion of how they may improve their communication, particularly in stressful situations.

Following this difficult discussion, the therapist reminded Molly about the first exposure task: Molly was to accompany the therapist to the waiting room for 5 minutes. Molly became very upset with the therapist and felt that the task was too difficult. In an effort to better understand his daughter's reaction, Molly's father asked, "Do you think we are going to leave you?" and she replied that she did worry about this. She then recalled an incident when the family was on vacation, and her parents told her that they would not leave the house but then went out for about 10 minutes. Molly indicated that since that time, she has felt that she could not trust her parents. The therapist explained to Molly and her parents that they may need to rebuild this trust and that the exposure tasks provide a good opportunity to do this. Although Molly refused to perform the proposed exposure task, she readily accompanied the therapist to her office to choose her reward for her homework. It became clear that Molly was able to separate from her parents when she was ready to and when there were few external pressures to do so. Also, although this is not atypical, the idea of doing an "exposure task" seemed to carry with it some anxiety. This would come up again in later sessions.

Molly and her mother attended the 11th session alone. One of the exposure tasks in this session was for Molly to accompany the therapist to the water fountain down the hall from the therapy room. Similar to the previous week, Molly was highly emotional and seemed confused about her feelings and their causes throughout the session. As the therapist and family discussed the STIC task, Mrs. L. informed the therapist that Molly's class had gone on a trip to the planetarium. Although Molly was too anxious to go on the trip, she coped well and got in line for the bus. She indicated that she might have been able to go if she had more time to think about and plan for it. The therapist used this opportunity to remind Molly and her mother of the importance of rating Molly's effort rather than the outcome and that this should be considered an initial attempt to cope. Discussion of this situation served to raise the issue of normality for Molly because she then reported that "everyone makes fun of me at school" and asks her questions about missing school once a week to see a doctor (come to therapy). Although Molly had some difficulty expressing her thoughts clearly, she seemed to have concerns that she was different from other children. In addition, it was clear that as she made attempts to become less anxious, her family continued to expect her to react to situations as she had in the past. The therapist commented that although she was making behavioral changes, there were some expectations (her own and her parents') that remained from the time before they began treatment. Mrs. L. agreed that they had become accustomed to believing that she was scared of certain situations but that this may not be true anymore. The therapist discussed with Molly that she needed to help her parents to understand the new feelings she was experiencing. Also, by expressing these emotions, she may come to understand them better and change her own expectations. Later in the session, Molly became upset again prior to the exposure task and refused to plan out the FEAR steps ahead of time. The therapist reminded her that this may make it easier, and she continued to refuse. Finally, the therapist held to the plan, and when it became clear that the session would not end until the task was completed, Molly agreed to do the task and did so successfully.

The discussion of Molly's feelings of anger, frustration, and confusion continued during the 12th session. During the discussion of the week's homework, Molly's parents reported that she had coped successfully during a long drive (about 45 minutes) to a farm to pick out pumpkins for Halloween. They further noted that Molly became very anxious about going on a hayride and refused to do it. Molly became upset during this discussion and cried, "I don't want people to talk about me anymore." Again, it was clear that Molly was feeling a lot of pressure from the therapist, her parents, and herself to overcome her anxiety and that she did not want to discuss instances when she had difficulty coping. The therapist tried to remind her that she is not expected to cope successfully every time but that she can still learn from these situations.

Molly became extremely upset when the therapist proposed the day's exposure task. Again, it was difficult for Molly to express her feelings, and this seemed to frustrate her mother, who tried to guess what Molly was afraid of. This seemed to be a common pattern between mother and daughter: Molly would become very upset and have difficulty expressing her feelings, which would lead her mother to try to figure them out. This would only frustrate Molly more because her mother would usually assume she was scared and would try to go through the FEAR steps. Again, the themes of anger, frustration, and sadness emerged, and it became clear that these related emotions were causing more distress than the anxiety itself. Molly was upset that she was different from other children. She told the therapist, "It's not fair" that other children do not have to come to therapy so people do not get disappointed in them. When asked to expand on this, Molly said, "Nobody cares" and indicated that she was afraid that her mother would yell at her later for being upset during the session. Mrs. L. began to feel angry and felt that Molly was wasting time in the session. It was clear to the therapist that Mrs. L.'s emotions regarding her daughter were playing an integral role in Molly's progress in therapy and needed to be addressed. She asked Mrs. L. about her feelings when she sees Molly upset and reminded her that although these sessions are difficult, and often address issues other than anxiety, expression of these emotions is important. She was encouraged not to think of these emotional outbursts as setbacks to be avoided but instead as opportunities to explore the emotional impact of the changes that were taking place. As the possibility of the scheduled exposure task (accompanying the therapist to another floor in the building) neared, Molly became more angry and upset and told the therapist, "I'm not going to go . . . because I don't feel like it." She was somewhat soothed by her mother but continued to refuse to complete the exposure task.

Despite the difficulty Molly experienced in the first three exposure sessions, she became more successful at coping with her anxiety both in and out of session over the next 2 weeks. Molly reported that she had been walking home from school every day and that she did not experience any anxious situations during the week between Sessions 13 and 14. She coped successfully during a scavenger hunt (exposure task) around the building in Session 13 and when her mother left the therapy room once to walk around the floor and once to walk anywhere in the building during Session 14. Although it is unclear exactly why Molly became less oppositional toward these tasks, it is likely that the discussions of the previous sessions had helped her to better understand her emotions and had allowed her to express them to her family. This may have relieved some of the pressure she was feeling to meet the expectations of her parents and the therapist and allowed her to focus her energy specifically on coping with her anxiety in these situations. In addition, it is likely that these conversations helped Molly to feel more comfortable in therapy and perhaps to feel more confident in the therapist's ability to help her.

Interestingly, as Molly became more successful and had fewer "panic attacks," the times during which she had difficulty coping became even more stressful because her own expectations and those placed on her by her parents had changed. During a discussion of the STIC task in Session 13, Molly described a situation in which she was extremely frustrated because she was unable to cope with her anxiety. She reported that she was very upset because her brother and sister were upset. She indicated that she tried to keep herself busy, think positively, and convince herself that she was okay, but these were not successful strategies. This was the first time in a few weeks when Molly had been unsuccessful at coping in a difficult situation. The therapist introduced the idea of differentiating between lapses and relapses and the importance of not confusing them. The therapist used examples of recent successes (i.e., walking home from school) to demonstrate that the previous incident was a lapse and not a relapse.

During Session 14, a new issue emerged regarding the burden felt by Molly from the pressure to meet these new expectations. She reported that she felt tired of pushing herself all the time and of people expecting things of her that she was unsure she could accomplish. Molly was frustrated that once she made significant gains, she could not sit back and was only pushed further. The therapist stressed the importance of continued challenges but also the importance of feeling proud of the present accomplishments and how they could balance these. This discussion of expectations also seemed related to Molly's difficulty planning exposure tasks ahead of time; it became apparent that she was unable to cope successfully when there were external pressures on her to do so but that she could do it on her own. At the end of Session 14, the therapist briefly addressed termination issues. Both Molly and her mother seemed anxious about this and asked the therapist a number of questions about what will happen after the program ends. The therapist reminded them that they had the tools they needed to cope effectively with anxiety and that it was simply up to them to continue to practice them so that they become easier to use.

Session 15 was an extremely difficult one for Molly. Again, a recent incident in which Molly had difficulty coping was made even more stressful because of the successes experienced in the past 2 months. It was again apparent that the expectations for success or failure were having dramatic effects on the emotional responses of Molly and her mother in anxiety-provoking situations and that these responses were affecting the outcome. Mrs. L. reported that she had not expected Molly to get very anxious or upset, and therefore, she became angry when this happened. Her response was to feel that Molly had not tried hard enough to cope. She admitted that by reacting with anger and frustration, she was unable to help Molly cope with the situation. Molly was similarly disappointed in the results of the situation. However, she indicated during the session that she felt misunderstood and that she was trying as hard as she could. She reported, "Everyone tells me I don't try hard enough, but I'm trying as hard as I can. . . . Who wouldn't try?" To her parents, she said, "You always say I'm not trying as hard as I could, but I'm giving my best effort every time. . . . I can't try any harder or my brains will fall out." In addition, she was upset because each time she tries her best and is successful, someone is there pushing her to try something more difficult and to put forth even more effort. She stated, "I don't feel like changing. Once I change, people expect different things from me; it's confusing." The therapist helped Mrs. L. understand these feelings and to think about ways to work with Molly during these difficult situations. Molly was finally able to verbalize that she does not like to make the FEAR plan ahead of time because she thought that it made her more anxious. When she makes a plan, she feels worried that she will not successfully follow the plan and this adds to the anxiety of the situation. This discussion was pivotal in helping the therapist and Mrs. L. to understand the pressure that Molly was feeling and the effort she was putting into helping herself overcome this anxiety.

Molly successfully completed her final three in vivo exposure tasks. First, she had some difficulty separating when her mother left the room to walk around the campus. However, her mother successfully refrained from allowing Molly to convince her to compromise the task (an exposure for Mrs. L. as well). It was finally agreed that Molly would hold onto her mother's car keys. She became tearful and upset when her mother got up to leave. However, once she left, she was able to talk to the therapist about her anxious thoughts ("What if I get sick and I can't find her?"). The therapist helped Molly to see that her anxiety was only at a severity of 2, which, according to her scale, was only mildly anxious, so the chances of her getting sick were low. In Session 17, Molly successfully left the building with the therapist to go down the street to the campus book store. For her homework, she designed a FEAR plan for this task, and she predicted that she would feel mildly to moderately anxious. However, when asked how she felt as she left the building, she only rated this task as a 1 and exhibited no signs of distress.

During Session 18, the final exposure task required Molly to get dropped off at the beginning of the session and meet the therapist in the lobby of the building. This was highly significant because this was the situation that Molly most feared during the first discussion of the exposure hierarchy 2 months earlier. Molly successfully coped and demonstrated little distress when she met the therapist and accompanied her to the therapy room. Following this, the therapist spent several minutes reviewing the program with the family and indicating areas in which she had seen dramatic progress. Molly reported that she had ridden the bus that afternoon with her class. She was extremely proud of this accomplishment, as were her parents. Molly was able to see the progress she had made since the beginning of therapy. She also reminded her parents that she might not have done this if she had been pressured by them to do so. The therapist encouraged Molly and her mother to set aside at least 30 minutes each week to catch up on the week's events and to talk so that Molly does not allow things to build up inside her. Mr. and Mrs. L. discussed the issue of Molly's medication and whether it could be reduced or eliminated all together. The therapist recommended that they discuss this with their physician, and they agreed. During this final session, the family completed a commercial: a video that allows the child to explain what she has learned throughout treatment. Molly chose to be a news anchorperson and included her sister in the production. Molly explained the FEAR steps and described the accomplishments that she had made. The therapist then showed the video and presented the family with certificates of accomplishment. She also reminded them that she was available by telephone or e-mail if they needed a booster session or if they simply wanted to share Molly's achievements with her.

Over the course of treatment, Molly was asked to complete two measures of anxiety each week, beginning at the 4th week of treatment. The first was composed of 10 items selected from the Negative Affectivity Self-Statement Questionnaire (Ronan, Kendall, & Rowe, 1994) for their ability to reliably differentiate anxious from nonanxious children. The second measure was the State-Trait Anxiety Inventory for Children (Spielberger, 1973), which was modified slightly to assess the child's feelings "over the past week." At Session 4, Molly endorsed all 10 anxious self-statements as occurring either "sometimes," "fairly often," or "often." By the 8th session, Molly endorsed only 3 self-statements as occurring "sometimes" and the other 7 "not at all." By the final 3 weeks of treatment, Molly failed to endorse that she was having any of the 10 anxious self-statements. This indicates a dramatic decrease over time. Similar changes were seen in Molly's weekly ratings of anxiety, although these seemed slightly more variable. At Session 4, Molly endorsed feeling "very troubled," "upset," and "worried." Seven weeks into treatment, Molly indicated that over the past week she had not felt troubled, upset, or worried. However, 3 weeks later she again endorsed feeling worried, scared, and nervous. This increase in anxiety coincided with Molly's class trip, which was an extremely anxiety-provoking situation for her. By the final three sessions, Molly received a score of 20, which indicates no feelings of worry, fear, or anxiety.

8. COMPLICATING FACTORS

There were few complicating factors in Molly's treatment. Her medication was maintained at a steady dosage throughout treatment and there was no need for changes. At times, logistic issues complicated treatment, such as scheduling and the distance to the clinic. However, these were addressed successfully. At times, particularly during the second half of treatment, Molly's behavior prevented the therapist from completing the goals of each session. Molly's emotional outbursts and oppositionality forced the therapist to struggle with balancing Molly's need to express herself and explore her feelings with the belief that by allowing Molly to avoid the exposure tasks, she would be undermining the core principles of the treatment. As a result, Molly had fewer opportunities to practice the FEAR steps during in-session exposure tasks than the manual suggests.

9. FOLLOW-UP

Following treatment, Molly and her parents participated in diagnostic interviews and again completed the questionnaire batteries. Information from the diagnostic interviews was again summarized into a composite diagnostic profile. Following treatment, Molly's three clinical diagnoses from pretreatment (separation anxiety disorder, agoraphobia, and generalized anxiety disorder) all showed reductions in severity ratings (see Table 9.1). The parent/child ratings of Global Interference from these disorders all reflected less severe symptoms, and the clinician severity ratings showed less severe symptoms for two of the three diagnoses. In addition, the two subclinical diagnoses that were assigned before treatment (school refusal, specific phobia–natural environment type) were no longer assigned following treatment. Finally, following treatment, Molly's CGAS score was rated as a 62. This score is indicative of some difficulty in a single area but of generally functioning well and reflects improvement in Molly's general functioning following treatment.

Examination of the posttreatment questionnaire measures revealed much less impairment than before treatment. Molly's RCMAS scores revealed striking reductions in her self-reported levels of anxiety. Indeed, her total score and subscale scores were reduced from above the 90th percentile before treatment to below the 15th percentile following treatment. Her total score was reduced from the 99th percentile before treatment to the 3rd percentile after treatment. Molly's scores on the MASC also revealed substantial reductions in self-reported anxiety. Indeed, T scores showed clinically meaningful improvements on all scales of the MASC (T score changes > 5; see March & Parker, 1999), and all scores were below the clinical range for same-age girls (see Kendall, Marrs-Garcia, Nath, & Sheldrick, 1999, for a discussion of these approaches to evaluating outcomes). In addition to reductions in reported levels of anxiety, ratings of Molly's ability to cope with anxiety also showed substantial improvement. On average, at posttreatment Molly and her parents rated her ability to cope close to a 4 on the scale from 1 to 7. This indicates that on average, they felt that she was "somewhat able to help myself/herself cope," reflecting an increase in their perceptions of her ability to cope with anxiety. Beyond anxiety, Molly also showed substantial reductions in levels of depressive symptoms following treatment. At posttreatment, Molly was virtually free of symptoms of depression according to the report of both herself and her parents. Finally, information from the CBCL and TRF forms revealed reductions in Molly's T scores. Molly's mother's report following treatment showed that Molly's score on the Internalizing scale was reduced, although it still fell in the clinical range. Similarly, the teacher reported a decrease in internalizing distress.

REPORT OF FAMILY FUNCTIONING AFTER TREATMENT

Following treatment, scores on the FAD revealed improvements in family functioning across the many domains measured by this scale. Across child, mother, and father reports, improvements in functioning were found on the majority of scales (improvements or maintenance of scores on 17 of 21 scales). Examination of these scores showed that Mr. L. indicated improvements across all domains of family functioning. Molly reported improvements on the majority of domains, and Mrs. L. indicated improvement on half of the domains. All three reporters indicated improvements on the communication and general functioning domains.

10. TREATMENT IMPLICATIONS OF THE CASE

The outcome of this case has implications for the use of FCBT for children with anxiety. First, consistent with the findings of treatment outcome research (Kazdin & Weisz, 1998; Ollendick & King, 1998), the

FCBT seemed to have been a successful approach to treating Molly's excessive anxiety. By the end of treatment, Molly was able to use the cognitive and behavioral skills that she had learned to cope with anxiety-provoking situations. Second, the use of a family treatment rather than an individual program allowed the therapist to address some issues concerning the parents' roles in maintaining their daughter's anxiety and the communication of emotions. In addition, it is likely that involving Molly's parents in treatment allowed for greater generalization of the coping skills outside of the therapy room. Although generally positive, FCBT may present potential problems. An example was provided when Molly did not want to be the public focus (as she was within a FCBT): A child may not want to be under the magnifying glass in such a public way, and an individual treatment may offer an opportunity to discuss difficult issues in a more private setting.

Finally, this case demonstrates the importance of applying a treatment manual in a flexible manner (Kendall et al., 1998). Although the manual provided important content and structure that was followed, there were times when flexibility was needed to address issues that arose. As indicated earlier, this often meant that material was carried over to a later session. However, by exploring such issues, the therapist was able to help the family recognize the complexity of the presenting issues and the roles that each member played in the maintenance of Molly's anxiety. It is likely that these discussions played a role in the success of the treatment.

11. RECOMMENDATIONS TO CLINICIANS AND STUDENTS

The outcome of this case is consistent with the existing support for cognitive-behavioral treatments for childhood anxiety. In light of this, our first recommendation to clinicians working with anxiety-disordered children is to consider adopting CBT, similar to that described here. Such treatment manuals allow clinicians to conduct therapy in an organized fashion and are widely available. Second, we continue to encourage that manuals be applied flexibly rather than in a mechanical manner. The clinician can take the time to address important issues even if they are not directly related to the goals of the session. It is likely that this helps to create a more personal therapeutic relationship, which in turn may foster treatment gains. In addition, as seen in the case described here, "outside" issues may be related both to the presenting problem and to its resolution. Last, it is often important to involve a child's parents in his or her treatment. In the current case, the mother played an integral role in her child's anxiety, and it was therefore important to include the mother in treatment. It is recommended that clinicians assess issues such as family interaction patterns and patterns of avoidance to determine the extent to which parents should be involved in their child's treatment.

SOURCE: Amy Krain, Jennifer L. Hudson, Meredith Coles, and Philip Kendall. (2002). The Case of Molly L.: Use of a Family Cognitive-Behavioral Treatment for Childhood Anxiety. *Clinical Case Studies, 4*, 271-298. © 2002 SAGE Publications.

NOTES

1. The case being presented was treated as part of a pilot program for the current randomized clinical trial of family cognitive-behavioral treatment.

2. School refusal is not a *Diagnostic and Statistical Manual of Mental Disorders* (4th ed.) (American Psychiatric Association, 1994) diagnosis; however, it is thoroughly assessed by the Anxiety Disorders Interview Schedule for *DSM-IV* Child Version and Parent Version and therefore is included here.

REFERENCES

Achenbach, T. M. (1991a). *Manual for the Child Behavior Checklist/4-18 and 1991 profile*. Burlington: University of Vermont.

Achenbach, T. M. (1991b). *Manual for the teacher's report form and 1991 profile*. Burlington: University of Vermont.

Barrett, P. M., Dadds, M. R., & Rapee, R. M. (1996). Family treatment of childhood anxiety: A controlled trial. *Journal of Consulting and Clinical Psychology, 64*, 333-342.

Barrett, P. M., Duffy, A. L., Dadds, M. R., & Rapee, R. M. (2001). Cognitive-behavioral treatment of anxiety disorders in children: Long-term (6 year) follow-up. *Journal of Consulting and Clinical Psychology, 69*, 1-17.

Beidel, D. C., Christ, M. G., & Long, P. J. (1991). Somatic complaints in anxious children. *Journal of Abnormal Child Psychology, 19*, 659-670.

Cobham, V. E., Dadds, M. R., & Spence, S. H. (1998). The role of parental anxiety in the treatment of childhood anxiety. *Journal of Consulting and Clinical Psychology, 66*, 893-905.

Epstein, N., Baldwin, L., & Bishop, D. (1983). The McMaster family assessment device. *Journal of Martial and Family Therapy, 9*, 171-180.

Howard, B. L., & Kendall, P. C. (1996). Cognitive-behavioral family therapy for anxiety disordered children: A multiple baseline evaluation. *Cognitive Therapy and Research, 20*, 423-443.

Hudson, J. L., & Rapee, R. M. (2001). Parent-child interactions and the anxiety disorders: An observational study. *Behaviour Research and Therapy, 39*, 1411-1427.

Kabacoff, R. I., Miller, I. W., Bishop, D. S., Epstein, N. B., & Keitner, G. I. (1990). A psychometric study of the McMaster Family Assessment Device in psychiatric, medical, and nonclinical samples. *Journal of Family Psychology, 3*, 431-439.

Kazdin, A., French, N., Unis, A., Esveldt-Dawson, K., & Sherick, R. (1983). Hopelessness, depression, and suicidal intent among inpatient children. *Journal of Consulting and Clinical Psychology, 51*, 504-510.

Kazdin, A. E., & Weisz, J. R. (1998). Identifying and developing empirically supported child and adolescent treatments. *Journal of Consulting and Clinical Psychology, 66*, 19-36.

Kendall, P. C. (1992). Childhood coping: Avoiding a lifetime of anxiety. *Behavioural Change, 9*, 1-8.

Kendall, P. C. (1994). Treating anxiety disorders in children: Results of a randomized clinical trial. *Journal of Consulting and Clinical Psychology, 62*, 100-110.

Kendall, P. C., Chu, B., Gifford, A., Hayes, C., & Nauta, M. (1998). Breathing life into a manual: Flexibility and creativity with manual-based treatments. *Cognitive and Behavioral Practice, 5*, 177-198.

Kendall, P. C., Flannery-Schroeder, E., Panichelli-Mindel, S., Southam-Gerow, M., Henin, A., & Warman, M. (1997). Therapy for youth with anxiety disorders: A second randomized clinical trial. *Journal of Consulting and Clinical Psychology, 65*, 366-380.

Kendall, P. C., & Marrs-Garcia, A. (1999). *Psychometric analyses of a therapy-sensitive measure of children's coping: The Coping Questionnaire (CQ)*. Manuscript submitted for publication, Temple University.

Kendall, P. C., Marrs-Garcia, A., Nath, S., & Sheldrick, R. C. (1999). Normative comparisons for the evaluation of clinical significance. *Journal of Consulting and Clinical Psychology, 67*, 285-299.

Kendall, P. C., & Ronan, K. R. (1990). Assessment of childhood anxieties, fears, and phobias: Cognitive-behavioral models and methods. In C. R. Reynolds & R. W. Kamphaus (Eds.), *Handbook of psychological and educational assessment of children: Personality, behavior, and context*. New York: Guilford.

Kendall, P. C., & Southam-Gerow, M. (1996). Long-term follow-up of treatment for anxiety disordered youth. *Journal of Consulting and Clinical Psychology, 65*, 883-888.

King, N. J., Hamilton, D. H., & Ollendick, T. (1988). *Children's phobia: A behavioural perspective*. Chichester, UK: Wiley.

Kovacs, M. (1981). Rating scales to assess depression in school aged children. *Acta Paedopsychiatrica, 46*, 305-315.

Kovacs, M. (1985). The Children's Depression Inventory (CDI). *Psychopharmacology Bulletin, 21*, 995-998.

March, J. S., & Albano, A. M. (1998). New developments in assessing pediatric anxiety disorders. In T. Ollendick & R. Prinz (Eds.), *Advances in clinical child psychology* (Vol. 20). New York: Plenum Press.

March, J. S., & Parker, J. D. A. (1999). The Multidimensional Anxiety Scale for Children (MASC). In M. Maruish (Ed.), *The use of psychological testing for treatment planning and outcome assessment* (2nd ed.). Hillsdale, NJ: Lawrence Erlbaum.

March, J. S., Parker, J., Sullivan, K., Stallings, P., & Conners, C. (1997). The Multidimensional Anxiety Scale for Children (MASC): Factor structure, reliability and validity. *Journal of the American Academy of Child and Adolescent Psychiatry, 36*, 554-565.

Ollendick, T. H., & Cerny, J. A. (1981). *Cognitive behavioral therapy with children*. New York: Plenum.

Ollendick, T. H., & King, N. J. (1998). Empirically supported treatments for children with phobic and anxiety disorders: Current status. *Journal of Clinical Child Psychology, 27*, 156-167.

Reynolds, C. R. (1982). Convergent and divergent validity of the Revised Children's Manifest Anxiety Scale. *Educational and Psychological Measurement, 42,* 1205-1212.

Reynolds, C. R., & Paget, K. D. (1983). National normative and reliability data for the Revised Children's Manifest Anxiety Scale. *School Psychology Review, 12,* 324-336.

Reynolds, C. R., & Richmond, B. O. (1978). What I think and feel: A revised measure of children's manifest anxiety. *Journal of Abnormal Child Psychology, 6,* 271-280.

Reynolds, C. R., & Richmond, B. O. (1985). *Revised Children's Manifest Anxiety Scale (RCMAS) manual.* Los Angeles: Western Psychological Services.

Ronan, K. R., Kendall, P. C., & Rowe, M. (1994). Negative affectivity in children: Development and validation of a self-statement questionnaire. *Cognitive Therapy and Research, 18,* 509-528.

Sawyer, M. G., Sarris, A., Cross, D. G., & Kalucy, R. S. (1988). Family assessment device: Reports from mothers, fathers, adolescents in community and clinic families. *Journal of Marital and Family Therapy, 14,* 287-296.

Silverman, W., & Albano, A. M. (1997). *The Anxiety Disorders Interview Schedule for Children (DSM-IV).* San Antonio, TX: Psychological Corporation.

Silverman, W., Kurtines, W., Ginsburg, G., Weems, C., Rabian, B., & Serafini, L. (1999). Contingency management, self-control, and education support in the treatment of childhood phobic disorders: A randomized clinical trial. *Journal of Consulting and Clinical Psychology, 67,* 675-687.

Siqueland, L., Kendall, P. C., & Steinberg, L. (1996). Anxiety in children: Perceived family environments and observed family interaction style. *Journal of Clinical Child Psychology, 25,* 225-237.

Spence, S. H., Donovan, C., & Brechman-Toussaint, M. (2000). The treatment of childhood social phobia: The effectiveness of a social skills training-based, cognitive-behavioural intervention, with and without parental involvement. *Journal of Child Psychology and Psychiatry, 41,* 713-726.

Spielberger, C. (1973). *Manual for State-Trait Anxiety Interview for Children.* Palo Alto, CA: Consulting Psychologists Press.

Amy Krain (M.A., Temple University, 1999) is a doctoral student in the clinical psychology program at Temple University. She recently completed her clinical psychology internship and is currently a research fellow at the New York University Child Study Center, where she is working on a multisite study of the treatment of anxiety disorders in youth. She is also working with researchers at the Institute of Pediatric Neuroscience to develop a research program that examines the neurobiological correlates of childhood anxiety.

Jennifer L. Hudson *(Ph.D., Macquarie University) is at the Department of Psychology, Macquarie University, in Sydney, Australia. Hudson has authored numerous papers on the nature and treatment of anxiety in youth. She recently coauthored a book on the topic of childhood anxiety and a cognitive-behavioral treatment for anxiety-disordered adolescents (C. A. T. Project). Hudson recently completed a postdoctoral research fellowship at the Child and Adolescent Anxiety Disorders Clinic at Temple University and is currently initiating a National Institute of Mental Health–funded project on the process of therapeutic change within cognitive-behavioral treatment of anxiety in youth.*

Meredith Coles *(M.A., Temple University, 1999) is a doctoral student in the clinical psychology program at Temple University. She is currently a clinical psychology intern at the Boston Consortium. Her research interests include the treatment of child and adult anxiety disorders and the cognitive processes involved in anxiety and worry. She has been a diagnostician and therapist at the Child and Adolescent Anxiety Disorders Clinic and Adult Anxiety Clinic of Temple University.*

Philip Kendall *(Ph.D., Virginia Commonwealth University, 1977) is Laura H. Carnell professor of psychology at Temple University, where he serves as director of the Child and Adolescent Anxiety Disorders Clinic. He is the editor of the* Journal of Consulting and Clinical Psychology. *The author of numerous research papers and monographs, his most recent book is titled* Child and Adolescent Therapy: Cognitive-Behavioral Procedures. *He has also authored treatment materials for youth, such as the* Coping Cat Workbook *and related therapist manuals. He is past president of the Society of Child and Adolescent Clinical Psychololgy of the American Psychiatric Association and the Association for the Advancement of Behavior Therapy. He is currently a principal investigator for two government-funded research studies examining treatments for anxiety-disordered youth.*

10 Narrative Family Therapy

Ethics of Family Narrative Therapy

Christopher Peyton Miller

Central Virginia Community Services

Alan W. Forrest

Radford University

Narrative therapy allows the family to create new meanings for each member of a family while integrating family history. Narrative family counseling should be examined by family counselors for its effects on families and individuals. Potential ethical issues arise when the counselor using narrative methods explores the family's knowledge of itself and each individual's experience within the family. In this article, ethical dilemmas in narrative family therapy are examined and discussed.

Keywords: *ethics; narrative; family therapy*

Goldenberg and Goldenberg (2004) stated, "Our sense of reality is organized and maintained through the stories by which we circulate knowledge about ourselves in the world we inhabit" (p. 343). Narrative family therapy has emerged as a metaphorical tool used by counselors working with families. Narrative methods may be used as an alternative to traditional systemic metaphor (White & Epston, 1990; Zimmerman &

AUTHORS' NOTE: Correspondence concerning this article should be addressed to Alan W. Forrest, Department of Counselor Education, Radford University, P.O. Box 6994, Radford, VA 24142; e-mail: aforrest@radford.edu.

Dickerson, 1994). In narrative family counseling, there are no "true" stories, no fixed "truths," and no master narratives (Freedman & Combs, 1996; Parry & Doan, 1994).

A narrative family counselor is not primarily interested in identifying problems. Rather, a narrative family counselor is focused on conversations produced by numerous possible narratives that coincide with each family member's perspective. Perceptions of life often become self-fulfilling constructs reinforced from within the family narrative (White, 1986). Each individual's story is determined, in part, by the stories of the others in the family with their differing narratives of the family. The narrative family counselor's goal is to assist clients in coconstructing narratives that better fit the individual's goals, while aligning with the family's goals and objectives.

Integrated into narrative family counseling is the deconstruction of the family story. This poststructural strategy can be dangerously disenfranchising to individual members of the family. For example, the primary client may have a narrative that is enveloped by the whole family narrative, thereby limiting an individual client's voice. Thus, an individual's perspective may be lost in the family's meaning-making process that occurs as the family uses narrative methods.

Angus and McLeod (2004) stated, "within this framework (dialectics of meaning making), we will suggest that the narrative framing of emotional processes, at both tacit and conscious levels of awareness, is important in promoting personal change experiences in psychotherapy" (p. 333). In the fictional case of Steve presented below, it should be noted that Steve may feel shame, which could silence his voice in counseling. Conversely, he may fear his private domain becoming public domain to his family. This consequence of narrative family therapy and dialectical meaning making should not be overlooked.

It is our contention that family counseling be critiqued according to its effects on both the family and the individual. Ethical dilemmas of narrative therapy, particularly in the case of Steve, are the focus of this article. It should be noted that a potential ethical issue arises when narrative counseling leads clients to explore the family's knowledge of itself while also encouraging each individual to explore his or her own experiences within the family context.

CASE STUDY

The American Counseling Association (ACA) *Code of Ethics* (2005, p. 7) B.1.d stated, "At initiation and throughout the counseling process, counselors inform clients of the limitations of confidentiality while seeking to identify foreseeable situations in which confidentiality must be breached." In the following fictional case study, the reader might note that it may become necessary for the counselor to disclose information, particularly if one or more family clients display harmful behavior to themselves or others. As it will be explained, Steve Barker, a fictional client, has a history of self-harm. Steve's diagnosis is depression with psychotic features. If Steve's self-destructive behavior manifests during the duration of the therapy relationship—or for that matter, some other harmful behavior or ideation of any member of the family occurs—a crisis plan will result, including an assessment for possible detainment or hospitalization. Clients should be informed that the counselor might disclose this information when the client gives informed consent at the outset of counseling. Furthermore, at the beginning of the counseling relationship, the family must be informed that if outside resources are deemed necessary and appropriate by the client(s) and the counselor, information may be disclosed. However, this information will only be disclosed with client consent on a situational basis with each situation being given written consent by the clients.

Some believe that deconstructionist methods ignore the physical reality of the past. Narrative counseling acknowledges that "animate bodies are already a system of meanings" (Sheets-Johnstone, 1990, p. 122). Our physical experience brings a narrative of descriptive discourse through the medium of feelings (e.g., feeling dirty) and behaviors, such as running away from our loved ones and ourselves. Steve's leaving is a part of the story that this family carries. In addition, the following family narrative includes somatic information that must not be ignored by the narrative counselor.

John and Judy Barker are a couple who have been married for 22 years. They have four children, two daughters, ages 20 and 18, and two sons, Joseph and Steve, ages 15 and 13. The family lives in a small town and the doors and windows of their house are always unlocked. Steve and his brother walk home from school every day. Both John and Judy have full-time jobs. Steve and his brother are latch-key children. As a child, Steve was abused physically by his older brother. One afternoon, Joseph, the older brother, had to stay after school because of misbehavior. Steve walked home alone. On his way home, Steve was taunted, abducted, and sexually assaulted by several men in their early 20s. Steve's parents did not become aware of the sexual abuse until beginning narrative family therapy. All family members described their family as "normal" with no unusual problems.

The family entered therapy per order of the Juvenile and Domestic Relations Court in their county. As a 13-year-old, Steve began to run away from home and experiment with marijuana and hallucinogenic drugs. Periodically, Steve would cut on himself. Steve reported experiencing somatic hallucinations that eventually crippled his mind and he spiraled into psychotic depression. Two weeks after the initial family therapy session, Steve attempted suicide and was hospitalized. He was initially diagnosed with major depressive episode with psychotic features. After a brief period of hospitalization, Steve was discharged and narrative family therapy resumed.

The family counselor began working with the Barkers using narrative family therapy approaches. The family counselor strongly believed that there is potential for people to reconstruct the oppressive story of their lives. However, it seemed very difficult to overcome the physical reality of Steve's trauma. For Steve, the sexual abuse that he endured resulted in his feeling very trapped. Changing his discourse about the trauma seemed to be an insurmountable task.

The family did not know what to do about Steve's trauma. They all proclaimed that they had lived a normal and simple lifestyle. The Barkers purported that they have had an unquestionably safe life history. The difficulty with this family narrative was that it contained elements of denial and did not accurately portray the family's story.

White's (1986) theory involving narrative metaphors and changing or shifting the family's thinking about themselves has its foundation clearly in reauthoring a family history. Peeling away the layers of cognitions, metaphors, and especially physical manifestations of Steve's abuse requires an aggressive use of narrative therapy. Once into the storytelling, the process of challenging metaphorical coherence becomes the focus of the therapy (Lackoff & Johnson, 1980). Lackoff and Johnson (1980, p. 41) reported that

> Charles Fillmore has observed (in conversation) that English appears to have two contradictory organizations of time. In the first, the future is in the front and the past is behind. In the second, the future is behind, the past is in front.

CONSIDERATION OF SELECTED ETHICAL CODES

This front/behind dichotomy is challenged by narrative therapy. When seen individually, each family member has his or her own front/behind metaphors. The history that this family presents challenges the counselor to see beyond the metaphors, helping the family to get beyond the story of the past. This reframe is accomplished by redefining the story in the present. When the counselor redefines the story to the present, he or she assumes several roles and uses techniques that may seem contradictory. The ACA *Code of Ethics* (2005, p. 5) A.7. Multiple Clients stated, "If it becomes apparent that the counselor may be called upon to perform potentially conflicting roles, the counselor will clarify, adjust, or withdraw from roles appropriately." As is the case with family counseling, there are multiple clients in the family. The Barker family must understand that the counselor may need to perform differing and multiple roles within the family story. Confidential information that is revealed by one member will not, without permission, be disclosed to the other members.

Storytelling becomes quite involved and individually challenging. The family counselor must clarify at the beginning and throughout the process of counseling that each individual within the family as well as the family as a whole is a client. In addition, the counselor should seek a there/then, a here/now, and a future narrative with the family. The nature of the family's relationship to the counselor and to one another must be clarified. Furthermore, how each member of the family and the counselor will be involved in the change process must be clarified by the counselor to the family. In the case example, Steve may meet with the counselor alone, face-to-face, and reveal his version of a family condition. Later in therapy, the family may broach this subject; however, the counselor should not reveal what Steve presented during his private meeting with the counselor.

In addition, the International Association of Marriage and Family Counselors (IAMFC) *Ethical Code* (2005) section A.7. stated, "Marriage and family counselors have an obligation to determine and inform counseling participants who is identified as the primary client" (p. 5). This is relevant to the Barker family. Although the precipitating event that led the family to accept counseling was Steve's abduction, assault, and eventual suicidal attempt, the entire family was undoubtedly affected. Yet, it was Steve who was the identified client throughout the period of his hospitalization. Family therapy conceptualizes the whole family as the identified client, yet there are issues that are idiosyncratic to Steve that he brings to the family sessions. For example, no one else in the family attempted suicide. Furthermore, the conditions surrounding the suicide attempt cannot be ignored throughout the treatment process. Steve's suicide attempt may, in fact, be the result of dysfunctional family relational dynamics, which are important to examine in a narrative family session. The counselor should hear each individual family member's narrative regarding the suicide attempt of Steve. However, the family counselor should remain mindful that it is his or her responsibility to clearly discern obligations to the individual member or members of the family while maintaining awareness of the family as a whole unit.

As the Barker family case indicates, family counseling was discontinued while Steve was hospitalized. The IAMFC *Ethical Code* (2005) A.10. specified, "Marriage and family counselors have an obligation to withdraw from a counseling relationship if the continuation of services would not be in the best interest of the client or would result in a violation of ethical standards" (p. 5). Thus, the family counselor must address whether or not counseling continues to be helpful and productive for the Barker family. The counselor should consider whether or not Steve requires ongoing individual counseling for a period of time before family counseling is resumed. The ethical dilemma is to determine what is therapeutically in the best interest of the Barker family. The IAMFC *Ethical Code* (2005) is clear that family counselors are obligated to assist in referring clients (and families) to appropriate services. Moreover, action must be initiated to address the needs of all family members, not just Steve.

The IAMFC *Ethical Code* (2005) presented another issue that needs to be considered in this case: Section B.1. stated, "Marriage and family counselors may disclose private information to others under specific circumstances known to the individual client or client family members" (p. 7). Steve may have disclosed information that had not been previously shared with his family. Subsequently, Steve may have revealed information that is particularly relevant to family understanding and healing. If information is to be introduced into the family sessions that he has discussed individually in counseling, the counselor has a responsibility to obtain an authorization from Steve releasing individual confidential information to all family members. If narrative family therapy is to be valuable and successful, all information needs to be available to the family because each family member may be reauthoring his or her own individual, personal, and family narrative.

Each family member may reveal his or her story to the counselor in individual sessions without concern for their own personal confidentiality. As the course of therapy progresses, these stories may become complicated and contradictory. As stated previously, the counselor should acknowledge that the family is the primary client, while each individual is also a client. The ACA *Code of Ethics* (2005) A.7. required that when there are multiple roles for the counselor, the counselor should discuss his or her multiple roles and any boundary issues that may arise. Furthermore, the counselor should document that he or she has had this discussion with clients including the date and time that the discussion took place.

The front/behind metaphor is especially applicable to the case of Steve. He may have no foresight into the future. The counselor helps to create an open, future-oriented space for Steve to elaborate his story. What has happened in the past will be deconstructed, while remaining a secondary part of Steve's narrative, as Steve begins his process of reauthoring his past. Thus, Steve will hopefully begin to see the past through a different lens, choosing to replace what he has previously encoded as a negative story with an optimal story, thereby facilitating a positive future outlook.

The space reserved for Steve's future unique outcomes may be elicited with appropriately phrased and carefully constructed questions. Using the idea metaphor as a resource, "let's pool our ideas" is a type of metaphor (Lackoff & Johnson, 1980) that may be used with Steve. In this metaphor, the counselor and client consider the ideas of Steve's narrative and the therapist being able to gather information together in a way that is inclusive of Steve's narrative, this metaphor is likened to this gathering together of important ideas. Denoting Steve's strengths as resources, the counselor should combine his or her resources with Steve so that the Barkers' family history is reframed showing the complementariness of the narrative approach while using a strengths-based approach.

Narrative therapy should only be practiced by those well trained in dealing with the entanglement of stories that can arise from a family situation. The ACA *Code of Ethics* (2005, p. 9) is clear about professional responsibility: C.2 f. continuing education; the counselor is "to maintain a reasonable level of awareness . . . maintain competence." The Barker family can only benefit from the further training of the counselor who expands his or her abilities to operationalize theory. Further research and investigation of narrative techniques and theory will prepare the counselor as new stories arise in the Barker family.

SUMMARY

The narrative therapy approach allows the family to create new meanings for each member of a family while recreating and reframing the past. New perspectives enhance family development, as the family counselor maintains a therapeutic posture abiding within the ethics of counseling and family therapy. This may be challenging to the counselor who integrates stories told by the identified client and the family. In this article, narrative approaches that adhere to the ethical demands of the ACA and the IAMFC have been discussed, thus presenting that these approaches are well grounded in theory and applicable to clinical settings.

The first principle of counseling is to do no harm. Narrative strategy offers an approach that deals with difficult issues. Indeed, in narrative approaches, clients may reauthor and restory previously harmful situations. The authors also discussed that counselors must respect confidentiality and honor boundaries of the family and its narrative. It is necessary for counselors to inform the family that each family member's territory or emotional grounding is important. In addition, the counselor should designate who the identified client is at times of family dysfunction.

As family counselors, we must continually be cognizant of what is in the best interest of the client and the family with whom we are working. In narrative family therapy, we must work assiduously toward creating a healthy redefined past while building a future that is protected, in the present, by a family counselor who is aware of professional counseling ethics.

SOURCE: Christopher Peyton Miller and Alan W. Forrest. (2009). Ethics of Family Narrative Therapy. *The Family Journal: Counseling and Therapy for Couples and Families, 17,* 156-159. © 2009 SAGE Publications.

REFERENCES

American Counseling Association. (2005). *Code of ethics.* Alexandria, VA: Author.

Angus, L., & McLeod, J. (Eds.). (2004). *The handbook of narrative and psychotherapy: Practice, theory, and research.* London: Sage.

Freedman, J., & Combs, G. (1996). *Narrative therapy: The social construction of preferred realities.* New York: Guilford.

Goldenberg, I., & Goldenberg, H. (2004). *Family therapy: An overview* (6th ed.). Pacific Grove, CA: Thomson Learning.

International Association of Marriage and Family Counselors. (2005). *Ethical code.* Alexandria, VA: Author.

Lackoff, G., & Johnson, M. (1980). *Metaphors we live by.* Chicago: University of Chicago Press.

Parry, A., & Doan, R. E. (1994). *Story re-visions: Narrative therapy in the postmodern world.* New York: Guilford.

Sheets-Johnstone, M. (1990). *The roots of thinking.* Philadelphia: Temple University Press.

White, M. (1986). Negative explanation, restraint, and double description: A template for family therapy. *Family Process, 25,* 169-184.

White, M., & Epston, D. (1990). *Narrative means to therapeutic ends.* New York: W. W. Norton.

Zimmerman, J. L., & Dickerson, V. C. (1994). Using a narrative metaphor: Implications for theory and clinical practice. *Family Process, 33,* 233-245.

_____

Christopher Peyton Miller, *Child and Family Center, Central Virginia Community Services, Bedford, Virginia.*

Alan W. Forrest, *Department of Counselor Education, Radford University, Radford, Virginia.*

Review of Narrative Therapy

Research and Utility

Mary Etchison
David M. Kleist
Idaho State University

Narrative therapy has captured the attention of many in the family counseling field. Despite the apparent appeal of narrative therapy as a therapeutic modality, research on its effectiveness is in its infancy. This article will review current research on narrative therapy and discuss why a broader research base has yet to be developed. Suggestions for practitioners also will be provided.

Narrative therapy is an increasingly used therapeutic modality (Cowley & Springen, 1995). Narrative approaches to therapy have been discussed in popular written media and academic journals ranging from the *Journal of Consulting and Clinical Psychology* and *Family Therapy Networker* to *The Family Journal*. Hevern (1999) reports more than 2,000 bibliographic narrative therapy resources of scholarly articles, book chapters and full texts, and doctoral dissertations. O'Hanlon (1994) posits that a narrative approach to therapy "represents a fundamentally new direction in the therapeutic world" and is "the third wave" (p. 22).

Narrative therapy refers to a range of social constructionist and constructivist approaches to the process of therapeutic change. Change occurs by exploring how language is used to construct and maintain problems. Interpretation of one's experience in the world serves as the essence of the narrative approach to therapy (Cowley & Springen, 1995). Experiences are collapsed into narrative structures or stories to give a frame of reference for understanding and making experiences understandable. White and Epston (1990) state that narrative therapy is based on the idea that problems are manufactured in social, cultural, and political contexts. To deepen understanding, problems have to be viewed from the context in which they are situated. Viewing the context includes exploring society as a whole and exploring the impact of various aspects of culture that help to create and/or maintain the problem. White and Denborough (1998) relate how people's lives and relationships are shaped by the stories they develop to give meaning to experiences. For example, in our culture, people who experience hardships are sometimes seen as failures or deficient in some ways. They may view themselves as the problem and create stories of themselves that depict a lack of power and worth. Problems may not be seen by them as external events that affect and influence their lives and, thus, are maintained. Narrative therapy deals specifically with these stories as the loci of effective therapeutic goal setting.

Narrative therapy is goal directed. Monk, Winslade, Crocket, and Epston (1997) comment that the primary goal of narrative therapy is to form an alliance with clients that accesses, encourages, and promotes abilities to enhance relationships with one's self and with others. Narrative therapy aims to refuse to see people as problems and to help them to see themselves as separate from problems. White and Epston (1990) state that once a person sees a problem as separate from the person's identity, the opportunity for change has been created. This change can take the form of behaving differently, resisting or protesting the problem, and/or negotiating the relationship with the problem in other ways. Narrative therapy's goals uniquely affect the therapeutic process.

The creation of alternative stories anchors narrative therapy's therapeutic process (Monk et al., 1997). It is a process that recognizes that humans are growing and that each moment offers opportunities to create an alternative story that builds on strengths and desired outcomes for a satisfying life. Historical acts of resisting damaging stories or depictions of self and relationships are explored as evidence of the person's ability to create alternative stories. Honoring everyday actions of resistance by externalizing conversations is depicted by narrative therapy as a way to begin to reclaim lives. Recognizing these actions as strengths can help people in the process of creating alternative stories. Anecdotal reports of the effectiveness of this process make narrative therapy attractive to clinicians.

Despite the apparent attraction to narrative therapy, research on its utility is sparse. A review of existing literature uncovered a limited number of studies. This review will examine these studies, explore possible reasons for the scarcity of research on the utility of narrative therapy, and discuss implications for practitioners.

REDUCING PARENT-CHILD CONFLICTS

Besa (1994) examined the effectiveness of narrative therapy in reducing parent-child conflicts. Besa initiated this research in response to anecdotal reports in the literature of dramatic success in the treatment of parent-child problems using narrative approaches. Parent-child conflict was defined as defiant behavior, keeping bad company, abuse of drugs, school problems, and other conduct problems. Participants consisted of six families with children between the ages of 8 and 17 years old. The families were selected from those families who presented with a parent-child conflict at a clinical setting providing individual, group, family, and marital therapy to low- to moderate-income clients.

The authors chose a single case research design to avoid using methods that relied on classification, pathologizing, or diagnostic categories to study the effectiveness of narrative therapy. Parents were trained to take baseline measurements of the targeted behavior and monitored their child's progress by counting the frequency of specific behaviors during baseline and intervention phases. The target behavior was the child's problem behavior that the family wanted to decrease and around which there was a parent-child conflict. The target behavior was defined in measurable terms, such as not doing chores, arguing, not doing homework, and so forth. A tracking form was developed to monitor the child's behavior, focusing on the specific behavior targeted for intervention. Results were evaluated using three multiple baseline designs.

Treatment used several narrative therapy techniques. Techniques included externalization (speaking of the problem as separate from the individual), relative influence questioning (exploring the influence of the problem on the individual and the individual on the problem), identifying unique outcomes and unique accounts (identifying times when there were exceptions to the problem), bringing forth unique redescriptions (attaching new meaning to behavior), and assigning between-session tasks (continuing work begun in session between sessions). Examples of these techniques included exploring exceptions to drinking and abuse, defining study habits as problems instead of the child as the problem, attaching new meaning to behavior as a desire to cooperate as opposed to attention seeking, and the assignment of engaging in cooperative activities instead of arguing.

Five of six families showed improvements, ranging from an 88% to a 98% decrease in parent-child conflicts with narrative therapy. No improvements were observed in the absence of narrative therapy. The authors concluded that in five of the six cases studied, narrative interventions were the probable cause for the changes observed. It suggests that narrative therapy was effective in reducing parent-child conflicts and would be applicable to families experiencing parent-child conflicts under conditions similar to the families involved in this study. The results supported anecdotal accounts of success in the literature.

CLIENT EXPERIENCE OF NARRATIVE THERAPY

St. James-O'Connor, Meakes, Pickering, and Schuman (1997) examined families' perceptions of their narrative therapy experience and the meaning that these families attributed to this experience. The study sought to discover what families found helpful and unhelpful in their therapeutic experience.

Eight families who were experiencing problems with children ranging in age from 6 to 13 participated in the study. Five families were headed by single parents and three were headed by more than one parent. The families selected presented with serious problems, including conduct disorders, family violence, grief associated with parental divorce and/or death, school problems, aggression with siblings and others, attention deficit/hyperactivity disorder (ADHD), and refusal to obey rules and direction. The researchers selected these families because they were currently being seen in family screenings by the narrative team at a university hospital outpatient clinic.

The researchers used an ethnographic research design guided by the question "What is the family's experience of narrative therapy?" The authors chose this design for three reasons: The research question required the possibility of complex responses, the practice and process of narrative therapy shared similarities with an ethnographic interview, and participants were viewed as coresearchers. The authors employed a semistandardized interview format using four questions aimed at developing a rich description of the families' perceptions: (a) What has been helpful in therapy? (b) What has not been helpful in therapy? (c) What is your overall experience of narrative therapy? and (d) What is an image or symbol to describe your experience of therapy? Each question included subsequent questions that could be used to facilitate a richer description. The interviewers were students who completed a graduate course in qualitative research and training in interviewing skills. The interviews were audiotaped and transcribed verbatim. Data were then coded using latent and manifest content analysis designed to recognize themes, commonalities, and differences.

Six major themes consistent with a narrative therapy paradigm emerged from the data. They were (a) externalizing conversation, (b) unique occurrence and alternate story, (c) developing personal agency, (d) consulting and reflecting teams, (e) building the audience, and (f) the helpful and unhelpful aspects of therapy. The following examples were noted by the clients:

1. "The therapist was not into blaming anyone for the problem. I like that. In our situation what was found was not one person in particular."

2. "The air is not so thick in the house anymore. It's more like a home . . . It's nice to hear her laugh and play like a kid should instead of sitting there watching TV."

3. "My therapist and the team behind the mirror told me that I was doing a good job and that I had a lot of solutions myself. I received a lot of compliments from the team and I believed them after a while."

4. "I found that they sat around together and talked to each other about what they saw instead of discussing it directly with me. They discussed it as if I were not there."

5. "So there is a sense that at least I'm on the right track. That is helpful. Solutions may come because there is a process to involve the family, the school."

6. "Both the therapists we had obviously cared. They were supportive and listened."

The authors concluded that the results supported the view of narrative therapy as empowering personal agency in family members. They observed that all of the family members reported some reduction in the presenting problem. The reduction of problems was greater in families involved in narrative therapy for longer periods than in families involved for shorter periods. The authors explain that this result may be due to the family making a number of cognitive shifts during the narrative therapy process. The results suggest that narrative therapy should continue as a viable therapeutic model for working with families. The results also indicate that an ethnographic method of inquiry is congruent with research on narrative therapy.

CHILDREN'S ATTRIBUTIONS ABOUT FAMILY ARGUMENTS

Weston, Boxer, and Heatherington (1998) initiated an exploratory descriptive study to examine children's attributions or stories about the causes of family arguments between marital partners and between parent and child. They sought to increase understanding of children's cognitions and their implications for therapeutic interventions.

Participants consisted of 92 children between the ages of 5 and 12 years old. The children were from predominately White, middle-class, two-parent families recruited by newspaper advertisements and pubic notices. Three single-parent families were unintentionally recruited, and these children participated in the parent-child argument group only.

The researchers used audiotaped family arguments and structured interviews to gather data from participant families. Two audiotaped arguments, one of a parent-parent conflict and one of a parent-child argument, were used as a stimulus for the children to recall arguments from their own families. Two identical versions of the parent-child conflict tapes were used to avoid confounding gender with the parent role. In one version, the parent was the mother, and in the other version, the parent was the father. The actors were a male and a female college student who were both theater majors and an 11-year-old female. The 11-year-old was depicted by the authors as having a gender-neutral voice. Children were randomly assigned to hear one or the other audiotape. In both the parent-parent script and the parent-child script, the argument was of low to medium intensity with a clear presence of conflict. Five structured interview instruments were used to gather data on arguments between parents, child's perceptions of parents' conflicts and parental divorce, parent-child arguments, and affect. Researchers used a pictorial scale to assist the children in identifying their perceptions.

The means from data obtained were rank ordered from the most strongly to the least strongly endorsed causes for parent-parent and parent-child arguments and their solutions. The data were statistically analyzed using a repeated-measures ANOVA.

The authors noted that, consistent with developmental literature, the use of open-ended questions was difficult for some of the children. They stated that the use of more creative information strategies, such as storytelling and the use of props, would be a more useful method. They found that the children between the ages of 6 and 12 were able to easily think about and respond to the structured questions concerning the causes of conflict between parent and parent and between parent and child. The 5-year-old children showed variation in their ability to comprehend the task. Some responded very thoughtfully, whereas others responded more briefly. Overall, the authors concluded that all of the children did make attributions in a meaningful way. There was consistency across ages in the ranking of the children's attributions. For example, in marital arguments, children of all ages viewed each parent differently. Father trait items were consistently ranked higher than father state items. The authors illustrated that children would rank "the dad is the kind of person that likes to argue" higher than "it's because the dad had a bad day." In contrast, mother state items were consistently rated higher than mother trait items. Attributing causes of parental conflict to mothers' traits was consistently low across all age groups. The authors noted that contrary to what would be predicted based on developmental literature and conventional wisdom, the children's stories about family conflict reflected a systemic perception of the conflict. Two highly ranked examples cited were "when parents argue, it's both of their faults" and "when parents and kids argue, it's because the parents want things one way and the kid wants them another way." The children also showed consistency in their hesitancy to rank a lack of affection as a cause of conflict. The authors recognized that this might be due to the sample of intact, nonclinical families who participated in the study. The authors also acknowledged that denial of such a cause might be defensive. They state that because children are unlikely to embrace this attribution, it could be clinically significant when they do. The authors found that the children's attributions concerning internal traits support literature that suggests that children are more likely to give a favorable attribution when evaluating inconsistent behaviors. They noted that "mom had a bad day" is more likely to be endorsed than "it's because mom is the kind of person who likes to argue." The authors also observed a gender/role difference in attributions. These different attributions may reflect a possible closer affective bond with the mother, more verbalization by the mother, or increased time spent with the mother. The study concluded that most children can easily incorporate the concepts of interpersonal causality and multiple perspectives about the causes of parent-parent and parent-child conflict when they are encouraged to think calmly about family arguments. These findings suggest a compatibility with constructivist clinical approaches, such as narrative therapy and family counseling. The authors posit that appreciating children's stories or attributions of causes of family conflict can aid therapeutic work with the family as a whole. The study demonstrated that a combination of quantitative and qualitative research methodology could be useful for studying narrative therapy.

TRANSFORMING INITIAL CONSTRUCTION OF THE PROBLEM

Coulehan, Friedlander, and Heatherington (1998) studied clients' processes of transforming their construction of the presenting problem from an individual intrapersonal perspective to an interpersonal systemic or relational perspective in initial therapy sessions. Building on the work of Carlos Sluzki's (1992) narrative approach to therapy, their exploratory study sought to make explicit the components of the change process involved in therapists facilitating family members' successful transformation of narratives.

Eight families and eight therapists (five Ph.D. psychologists, one psychiatrist, and five master's-level counselors/social workers) participated in the study conducted at an outpatient clinic of a major teaching hospital in the east. The eight families included two intact, one remarried, four single-parented, and one family headed by grandparents. The criteria for inclusion as a participant family were as follows: (a) An adult family member requested help and identified an adolescent or child older than age 8 as the source of the problem and (b) on the basis of the initial telephone call, the therapist believed a transformation was warranted. Multiple problems were identified by the parents during the initial telephone contact, including problems of academic failure, noncompliance, violence, eating disturbances, and so forth. Several of the children were currently or previously placed in foster home or residential settings. All of the therapists were extensively trained in Sluzki's (1992) approach to narrative family therapy. Sluzki asserts that problems are maintained and embedded in the stories that family members use in describing the problem and that the therapist and family members cogenerate qualitative changes in those stories as part of the therapeutic process. Success is achieved when "a transformation has taken place in the family's set of dominant stories so as to include new experiences, meanings, and actions, with the effect of loosening of the thematic grip of the set of stories on symptomatic-problematic behavior" (p. 219). When possible, reflecting teams were used during intake interviews.

Participant families' initial interviews were videotaped, with postsession questionnaires designed to elicit the parent's descriptions of the problems. The researchers also administered questionnaires to the therapist, staff observers, and three master's-level therapists not affiliated with the clinic at the time of data collection to identify sessions in which a shift in constructions did or did not take place.

In addition, researchers used an observational coding system to provide an alternative indicator of the parents' construction of the problem. The coding system was used to code the referring parent's description of the problem during the initial telephone contact and all parents' descriptions in the actual session. The coding process involved locating the problem and causes. The judges first read the transcript in its entirety and then reread it carefully line by line. Three criteria were identified for locating a problem description: when the speaker (a) used words such as difficulty, problem, or conflict; (b) responded to inquiry about the problem; or (c) described a negative emotional state or attitude, problematic reaction, condition, diagnosis, or impasse, implying a need for change. Only those problems coded identically by at least two of the three judges were retained for analysis.

Videotapes were transcribed verbatim. A qualitative method of constant comparison was used to analyze the data. The authors chose this method to mirror the theoretical foundations of the narrative approach under investigation. A multiple perspective and consensual procedure was used to develop the model from the data and reduce the potential of bias.

Twenty-five verbatim problem statements, all involving children, were transcribed and coded for the initial telephone screenings; 76% were coded as intrapersonal. There was no difference in the number of problem statements made by parents in the successful and unsuccessful groups. In all of the sessions, coding of the problems' descriptions made by the parents early in the therapy session reflected the intrapersonal view expressed in the telephone contact. The authors observed that at the conclusion, in three of the four successful sessions, the parents' descriptions had shifted to an interpersonal and systemic view. In the additional successful session, the parents' descriptions remained intrapersonal, but the description of the problem behavior focused on a different child.

The authors reported, in contrast, that in three of the four unsuccessful sessions, the parents' descriptions remained intrapersonal throughout the session with a tendency for the parents to express individual problems of their own, such as "I have a tendency to scream," as well as those of the children. The parents in the remaining unsuccessful session did not express constructions during the interview.

The study resulted in a three-stage conceptual model of transformation that was consistent with, yet added to, Sluzki's (1992) pioneering work. The first stage describes the process of family members' articulation of multiple views and descriptions of the problem. These multiple descriptions and views formed an expanded content to base alternate descriptions, attributions, and meanings of the problem. The second stage describes the process of a shift in family members' affective tone. The third stage describes the process of family members' exploration of positive aspects of both individual family members and the family as a whole. The authors instruct that successful transformations of the problem will move through each of the three stages, whereas unsuccessful transformations will not. They also posited that the presence of reflecting teams in successful families might have contributed equally or more influentially to transforming problems.

The aforementioned studies provide support for the use of narrative approaches to working with families. However, support for the use of narrative approaches with families is at best tentative given the small number of clinical studies. A variety of reasons for this small number of studies are possible.

POSSIBLE REASONS FOR SCARCITY OF STUDIES

Neimeyer (1993) has stated that meaningful attention to research on the utility of language-based therapy modalities, such as narrative therapy, is limited by the recent emergence of constructivism as a clinical and empirical paradigm. Unique epistemological and methodological requirements for researchers embracing such a constructivist orientation exist that are sometimes inconsistent with traditional quantitative empirical research methods (Gale, 1993), leading to very few outcome studies (Neimeyer, 1993), for example, constructivists' denial of the possibility of objectivity, which forms the foundation of quantitative empiricism (Kelley, 1998). In contrast, constructivist approaches to researching therapy emphasize a qualitative understanding of one's meaning given to experience (Nelson & Poulin, 1997) in context, without imposing the requirement of researcher objectivity. Participants and researchers in qualitative inquiry are regarded as coresearchers (Gale, 1993) who together explore the meaning of experience. Constructivist-based research places importance on the interaction between participants and researcher as a necessary component for quality data gathering and analysis (Merchant, 1997). Qualitative research looks thoroughly into how people make meaning as well as how and why they think and behave as they do (Ambert, Adler, Adler, & Detzner, 1995). The essence of narrative therapy approaches, as stated earlier, is interpreting and giving meaning to experience. Because qualitative approaches to inquiry emphasize understanding experience (Nelson & Poulin, 1997), they are particularly suited to researching the effectiveness of narrative therapy.

Another reason for the shortage of research on the utility of narrative therapy may be researchers' lack of training in qualitative methodology. Merchant (1997) depicts most counseling training programs as emphasizing quantitative research methodology, almost to the exclusion of quantitative modes of inquiry. Because most journal editorial boards are composed of graduates of such programs, journals may be reluctant to accept research using alternative modes of inquiry. According to Ambert et al. (1995),

> Editorial boards of high-profile journals in family studies, psychology, and sociology are composed of well-published scholars, only a minority of whom are experienced qualitative researchers. The result is that a majority of the qualitative articles submitted have to be evaluated by scholars who have little experience in qualitative research, or who have little experience in the substantive area of a submitted article or who subscribe to a different epistemology. (pp. 879-880)

IMPLICATIONS FOR PRACTITIONERS

The studies reviewed in this article demonstrate that narrative approaches to therapy have useful application when working with a variety of family therapy issues. However, the breadth of research on the utility of narrative therapy approaches is limited. Certainly no statement can be made about narrative therapy as the approach to use for any particular family problem. This, however, should not preclude family counselors from using narrative approaches. As has been argued, narrative therapy is based on principles that are congruent with context-sensitive research methodologies (e.g., ethnography, grounded theory) that de-emphasize generalizability. For family counselors, the issue, then, turns to tailoring treatment to fit your client. Call yourself a narrative-based family counselor but be prepared to modify (i.e., tailor) your way of doing narrative-based family counseling to the unique dynamics of your clients. These unique counseling contexts can provide practitioners an opportunity to become researchers, potentially leading to unique outcomes and redescriptions of how narrative therapy can inform the work of family counselors.

SOURCE: Mary Etchison and David M. Kleist. (2000). Review of Narrative Therapy: Research and Utility. *The Family Journal: Counseling and Therapy for Couples and Families, 8,* 61-66. © 2000 SAGE Publications.

REFERENCES

Ambert, A., Adler, P. A., Adler, P., & Detzner, D. F. (1995). Understanding and evaluating qualitative research. *Journal of Marriage & Family, 57,* 879-893.

Besa, D. (1994). Evaluating narrative family therapy using single system research designs. *Research on Social Work Practice, 4,* 309-326.

Coulehan, R., Friedlander, M., & Heatherington, L. (1998). Transforming narratives: A change event in constructivist family therapy. *Family Process, 37,* 17-33.

Cowley, G., & Springen, K. (1995). Rewriting life stories. *Newsweek, 125*(16), 70-74.

Gale, J. (1993). A field guide to qualitative inquiry and its clinical relevance. *Contemporary Family Therapy, 15*, 73-92.

Hevern, V. W. (1999). *Narrative psychology: Internet and resource guide*. Syracuse, NY: Author. Retrieved from the World Wide Web: http://maple.lemoyne/narpsych.html

Kelley, P. (1998). Narrative therapy in a managed care world. *Crisis Intervention and Time Limited Treatment, 4*, 113-123.

Merchant, N. (1997). Qualitative research for counselors. *Counseling & Human Development, 30*(1), 1-20.

Monk, C., Winslade, J., Crocket, K., & Epston, D. (1997). *Narrative therapy in practice, the archaeology of hope*. San Francisco: Jossey-Bass.

Neimeyer, R. A. (1993). An appraisal of constructivist psychotherapies. *Journal of Consulting & Clinical Psychology, 61*(2), 221-234.

Nelson, M. L., & Poulin, K. (1997). Methods of constructivist inquiry. In T. L. Sexton & B. L. Griffin (Eds.), *Constructivist thinking in counseling practice, research, and training* (pp. 157-173). New York: Teachers College Press.

O'Hanlon, B. (1994). The third wave. *Family Therapy Networker, 18*, 19-29.

Sluzki, C. E. (1992). Transformations: A blueprint for narrative changes in therapy. *Family Process, 31*, 217-230.

St. James-O'Connor, T., Meakes, E., Pickering, M., & Schuman, M. (1997). On the right track: Client experience of narrative therapy. *Contemporary Family Therapy: An International Journal, 19*, 479-495.

Weston, H. E., Boxer, P., & Heatherington, L. (1998). Children's attributions about family arguments: Implications for family therapy. *Family Process, 37*, 35-49.

White, C., & Denborough, D. (1998). *Introducing narrative therapy, a collection of practice based writings*. Adelaide, South Australia: Dulwich Centre Publications.

White, M., & Epston, D. (1990). *Narrative means to therapeutic ends*. New York: Norton.

Mary Etchison is a doctoral student in the Department of Counseling at Idaho State University.

David M. Kleist is an assistant professor in the Department of Counseling at Idaho State University.

11 Phases of Family Therapy

Basic Principles of Intervention

Mark S. Carich

Adler School of Professional Psychology
Big Muddy River Correctional Center

Karen Spilman

Big Muddy River Correctional Center

This is Dr. Robert Sherman's final column as editor of the Techniques to Share column. We appreciate the significant time and effort that Robert has devoted to making the column such a valuable section of The Family Journal. Thank you, Robert, for an excellent job.

Psychotherapy can be a complex process, as noted by a number of writers in the field. Each view consists of a specific theoretical perspective with techniques espoused from that particular author. There are literally thousands of techniques, ranging from cognitive, cognitive-behavioral, and behavioral to hypnotic. In this article, 12 generic principles of interventions were distilled from across the field of therapeutic models. These are generic in the sense that each principle can be applied to almost any technique or therapeutic situation. The principles can be applied to techniques. These 12 principles include respect, rapport, joining, compassion, cooperation, flexibility, utilization principle, safety principle, generative change, metaphoric principle, goal orientation, and multi-level communication principle. Collectively, they provide a practical framework and guide for the practitioner to conduct the treatment in a way that is appropriate to most popular theories.

Keywords: *principles; intervention; therapy*

Psychotherapy of any type involves a process or exchange of information (communication) between the therapist and client in a therapeutic context. Zeig and Munion (1990) stated, "Psychotherapy is a change-oriented process that occurs in the context of a contractual, empowering, and empathetic professional relationship . . . the process is idiosyncratic and determined by the interaction of the patients' and therapists' preconceived positions" (p. 14). They further emphasized that the principles and views of the therapists (or models) affect how data is organized. Zeig and Munion stated, "The model is not only a philosophy, it is also perceptual in that it becomes a lens. This lens tells the practitioner what to look for and respond to in the therapeutic encounter" (p. 14).

Therapy involves communication or an exchange of behaviors (or information) between the therapist and client within a specific context (Becvar & Becvar, 1982). The context is defined by the goal of helping the client system create change. The authors emphasize that any therapy session can be segmented or arbitrarily divided into a series of techniques or communicative behaviors because all behavior is considered communicative (Becvar & Becvar, 1982; Zeig & Munion, 1999). A therapeutic technique is a behavior aimed at evoking a therapeutic response toward treatment goals.

Thus, when using any therapeutic technique, it is important to keep in mind the basic principles that help facilitate the delivery and input of interventions. Such principles are guidelines in the delivery of interventions.

There are a variety of principles of intervention depending on the specific theory of therapy and unique style of the clinician. There is such diversity among these theories that over the past 100 years there has been little consensus among therapists on problem formation (Haley, 1997), let alone treatment principles.

The principles were selected from a variety of models. They are generic because these principles transcend any theoretical/therapeutic model. They are considered generic because they can be applied to almost any technique originating from a given model.

To cut through this confusion, we have examined many theories and models and abstracted from them 12 selected principles that are essential. These selected principles are generic in that they are found in many models and orientations, including, but not exclusively, in Adlerian, cognitive, cognitive-behavioral, Ericksonian, existential, systemic/cybernetics, and Rogerian, among others. Some of the principles overlap with each other in that they may be differently labeled within any given theory. They are presented below.

PRINCIPLES

Many clinicians assume a rather eclectic method of practice. Therefore, the theme of this article is to present 12 generic principles that can be used with any therapeutic technique to enhance a successful response or treatment outcome.

These 12 principles include: respect, rapport, joining, compassion, cooperation, flexibility, utilization principle, safety principle, generative change, metaphoric principle, goal orientation, and multi-level communication principle (Keeney, 1983; Zeig, 1980, 1987; Zeig & Munion, 1999). Collectively, they provide a practical framework and guide for the practitioner to conduct the treatment in a way that is appropriate to most popular theories.

Respect

Respect occurs in different levels and dimensions, as outlined by Carkhuff's (1969) five levels: attention to, informing and consulting with, suggesting rather than commanding, and listening carefully to the client. Respect is defined as acknowledging, recognizing, and accepting the individual as one is (Carkhuff, 1969; Zeig & Munion, 1999). This involves accepting clients as troubled persons with behaviors, problems, lifestyles, and so on, which may not be acceptable to the clinician. Clients are viewed as manifesting unique lifestyles and personal or cultural characteristics that may be unfamiliar or unacceptable to the clinician. Clients should also be viewed as individual beings with differences (Zeig & Munion, 1999). For example, when working with sex offenders, the clinician does not accept or condone the offending behaviors but accepts the client as a person to facilitate therapeutic change and is, somehow, respectful of the offender.

In general, clients are sensitive to and perceptive of the clinician's behavior. They unconsciously perceive and react to the clinician's attitude toward them. Disrespect, or lack or respect, will lead to hindrances in therapeutic work. Most orientations have long emphasized the need to respect the client (Corsini, 1979; Corsini & Wedding, 1989; de Shazer, 1985; Dinkmeyer, Dinkmeyer, & Sperry, 1987; Dreikurs, 1967; Haley, 1967; Manaster & Corsini, 1982; Minuchin, 1974; Zeig & Munion, 1999).

Rapport

Rapport is a relationship that is essential to therapeutic work and change (Dinkmeyer et al., 1987; Dreikurs, 1967; Zeig & Munion, 1999). Rapport is the relationship in which involved parties have developed common psychological understanding. In the context of therapy, rapport is the harmonious relationship with the client that will promote understanding of the client's issues and facilitates the delivery of interventions. A harmonious relationship is one that includes trust, connectedness, willingness to be together, and general good feelings toward the other person. For example, a client will tolerate intense confrontation as long as there is rapport. Rapport is developed and facilitated by identifying with and joining the client

(Carich, 1989b). It is necessary that the connection is an emotional tie between therapist and client.

Joining

Joining the client refers to the way in which the clinician identifies with the client. Client identification, originated by Adler (Carich, 1989a; O'Connell & Gomez, 1990), has more recently been referred to as joining the client. Joining is psychologically entering the client's frame of reference to add dimension in helping or guiding the client toward constructive goals. Minuchin (1974), Minuchin and Fishman (1981), and Erickson (Zeig, 1987; Zeig & Munion, 1999) have more fully developed joining as a technique, principle, and attitude.

Joining occurs in levels. To join the client, the clinician accepts, identifies, and adapts to the client. The therapist adapts to the client by acknowledging and enjoying the client within his or her own world (Zeig & Munion, 1999). The client's behavior is utilized toward therapeutic goals (Zeig, 1992). This does not mean that the clinician is in complete agreement with the client but rather accepts the client's position at face value (i.e., the clinician accepts whatever is presented by the client in an objective manner, can equate or associate with the issues of the client, and adapts therapeutic goals to fit the specific position of the client). For example, if the client reports being in a state of depression, the therapist enters the client's world of depression. The client's depressive world is entered by matching the client's depressive language, demeanor, and nonverbal behaviors. Joining is identifying with the client system, which may mimic or just acknowledge and show understanding of the client's world, which is a form of overt empathy.

Compassion

Compassion is another important principle of intervention (Zeig & Munion, 1999). Compassion is the empathetic understanding of the client and refers to the affective cognitive response and behavioral display of care and concern. Carkhuff (1969) divided empathy into five levels, as follows:

- Level 1: The verbal and nonverbal expressions of the clinician neither enhance nor detract from what is being communicated by the client. They simply are an indication to the client that the clinician is actively and attentively listening.
- Level 2: The clinician responds to the affect (unspoken or implied communications) of the client.
- Level 3: The clinician recognizes that the client has deeper feelings than those being expressed but responds only to what is being communicated by the

client at that moment. The response of the clinician is controlled so as not to add to or subtract from the expressions of the client.

- Level 4: The response from the clinician is stated in such a way as to lead the client to seek deeper feeling or meaning in his or her expression.
- Level 5: The clinician responds to the client with a full sense of awareness of who the client is and with a comprehensive and accurate empathetic understand of the client's deepest feelings (insight).

Empathy is perspective-taking; based on understanding the client and communicating that understanding back to the client.

Likewise, compassion can arbitrarily be divided into levels. Compassion and empathy can be an emotional trap if the clinician becomes overly involved or enmeshed within the client system. This is considered to be sympathy. The clinician's involvement with the client is subjective and is carefully managed so as to avoid client traps or becoming ensnarled in the client's problematic context. De Shazer (1985) claimed that the clinician automatically becomes part of the client's problematic context on entering into the therapeutic interactional level of the client/clinician system. This initially occurs at the interactional level of the client's problematic system. The clinician then becomes the catalyst for changing a problematic system into a nonproblematic system.

Another aspect of compassion is subjectivism. Therapy, like any human phenomena, is a subjective process. Objectivity is only relative to the observer (Keeney, 1983; Keeney & Rossi, 1983). Keeney (1983) used the concept of self-reference to describe the relationship between subjectivity and objectivity. Self-reference means that the observer is attached to the observation or the perceiver to the perception. In therapy, total objectivity is a myth, as the clinician expresses his or her attitudes unconsciously and/or non-verbally to the client. It is important for clinicians to be aware of their own biases as well as the disposition of the client. Being empathetic helps clinicians maintain impartiality and identify more closely with the client. Empathy involves a "willingness to understand the client's perceptual frames and motivation" (Zeig & Munion, 1999).

Cooperation

Cooperation is a central Adlerian principle (Dreikurs, 1959, 1967, 1972; Dinkmeyer et al., 1987) from which one of the goals in therapy is to gain cooperation with the client. Cooperation involves respect and a willingness to participate and is a mutual agreement at some level. Positive cooperation is based on equality and is not a game of one-upmanship, as is negative cooperation. Therapy is a win/win relationship, not a win/lose relationship. Win/lose relationships lead to power struggles, which in turn lead to revenge. Power struggles, revengeful interactions, equality or win/win, and win/lose relationships all require continuous cooperation (Dreikurs, 1959).

Dreikurs (1959, p. 13) contended that all parties in a relationship cooperate fully, stating,

> Every relationship, regardless of its kind and pattern, requires such cooperation that unless two people agree about the way in which they intend to treat each other, they could not deal with each other. Cooperation is the basis of all human relationships,

including conflict. Cooperation, in a process of change, may involve discomfort or risk taking and requires the commitment of the client.

Flexibility

Flexibility is the key principle in therapeutic work, whereas rigidity leads to restricted responses or interventions (Bandler & Grinder, 1979). Flexibility is defined as pliability. It allows the clinician more movement and thus a wider range of intervention. Bandler and Grinder (1979, p. 74) described flexibility as follows:

> In cybernetics there is a law called the Requisite Variety. It says that in any system of human beings or machines, the element in that system with the widest range of variability is going to allow you to elicit responses and control the situation. (p. 74)

Haley (1967) furthered the usefulness of flexibility in discussing Don Jackson and Milton Erickson's work as he stated,

> To deal with the varieties of human dilemmas, a therapist must be capable of a wide range of behavior with patients. Don A. Jackson once characterized one of his major goals in therapy as memorizing his own freedom to maneuver with patients; this theme is apparent throughout Erickson's own work. (p. 534)

A therapist must be wary of specific comments, responses, or models of practice so as not to unnecessarily limit interventions and interaction with clients.

Flexibility relates to utilization, as stated by Zeig and Munion (1999), "Utilization is the readiness of the therapist to respond strategically to any and all aspects of the patient or the environment" (p. 42). It is the willingness to adapt.

Utilization Principle

Utilization is an ongoing process whereby the client's observed or expressed values, symptoms, situations, or behaviors become tools for the therapist to assist the client in achieving therapeutic goals. Zeig's (1992) principles of utilization are summarized below.

1. A therapist accesses, within himself or herself, a readiness to respond constructively to the patient's responses.

2. Whatever the client brings to the session can be utilized.

3. Whatever technique the patient uses to be a patient can be harnessed by a therapist.

4. A therapist can develop the patient's responses into something useful therapeutically.

The utilization principle stems from the work of Milton H. Erickson (Zeig, 1987). Erickson used whatever behavior, attitude, problem, or resistance and redirected it toward therapeutic goals (O'Hanlon, 1988). In Ericksonian therapy, the client's symptoms or problematic behaviors are used to facilitate change. Mathews (1985) described the utilization principle as follows: "Utilization involves using and accepting the client's ongoing behavior, perception and attitudes . . . the client is not asked to conform to the therapists' modes of interaction but rather the client's behavior is accepted and utilized in treatment" (p. 49).

Concerning interventions, it is important for the clinician to use any outcome of a technique and redirect it toward therapeutic goals. The outcome of an intervention that did not meet its objectives can be further utilized toward change. Zeig and Munion (1999) stated, "Effective therapy is predicated upon the utilization of aspects of the patient's problems, life, behavior and functioning" (p. 26). Thus, effective treatment can be enhanced by "anything that the patient brings to, or exists in, the therapeutic encounter" (Zeig & Munion, 1999).

Safety Principle

The safety principle is based on the cybernetic process and on change through homeostasis and/or equilibrium. Under the cybernetic systemic lens, homeostasis consists of both patterns of stability and change (Keeney, 1983; Keeney & Rossi, 1983). More specifically, any living system is based on calibrated patterns of stability and change. Stability consists of and is based on patterns of change. Both create or facilitate a continuous steady state of balance. At any rate, the system maintains a continuous state of stability as it strives for self-preservation via compensation (Ansbacher & Ansbacher, 1956).

When using any intervention, it is important to maintain patterns of stability, while inducing change, by creating a safe, therapeutic context (Dreikurs, 1967; Havens, 1985; Rossi, 1973). Rossi (1973) emphasized the importance of a safe context by protecting the client. Rossi (1973) stated, "The patient must be protected at all times" (p. 11). Similarly, Dreikurs (1967) stressed the importance of not hurting the clients to the point of destroying cooperation. Although inducing a pattern of stability, it is also important to induce patterns of change or "differentness." In essence, there are two levels of client safety: (a) psychological safety and (b) emotional vulnerability to change.

Client safety issues can surface at any time during the therapeutic process when the client is in a fragile emotional state, is self-abusing, or is living in a physically threatening environment. When considering interventions for change, clinicians should be very aware of the vulnerability of the client and client accessibility to a support system. An example of applying the safety principle would be implementing some form of follow-up care or support plan after an intense therapy session with a client expressing suicidal ideology. It is likely that such a client will go through many such sessions to achieve significant patterns of change, but the client cannot be further damaged during the change process.

The best opportunity for change occurs when the client feels safe enough to go to an emotionally vulnerable level within the therapeutic relationship. Change can be very frightening for some clients. It is important to be supportive of the client during this process.

Generative Change

Generative change is a futuristic view of change in which small changes create or facilitate larger changes (DeShazer, 1985; Lankton, 1985; Zeig & Munion, 1999). Adlerian approaches are generally futuristically oriented, centering on Adler's concept of guiding fictional goals and the "as if" philosophy (Adler, as cited in Ansbacher & Ansbacher, 1956; Carich, 1989b; Manaster & Corsini, 1982). Generative change is based on the systemic notion of holism or a holistic view of change. Systems form Gestalt wholes in which each part interacts with the other and forms a homeostatic balance (Adler, as cited in Ansbacher & Ansbacher, 1956; Carich & Willingham, 1987). A change in one part impacts the other part of the whole at different levels of influence (Becvar & Becvar, 1982), much as throwing a stone into a pond generates repercussions throughout the pond. The degree of impact generated by a client depends on the receptivity of other individuals.

Lankton (1985) summarized generative change as follows: "Generative change can be simply defined as change which stimulates and encourages, inspires and brings forth additional changes" (p. 140). He also stated, "This ripple or snowball effect will, of course, be dramatic to the extent that pervasive personality factors are also affected, and the dynamics or operation of the presented symptoms take on new meaning" (p. 147).

With generative change in mind, some interventions can be aimed at planting small seeds of change that can be followed up later.

Metaphoric Principle

Although Erickson, Havens (1985), and Adler (as cited in Ansbacher & Ansbacher, 1956), among others, consistently used metaphors as a means of intervention, metaphors, in this context, are meant to be used as a guiding principle.

Zeig and Munion (1999) defined metaphor as "a figure of speech in which a word or phrase literally denoting one kind of object or idea is used in place of another to suggest a likeness, or analogy, between them" (p. 65). Metaphors are symbolic series of representations used in the therapeutic process within a social context. The metaphoric principle refers to using the appropriate therapeutic frame that pertains to the client's situation. More specifically, the clinician chooses communicational frames that have meaning for the client. For example, the impact of one family member on the remainder of the family might be compared to the waves that are created when one throws a rock into a pond. The repercussions of the rock's impact are felt throughout the system at various levels. In other words, interventions create different impacts with the client system, which can be followed up at a later time.

Therapeutic messages are packaged within specific interventions. Interventions are based on and derived from specific metaphors of the client. The metaphors involve the client's language and frame of reference. For example, the clinician typically does not use technical, academic jargon when trying to develop a therapeutic relationship. Typically, conversations that both understand are used.

Goal Orientation

Because behaviors are goal oriented and purposeful (Dinkmeyer et al., 1987; Dreikurs, 1967; O'Hanlon, 1988), interventions are, likewise, goal oriented.

It is important for the clinician to be aware of his or her particular goal or purpose for a given intervention. The clinician's awareness includes the type of treatment experience necessary for the client to resolve his or her problems or at least move in that direction. The specific type of experience then dictates the type of persuasiveness or influence of the intervention implemented by the clinician.

Multilevel Communication

Life is quite complex. Causality and life in general can be viewed from a meta perspective consisting of logical levels (Carich, 1998). Communication has been subdivided into different levels and dimensions (Keeney, 1983; Zeig, 1980, 1985, 1987; Zeig & Munion, 1999). This subdivision occurs in the realm of awareness and meaning. Communication occurs in levels, as messages may have different meanings. Likewise, interventions may impact the client at different levels of awareness and meaning (Zeig & Munion, 1999). Interventions may consist of different meanings, such as are embodied in implications, metaphors, and paradoxical messages.

CONCLUSION

Principles and interventions were differentiated in this article. Interventions are behaviors aimed at producing change, referred to as therapeutic response, whereas principles are guidelines for the use of interventions. It appears to the authors that many graduate educational programs focus only on one or two specific therapeutic models, based on the professors' orientation. There is little emphasis on the variety of techniques that exist outside of the specified models.

In conclusion, several generically oriented principles of intervention were briefly reviewed and applied to therapy. Although many of the citations came from the Adlerian, Ericksonian, systemic, cybernetic, strategic, and other literature, they can be applied to most any therapeutic system or approach. These principles play a key role as they help the clinician create a context of change and facilitate the setup and delivery of any intervention. The principles of intervention assume a complementary role with the intervention.

SOURCE: Mark S. Carich and Karen Spilman. (2004). Basic Principles of Intervention. *The Family Journal: Counseling and Therapy for Couples and Families, 12,* 405-410. © 2004 SAGE Publications.

REFERENCES

Ansbacher, H., & Ansbacher, R. (Eds.). (1956). *The individual psychology of Alfred Adler: A systematic presentation in selections from his writings.* New York: Harper & Row.

Bandler, R., & Grinder, J. (1979). *Frogs into princes: Neurolinguistic programming.* Moab, UT: Real People Press.

Becvar, R., & Becvar, D. (1982). *Systems theory and family therapy: A primer.* Washington, DC: University Press of America.

Carich, M. S. (1989a). *The joining technique: Utilizing the cooperative principle.* Manuscript submitted for publication.

Carich, M. S. (1989b). Variations of the "as if" technique. *Individual Psychology, 45*(4), 537-545.

Carich, M. S. (1998). The third alternative: A meta-recursive view. *The Milton H. Erickson Foundation Newsletter, 18*(3), 2.

Carich, M. S., & Willingham, W. (1987). The roots of family systems theory in individual psychology. *Individual Psychology, 43*(1), 71-78.

Carkhuff, R. R. (1969). *Helping and human relations: Vol. 1. Selection and training.* New York: Holt, Rinehart & Winston.

Corsini, R. (Ed.). (1979). *Current psychotherapies* (2nd ed.). Itasca, IL: F. E. Peacock.

Corsini, R., & Wedding, D. (Eds.). (1989). *Current psychotherapies* (4th ed.). Itasca, IL: F. E. Peacock.

de Shazer, S. C. (1985). *Keys to solution in brief therapy.* New York: Norton.

Dinkmeyer, D., Dinkmeyer, D., & Sperry, L. (1987). *Adlerian counseling and psychotherapy.* Columbus, OH: Merrill.

Dreikurs, R. (1959). Communication within the family. *Central States Speech Journal, 11*(1), 11-19.

Dreikurs, R. (1967). *Psychodynamics, psychotherapy and counseling.* Chicago: Alfred Adler Institute.

Dreikurs, R. (1972). Technology of conflict resolution. *Journal of Individual Psychology, 28*(2), 203-206.

Haley, J. (1967). *Advanced techniques of hypnosis and therapy: Selected papers of Milton H. Erickson.* New York: Grune & Stratton.

Haley, J. (1997). Changes in therapy. In J. K. Zeig (Ed.), *The evolution of psychotherapy: The third conference* (pp. 245-255). New York: Brunner/Mazel.

Havens, R. (1985). *The wisdom of Milton H. Erickson.* New York: Irvington.

Keeney, B. P. (1983). *Aesthetics of change.* New York: Guilford.

Keeney, B. P., & Rossi, J. (1983). Cybernetics of brief family therapy. *Journal of Marital & Family Therapy, 9,* 375-382.

Lankton, C. (1985). Generative change: Beyond symptomatic relief. In J. Zeig (Ed.), *Ericksonian Psychotherapy: Vol. 1. Structures* (pp. 137-170). New York: Brunner/Mazel.

Manaster, G., & Corsini, R. (1982). *Individual psychology: Theory and practice.* Itasca, IL: F. E. Peacock.

Mathews, W. J. (1985). A cybernetic model of Ericksonian hypnotherapy: One hand draws the other. In A. S. Lankton (Ed.), *Ericksonian monographs no. 1: Elements and dimensions of an Ericksonian approach* (pp. 42-60). New York: Brunner/Mazel.

Minuchin, S. (1974). *Families and family therapy.* Cambridge, MA: Harvard University Press.

Minuchin, S., & Fishman, C. (1981). *Family therapy techniques.* Cambridge, MA: Harvard University Press.

O'Connell, W., & Gomez, E. (1990). Dieletics, trances and the wisdom of encouragement. *Individual Psychology, 46*(4), 431-442.

O'Hanlon, W. (1988). Solution-oriented therapy: A megatrend in psychotherapy. In J. K. Zeig & S. R. Lankton (Eds.), *Developing Ericksonian therapy* (pp. 93-111). New York: Brunner/Mazel.

Rossi, E. L. (1973). Psychological shocks and creative moments in psychotherapy. *American Journal of Clinical Hypnosis, 16*, 9-22.

Zeig, J. K. (1980). Symptom prescription technique: Clinical applications using elements of communication. *The American Journal of Clinical Hypnosis, 23*(1), 23-32.

Zeig, J. K. (1985). *Experiencing Erickson: An introduction to the man and his work.* New York: Brunner/Mazel.

Zeig, J. K. (1987). Therapeutic patterns of Ericksonian influence communication. In J. K. Zeig (Ed.), *The evolution of psychotherapy* (pp. 392-405). New York: Brunner/Mazel.

Zeig, J. K. (1992). The virtue of our faults: A key concept of Ericksonian therapy. In J. K. Zeig (Ed.), *The evolution of psychotherapy: The second conference* (pp. 252-266). New York: Brunner/Mazel.

Zeig, J. K., & Munion, M. W. (1990). What is psychotherapy? In J. K. Zeig & M. W. Munion (Eds.), *What is psychotherapy: Contemporary perspectives* (pp. 1-14). San Francisco: Jossey-Bass.

Zeig, J. K., & Munion, M. W. (1999). *Milton H. Erickson.* Thousand Oaks, CA: Sage.

Mark S. Carich, Ph.D., is coordinator of the Sexually Dangerous Persons Program with the Illinois Department of Corrections at Big Muddy River Correctional Center. He is on both the teaching and dissertation faculties of the Adler School of Professional Psychology in Chicago. His most recent book (co-authored with M. Calder) is Contemporary Treatment of Adult Male Sex Offenders *(Russell House Publishing, 2003). Dr. Carich has co-authored or created numerous treatment and assessment inventories, articles, and chapters as well as conducted training workshops nationwide. His clinical research interests include therapy techniques, contemporary sex offender treatment processes, cognitive restructuring, victim empathy, arousal control, the assault cycle, assessment, relapse prevention, and recovery.*

Karen Spilman, MSW, is a colleague of Dr. Carich and his co-therapist in the Sexually Dangerous Persons Program at Big Muddy River Correctional Center. She co-authored the 2002 article "Can Guilty Committed Sex Offenders Recover? Part I: Criteria to evaluate recovery," which appeared in the journal The Forensic Therapist, *with Dr. Carich. She has previously worked as a legal advocate for sexually abused children and facilitated therapy and behavior modification groups for children and adolescents at an in-patient treatment program for severe behavior disorders. She has conducted many training events for foster and adoptive families and has presented seminars on victim impact to multidisciplinary audiences. Her clinical research interests include sex offender management, victim empathy/victim impact issues, relapse prevention, and recovery.*

12 Families in Transition:
Alternative Family Patterns

Parental Divorce and Family Functioning

Effects on Differentiation Levels of Young Adults

Patrick Johnson
Jill M. Thorngren
Adina J. Smith
Montana State University

This study examined the effect of parental divorce and various dimensions of functioning in the family of origin on young adult development. A total of 813 participants completed the Self-Report Family Inventory, the Differentiation of Self Inventory, and demographic questions. Results indicate that parental divorce and family functioning significantly affect differentiation levels of young adults. Implications of the results for counselors and future researchers are provided.

The number of families affected by divorce has grown tremendously in the past 50 years. Almost 50% of marriages end in divorce in the United States, and 1 million children are affected by their parents' divorce each year (Bureau of the Census, 1992). Although not conclusive, existing literature has found that children from divorced families experience varied effects due to divorce. Children from divorced families, for example, are more likely than children from intact families to have academic problems,

AUTHORS' NOTE: Correspondence concerning this article should be addressed to Dr. Patrick Johnson, Montana State University, Department of Health and Human Development, 210 Herrick Hall, Bozeman, MT, 59717-3540; e-mail: rjohnson@montana.edu.

exhibit problematic externalizing and internalizing behaviors, be less socially responsible and competent, and have lower self-esteem (Amato & Keith, 1991; Cherlin & Furstenberg, 1994; Hetherington, 1989). Furthermore, developmental tasks of adolescence and young adulthood, such as forming intimate relationships, individuating from parents, and increasing social and economic autonomy, seem to be somewhat more arduous for youths from divorced families than those from intact families (Hetherington, Bridges, & Insabella, 1998; Johnson & Nelson, 1998). These children are also at higher risk for lower levels of school achievement, unemployment, being sexually active at an early age, delinquent behavior, substance abuse, and association with antisocial peers (Amato & Keith, 1991; Chase-Lansdale, Cherlin, & Kiernan, 1995; Hetherington & Clingempeel, 1992).

In addition to psychosocial adjustment difficulties, it appears that parent-child relationships are perceived differently by young adults from divorced and intact families. College-age students from divorced families perceive their parental relationships, particularly with fathers, less positively than children from intact families (Fine, Moreland, & Schwebel, 1983; Fine, Worley, & Schwebel, 1986; White, Brinkerhoff, & Booth, 1985), with relationship deficits being stronger for noncustodial than custodial parents (Amato & Booth, 1991). Other research has shown that adult children of divorced parents feel less affection for their parents, have less contact with them, and engage in fewer intergenerational exchanges of assistance than adults from intact families (Amato & Booth, 1991; Booth & Amato, 1994; White, 1992, 1994). In a qualitative study, Bonkowski (1989) indicated that young adults from divorced families have difficulty establishing feelings of trust in their own relationships, continue to mourn the loss of their family unit, have difficulty individuating, and view postdivorce emotional closeness to their parents as burdensome.

Although parental divorce has varied effects on children, family factors seem to moderate the influence of those effects (Amato & Booth, 1991; Johnson & McNeil, 1998; Lopez, Campbell, & Watkins, 1988). For example, when members of divorced families demonstrate warmth, harmony, and cohesion with each other, the differences between the adjustment of children in these families and those in intact families are decreased (Hetherington, 1989). Higher levels of postdivorce family functioning also appear to moderate the emotional cutoffs that have been associated with parental divorce (Johnson & Nelson, 1998; Johnson, Wilkinson, & McNeil, 1995). Furthermore, young adults' perceptions of triangulation and intimidation by their parents appear to be reduced by higher levels of family functioning while feelings of equality between the young adults and their parents are increased (Johnson & McNeil, 1998). Others have identified variables such as frequency of contact with noncustodial parents (Johnson & McNeil, 1998; Kinnaird, 1987), timing of parental divorce (Bulcroft & Bulcroft, 1991), gender (Booth & Edwards, 1989; Kalter, 1987), and family structure (Aquilino, 1990) that along with family functioning seem to moderate the effects of parental divorce on children.

Thus, the effect of parental divorce and family factors on children is becoming more clear, although research is needed to further assess longer term developmental outcomes for young adults. In addition, although family factors have been shown to moderate the effects of parental divorce, there is a need for a comprehensive assessment of the family variables that might influence developmental task attainment for young adults from divorced families. To these ends, the present study was designed to assess the effect of parental divorce on developmental task attainment for young adults and to assess the effects of multiple family factors for young adults from divorced families. Specifically, the present study tested the following research hypotheses. First, it was expected that young adults from divorced families would exhibit more difficulty with developmental task attainment than would those from intact families. Next, it was expected that specific family factors would moderate the effects of parental divorce. Most notably, higher levels of family functioning were expected to predict higher levels of developmental task attainment for young adults from divorced families. For the present study, the tasks associated with young adult development were conceptualized via intergenerational family theory.

YOUNG ADULT DEVELOPMENT: CONCEPTUAL FRAMEWORK

Intergenerational family theory offers a broad-based perspective on young adult development. Following Bowen (1976, 1978), Carter and McGoldrick (1989) indicated that the primary developmental task for young adults is to successfully differentiate from their families of origin. According to Bowen, an individual's level of differentiation is largely determined by the degree to which the child is the recipient of the family's projected anxiety, a process with both intrapsychic and interpersonal outcomes for the offspring. Individuals with higher amounts of intrapsychic differentiation are able to separate thoughts from emotions, whereas poorly differentiated individuals become flooded by emotions. Well-differentiated individuals can choose to make thoughtful decisions based on intellect or to follow their "gut-level" emotions or instincts. The ability to make this an active choice versus a reaction to anxiety and emotionality separates differentiated from undifferentiated individuals. Intrapsychic differentiation, then, is characterized by the ability to experience strong affect as well as shift to calm, logical reasoning when circumstances dictate (Skowron & Friedlander, 1998).

Interpersonal differentiation of self refers to the ability to experience intimacy with and independence from others. Differentiation of self in this context includes adhering to strong personal beliefs despite contrary pressure from others and the ability to engage in physical and intimate relationships without endangering one's own sense of identity (Skowron & Friedlander, 1998). In contrast to the balance displayed in individuals with higher levels of differentiation, those who are less differentiated are more likely to engage in fused relationships and/or are emotionally cut off when they experience anxiety (Johnson & Waldo, 1998). Fusion has been characterized as the tendency of undifferentiated persons to remain "stuck" in the positions they held in their families of origin, have few firmly held convictions, be dogmatic or compliant, and seek approval above all other goals (Bowen, 1976, 1978; Kerr & Bowen, 1988; Skowron & Friedlander, 1998). Emotional cutoff, on the other hand, is demarcated by reactive emotional distance, a tendency to deny family importance, and a facade of independence (Skowron & Friedlander, 1998).

Thus, fusion and emotional cutoff are hallmark traits of individuals who did not attain a high level of differentiation from their families of origin. Whether exhibiting dependency or pseudo-independence, these individuals are reactive to anxiety in the environment and are less able to make decisions based on choice and reasoning. People with fusion tendencies will seek refuge in relationships at all costs; those with cutoff tendencies may flee from interconnectedness. Neither type is able to maintain a healthy balance between separateness and togetherness needs, described by Bowen (1976, 1978) as the two basic life forces.

METHOD

Procedures and Participants

Participants were 813 undergraduate student volunteers who were enrolled in classes at a large university in the Rocky Mountain region. After providing written consent, participants completed standardized instruments and demographic questions. The participants included 563 females (69%), 222 males (27%), and 28 (4%) participants who did not identify their gender. Of the participants, 795 provided information on age ($M = 21.26$, $SD = 5.91$). In terms of ethnicity, 805 participants provided information, with 727 (89%) identifying themselves as Caucasian/Anglo Americans, 29 (4%) identifying themselves as Native Americans, 14 (2%) identifying themselves as Asian Americans, 11 (1%) identifying themselves as Hispanic/Latino Americans, 7 (2%) identifying themselves as African Americans, and 17 (2%) identifying themselves as "other." Of the participants, 796 provided information about their parents' marital status, with 584 (73%) indicating that they were from intact families and 212 (27%) indicating that they had parents who were divorced.

The divorced group ($n = 212$) included 53 (25%) males, 152 (71%) females, and 9 (4%) participants who did not identify their gender. The mean age of respondents at the time of their parents' divorce was 8.32, with a standard deviation of 5.52. Regarding family structure, 131 (59%) participants were from single-parent families, 90 (40%) lived with stepfamilies, and 2 (1%) responded as "other." The mean frequency of contact with noncustodial parent during the past year was 27.11 times (*SD* = 25.87).

INSTRUMENTS

The Differentiation of Self Inventory (DSI). The DSI (Skowron & Friedlander, 1998) is comprised of 43 items that are rated on a 6-point scale to generate a total differentiation score and four subscale scores. Factor analyses demonstrated support for the four subscales as being "empirically distinct dimensions of a single construct, differentiation of self" (Skowron & Friedlander, 1998, p. 241). The first subscale, Emotional Reactivity, reflects the degree to which a person responds to environmental stimuli with emotional flooding, emotional lability, or hypersensitivity. The second subscale, I Position, reflects a clearly defined sense of self and the ability to thoughtfully adhere to one's convictions when pressured to do otherwise. The third subscale, Emotional Cutoff, reflects feeling threatened by intimacy and feeling excessive vulnerability in relations with others; this vulnerability leads to fears of engulfment and defensive behaviors such as distancing and denial. The fourth subscale, Fusion With Others, reflects emotional overinvolvement with others, including triangulation and over-identification with parents. Higher scores on the DSI reflect higher levels of differentiation (i.e., more total differentiation, less fusion, less reactivity, less cutoff, and more I position).

Skowron and Friedlander (1998) provided information about the psychometric properties of the DSI. Initial construct validity of the DSI was supported as the DSI correlated highly and in the expected direction with a measure of chronic anxiety and with amount and intensity of symptomatic distress. Across several studies, internal consistency coefficients, using Cronbach's alpha, supported moderate to high reliabilities for the DSI total score and each of the four subscales (e.g., DSI = .88, Emotional Reactivity = .88, Emotional Cutoff = .79, Fusion With Others = .70, and I Position = .85). For the present study, internal consistencies were calculated, and the resulting reliability coefficients were .83 for the total DSI scale, .81 for the Emotional Reactivity subscale, .84 for the Emotional Cutoff subscale, .68 for the Fusion subscale, and .78 for the I Position subscale.

The Self-Report Family Inventory Version II (SFI). The SFI (Beavers & Hampson, 1990) is comprised of 36 items rated on a 5-point scale that assess individuals' perceptions of family competence and style. Factor analyses revealed five factors that measure consistent themes of family life across different samples, from which the subscales for the SFI were developed. The first subscale, Health/Competence, is a global measure of family functioning that assesses themes of happiness, optimism, problem-solving and negotiation skills, family love, strength of adult coalitions, autonomy/individuality emphasis, and blaming/responsibility patterns. The second subscale, Conflict, assesses the level of overt unresolved conflict, fighting, blaming, and arguing.

The third subscale, Cohesion, assesses the level of satisfaction and happiness attained through togetherness and emphasis on family closeness. The fourth subscale, Leadership, assesses the level of strong and consistent patterns of adult leadership in the family. The fifth subscale, Emotional Expressiveness, assesses feelings of closeness, physical and verbal expressions of positive feelings, and the ease with which warmth and caring are expressed by family members.

Beavers and Hampson (1990) provided psychometric information about the SFI. At a 3-month follow-up, test-retest coefficients for each scale were as follows: Health/Competence $r = .84$, Conflict $r = .52$, Cohesion $r = .50$, Leadership $r = .49$, and Expressiveness $r = .79$. Construct validity was generally found to be sufficient for the SFI subscales through moderate correlations with other conceptually similar measures (i.e., Locke-Wallace Marital Satisfaction Scale, FACES II, FACES III, and Family Environment Scale). For the present study, internal consistencies were calculated, and the resulting reliability coefficients were .93 for the Health/Competence subscale, .88 for the Conflict subscale, .78 for the Cohesion subscale, .31 for the Leadership subscale, and .86 for the Expressiveness subscale. Thus, all subscales, except Leadership, exhibited sufficient internal consistency.

RESULTS

To assess differences between young adults from divorced families and those from intact families across the various components of differentiation, MANOVA and univariate follow-ups were calculated. A multivariate F ratio was generated from Wilks's lambda statistic; significant differences between those from divorced families and those from intact families across the four DSI subscales and the total DSI score were found, $F(4, 763) = 5.48, p < .001$. See Table 12.1 for the univariate analyses of variance, means, and standard deviations for each DSI subscale and the total DSI score as a function of parental marital status.

To assess the unique effects of select variables (i.e., family health/competence, family structure, frequency of contact with noncustodial parent, age at time of parental divorce, and gender) on differentiation levels of young adults from divorced families, multiple regression analyses were used for each DSI subscale and the total DSI score. Family health/competence significantly predicted all four DSI subscales and the total DSI score such that higher levels of family health predicted higher levels of total differentiation, $F(1, 188) = 4.45, p < .05$; higher levels of I position, $F(1, 197) = 5.98, p < .01$; higher levels of fusion, $F(1, 196) = 28.34, p < .001$; lower levels of emotional cutoff, $F(1, 191) = 19.84, p < .001$; and lower levels of emotional reactivity, $F(1, 195) = 3.01, p < .05$. Gender was

Table 12.1   Univariate Analyses, Means, and Standard Deviations for Each Differentiation of Self Inventory (DSI) Subscale and the Total DSI Score as a Function of Parental Marital Status

		Parental Marital Status			
	Univariate Analyses	Intact		Divorced	
Variable	F(1, 766)	M	SD	M	SD
Total DSI score	2.76*	161.61	21.14	158.67	23.17
Emotional Cutoff	6.27**	55.29	10.37	53.16	11.13
Fusion	7.78**	23.13	6.86	24.77	7.69
Emotional Reactivity	5.03*	37.33	9.21	35.79	10.53
I Position	0.76	45.77	8.59	45.20	9.20

NOTE: Higher scores indicate more differentiation (i.e., more total differentiation, less emotional cutoff, less fusion, less emotional reactivity, and more I position).

*$p < .05$. **$p < .01$.

significant on three DSI subscales and the total DSI score such that males had higher levels of total differentiation, $F(1, 188) = 5.60$, $p < .01$; lower levels of fusion, $F(1, 196) = 13.45$, $p < .001$; higher levels of emotional cutoff, $F(1, 191) = 5.67$, $p < .01$; and lower levels of emotional reactivity, $F(1, 195) = 14.87$, $p < .001$, than females. Family structure, frequency of contact with noncustodial parent, and age at time of parental divorce did not significantly predict any of the DSI subscales or the total DSI score.

To assess the unique effects of each family relationship factor that contributes to overall family health (i.e., conflict, cohesion, leadership, and emotional expressiveness) on differentiation levels of young adults from divorced families, multiple regression analyses were used for each DSI subscale and the total DSI score. Conflict significantly predicted three DSI subscales and the total DSI score such that higher levels of conflict predicted lower levels of total differentiation, $F(1, 197) = 15.22$, $p < .001$; lower levels of I position, $F(1, 206) = 17.97$, $p < .001$; higher levels of emotional cutoff, $F(1, 200) = 12.26$, $p < .01$; and higher levels of emotional reactivity, $F(1, 204) = 3.18$, $p < .05$. Cohesion was significant on one DSI subscale such that higher levels of cohesion predicted lower levels of emotional reactivity, $F(1, 204) = 4.32$, $p < .05$. Emotional expressiveness was significant on three DSI subscales such that higher levels of expressiveness predicted lower levels of emotional cutoff, $F(1, 200) = 6.18$, $p < .01$; higher levels of fusion, $F(1, 205) = 15.31$, $p < .001$; and higher levels of emotional reactivity, $F(1, 204) = 4.24$, $p < .05$. Leadership did not significantly predict any of the DSI subscales or the total DSI score.

DISCUSSION

Results of the study show that parental divorce has an effect on differentiation levels of young adults. Specifically, results indicate that young adults from divorced families are more emotionally cut off from significant others than are young adults from intact families. This finding provides some confirmation of the conclusions drawn by previous researchers (i.e., Johnson & Nelson, 1998; Johnson et al., 1995) who conceptualized the lower levels of intimacy and individuation with parents and significant peers that have been found in young adults from divorced families as being reflective of emotional cutoffs. Results also suggest that young adults from divorced families are more emotionally reactive than are young adults from intact families, supporting previous research that has shown higher levels of reactivity for young adults after parental divorce (Buboltz, Johnson, & Woller, in press). In addition, parental divorce seems to lead to less inter-personal fusion for young adults. Although less fusion is theoretically characteristic of higher levels of differentiation, it may be that young adults who experienced parental divorce remain in a more disengaged interpersonal position rather than risk intimacy and thus appear less fused. This possible conclusion is supported by the lack of intimacy with significant others that young adults from divorced families have exhibited in previous research (Johnson & Nelson, 1998; Johnson et al., 1995). Thus, young adults from divorced families seem to have more difficulty with the developmental tasks associated with attaining a separate sense of self without emotionally and reactively cutting off from significant others.

Results of the study also support previous findings (Amato & Booth, 1991; Johnson & McNeil, 1998) that suggest the quality of family functioning in the family of origin moderates the effects of parental divorce for young adults. Specifically, greater amounts of family health/competence seem to increase overall levels of differentiation, increase levels of I position, decrease levels of emotional cutoff, and decrease levels of emotional reactivity for young adults from divorced families. Thus, whereas parental divorce was found to have a detrimental effect on several indices of differentiation, greater amounts of family health seem to moderate those effects. Interestingly, higher levels of family health also predicted higher levels of interpersonal fusion for young adults from divorced families. As discussed previously, young adults from divorced families have been found to have lower levels of intimacy with significant others than young adults from intact families; consequently, greater amounts of family health may moderate this tendency and increase interpersonal closeness. It is not clear whether the increase in interpersonal intimacy reaches a dysfunctional level; this will be discussed further in the Limitations and Suggestions for Future Research section.

Results of the study indicate that family structure (i.e., single parent or stepfamilies), frequency of contact with noncustodial parent, and age at time of parental divorce do not affect differentiation levels of young adults from divorced families. Specifically, results suggest that there are no differences between single-parent families and stepfamilies related to young adult development, not an unexpected finding considering that previous research has shown that the type of family structure is less important than the quality of family interactions within a specific structure (Johnson & McNeil, 1998). The lack of significance of frequency of contact with noncustodial parent and age at time of parental divorce, however, is surprising considering that both of these variables have been shown to affect young adult development (Bulcroft & Bulcroft, 1991; Johnson & McNeil, 1998; Johnson et al., 1995; Kinnaird, 1987). It may be that these variables lose their predictive power in a multivariate analysis when a factor as potent as family health is taken into account.

Results also suggest that gender has an effect on differentiation levels of young adults from divorced families, with men exhibiting higher overall differentiation levels, less fusion, less emotional reactivity, and more emotional cutoffs than women. Previous research has been mixed regarding the effects of gender after parental divorce (Booth & Edwards, 1989; Johnson & McNeil, 1998; Kalter, 1987; Wallerstein, 1985). It is unclear whether the effects found in the present study represent differences based on postdivorce outcomes or on gender differences inherent in the way the theoretical constructs associated with differentiation have been operationalized in the DSI by Skowron and Friedlander (1998). Issues related to the various theoretical constructs discussed in this study will be explored in greater detail in the Limitations and Suggestions for Future Research section.

In addition, results suggest that specific dimensions of family health (i.e., conflict, cohesion, and emotional expressiveness) have unique effects on differentiation levels of young adults from divorced families, although leadership does not seem to have an effect. In support of previous research (Johnson & McNeil, 1998; Johnson et al., 1995), family cohesion appears to reduce emotional reactivity, whereas family conflict seems to have a deleterious effect on overall differentiation levels by increasing levels of emotional cutoff, increasing levels of emotional reactivity, and decreasing levels of I position for young adults from divorced families. Thus, the effects of conflict and cohesion are clear and consistent with expectations. The effects of emotional expressiveness, however, are less consistent. Specifically, higher levels of emotional expressiveness seem to lead to lower levels of emotional cutoff, higher levels of fusion, and higher levels of emotional reactivity for young adults from divorced families. These mixed results may be related to the theoretical operationalization of the emotional expressiveness variable in the SFI (Beavers & Hampson, 1990). Again, issues related to theoretical constructs in this study will be discussed further in the Limitations and Suggestions for Future Research section.

LIMITATIONS AND SUGGESTIONS
FOR FUTURE RESEARCH

As noted, a possible limitation, which may prove constructive in directing future research, is the operationalization of some of the theoretical constructs used in the study. Specifically, the ways in which conflict, expressiveness, cohesion, and fusion were defined via the assessment measures may have produced conflicting results. In this study, more family expressiveness predicted less emotional cutoff while it also predicted more fusion and more emotional reactivity. These results initially appear contradictory; less cutoff signifies higher levels of differentiation, but fusion and emotional reactivity are associated with lower levels of differentiation. A common assumption in most theories of family counseling is that enhancing expressiveness between family members leads to healthier family functioning; this study only partially supported that assumption. Previous research (Johnson & McNeil, 1998) that used the expressiveness scale of the Family Environment Scale (FES) (Moos & Moos, 1981) indicated that "expressiveness is the most important post-divorce variable for promoting healthy differentiation for young adults" (p. 245). Perusal of questions assessing expressiveness in the FES and SFI suggests a philosophical difference between the two measures. The FES assesses expressiveness with items such as "We tell each other about our personal problems," "Money and paying bills is openly talked about in our family," and "There are a lot of spontaneous discussions in our family." In contrast, the SFI assesses expressiveness with items such as "Our family members touch and hug each other," "Our family is proud of being close," and "Family members easily express warmth and caring toward each other." It appears that the FES views expressiveness as inclusive of a range of emotions and topics including anger and problem solving. The SFI, conversely, views expressiveness as being primarily warm and conflict free. Given this perspective, it may be understandable that those scoring higher on the SFI expressiveness subscale may also exhibit more tendencies toward fusion and emotional reactivity. Additional research may further illuminate the various definitions of family expressiveness and the corresponding ramifications for individual and family functioning.

Results also indicate that higher levels of cohesion are associated with less emotional reactivity. Thus, cohesion is associated with less emotional reactivity, whereas expressiveness is associated with more emotional reactivity. On the surface, it would appear that cohesion and expressiveness would both lead to similar types of healthy family functioning. As defined by the instruments in this study, however, cohesion led to higher levels of differentiation while expressiveness generally led to lower levels of differentiation. Again, the operational definitions of these two constructs may have had an effect on the results.

In addition, in the present study, conflict in the postdivorce family predicted lower levels of the various components of differentiation. Although this is an expected finding, future research may focus on the definition of conflict and examine the possibility of healthy conflict that may lead to change and growth.

Finally, the construct of fusion warrants further examination. Parental divorce predicted less interpersonal fusion in young adults, although higher levels of family health in postdivorce families predicted more interpersonal fusion. It may be that divorce in general produces less closeness or intimacy, which is construed as less fusion, and that family health moderates this effect, producing what appears to be more fusion. What is not clearly defined is the level at which fusion can be considered unhealthy. Perhaps given the circumstances surrounding divorce, healthier families engage in behaviors that are characteristic of fusion that are in reality effective and necessary coping mechanisms in that context. Neither Bowen's (1976, 1978) original work or Skowron and Friedlander's (1998) subsequent conceptualizations of fusion and differentiation designate an ideal amount of differentiation. Counselors are cautioned against assuming that higher levels of fusion automatically denote a lower level of mental health. Future research warrants investigating those characteristics of fusion that may be considered healthy in certain contextual situations.

Similarly, feminist scholars have frequently criticized Bowen's (1976, 1978) conceptualization of differentiation. The focus on togetherness that is frequently considered a characteristic of many females may be perceived as fusion from Bowen's perspective (Knudson-Martin, 1994). This study indicates that males from divorced families exhibit less fusion and less reactivity than their female counterparts; however, males also exhibited more emotional cutoff. It appears that females and males react differently to parental divorce. What is not evident is at what point each style of coping becomes dysfunctional. Additional research is needed to explore the multiple factors that influence individuals' styles of coping and what determines healthiness or unhealthiness in each style. This in turn may lead to a reconceptualization of the construct of fusion.

IMPLICATIONS FOR COUNSELORS

Despite limitations, results of the study have implications for counselors. In general, counselors are advised to be aware of issues regarding differentiation when working with young adults from divorced families. Broadly speaking, it appears that young adults who experience divorce in their families of origin attain a lower level of differentiation than their counterparts from intact families. As young adults struggle with monumental decisions such as attending college, pursuing career options, and seeking intimate partners, their levels of differentiation may have a significant effect. For example, those who are prone to emotional reactivity may make decisions based almost exclusively on "what feels right" without accessing more objective measures. Another example is that young adults may reactively choose to pursue career or college options as far from home as geographically possible based on a tendency to emotionally cut off versus a well-thought-out and active choice to relocate.

Counselors are encouraged to validate the feeling aspect of their clients' decision-making style and also help their clients explore decisions from more objective stances. Processing the reasons that their clients are making decisions, especially reactive ones, is invaluable in enhancing self-awareness and expanding options in more than one direction.

Differentiation levels also influence issues related to couples. Based on their experiences, young adults from divorced families may either attempt to imitate their parents' choices in mate selection or conversely, choose partners whom they presume to be very different from their parents. If made from a place of emotional reactivity, these decisions represent examples of fusion and cutoff. As partners in these types of relationships are faced with the everyday stresses of couplehood, the anxiety that is created may perpetuate extreme positions of fusion and cutoff, leading to less satisfying marriages. As noted by Skowron (2000), couples who are less reactive, cut off, or fused with others and are better able to take I positions in relationships experience greater levels of marital satisfaction than those who are less differentiated. Greater differentiation, then, appears to lead to a greater tolerance of the anxiety that is inherent within couple relationships. Numerous counselors have suggested ways to assist clients in increasing their differentiation levels in the context of couples counseling (e.g., Bray, Williamson, & Malone, 1986; Framo, 1981; Waldo & Harman, 1993).

If young adults from divorced families choose to have children of their own, many additional issues related to differentiation become salient points for exploration in counseling. Beginning with how the choice is being made to have children, counselors can explore clients' expectations regarding parenting and roles that each parent will take. As differentiation is considered to be a product of multigenerational transmission (Bowen, 1976, 1978), it is important for counselors to work with clients by exploring their family-of-origin experiences. Specifically, counselors may want to discuss with their clients the ways in which their parents' divorce has affected them and to explore which family patterns and roles they hope to perpetuate with their own children and which they hope to alter.

In general, counselors who work with families after or during divorce are encouraged to recognize the effect of divorce on family members and to encourage those behaviors that moderate the effects of divorce. Suggested goals include working with families to decrease the amount of overt conflict and increase cohesion between family members. Counselors may achieve these goals by teaching family members effective conflict resolution skills and assisting families in reorganizing their boundary structures and planning activities among members that recognize changes in boundaries while still enhancing interactions between newly formed subsystems. It is specifically advisable to work with young adults in forming separate but healthy relationships with each of their parents.

In sum, when working with young adults from divorced families, counselors should be particularly aware of tendencies their clients may have toward emotional reactivity and/or emotional cutoff. By promoting behaviors associated with differentiation, counselors can help young adults access both emotional and rational faculties in making thoughtful rather than reactive decisions related to their families of origin, careers, and intimate relationships.

SOURCE: Patrick Johnson, Jill M. Thorngren, and Adina J. Smith. (2001). Parental Divorce and Family Functioning: Effects on Differentiation Levels of Young Adults. *The Family Journal: Counseling and Therapy for Couples and Families, 9*, 265-272. © 2001 SAGE Publications.

REFERENCES

Amato, P. R., & Booth, A. (1991). Consequences of parental divorce and marital unhappiness for adult well-being. *Social Forces, 69*, 895-914.

Amato, P. R., & Keith, B. (1991). Parental divorce and adult well-being: A meta-analysis. *Journal of Marriage and the Family, 53*, 43-58.

Aquilino, W. (1990). The likelihood of parent-child coresidence: Effects of family structure and parental characteristics. *Journal of Marriage and the Family, 52*, 405-419.

Beavers, W. R., & Hampson, R. B. (1990). *Successful families*. New York: Norton.

Bonkowski, S. E. (1989). Lingering sadness: Young adults' response to parental divorce. *Social Casework: The Journal of Contemporary Social Work, 70*, 219-223.

Booth, A., & Amato, P. R. (1994). Parental marital quality, divorce, and relations with offspring in young adulthood. *Journal of Marriage and the Family, 56*, 21-34.

Booth, A., & Edwards, J. N. (1989). Transmission of marital and family quality over the generations: The effect of parental divorce and unhappiness. *Journal of Divorce, 13*, 41-58.

Bowen, M. (1976). Theory in the practice of psychotherapy. In P. J. Guerin Jr. (Ed.), *Family therapy: Theory and practice* (pp. 42-90). New York: Garner.

Bowen, M. (1978). *Family therapy in clinical practice*. Northvale, NJ: Jason Aronson.

Bray, J. H., Williamson, D. S., & Malone, P. E. (1986). An evaluation of an inter-generational consultation process to increase personal authority in the family system. *Family Process, 25*, 423-435.

Buboltz, W. C., Johnson, P., & Woller, K. (in press). Psychological reactance in college students: Family of origin predictors. *Journal of Counseling and Development*.

Bulcroft, K. A., & Bulcroft, R. A. (1991). The timing of divorce: Effects on parent-child relationships later in life. *Research on Aging, 1*, 226-243.

Bureau of the Census. (1992). *Marital status and living arrangements: March, 1992* (No. 468, Tables G & 5, Current Population Reports, Series P-20). Washington, DC: Government Printing Office.

Carter, B., & McGoldrick, M. (Eds.). (1989). *The changing family life-cycle: A framework for family therapy* (2nd ed.). Boston: Allyn & Bacon.

Chase-Lansdale, P. L., Cherlin, A. J., & Kiernan, K. E. (1995). The long-term effects of parental divorce on the mental health of young adults: A developmental perspective. *Child Development, 66,* 1614-1634.

Cherlin, A. J., & Furstenberg, F. F. (1994). Stepfamilies in the United States: A reconsideration. In J. Blake & J. Hagen (Eds.), *Annual review of sociology* (pp. 359-381). Palo Alto, CA: Annual Reviews.

Fine, M. A., Moreland, J. R., & Schwebel, A. I. (1983). Long-term effects of divorce on parent-child relationships. *Developmental Psychology, 19,* 703-713.

Fine, M. A., Worley, S. M., & Schwebel, A. I. (1986). The effects of divorce on parent-child relationships. *Journal of Social Behavior and Personality, 1,* 451-463.

Framo, J. L. (1981). The integration of marital therapy with sessions with the family of origin. In A. S. Gurman & D. P. Kniskern (Eds.), *Handbook of family therapy* (pp. 133-158). New York: Brunner/Mazel.

Hetherington, E. M. (1989). Coping with family transitions: Winners, losers, and survivors. *Child Development, 60,* 1-14.

Hetherington, E. M., Bridges, M., & Insabella, G. M. (1998). What matters? What does not? Five perspectives on the association between marital transitions and children's adjustment. *American Psychologist, 53,* 167-184.

Hetherington, E. M., & Clingempeel, W. G. (1992). Coping with marital transitions: A family systems perspective. *Monographs of the Society for Research in Child Development, 57*(2-3, Serial No. 227).

Johnson, P., & McNeil, K. (1998). Predictors of developmental task attainment for young adults from divorced families. *Contemporary Family Therapy, 20,* 237-250.

Johnson, P., & Nelson, M. D. (1998). Parental divorce, family functioning, and college student development: An intergenerational perspective. *Journal of College Student Development, 39,* 355-363.

Johnson, P., & Waldo, M. (1998). Integrating Minuchin's boundary continuum and Bowen's differentiation scale: A curvilinear representation. *Contemporary Family Therapy, 20,* 403-413.

Johnson, P., Wilkinson, W. K., & McNeil, K. (1995). The impact of parental divorce on the attainment of the developmental tasks of young adulthood. *Contemporary Family Therapy, 17,* 249-264.

Kalter, N. (1987). Long-term effects of divorce on children: A developmental vulnerability model. *American Journal of Orthopsychiatry, 57,* 587-600.

Kerr, M. E., & Bowen, M. (1988). *Family evaluation: An approach based on Bowen theory.* New York: Norton.

Kinnaird, K. L. (1987). Attitudes toward marriage, divorce, and premarital sexual activity among women as a function of parents' marital status. *Dissertation Abstracts International, 48*(5), 1516B.

Knudson-Martin, C. (1994). The female voice: Applications to Bowen's family systems theory. *Journal of Marital and Family Therapy, 20,* 35-46.

Lopez, F. G., Campbell, V. L., & Watkins, C. E. (1988). The relation of parental divorce to college student development. *Journal of Divorce, 12,* 83-98.

Moos, R. H., & Moos, B. S. (1981). *Family Environment Scale manual* (3rd ed.). Palo Alto, CA: Consulting Psychologists Press.

Skowron, E. A. (2000). The role of differentiation of self in marital adjustment. *Journal of Counseling Psychology, 47,* 229-237.

Skowron, E. A., & Friedlander, M. L. (1998). The Differentiation of Self Inventory: Development and initial validation. *Journal of Counseling Psychology, 45,* 235-246.

Waldo, M., & Harman, M. J. (1993). Relationship enhancement therapy with borderline personality. *Family Journal, 1,* 25-30.

Wallerstein, J. S. (1985). Children of divorce: Preliminary report of a ten-year follow-up of older children and adolescents. *Journal of the American Academy of Child Psychiatry, 24,* 545-553.

White, L. (1992). Children of divorce: Preliminary report of a ten-year follow-up of older children and adolescents. *Journal of the American Academy of Child Psychiatry, 24,* 545-553.

White, L. K. (1994). Growing up with single parents and stepparents: Long-term effects on family solidarity. *Journal of Marriage and the Family, 56,* 935-948.

White, L. K., Brinkerhoff, D. B., & Booth, A. (1985). The effect of marital disruption on children's attachment to parents. *Journal of Family Issues, 6,* 5-22.

Patrick Johnson, Ph.D., is an assistant professor and the program leader for the mental health counseling program at the Department of Health and Human Development at Montana State University. He received his doctoral degree in counseling psychology at New Mexico State University.

Jill M. Thorngren, Ph.D., is an assistant professor and the program leader for the marriage and family counseling program at the Department of Health and Human Development at Montana State University. She received her doctoral degree in counseling and counselor education at Idaho State University.

Adina J. Smith, Ph.D., is an assistant professor and the director of the Human Development Clinic at the Department of Health and Human Development at Montana State University. She received her doctoral degree in clinical psychology at the University of Georgia.

Counseling Gay and Lesbian Families

Theoretical Considerations

Jennifer L. Adams

Jodi D. Jaques

California Polytechnic State University,

San Luis Obispo

Kathleen M. May

University of Virginia

There are an estimated 2 to 10 million gay and lesbian parents raising from 6 to 14 million children in the United States. Research has revealed few measurable differences between gay and lesbian families and heterosexual families. However, as a result of living in a homophobic and heterosexist society, gay and lesbian families face unique concerns. In this column, family counselors and therapists are challenged to consider whether the theoretical model that influences their work considers the broader social context and the impact that marginalization and discrimination may have on gay and lesbian families.

Keywords: gay; lesbian; families; counseling

There are an estimated 2 to 10 million gay and lesbian parents raising from 6 to 14 million children in the United States (Lamme & Lamme, 2001; Strong & Callahan, 2001). Lesbian and gay families are as diverse as heterosexual families. Each family is unique, whether heterosexual or homosexual. Gay and lesbian families share many of the same concerns as households headed by heterosexuals and in addition, deal with issues specific to being members of an oppressed group.

Gays and lesbians experience oppression in the forms of *homophobia* and *heterosexism*. Homophobia is an irrational fear, intolerance, or hatred of gay men and lesbians. Sanders and Kroll (2000) stated that homophobia can be an attitude or action directed at a person based on her or his homosexual orientation. Overt acts can include gay bashing (where people are beaten and even killed because they are believed to be homosexual) or acts of hatred (where people's integrity is attacked based on their perceived orientation). Covert displays include laws that deprive gays and lesbians equal rights due to their orientation (i.e., marriage, adoption, or antidiscrimination). Heterosexism is defined as "a belief in the inherent superiority of one form of loving (male with female) over all others and thereby the right to cultural dominance" (Sanders & Kroll, 2000, p. 435). Even though homophobia may appear to be the more obvious issue, it is actually heterosexism that causes more problems for gays and lesbians. As Sanders and Kroll stated,

> In working with youth and families, heterosexism is extremely impor-tant to address. It is the pervasiveness of the heterosexist belief that homosexuality is somehow lesser—less valid, less fulfilling, less cele-bratory than heterosexuality—which is the larger social (and therefore clinical) problem. (p. 435)

UNIQUE CONCERNS OF LESBIAN AND GAY FAMILIES

Research has revealed few measurable differences between gay and lesbian families and heterosexual families. However, our largely unaccepting society makes same-sex family life less comfortably visible to the dominant heterosexual world. Consequently, issues such as "coming out," safety, and isolation are real for many gay and lesbian families. These concerns are not discrete and interact with one another to form complex dynamics.

Families make different choices about being "out" in their communities. Gays and lesbians may deal with coming out either before or after becoming parents. When considering telling their children, concerns include child-custody disputes, family-of-origin reaction, fear of discrimination, peer ostracism, and how and when to tell (Ryan & Martin, 2000; Strong & Callahan, 2001). "Threats to legal custody are perhaps the most feared of all legal sanctions" (Parks, 1998, p. 385) and must be carefully researched before revealing a parent's sexual orientation. The gay or lesbian parent's family of origin can be a source of support or a source of conflict depending on their reaction to the coming out. Many parents fear discrimination in their employment, their neighborhoods, or their children's schools and must give careful consideration before revealing their sexual orientation (Ryan & Martin, 2000).

Lamme and Lamme (2001) stressed the significance of the decision regarding coming out:

> The difference between gay families that are "out" and those that are closeted or partially closeted is vital to understand. Children from "out" families may feel like representatives of their community, constantly required to explain their situation and defend their home life. If a family is even partially "in the closet," the children are often doubly afraid: They fear that they could be harassed and lose friends if the family secret becomes known, and they fear that their parents could be persecuted—perhaps losing their jobs or home—if they let the secret slip. This fear can be a paralyzing burden. Besides carefully choosing their words every time they speak of their parents, children from closeted families can be afraid to invite friends over to their house or to form any close friendships. (p. 66)

Children need to express their concerns about coming out and may need assistance in making important choices about this issue. It is essential for both counselors and families to understand that coming out is not a single event but a lifelong process for both parents and their children.

With regard to personal safety, McPherson (2001) observed that as gays and lesbians, "Wherever we go, [we] have to ask ourselves, 'Are we safe here?' When you are a parent, your stress is multiplied as you constantly worry about the safety of your children" (p. 11). Safety concerns affect not only parents but children as well, and family therapists may need to assist gay and lesbian parents in understanding their children's needs. For example, children may want their parents to hide their sexual orientation while at a school function. The therapist can help the parents understand the child's need as reaction to a homophobic culture and not the child's dislike for the parent.

Gay and lesbian families who are not White and middle class to upper class or who do not belong to the dominant culture must be viewed in the context of other oppressions. Racism and classism affect gay and lesbian families of color and families living in poverty. White families may have the advantages of White privilege while at the same time experiencing heterosexism and homophobia. A gay and lesbian family who happens to be African American and poor may live with heterosexism, racism, and classism. All forms of oppression as well as conflicting loyalties should be considered.

Lesbian and gay families face unique challenges as a result of living in a homophobic and heterosexist society. They also address issues that are universal to being a part of any family. Family therapists have a responsibility to provide services using a theoretical approach that considers the social context and which does not assume that all problems are within the family itself.

THEORETICAL CONSIDERATIONS AND CHALLENGES

There are several considerations for the family therapist when providing services to lesbian and gay families. Prevailing stage models of family development and theories of family therapy based on cybernetics are merely by-products of mid-20th century modernist culture and reflect the biases and underlying assumptions regarding what constitutes truth and reality (Doherty, 1991). These models still offer a valuable context for understanding families, including gay and lesbian families; however, their limitations must be acknowledged.

"Theory" determines what therapists see and how they think about their clients' difficulty. The underlying assumptions of any theoretical approach can be unconscious or made conscious. When counseling gay and lesbian families, it is critical to make the underlying assumptions conscious. Theories that are based on a belief that heterosexuality is the only legitimate form of sexual identification, that monogamy is the norm, and that any other type of relating is deviant are not only inappropriate but may cause actual harm.

Theoretical models that assume "the problem" is entirely within the family and focus solely on family interactions should be avoided. The broader social context must be considered when counseling gay and lesbian families. The impacts of marginalization, social disapproval, and discrimination by the dominant culture need to be acknowledged. Theoretical approaches that help the family understand how they have been taught to cooperate in their own oppression and help them deconstruct their thinking by challenging learned descriptions of healthy and pathological relationships may be the most helpful (Seem, 2001).

Other challenges to providing appropriate services to gay and lesbian families are closely related to the consideration of the underlying assumptions in the theories that guide our interventions. These challenges include recognizing gay and lesbian families, the political/social climate, a lack of institutional support, and the personal beliefs, attitudes, and prejudices of the family therapist.

As previously addressed, there are many gay and lesbian family constellations and their identity may not be readily obvious. Families may be open about their makeup or they may choose to remain invisible due to the possible negative effects of homophobia.

The political/social climate also is an obstacle to working with lesbian and gay families. Although there have been advancements in the gay rights movements, there has been a backlash as well. The religious right and right-wing organizations believe that homosexuals are "threatening the fabric of family life" and "some religious fundamentalists believe that homosexuality is against the will of God" (Ariel & McPherson, 2000, p. 424). There also exists a conservative element of society that adheres to the patriarchal family structure dictating the male figure as central and all powerful.

Finally, many people fear nonconformity and difference and become prejudiced toward homosexuality in general. These factors create a difficult atmosphere in which to provide services for gay and lesbian families. Although it is too early to foresee the full impact of the recent decision of the Supreme Court striking down the Texas sodomy law, that may foretell increasing societal acceptance of homosexuality.

Family therapists and counselors must address personal challenges regarding their own beliefs, attitudes, and prejudices. Homophobic beliefs and heterosexist attitudes can negatively affect the quality of the helping relationship. Ryan and Martin (2000) described additional obstacles that included "the desire to appear . . . liberal-minded, because it results in an unwillingness to acknowledge views that may be biased" (p. 210); an investment in traditional gender roles for males and females; and finally, the belief that homosexual relationships are more sexually focused than heterosexual relationships and therefore require talking about uncomfortable sexual issues. Sanders and Kroll (2000) suggested that therapists "view what has been called sexual orientation through the lens of human affiliation" (p. 434). *Affiliative orientation* is defined as "the involuntary inner experience of 'romantically falling in love,' which we all experience from time to time in our lives" (Sanders & Kroll, 2000, p. 434).

SUGGESTIONS FOR FAMILY COUNSELORS AND THERAPISTS

Difficulty in identifying gay and lesbian families, a negative political and social climate, and personal beliefs and attitudes are obstacles that can be overcome. Researchers have provided numerous suggestions for helping professionals to improve their skills in counseling gay and lesbian families (Ariel & McPherson, 2000; Lamme & Lamme, 2001; Parks, 1998; Ryan & Martin, 2000; Sanders & Kroll, 2000). Awareness of personal beliefs and biases is fundamental and must be examined and when necessary, modified. Family therapists should be intolerant of antigay language and be willing to speak out when it is encountered. They should be careful to use inclusive language and materials in their practices and not those that reflect heterosexism. Formal policies, forms, and brochures ought to reflect this same acceptance and inclusivity. Books and posters that affirm gay and lesbian families help to ensure welcoming surroundings. Awareness of specific issues that may affect gay and lesbian families and knowledge of resources and support groups is the therapist's responsibility.

Ariel and McPherson (2000) stated that a counselor or therapist "has a profound responsibility to obtain the training, education, and experience necessary to understand the lived experience of lesbian and gay parents, their children, their extended families, and their families of choice" (p. 431).

Family therapists and counselors are in a position to provide much needed support and recognition to this population. As Ariel and McPherson observed,

> One of the most remarkable aspects of working with gays and lesbians is the continual awareness of two realities. The first is the universal reality of ordinary human beings struggling together to create intimate bonds that allow both individual freedom and family cohesion. The second is the particular reality of societal prejudice: at any moment, a gay or lesbian family can become the object of hate or derision that powerfully affects self-esteem and the level of stress within the family. Being able to hold both of these realities is primary to intervening effectively with any oppressed group. (p. 430)

SOURCE: Jennifer L. Adams, Jodi D. Jaques, and Kathleen M. May. (2004). Counseling Gay and Lesbian Families: Theoretical Considerations. *The Family Journal: Counseling and Therapy for Couples and Families,* 12, 40-42. © 2004 SAGE Publications.

REFERENCES

Ariel, J., & McPherson, D. W. (2000). Therapy with lesbian and gay parents and their children. *Journal of Marital and Family Therapy, 26,* 421-432.

Doherty, W. (1991). Family therapy goes postmodern. *Family Therapy Networker, 15,* 36-42.

Lamme, L. L., & Lamme, L. A. (2001). Welcoming children from gay families into our schools. *Educational Leadership, 59*(4), 65-69.

McPherson, D. (2001). Queer as parents [Essay]. *In The Family, 7*(1), 11-13.

Parks, C. A. (1998). Lesbian parenthood: A review of the literature. *American Journal of Orthopsychiatry, 68,* 376-389.

Ryan, D., & Martin, A. (2000). Lesbian, gay, bisexual, and transgender parents in the school systems. *School Psychology Review, 29,* 207-216.

Sanders, G. L., & Kroll, I. T. (2000). Generating stories of resilience: Helping gay and lesbian youth and their families. *Journal of Marital and Family Therapy, 26,* 433-442.

Seem, S. R. (2001). Feminist family therapy: For heterosexual couples and families only? In K. M. May (Ed.), *Feminist family therapy* (pp. 29-51). Alexandria, VA: American Counseling Association.

Strong, S., & Callahan, C. J. (2001). Professional responsibility to gay, lesbian, bisexual, and transgendered (GLBT) youths and families. In D. S. Sandhu (Ed.), *Elementary school counseling in the new millennium* (pp. 249-258). Alexandria, VA: American Counseling Association.

Jennifer L. Adams is a graduate student in counseling at California Polytechnic State University, San Luis Obispo, California. Her interests include social justice and feminist theory and practice.

Jodi D. Jaques is an assistant professor of counselor education at California Polytechnic State University, San Luis Obispo, California. Her interests include social justice and feminist theory and practice.

Kathleen M. May is an associate professor of counselor education at the University of Virginia, Charlottesville. Her interests include social justice and feminist theory and practice.

13

Family Stress, Crisis, and Trauma:
Building Family Resilience

Trauma Symptoms in Preschool-Age Children Exposed to Domestic Violence

Alytia A. Levendosky

Alissa C. Huth-Bocks

Michael A. Semel

Deborah L. Shapiro

Michigan State University

The posttraumatic stress symptoms of 39 children who had witnessed domestic violence and 23 children who were living in families with domestic violence were assessed by maternal report. Two measures of PTSD were used and compared, one based on the DSM-IV symptom list and one from the CBCL. Although all children had experienced at least one symptom of trauma, only 3% or 24% of the children, depending on the measure used, met criteria for PTSD based on the DSM-IV. Children with reexperiencing trauma symptoms also had more externalizing behavior problems. The applicability of DSM-IV criteria for young children and the use of the CBCL to assess trauma symptoms were questioned.

AUTHORS' NOTE: This research was supported by an NIMH B/START grant to the first author. The authors would like to thank the following graduate and undergraduate students for their assistance in data collection and management: Sarah Arnold, Kristin August, Jenni Clift, Waseya Cornell, Jocelyn Cramer, Betsy Grego, Deborah Kraus, Daniel Lake, Barbara Leibson, Julie Maleski, Susan Marsiglia, Brian McManus, Amanda McClintock, Suzanne Morton, Lisa Pahl, Michael Popovich, Elizabeth Primeau, Sarah Preus, Jacqueline Rieth, Deirdre Shires, Kimberly Sharky, and Sally Theran.

A handful of studies have found that preschool children living in families with domestic violence exhibit higher levels of social, behavioral, and cognitive problems than children in nonviolent homes (Davis & Carlson, 1987; Fantuzzo et al., 1991; Graham-Bermann & Levendosky, 1998a). However, there has been little research on the traumatic symptoms that these children may develop as a result of witnessing domestic violence. A few studies of school-age children witnessing domestic violence have documented that children 6 and older do experience traumatic symptoms as a result of these experiences (Graham-Bermann & Levendosky, 1998b; Kilpatrick & Williams, 1997; Lehmann, 1997; Rossman, 1998). Research on trauma symptoms in children younger than 6 who have experienced any traumatic events is very minimal, perhaps due to problems in conceptualizing traumatic symptomatology in young children (cf. Scheeringa, Zeanah, Drell, & Larrieu, 1995).

Trauma perpetrated by another person, as opposed to experiencing severe illness or natural disasters, is simultaneously a psychological, physiological, and relational event. Trauma overwhelms the person's ego capacities to understand what has happened (Herman, 1992). Fundamental assumptions about the safety of the world and trust in the relationships are undermined as the individual struggles to assimilate this experience (Herman, 1992). Normal physiological reactions to stress, such as hyperarousal, may repeat themselves in an altered and exaggerated form, even after the trauma is over. In adults and older children, these physiological responses have been linked to changes in the hypothalamic-pituitary-adrenal axis and associated neurotransmitters (Charney, Deutch, Krystal, Southwick, & Davis, 1993; van der Kolk, Boyd, Krystal, & Greenberg, 1984; van der Kolk, 1987). Child and adult trauma survivors often have difficulty modulating arousal, possibly due to the effects of the trauma on serotonin levels (Ornitz & Pynoos, 1989; van der Kolk, 1994). Relationally, survivors of interpersonal trauma suffer from a loss of trust and a sense of betrayal from a person who is loved (Janoff-Bulman, 1992; Terr, 1990).

The Diagnostic and Statistical Manual for Mental Disorders, Version IV *(DSM-IV)* criteria for post-traumatic stress disorder (PTSD) focus on three types of symptoms, reexperiencing, avoidance, and hyperarousal (American Psychiatric Association [APA], 1994). The specific symptoms, however, are adult-focused, for example, "intense psychological distress at exposure to internal or external cues that symbolize or resemble an aspect of the traumatic event" or "feelings of detachment or estrangement from others" (APA, 1994, p. 428). These, among other symptoms listed in the *DSM-IV*, would be difficult to measure in a young child. Several authors have suggested that there needs to be criteria for PTSD that are child-focused (Fletcher, 1996; Graham-Bermann & Levendosky, 1998b; Scheeringa et al., 1995). The Zero to Three National Center for Infants, Toddlers, and Families (1994) has developed such criteria for children age 0 to 3. However, there is still a large gap for children age 3 to 12, for whom there are no child-focused criteria for a PTSD diagnosis.

The *DSM-IV* gives some guidance on this, suggesting that children's reexperiencing symptoms may include repetitive play with traumatic themes, frightening dreams, and trauma-specific reenactment (APA, 1994). A review of the studies of PTSD symptomatology in children finds that about 25% to 40% of children of all ages exposed to traumatic events fit diagnostic criteria for PTSD, according to the *DSM-IV* (Fletcher, 1996). However, this review included only a handful of studies of children 5 and younger, thus the rates in young children are less clear.

TRAUMA AND DOMESTIC VIOLENCE

Numerous studies have documented the effects of domestic violence on women's psychological functioning, including trauma symptomatology (Cascardi & O'Leary, 1992; Khan, Welch, & Zillmer, 1993; Rounsaville & Lifton, 1983; Sato & Heiby, 1992; Testa, Miller, & Downs, 1993). Rates of PTSD are high, ranging from 45% to 85% in the samples of battered women (Astin, Ogland-Hand, Coleman, & Foy, 1995; Houskamp & Foy, 1991; Kemp, Rawlings, & Green, 1991; Vitanza, Vogel, & Marshall, 1995). A few studies indicate that greater severity and frequency of violence is associated with more serious symptomatology (e.g., Kemp, Green, Hovanitz, & Rawlings, 1995). Some theorists (e.g., Herman, 1992; Walker, 1991) have focused on the chronic nature of domestic violence trauma in comparison with the solitary event traumas, such as natural disasters, stranger rape, and stranger assault. Many women living with abusive partners experience trauma and the resulting psychological and physiological reactions to trauma over and over again (Herman, 1992). Thus, due to the prolonged, unpredictable, and repetitive nature of domestic violence, persistent affective, cognitive, and even personality changes may occur (Herman, 1992; van der Kolk, 1987). In other words, women who live in violent homes may never have the chance to recover while they remain in these physically and/or psychologically abusive environments.

One would also expect that children living in domestic violence situations would struggle with similar cognitive and affective responses to the trauma of witnessing serious harm to their mothers. For example, persistent trauma may provoke frequent posttraumatic play (Davies, 1992; Terr, 1990). There have been only four published studies of the impact of domestic violence on PTSD in school-age children. In the first published study, Rossman (1994) found that child witnesses to domestic violence had much higher levels of trauma symptoms than nonwitnesses. However, this study was quite small and included children from age 4 to 9. Lehmann (1997) found that 56% of a sample of 84 child witnesses of domestic violence met diagnostic criteria for PTSD. Aspects of the assaults, including the frequency of assault and duration of the abusive relationship, predicted PTSD symptomatology. These children were age 9 to 15 and were living in a domestic violence shelter at the time of the assessment. In a small sample of child witnesses to domestic violence (n = 20), Kilpatrick and Williams (1997) found that these children (age 6 to 12) were more likely to experience traumatic symptoms in response to parental conflict than nonwitnesses (n = 15). Finally, Graham-Bermann and Levendosky (1998b) found that 13% of 64 child witnesses to domestic violence (age 7 to 12) met diagnostic criteria for PTSD. However, 52% suffered from intrusive and unwanted memories of the traumatic event, 19% experienced traumatic avoidance, and 42% were reported to have symptoms of hyperarousal. PTSD symptoms were associated with more severe violence and more internalizing and externalizing behavior problems.

The current study was designed to examine the effects of domestic violence on trauma symptoms in an understudied population, that of preschool children age 3 to 5. This is the first empirical study on PTSD focusing on only preschool-age children witnessing domestic violence. It was hypothesized that these children would experience trauma symptoms as a result of the violence that they witnessed, and their level of PTSD symptomatology would be related to their level of behavioral problems. It was hypothesized that children who had witnessed domestic violence would have higher PTSD and behavior problem scores than children who were living in families with domestic violence but had not directly witnessed it.

METHOD

Participants

The participants included 62 preschool children and their mothers living in families with domestic violence in a midsize Midwestern city. These participants were part of a larger study that was examining the effects of domestic violence on children's family relationships and behavioral functioning (Levendosky, Huth-Bocks, Shapiro, & Semel, 2000). For the purposes of the current article, only data from those children living in families in which domestic violence was currently occurring were used. These children included 25 boys and 37 girls age 3 to 5. The mean monthly income was $1,321 ($SD$ = 871). Twenty-four percent were Caucasian, 42% were African American, 19% were biracial, and 15% were from other minority groups. Marital status was 39% single, 37% married/living with a partner, and 24% separated/divorced. The families were recruited from the community through flyers at Head Start Family Independence Agency (DSS) offices and in apartment complexes, bus stops, and retail stores.

Measures

Domestic violence. The 46-item Severity of Violence Against Women Scales (SVAWS) (Marshall, 1992) was used to assess the mothers' experiences of domestic violence, including threats of violence, violent acts, and sexual abuse. Women completed this questionnaire for violence experienced in the past year. The original nine categories (Marshall, 1992) were combined so that four scales of different types of violence were used in this study: threats of violence, mild, severe, and sexual violence. Items in each category were summed to produce a frequency score. Higher scores indicate more frequent abuse. The reliability alpha was .93, .95, .97, and .85, respectively.

Children's behavioral functioning. Children's emotional and behavioral functioning was assessed through maternal report on the Child Behavior Checklist (CBCL) (Achenbach, 1992). Mothers with children age 3 years completed the 100-item CBCL for 2- to 3-year-old children (Achenbach, 1992), and mothers with children age 4 to 5 completed the 113-item CBCL for children older than 4 years of age. Children's raw scores were transformed to *T*-scores, allowing all children's scores to be grouped together. Two broadband subscales—internalizing and externalizing behaviors—were used in this study. This measure has high reliability and validity (Achenbach, 1991).

Children's trauma symptoms. Children's trauma symptoms were assessed by maternal report on two instruments. The first was the PTSD scale from the CBCL, developed by Wolfe, Gentile, and Wolfe (1989). This scale was adapted for the two different age versions of the CBCL used in this study. There were 14 items on the 2- to 3- year-old CBCL and 22 items on the 4- to 18-year-old CBCL for the PTSD scale. The 3-point scale on the CBCL was recoded into presence or absence, and then items were summed. Items on the 2- to 3-year-old CBCL PTSD scale were weighted so that the scales were equivalent and means could be compared. The alpha was .80 for the 2- to 3-year-old scale and .67 for the 4- to 18-year-old scale.

The second was an 18-item measure of PTSD symptoms in preschool children (PTSD-PAC) developed for this study based on the *DSM-IV* criteria for PTSD symptoms, with the addition of symptoms relevant to young children's traumatic responses. Several of the additional items were from Scheeringa et al.'s (1995) PTSD scale for children age 0 to 3. See Table 13.1 for a list of the items on this measure. Mothers were asked to complete this measure only if they indicated that their child had witnessed at least one domestic violent event. To qualify for a PTSD diagnosis, symptoms must have been present for more than a month. Mothers rated the presence or absence of these symptoms. The total number of symptoms was summed. The alpha for this scale was .79.

Procedure

Mothers contacted the project office if they were interested in participating. A brief screening was conducted to determine eligibility, based on the child's age (between 3 and 5) and lack of developmental disabilities.

Table 13.1   Percentage of Child Witnesses to Domestic Violence Who Exhibit Trauma Symptoms

Symptom	Total (n = 39)	%
1. Playing out violent event with toys, himself/herself, or siblings/friends	9	23
2. Talking about violent event	30	77
3. Having frightening dreams/nightmares that have increased in frequency and/or are about the violent event or similar to it	8	21
4. Becoming upset when seeing something reminding him/her of the violent event	17	44
5. Having flashbacks of the event	5	13
6. Being less interested in playing or talking with others since the violent event	0	0
7. Showing less feelings since the violent event (e.g., less anger or loving feelings)	3	8
8. Showing a loss of previously acquired skills since the event, including toilet training or language development	1	3
9. Playing with less imagination and/or seeming to have less fun when playing	0	0
10. Avoiding activities, places, persons, thoughts, or conversations associated with the violence since the violent event	10	26
11. Increased irritability, moodiness, or temper tantrums since the violent event	6	15
12. Decreased ability to concentrate since the violent event	3	8
13. Increased awareness of what is going on around him/her since the violent event	16	41
14. Becoming easily startled since the violent event	3	8
15. Developing new fears (e.g., of the dark, strangers, going to the bathroom alone) since the violent event	10	26
16. Difficulty going to sleep since the violent event (not afraid of the dark)	1	3
17. Developing fear of separation from primary caregiver since the violent event	14	36
18. Increased aggressiveness since the violent event	7	18

Interviews were conducted either in the family's home or the university offices. Interviews lasted approximately 2 hours. The mother completed an informed consent and was told that a report would be made to Child Protective Services if any unreported child abuse or neglect were discovered during the interview. Three reports were made to Child Protective Services based on observation or child report of abuse. Mothers were paid $50 for participation.

RESULTS

The means and standard deviations for the frequency of violence events and child adjustment scores are shown in Table 13.2. Mothers experienced about 10 physical threats during the past year from their partners, 4 episodes of mild violence, 2 episodes of severe violence, and 1 to 2 episodes of sexual violence. Violence and adjustment scores did not differ by sex of the child.

Posttraumatic Stress Symptoms in the Children

All of the mothers in this sample reported that they had experienced domestic violence during the past year. Of the 62 children in the sample, mothers reported that 63% ($n = 39$) had actually witnessed the domestic violence events and that the rest ($n = 23$) were living in the home during the time period of the abusive relationship. The group of children who had witnessed the domestic violence events also included 3 children who had been physically abused themselves in addition to witnessing domestic violence. All of the mothers whose children witnessed the event felt that their children had been intensely upset by the violence, the first criterion of PTSD, according to the *DSM-IV*. The mothers of the 39 children who had witnessed the domestic violence reported on their PTSD symptoms in reaction to the violent event(s) using the PTSD-PAC. These results are reported separately from the results of the CBCL PTSD scale that was completed by the mothers of all 62 children living in domestic violence families.

On the PTSD-PAC, the most frequently reported symptoms were talking about the violent event, an upset reaction in response to memory triggers, hypervigilance, and new separation anxiety (see Table 13.1). On the CBCL PTSD scale, the most frequently reported symptoms were "argues a lot," "can't sit still, restless, or hyperactive," and "fears certain animals, situations, or places." No significant sex differences were found in PTSD symptomatology on either scale.

To examine the symptomatology from a diagnostic perspective, the symptoms were divided into the three groups described in the *DSM-IV* (APA, 1994). The first set of symptoms is described as traumatic reexperiencing of the trauma. The subject must have experienced at least one

Table 13.2   Frequency of Violence Experienced by the Mothers and Mean
Adjustment Scores of the Preschool Children

	M	SD
Mother's violence experiences		
Threats of violence	10.12	10.90
Mild violence	4.15	5.25
Severe violence	2.03	5.26
Sexual violence	1.45	3.33
Children's adjustment		
Internalizing behavior	54.00	9.38
Externalizing behavior	58.90	9.30

of these symptoms to satisfy this set of criteria. For the PTSD-PAC, these include the first 5 items listed in Table 13.1. These items were translated from the *DSM-IV* to be more specifically appropriate for young children. Eighty-five percent of the preschool children had at least one of these symptoms. Using the PTSD scale from the CBCL, 92% of the total sample had at least one reexperiencing symptom.

The second set of symptoms includes persistent avoidance of the stimuli that are associated with the traumatic event(s), and three or more symptoms are necessary to satisfy diagnostic criteria. For the PTSD-PAC, these include items 6 through 10 listed in Table 13.1. In this set, some questions were added (e.g., loss of previously acquired skills) and others translated to be more specific for young children. Only 3% of the preschool children had at least three symptoms. In contrast, using the CBCL PTSD scale, 47% of the preschool children had at least three avoidance symptoms.

The third set of symptoms includes increased arousal following the traumatic event(s), and two or more symptoms are needed to satisfy diagnostic criteria. For the PTSD-PAC, these symptoms include items 11 through 18 listed in Table 13.1. In this set, 3 items were added that specifically pertain to young children, including increased aggressiveness, development of new fears, and separation anxiety. Thirty-nine percent of the preschool children had at least two symptoms. Using the CBCL PTSD scale, 91% of the preschool children had at least two symptoms of hyperarousal.

To satisfy all of the criteria for a PTSD diagnosis, children had to have at least one reexperiencing symptom, three avoidance symptoms, and two hyperarousal symptoms. Based on the PTSD-PAC, although all of the

39 children had at least one symptom of PTSD, only 1 child, or 3% of the sample, met diagnostic criteria according to the *DSM-IV* (APA, 1994). Using the PTSD scale from the CBCL, 24% met diagnostic criteria according to the *DSM-IV*. Strikingly, there were no significant correlations between the CBCL PTSD scales and those from the PTSD-PAC.

PTSD Symptoms and Maternal Experiences of Domestic Violence

The four types of violence experiences were correlated with the scores for the trauma symptoms from the PTSD-PAC (see Table 13.3). Reexperiencing symptoms in preschool children were associated with increased violence of all types. Hyperarousal symptoms in preschool children were associated with increased threats of violence, mild violence, and sexual violence (a trend) experienced by their mothers. The total number of PTSD symptoms was associated with all four types of violence experiences. In contrast, there were no significant relationships between the CBCL PTSD scales and the types of violence experiences of the mothers.

PTSD Symptoms and Children's Adjustment

Only reexperiencing symptoms from the PTSD-PAC were associated with children's functioning, so that more symptoms were associated with increased levels of externalizing behaviors ($r = .32$, $p < .05$). However, the whole group of 62 preschool children had highly elevated externalizing behaviors compared with the normal population, so that 42% of the sample had T-scores of at least 60, and 29% of the sample fell into the clinical range (Achenbach, 1991). In contrast, these children did not have elevated internalizing behaviors. Neither the internalizing nor the externalizing scores were related to the CBCL PTSD scores when the relevant PTSD items were removed from the behavior scales.

Comparisons Between Witnesses and Nonwitnesses

The 39 children who had witnessed domestic violence were compared with the 23 children who had not witnessed domestic violence but were living in families with domestic violence, on externalizing and internalizing behavior scores and the PTSD scales from the CBCL, using t tests. There were no significant differences between the groups. In addition, the frequency of the four types of violence was compared using t tests between these two groups. There was no significant difference in frequency of violence experienced by the mothers of these two groups of children.

Table 13.3   Correlations Between Types of Mothers' Domestic Violence Experiences and PTSD
Symptoms of the Preschool Children From the PTSD-PAC

	Reexperiencing	Avoidance	Hyperarousal	Total PTSD Score
Threats of violence	.61***	.10	.50***	.55***
Mild violence	.45*	−.03	.34**	.38**
Severe violence	.56***	.02	.20	.36**
Sexual violence	.50***	.12	.27*	.39**

NOTE: PTSD = post-traumatic stress disorder; PTSD-PAC = PSTD symptoms in preschool children.

$*p < .10.$ $**p < .05.$ $***p < .001.$

DISCUSSION

The results of this study indicate that preschool children who witness domestic violence or live in domestic violence families without directly witnessing it suffer from symptoms of PTSD. In particular, preschool children appeared to be most vulnerable to symptoms of reexperiencing the trauma and hyperarousal. However, few of these children met criteria for the diagnosis of PTSD using the *DSM-IV* criteria (APA, 1994) based on either measure of PTSD used in this study.

These findings are similar to the findings of Graham-Bermann and Levendosky (1998b), who found that although the majority of school-age children exposed to domestic violence experienced symptoms of PTSD, only 13% of the sample met criteria for the diagnosis. Both the current study and the one by Graham-Bermann and Levendosky (1998b) were conducted on a community sample of children. The other studies of children exposed to domestic violence have found higher rates of PTSD (e.g., Lehmann, 1997; Kilpatrick & Williams, 1997); however, these studies were conducted on children living in shelters. Children in shelters are suffering not only from the trauma of the violent events but also from moving suddenly; being separated from family, friends, school, and community; and the often chaotic experience of shelter life. Thus, their level of trauma symptomatology is, not surprisingly, higher.

However, the results of the current study also lend support to concerns that the current criteria for a diagnosis of PTSD are not appropriate for young children. Avoidant symptoms appear to be particularly unusual in this sample. Perhaps this is a developmental phenomenon: Young children may respond by clinging to their mother or other attachment figures in response to trauma rather than avoiding feelings, people, or places. It is also noteworthy that some of the symptoms most frequently endorsed by the mothers on the PTSD-PAC were ones specifically created in response to concerns about the developmental criteria for the disorder (e.g., developing new fears, developing separation anxiety, and increased aggressiveness). For the purposes of this study, these were all grouped under hyperarousal symptoms. The findings in this study were similar to those of Graham-Bermann and Levendosky, who found that only 19% of their sample of school-age children met criteria for avoidant symptoms, whereas 52% met criteria for reexperiencing and 42% for hyperarousal. These rates are also much lower than rates of PTSD seen in women who are abused. Thus, it is also possible that children respond differently to traumatic events than adults because of their lesser cognitive and emotional capacities to perceive them, and thus they more rarely respond by developing a full-blown PTSD.

Another alternative is that young children display clinical levels of trauma in different ways. Scheeringa et al. (1995), who studied PTSD in infants age 0 to 3, recommend that the original three categories be maintained for young children (i.e., reexperiencing, avoidance, and hyperarousal) but that only one symptom of each of these be required. In addition, they group the new fears, separation anxiety, and increased aggressiveness in a new category labeled "new fears and aggression" and requires one symptom from this group. In the current study, using Scheeringa et al.'s criteria, 26% of the sample would then be considered to have PTSD based on the PTSD-PAC and 50% based on the CBCL-PTSD. Rates of 26% to 50%, rather than 3%, are consistent with other studies of children experiencing traumatic events. Thus, Scheeringa's criteria may be more useful for young children, including preschoolers, than the criteria in the *DSM-IV*.

Furthermore, in this study, symptoms of PTSD were associated with increased severity of the four types of violence. In particular, symptoms of reexperiencing were positively associated with all four types of violence and symptoms of hyperarousal were positively associated with all but the severe violence category. These findings mirror studies on older children (Graham-Bermann & Levendosky, 1998b) and battered women (Kemp et al., 1995) finding that more abuse toward the mother is associated with higher levels of trauma symptoms in both children and their mothers. Thus, it is not merely the presence of violence in the parental relationship but also the extent and frequency of it. The lack of association of avoidant symptoms with any of the violence types lends further support to the hypothesis that the avoidant symptoms are not as reflective of trauma in this age group.

Another interesting finding that is different from the results of the Graham-Bermann and Levendosky (1998b) study is that there was only one relationship between traumatic symptoms and behavior problems. In the prior study with older children, all three types of trauma symptoms were associated with both internalizing and externalizing symptoms. In this study, only reexperiencing symptoms were associated with externalizing behaviors. Reexperiencing symptoms were the most frequently reported symptoms by mothers, and these children appear to demonstrate more aggressive, delinquent, and acting-out behaviors as well. Perhaps the intrusive nature of reexperiencing the trauma upsets the child and arouses a parasympathetic response, causing either aggression toward the self or others. Thus, trauma not only impacts children's intrapsychic life but also their interpersonal functioning. However, it occurs in a more limited way than for older children. It appears that trauma symptoms for young children are not necessarily manifested in behavioral pathology, as measured by the CBCL, and thus may have less of an impact on their development than they do for older children.

In addition, it is noteworthy that these children generally had elevated externalizing behavior scores compared with national norms. This suggests that living with domestic violence is related to more aggressive and acting-out behavior, possibly due to modeling. However, trauma symptomatology seems to play only a minor role in behavior problems for children this age.

Finally, the lack of concordance between the measure of trauma derived from the *DSM-IV* (PTSD-PAC) and the CBCL PTSD scale and the lack of association of the CBCL PTSD scale with the violence or behavior problems suggests some problems with using the CBCL PTSD scale. Although many of the behaviors listed on the two scales are similar, the first measure is administered in response to the mother thinking about changes in the behaviors following the violent events. The CBCL PTSD scale is part of the whole measure that simply asks mothers to respond about the frequency of each behavior exhibited by their child in the past 6 months. The CBCL PTSD scale has been used in several studies of trauma in children, but there is a significant concern as to whether it is actually assessing a response to a traumatic event.

There are several limitations in the current study. First, we relied on maternal reports of their child witnessing the domestic violence to ask mothers to assess the PTSD symptoms. Unfortunately, this meant that 23 of the children living in domestic violence homes were excluded from these analyses. Given the likelihood of underreporting and minimizing of the impact of domestic violence on their children, it is possible that many of the other 23 children may have also been exhibiting trauma symptoms. In addition, the PTSD-PAC is a measure that has not yet been subjected to tests of reliability and validity. Finally, the diagnostic criteria based on the *DSM-IV* includes symptomatology that may be indicators of depression in addition to or rather than PTSD, including items 11 and 12 from Table 13.1. This is a potential problem for differential diagnosis using the *DSM-IV* criteria.

The results from this study call for further research on trauma symptomatology in young children. Appropriate diagnostic criteria need to be developed to assess accurately the impact of traumatic events on preschool-age children. In addition, it is clear that trauma symptoms are a common reaction in young children who witness domestic violence. Thus, it is important for clinicians and school counselors working with preschool-age children to assess for family violence when attempting to understand the nature of the child's behavioral and emotional problems.

SOURCE: Alytia A. Levendosky, Alissa C. Huth-Bocks, Michael A. Semel, and Deborah L. Shapiro. (2002). Trauma Symptoms in Preschool-Age Children Exposed to Domestic Violence. *Journal of Interpersonal Violence, 17,* 150-154. © 2002 SAGE Publications.

REFERENCES

Achenbach, T. M. (1991). *Manual for the Child Behavior Checklist/4-18 and 1991 profile.* Burlington: University of Vermont, Department of Psychiatry.

Achenbach, T. M. (1992). *The Child Behavior Checklist: 2- to 3-year-old version.* Unpublished manuscript, University of Vermont, Burlington, VT.

American Psychiatric Association. (1994). *Diagnostic and statistical manual of mental disorders–IV.* Washington, DC: Author.

Astin, M. C., Ogland-Hand, S. M., Coleman, E. M., & Foy, D. W. (1995). Post-traumatic stress disorder and childhood abuse in battered women: Comparisons with maritally distressed women. *Journal of Consulting and Clinical Psychology, 63,* 308-312.

Cascardi, M., & O'Leary, K. D. (1992). Depressive symptomatology, self-esteem, and self-blame in battered women. *Journal of Family Violence, 7,* 249-259.

Charney, D. S., Deutch, A. Y., Krystal, J. H., Southwick, S. M., & Davis, M. (1993). Psychobiological mechanisms of post-traumatic stress disorder. *Archives of General Psychiatry, 50,* 294-305.

Davies, D. (1992). Intervention with male toddlers who have witnessed parental violence. *Families in Society: The Journal of Contemporary Human Services, 72,* 515-524.

Davis, L. V., & Carlson, B. E. (1987). Observations of spouse abuse: What happens to the children? *Journal of Interpersonal Violence, 2,* 278-291.

Fantuzzo, J. W., DePaola, L. M., Lambert, L., Martino, T., Anderson, G., & Sutton, S. (1991). Effects of interparental violence on the psychological adjustment and competence of young children. *Journal of Clinical and Consulting Psychology, 59,* 258-265.

Fletcher, K. E. (1996). Childhood post-traumatic stress disorder. In E. J. Mash & R. A. Barkley (Eds.), *Child psychopathology* (pp. 242-276). New York: Guilford.

Graham-Bermann, S. A., & Levendosky, A. A. (1998a). The social functioning of preschool-age children whose mothers are emotionally and physically abused. *Journal of Emotional Abuse, 1*(1), 59-84.

Graham-Bermann, S. A., & Levendosky, A. A. (1998b). Traumatic stress symptoms in children of battered women. *Journal of Interpersonal Violence, 14,* 111-128.

Herman, J. L. (1992). *Trauma and recovery.* New York: Basic Books.

Houskamp, B. M., & Foy, D. W. (1991). The assessment of post-traumatic stress disorder in battered women. *Journal of Interpersonal Violence, 6,* 367-375.

Janoff-Bulman, R. (1992). *Shattered assumptions: Toward a new psychology of trauma.* New York: Free Press.

Kemp, A., Green, B. L., Hovanitz, C., & Rawlings, E. I. (1995). Incidence and correlates of posttraumatic stress disorder in battered women. *Journal of Interpersonal Violence, 10,* 43-55.

Kemp, A., Rawlings, E. I., & Green, B. L. (1991). Post-traumatic stress disorder (PTSD) in battered women: A shelter sample. *Journal of Traumatic Stress, 4,* 137-148.

Khan, F. I., Welch, T. L., & Zillmer, E. A. (1993). MMPI-2 profiles of battered women in transition. *Journal of Personality Assessment, 60,* 100-111.

Kilpatrick, K. L., & Williams, L. M. (1997). Post-traumatic stress disorder in child witnesses to domestic violence. *American Journal of Orthopsychiatry, 67,* 639-644.

Lehmann, P. (1997). The development of post-traumatic stress disorder (PTSD) in a sample of child witnesses to mother assault. *Journal of Family Violence, 12*(3), 241-257.

Levendosky, A. A., Huth-Bocks, A. C., Shapiro, D. L., & Semel, M. A. (2000). *The impact of domestic violence on the maternal-child relationship and preschool-age children's functioning.* Manuscript submitted for publication.

Marshall, L. (1992). Development of the severity of violence against women scales. *Journal of Family Violence, 7,* 103-121.

Ornitz, E. M., & Pynoos, R. S. (1989). Startle modulation in children with post-traumatic stress disorder. *American Journal of Psychiatry, 146,* 866-870.

Rossman, B. B. R. (1994). Children in violent families: Diagnostic and treatment considerations. *Family Violence and Sexual Assault Bulletin, 10,* 29-34.

Rossman, B. B. R. (1998). Descartes' error and post-traumatic stress disorder: Cognition and emotion in children who are exposed to parental violence. In G. W. Holden, R. Geffner, & E. N. Jouriles (Eds.), *Children exposed to marital violence: Theory, research, and applied issues.* Washington, DC: American Psychological Association.

Rounsaville, B. J., & Lifton, N. (1983). A therapy group for battered women. In M. Rosenbaum (Ed.), *Handbook of short-term therapy groups* (pp. 155-179). New York: McGraw-Hill.

Sato, R. A., & Heiby, E. M. (1992). Correlates of depressive symptoms among battered women. *Journal of Family Violence, 7,* 229-245.

Scheeringa, M. S., Zeanah, C. H., Drell, M. J., & Larrieu, J. A. (1995). Two approaches to the diagnosis of post-traumatic stress disorder in infancy and early childhood. *Journal of the American Academy of Child and Adolescent Psychiatry, 34,* 191-200.

Terr, L. C. (1990). *Too scared to cry.* New York: Basic Books.

Testa, M., Miller, B. A., & Downs, W. R. (1993, August). *Women's self-esteem predicts subsequent violent victimization by partner.* Paper presented at the American Psychological Association conference, Toronto, Canada.

van der Kolk, B. A. (1987). *Psychological trauma.* Washington, DC: American Psychiatric Press.

van der Kolk, B. A. (1994). The body keeps score: Memory and the evolving psychobiology of post-traumatic stress. *Harvard Review of Psychiatry, 1,* 253-265.

van der Kolk, B. A., Boyd, H., Krystal, J., & Greenberg, M. (1984). Post-traumatic stress disorder as a biologically based disorder: Implications of the animal model of inescapable shock. In B. A. van der Kolk (Ed.), *Post-traumatic stress disorder: Psychological and biological sequelae* (pp. 124-134). Washington, DC: American Psychiatric Press.

Vitanza, S., Vogel, L. C. M., & Marshall, L. L. (1995). Distress and symptoms of post-traumatic stress disorder in abused women. *Violence and Victims, 10*(1), 23-34.

Walker, L. E. (1991). Post-traumatic stress disorder in women: Diagnosis and treatment of battered woman syndrome. *Psychotherapy, 28,* 21-29.

Wolfe, V. V., Gentile, C., & Wolfe, D. A. (1989). The impact of sexual abuse on children: A PTSD formulation. *Behavior Therapy, 20,* 215-228.

Zero to Three National Center for Infants, Toddlers, and Families. (1994). *Diagnostic classification of mental health and developmental disorders of infancy and early childhood.* Washington, DC: Author.

Alytia A. Levendosky received her Ph.D. from the University of Michigan in 1995. She is currently an associate professor at Michigan State University in the Department of Psychology. Her research interests include the intergenerational transmission of domestic violence and the impact of domestic violence on women and children. She is currently conducting a prospective longitudinal study of the risk and resilience factors for domestic violence.

Alissa C. Huth-Bocks is currently finishing her doctoral program in clinical psychology at Michigan State University. Her research interests include parent-child relationships and young children's mental health in high-risk families. Her dissertation is examining prenatal and postnatal predictors of mother-infant attachment in families experiencing domestic violence.

Michael A. Semel is currently completing the requirements for his Ph.D. in clinical psychology at Michigan State University. He completed a predoctoral internship in clinical psychology at Cambridge Hospital in 1999 and a child clinical psychology fellowship at Cambridge Hospital in 2000. He continues to provide outpatient psychiatric care and crisis evaluations as a Harvard Medical School fellow at Cambridge Hospital while coordinating care and providing treatment for a group of severely disturbed adolescents through the Children's Community Support Collaborative of the New England Home for Little Wanderers.

Deborah L. Shapiro received her Ph.D. in clinical psychology at Michigan State University in August 2001, after completing a predoctoral internship at the Indiana University School of Medicine. Her clinical work has focused on the treatment of trauma, and her research interests include the effects of childhood sexual abuse and domestic violence and health care. She plans to continue working on the prevention and therapeutic intervention of violence and trauma.

"It's the Little Things"

Women, Trauma, and Strategies for Healing

Vanja M. K. Stenius

Bonita M. Veysey

Rutgers University

Women recover and heal from traumatic violent experiences in many different ways. This study, which is part of the Franklin County Women and Violence Project, explores the healing experiences of 18 women who have histories of violence, substance abuse, and involvement in the mental health and/or substance abuse treatment system. Ethnographic interviews suggest that while professional intervention can be beneficial, it may not be adequate. In fact, it can be retuamatizing. The means of service delivery and treatment by individuals, service providers and others, may be more important than the actual service. Often women find that caring individuals and a safe environment yield the greatest benefit. It is not so much what people do to help, but how they do it.

Keywords: trauma; healing strategies; women/ social supports; recovery; service delivery; substance abuse

Interpersonal violence, including physical and sexual assault, such as rape, incest, battering, and murder, is so common for women as to be described as a normative part of female experience in the United States today (Salasin & Rich, 1993). In fact, 20% to 30% of women in the general population report experiencing sexual and/or physical abuse during their lifetime (Commonwealth Fund, 1997; Mowbray, Oysermann, Saunders, &

Rueda-Riedle, 1998). One million women report episodes of domestic violence each year in the United States (Manley, 1999). Furthermore, these
numbers underestimate the prevalence of violence because the silencing that
results from fear, shame, and stigma creates a gross underreporting of incidents (Alexander & Muenzenmaier, 1998; Commonwealth Fund, 1997).

The violence that women experience has profound effects. Early
childhood sexual and physical abuse rips at the core of an individual's
developing sense of self. It violates fundamental assumptions about the
integrity and control of the body. The world no longer appears safe, just,
and orderly (Carmen & Rieker, 1989; Herman, 1992; Prescott, 1998).
Women who experience physical and sexual abuse as children are at
increased risk for mental health problems, such as depression, posttraumatic
stress and other anxiety disorders, suicidal ideations and attempts, poor self-
esteem, eating disorders, and self-inflicted injury (Alexander &
Muenzenmaier, 1998; Bassuk, Melnick, & Browne, 1998; Commonwealth
Fund, 1997, 1998; Herman, 1992; Miller, 1996; van der Kolk, 1996a,
1996b); substance abuse (Alexander, 1996; Amaro & Hardy-Fanta, 1995;
Najavits, Weiss, & Liese, 1996); and chronic medical conditions such as
pelvic pain, gastrointestinal problems, fibromyalgia, epilepsy, migraines,
respiratory-related ailments, and cardiovascular problems in later life
(Bassuk et al., 1998; Felitti, Anda, & Nordenberg, 1998; Green, Epstein,
Krupnick, & Rowland, 1997; van der Kolk, 1996a, 1996b; Zlotnick et al.,
1997). Women who were abused as children are also at increased risk of
rape and domestic violence as adults (Alexander & Muenzenmaier, 1998;
Lipschitz et al., 1996; Walker et al., 1999).

The consequences and subsequent costs of violence may be assumed by
estimates from within treatment systems. The percentages of women with a
history of interpersonal violence within the psychiatric system vary between
48% and 90% (Alexander, 1996; Jennings, 1997; Kalinowski & Penney,
1998). A history of interpersonal violence among women with drug and
alcohol problems is very common, with percentages ranging from 55% to
99% (Jennings, 1997; Miller, 1994, 1996; Najavits et al., 1996). This
suggests that trauma is central and causally related to addiction and
symptoms of traumatic stress, which are often misunderstood as symptoms
of non-trauma-related mental illnesses (Alexander & Muenzenmaier, 1998;
Amaro & Hardy-Fanta, 1995; Miller, 1996).

However, women who receive mental health, substance abuse, and/or
emergency medical services are rarely asked about histories of physical and
sexual abuse (Browne & Bassuk, 1997; Commonwealth Fund, 1998; Miller,
1996). Of the few women whose abuse histories are known, only 10% to
20% report that their trauma has been adequately addressed in treatment
(Alexander & Muenzenmaier, 1998). There is an acute lack of trauma-
informed, gender-specific care for women. In addition, systems serving
women in need of mental health and/or substance abuse services generally
have been fragmented, poorly organized, or nonexistent (Blanch & Levin,

1998). Exclusionary practices within the mental health and substance abuse systems serve to further fragment women's care as each particular service setting focuses on narrowly defined, service-specific symptoms rather than addressing women in their wholeness and complexity. Treatment systems have also caused harm to women through a legacy of disbelieving, misdiagnosing, overmedicating, and engaging in retraumatizing practices, such as forced disrobing and the use of seclusion and chemical and physical restraints (Carmen & Rieker, 1989; Jennings, 1997; Kalinowski & Penney, 1998; Ridgely & van der Berg, 1997).

Several factors are known to help women in the healing process, including adequate and early identification of co-occurring problems, a treatment philosophy based on competency building and empowerment, and services and supports provided in safe, accessible, and community-based locations (Alexander & Muenzenmaier, 1998). Other essential components include the establishment of mutual relationships built on trust (Harris, 1994; Maine Trauma Advisory Report Group, 1997; Prescott, 1998), notably in the form of peer relationships (Dunn, Steginga, Occhipinti, & Wilson, 1999) and peer-run groups (Baxter & Diehl, 1998), establishing and maintaining safety (Hedges, 2000; Talbot et al., 1998), and trauma-specific treatment (Harris, 1994; Harvey, 1996; Miller, 1994, 1996).

The purpose of the current study was to understand how women with histories of violence view and participate in their own healing process, allowing them to define how formal treatment systems and informal resources interact to support them in their recovery. The current study utilized an ethnomethodological stance, which recognizes that objects and events have equivocal meanings and that social realities are reflexive (i.e., they are constituted and constituting; Gubrium & Holstein, 1995). Whereas quantitative and positivistic research methods are limited in their ability to get a complete picture of the phenomena or lives under study (Feldman & Aldrich, 1990), ethnographic case studies provide women with the opportunity to tell their stories with their own voices, giving the researcher a view of how the women's lives interact with the service system and other supports to influence their recovery and healing without limiting responses to already developed concepts.

METHOD

The Franklin County Women and Violence Project (FCWVP) was one of nine sites nationally that tested the effectiveness of comprehensive and integrated services for women with histories of trauma and co-occurring disorders.[1] The study defined *trauma* as at least one occurrence of physical or sexual abuse at any time during the woman's life. In childhood, this includes hitting, punching, kicking or burning, extreme punishment, sexual touching, exposure, or rape. In adulthood, this includes physical assaults, coerced sex,

Table 13.4   Participant Characteristics

Participant	Age	Ethnicity	Children	Port of Entry	Trauma Type[a]
E1	30s	White	No	Domestic violence	Childhood physical
E5	30s	White	No	Mental health	All but one
E6	50s	White	Yes	Domestic violence and/or substance abuse	All
E8	40s	White	No	Domestic violence	All
E9	40s	White	Yes	Mental health	All but one
E13	30s	White	Yes	Domestic violence	Adult physical
E15	40s	White	Yes	Domestic violence	All
E18	40s	White	Yes	Domestic violence	All
E20	40s	White	Yes	Domestic violence	All but one
E21	20s	Latina	No	Substance abuse	All
E22	30s	White	Yes	Substance abuse	All but one
E23	30s	White	Yes	Substance abuse	All
E24	Missing	White	Yes	Substance abuse	Childhood and adult sexual abuse
E25	Missing	White	No	Substance abuse	Childhood physical and sexual
E26	30s	White	Yes	Homeless	All
E28	20s	White	Yes	Homeless	All but one
E29	30s	White	Yes	Homeless	All but one
E31	30s	White	Yes	Homeless	All

NOTE: a. Trauma types include childhood physical, childhood sexual, adult physical, and adult sexual.

or rape. In addition to a quasi-experimental outcome study, the evaluation also included a series of in-depth interviews with 18 women who met the criteria for the larger study. All women in the interview sample have diagnoses of mental and substance use disorders, a history of physical and/or sexual abuse, and two or more treatment episodes within the mental health or substance abuse systems. The participants for these interviews were selected from a stratified sampling frame of women currently using services. The sample was stratified by portal of entry (i.e., substance abuse, mental health, domestic violence, and homeless services), race and/or ethnicity, and motherhood status. All of these factors are believed to influence how women perceive themselves, how they participate in services, and their patterns of recovery. The resulting sample comes primarily from domestic violence and substance abuse portals (see Table 13.4). The women range in age from their 20s to their 50s; 72% are in their 30s or 40s. Of the women, 72% are mothers. All but one woman is White, which reflects the demographics of Franklin County. In terms of experiences with physical and sexual abuse in childhood and adulthood, 44% experienced all four. Of the remainder, all but one experienced two or more forms of trauma.

Interviews

Field researchers were trained in techniques of interviewing, observation, and taking field notes. A clinician with expertise in trauma and addiction provided supervision. Teams of two interviewers, one with doctoral level[2] training in clinical psychology and one personal experience with trauma and co-occurring mental health and substance abuse disorders, conducted the interviews. All of the interviewers were women and had personal and/or clinical knowledge of trauma, substance use, and mental health. The inclusion of interviewers with a history similar to the women's was intended to foster an atmosphere in which the women felt that they would be heard and understood. Prior to beginning the interview, respondents were informed that one or more of the interviewers was also a consumer/survivor/recovering (CSR) person.

The researchers approached potential participants and requested participation in the study, explaining the purpose, activities, and human subjects protections of the research. Persons consenting to participate were interviewed every 3 months for a total of four interviews each. Interviews consisted of open-ended questions and varied in length from 1 to 2 hr. Interviews were held in a location that the women felt comfortable with and conducted in private; most were conducted at a local women's drop-in center. All interviews were audiotaped and then transcribed. The interviewers and a researcher (one of the authors) reviewed the transcriptions for accuracy. The study's findings are from the first interview that focused on how the women take care of themselves during difficult times and their experiences with supports and services that have and have not been helpful.

The semistructured interviews examined the healing and recovery process from the unique and varied viewpoints of the women. Through the course of several interviews, the case studies examined what does and does not help women heal physically, mentally, and spiritually by providing a narrative of their lives and experiences. The overarching goal of the project was to better understand what helps women heal in their entirety, not just how they address one aspect of themselves but also how they may become whole.

Analysis

Analyses for this article were conducted for the women's responses that address each of the following issues: how women take care of themselves during times of crisis, what formal supports have been harmful, and what formal supports have been helpful. Responses related to each of these issues were identified and then coded for common themes using a grounded theory approach (Glaser & Strauss, 1967). An initial list of themes was identified through open coding (Strauss & Corbin, 1990) and refined using a constant comparative approach (Glaser & Strauss, 1967). The organization of themes into categories, or domains (Spradley, 1979), and subcategories was central to the process, with constant reference to the data to develop categories that fit the women's conceptualizations of what differentiates their helpful and hurtful experiences and the linkages between helpful and hurtful experiences and supports. The first author completed the initial theme development and coding. The second author independently confirmed the themes and coded the statements.

FINDINGS

How Women Take Care of Themselves During Difficult Times

Women who have histories of trauma and co-occurring mental health and substance use disorders take care of themselves in a variety of ways when they have difficult times. Most of the women identify informal resources and supports that they use to take care of themselves. The women who report the most difficulty in taking care of themselves cite the need to recognize that they are worthy of being taken care of, and the necessity of taking care of themselves first rather than investing all of their energy in caring for others. One of the women illustrated this in saying, "I'd forget about me, so I didn't really do anything. But I've been learning now how to [take care of myself]." The recognition by women that they can and need to take care of themselves changes over time as do the means they use to do so. However, substantial commonalities exist in the methods that women use. These are connections with others, spirituality and belief systems, body work and restorative activities, and decision making and setting limits. In addition, women continue to use numbing and dissociation techniques to regain control when a situation is overwhelming, and they also set a limit on how sick they will allow themselves to become. These last two points are significant within the context of mental health practice.

Connections With Others

All of the women relied on various groups of individuals, including professionals, peers, family, and friends, to help them take care of themselves. To whom they turned depended partly on the specific situation but also on the types of supports present in women's lives. Professional service providers are a means of support for many of the women; for some it is their only source of assistance. Those who have family and peer networks report that these provide a level of understanding and trust that is not always possible in professional relationships. One woman stated, "I use the support network and it's just incredible. I don't feel like I'm alone and that's a huge thing." Women report feeling more comfortable expressing their feelings and talking about their experiences with other women, especially those who have had similar experiences. One woman indicated this in saying, "The most helpful for me, I think, is when people share what they are doing, because it validates my experience and it also opens other possibilities for me." Empowering interpersonal relationships place a woman's life in context. They validate her experiences, place the injury in perspective, reflect back her worth, and give value to her personhood. One woman highlighted this in saying, "The greatest gift for anyone in pain is compassion. It's just to totally validate them and give them compassion."

Spirituality and Beliefs

Of the women, 72% found that a spiritual connection helps them stay sober and maintain their emotional balance. The nature of the spiritual connection varies from formal religious practices to more general belief systems. However, each serves the same essential purpose—providing women with a source of support, a sense of hope, and a feeling of inner peace. In contrast to seeking out support from others, which depends on the availability and accessibility of others, spirituality is a constant presence. Women pray, meditate, reflect on their belief in a larger purpose, or engage in other practices whenever they need to. One woman described how she drew strength even in her weakness:

> I had come to a much greater understanding . . . that [forgiveness] didn't depend upon my drug addiction and whether I died a drug addict or got into recovery. God was faithful, and he was in my heart even though I was caught up in addiction.

In essence, the importance of spirituality is threefold. It is critical that women believe that they are good people, that they are not responsible for the bad things that happened to them, and that life is ultimately just. These concepts reestablish a sense of order and fairness, while reducing shame and hurt. Redefining the past and placing blame where it belongs to transform the present takes the hurtful events and not only neutralizes their effects but also, in fact, turns them into assets. One woman illustrated this in saying:

The concept that AA was founded on is . . . that you use your bad thing that happened to help someone else. It turns it into a positive thing in a funny way. It actually transforms that event from something that happened to you to something that gave you the ability to help others. It just changes where you are coming from in the world, and that has got to change how you feel about yourself. Instead of being a worthless, broken thing, you are actually a helping, worth-full thing.

Body Work and Other Restorative Activities

During times of crisis, one half of the women used different types of body work and physical activities to reduce stress and to calm, center, and balance themselves. Three themes emerged, including the importance of pets and nature, physical care, and volunteerism. Pets are fully accepting of their owners and give love unconditionally. They are not fickle and can be relied on to always be there. Walking and enjoying nature seem to be elemental. One woman's comment illustrates this point: "Aesthetics and the beauty of nature heal all. I went into the outdoors to heal from my abuse." During difficult times, women may engage in activities that relax the mind and body such as taking baths, listening to music, burning candles, using self-relaxation techniques, exercise, getting massages, and practicing yoga or other mind-body movement. Some women focused on keeping their bodies healthy through adequate sleep, exercise, and healthy eating, thus taking care of and reclaiming their bodies. Women who use this as a means of taking care of themselves believe that a reciprocal connection exists between their physical and emotional health.

Women also commonly become involved in activities that are meaningful and provide them with something healthy on which to focus (e.g., volunteering). One woman stated, "There's something about helping other people when you're not feeling real good that helps." Volunteering serves multiple purposes, including altruistic service, connecting with others, redefining social roles, and having a set schedule.

Decision Making and Limit Setting

Even if it's not explicit, everything that a woman does to take care of herself involves decision making. Of the women, 78% explicitly pointed to the importance of making their own decisions or setting limits. Explicit and active decision making entails numerous aspects but generally involves a sense of awareness of themselves, their needs, and what is and is not good for them, and then acting on that knowledge. One woman stated, "In the past, I stopped my life and took care of everybody else. This is the first time that I really have made some boundaries and have honored them."

Choice is crucial. For women this means choosing the pace at which they heal; determining when they work on which issues and with whom; being honest with themselves about what they do and do not need; setting and maintaining boundaries, whether emotional or physical; establishing a safe space, emotionally and physically; and not accepting things, whether they be friends, service providers, services, partners, or family, that are not good for them and finding ones that are: in essence, assessing the situation, making beneficial decisions, and then taking action.

Other Strategies for Taking Care of Self

Many girls and women use emotional and behavioral coping strategies to survive violent situations. Of the women in this study, 56% reported engaging in some form of coping strategy. Some strategies help them gain some degree of invisibility, such as flat affect or immobilization. Some strategies help them maintain a sense of meaning and order in the world by suppressing memories, dissociating, or by the fracturing of self (i.e., creating new identities to cope with daily trauma, each with its own memories and personality characteristics). The use of substances for the purposes of suppressing feelings and memories was cited by a number of women. Others spoke of sex and food as helping them cope with poor self-esteem. Most women acknowledged that these substances and behaviors were addictive and counterproductive. However, many of the women in the sample continue to use dissociation as a means of calming themselves and taking control of bad situations. For example, one woman stated, "I just won't let myself freak out. Now I just breathe and wait before I react. And sometimes I dissociate." Another added, "Sometimes I just numb up and I won't let myself feel nothing."

It is not surprising to note, many of these creative survivors understand how much control they really have over biologically based illnesses, such as physical health problems and psychiatric disorders. These women understand what they need to do to heal and what they need to do to prevent deterioration. In discussing her fear that her psychiatrist would use electroconvulsive therapy (ECT) one woman was afraid that "they're going to erase my memory and I'm going to come out a vegetable. And I think that's the only reason I have never allowed myself to fully break down. . . . It was out of fear." Other women anchored themselves to people or pets. Some of the women discussed how their family responsibilities keep them from getting ill, or forced them to continue despite emotional turmoil.

Finally, through these interviews it became clear that success can be as problematic as any other trauma symptom. One woman described her experiences with therapists as follows: "[The therapists] sit there and go, 'Oh, my God, you've done so well.' [The next time] I am going to say, 'Look, I probably am going to try to impress you, but please don't fall for it. I really need help.'" She concluded by saying, "The periods when it looks to the world like I am not functioning well are actually the periods when I am doing the most healing on myself and I'm actually the more finished product."

Formal Treatment Services That Have and Have Not Been Helpful in the Past

No specific support or service was uniformly identified as helpful or not helpful. Life experiences, personal preferences, and interpersonal styles dictate which service system women use most frequently and, to a large degree, how helpful they perceive those services to be. Some women reported experiences with inpatient and partial hospitalization as very helpful, while others stated just the opposite. Similarly, some women rely on Alcoholics Anonymous (AA) meetings to maintain their sobriety, while others have had problems with the meetings. The service per se does not matter as much as the means of delivery and the characteristics of those offering the service. Most of these characteristics hold irrespective of whether the service is for health care, mental health, or substance abuse treatment.

The elements in services that women found harmful to their healing are system barriers and insurance limits, lack of trauma sensitivity, lack of professional cross-training in dual diagnoses, and individual therapists' attitudes and behaviors. The primary themes of services that women reported as helpful are individual therapists' skills and relational styles, availability and institutional responsiveness, female therapists and women-only groups, and shared experience and empathy.

Harmful Service Elements

System barriers and insurance limits. System constraints present significant barriers to effective service delivery. Of the women, 72% reported problems in receiving services. Treatment services offer minimal benefit if women cannot receive the specific services they need or have to change providers because of insurance limits, catchment area restrictions, or program eligibility requirements. Insurance constraints may inhibit the receipt of necessary services, limit options in selecting service providers, or force women to choose between changing providers and losing coverage. This often means that women must either find another means of paying for the service or leave a provider with whom they have a good relationship. For example, one woman described her situation by saying,

> [The insurance company] has their own professional preferred providers. I need to lay it all out financially to see what's better and what I need to pay out of pocket to stay with the same person or if [the therapist] can get covered elsewhere.

Starting over is difficult and requires a large emotional investment to develop a relationship with a new therapist. As one woman stated,

> I've changed a lot of individual therapists in mental health over the past 3½ years. I've had to change some of them because they left to go

into [private] practice. I don't weather it well because I [have to] start
all over again.

Another woman put it succinctly and eloquently, saying, "It happens all
the time, so much transition. But it's hard for people who've had trauma and
rejection."

Availability is an additional concern. The 9-to-5 structure of much service
delivery is difficult, particularly if something unexpected arises or the
woman has a crisis. As one woman noted, "There are times in my life, when
I feel like, 'Okay, I need some assistance right now.' And I don't get it, and
then by the time I do get it, I feel like I don't need it anymore." Women
appreciate flexible access to providers, being able to contact them on a
24-hr basis if necessary. Finally, session limits are perceived as arbitrary
restrictions that interfere with healing and, when the content of the session
is emotionally intense, can be dangerous. One woman illustrated this by
saying, "I can't stand going to a therapist for an hour and then, 'Oh, time's
up.' And then I'm left shaking in my car trying to get it together."

Lack of trauma sensitivity. Without a doubt, the most deleterious effects
occur when treatment providers do not take into consideration a woman's
trauma history. Of the women, 40% shared an experience that touched
them deeply. Profound stories of clinical maltreatment demonstrate this.
One woman told the interviewers:

> This last suicide attempt . . . was definitely all related to trauma,
> brought on by a traumatic experience that was not sexual or anything.
> It was a car accident. Then it was culminated and fed by what I con-
> sidered really wrong treatment by the respite staff. They didn't
> help . . . Right after that, within 2 hours, I took 100 Tegretols. So, [the
> treatment] really spurred [the attempt].

The application of traditional substance abuse and mental health services
in a non-trauma-informed manner causes significant emotional distress and
a loss of sense of safety. Services that are designed to provide safety, such as
inpatient care, can be perceived as death sentences. Coercion, therapists
challenging the veracity of women's accounts (i.e., loss of credibility),
confrontational styles, ultimatums, male therapists, and coed groups may
trigger women. One woman related her experiences:

> I freaked the first time I went to a dialectical behavior therapy (DBT)
> group because I assumed it was all women, and there were two men there.
> I sat as far away as possible and with a clear view of the door to get out.

Their resulting reaction, such as rage, agitation, aggression, or
dissociation, further exacerbates the problem, increasing institutional
interventions.

The lack of training in this area compounds existing mental health problems. One woman described one of her therapists: "I had a very bad therapist. He just made me feel like a lot of things that happened to me were my fault. We were talking about the sexual abuse when I was a child." The presenting problem can be exacerbated or other symptoms may emerge, when the trauma is not taken into consideration.

Lack of cross-training. Similarly the lack of cross-training between mental health and substance abuse providers can have significant negative effects on women. Of the women, 44% reported some problem with lack of cross-training. Some women experienced multiple mental health and substance abuse treatment episodes without providers considering how substance abuse and mental health issues affect each other. This lack of knowledge can put service recipients at risk. One woman described a situation that illustrates the potential dangers when providers do not consider how substance abuse and mental health issues interrelate:

> He was actually the physician who would adjudge a person alcoholic or drug-addicted or whatever, . . . but he was really dangerous. He didn't have a freakin' clue, not a clue. He would give drunks barbiturates, so they could sleep at night. I mean, please. Some people died because of him.

Individual therapists' attitudes and behaviors. Therapists' interaction styles have a significant impact on whether treatment services are beneficial, detrimental, or have no impact. Of the women, 61% discussed harmful experiences with individual service providers. A level of acceptance and respect accompany helpful experiences. Conversely, women found that professionals who do not listen, tell them what to do or what is best for them, blame, dismiss their ideas, judge, or stigmatize are not helpful.

One woman illustrates this in describing her experiences with a former therapist, stating,

> I had a therapist who mocked me and made fun of me. . . . She was used to working with hardened drug addicts, I guess—this was the explanation as it was told to me—and was used to having that confrontational style. I guess it's a style to mock and belittle you. I was so suicidal after seeing her.

Many women are discouraged when they are not able to address the trauma and their feelings but forced into a therapeutic model in which the therapist determines what should be addressed, when, and how. Several women discussed the fact that certain settings, most notably psychiatric inpatient care and in psychiatric evaluations, will not allow women to discuss trauma experiences or topics that are emotionally charged. One woman recounted her experience, saying,

> When you are in [Inpatient], the only options you really have are what they give you. It's not help with what's going on, but dealing more with the medication and waiting until you're under control. [Inpatient] won't give you the option of dealing with the emotional stuff.

Similarly, overuse of medications and constant switching of medications exacerbates existing problems or contributes to new ones. This generally occurs in conjunction with service delivery in which women are rushed in and out of sessions and not given an opportunity to talk and be heard. Such treatment promotes the sense that service providers do not care and are not interested in helping, but are just doing a job.

Helpful Service Elements

Individual therapists' skills and relational styles. Therapeutic modality and content were rarely mentioned as important factors; however, interpersonal style and behavior was the focus of discussion for a majority of subjects. All of the women provided some insight into what helps them and identified several core characteristics of a good therapist. It is important that therapists demonstrate genuine caring, treat the woman as capable and intelligent, respect her ideas and choices, and interact in a respectful and courteous manner. Women stress the importance of providers affirming their ability to assess situations and make good decisions for themselves rather than having their choices dictated for them. This mutual trust helps the women help themselves. One woman explained,

> A good therapist can just open the door for you. She didn't tell me what to do. She just shared what she had done. I've had other epiphany experiences from when someone shared their own experience in a non-preachy way.

Another says, "A good therapist asks the right questions and doesn't tell you or judge you or give you ultimatums. It's really important to be supportive and believed and not questioned."

Open communication is an important aspect of this relationship in which the woman can present her knowledge and assessment of the situation. The provider either affirms the woman's view or offers another perspective and additional information while being respectful of the woman. In this way, the therapist provides her client with information and ultimately supports the woman's choice. Having a reliable, caring professional can result in a notably different experience than traditional therapy. One woman described the benefits of such an experience with a therapist, stating,

> Just knowing someone is there. Even though she has to play the role of therapist, there is that part of her, that universal part of her, that I feel

really cares about me. She has just been there for everything—dealing with me, staying up at night, calling me and making sure that things are going okay.

Availability and institutional responsiveness. Around-the-clock availability played a significant role in formal treatment relationships with 56% of the women discussing this to some extent. Women value the ability to contact someone when needed even if they never do. The crucial aspect is knowing that the support is "always there." Around-the-clock response also provides a sense of safety, as another woman described:

I think Crisis Services has been incredible for me since I've been here. When you're in a really bad place, when you're in the worst place you can be, they're right there. They'll even come and pick you up if you need to be picked up. So knowing that that safe place is there has been real helpful.

Similarly, women stated they need practical support from professionals to access services. This may mean finding ways to get around insurance limits or altering the fee structure to ensure that women can continue to receive services. Providing necessary follow-up care ensures continuity of care between settings and allows a woman to transition in a safe manner. One woman described this in saying, "For some reason the last [hospitalization] was all mapped out—the aftercare, the after discharge care. I think that was extremely important to keep in touch with the social worker."

The therapist is perceived as someone with whom the woman can connect and who genuinely cares, particularly when the therapist goes beyond the strictures of traditional service delivery. One woman noted, "I had a really good therapist, and she fought with insurance companies to get me more services because my situation was so stressful." Another added, "He volunteered, because I couldn't get DSS or anybody to help me. I really think that was a big boost that he took time without getting paid to help us." Both of these respondents believed that their therapists' willingness to extend themselves beyond their given role had a profound impact on their recovery. Women appear to feel that this reaffirms their worth.

Female therapists and women-only groups. Because of the nature of the violence girls and women experience (i.e., largely male perpetrators), many women must be in all-female environments to work on aspects of their trauma recovery. One half of the women discussed the value of female-only groups and female therapists. One woman clearly stated, "I think having all women support groups that are just totally run by women therapists is an absolute must for certain parts of the healing process." Many women share their adverse reactions to coed dialectical behavioral therapy (DBT) groups and their reluctance to attend mixed AA meetings. Two themes emerge relating to the need for women-only groups: (a) the groups increase participants' sense of safety and (b) women feel free to discuss issues related to their trauma within the groups.

Most of the interviewed women report experiences with male and female therapists. They had good and bad experiences with therapists of both genders. The women who had good, therapeutic relationships with male therapists often talk about their interior thoughts about working with a man, although this does not appear in their discussions of female therapists. In regard to experiences with male therapists some women acknowledged their trepidation, some reported having wonderful experiences, while some stated that they refused to continue in treatment. One woman described her thinking: "I had a lot of trouble with men. [But] his energy is soft. He's tall, and his energy is very soft, so I was okay with him."

Shared experience and empathy. Of primary significance is a nonjudgmental attitude that validates the woman's experiences and feelings. Almost 90% of the women highlighted the importance of common experiences and empathy. Women need to trust and feel comfortable in a therapeutic environment. For many women, this means talking to others who have had similar experiences and can empathize with them. Women value interactions with others who have had similar experiences. Peer supports, whether in groups or other settings, offer several benefits. The interactions demonstrate to women that they are not alone and that others have experienced similar traumatic events and responded in a like manner, behaviorally, emotionally, or both. For example, one woman stated,

> I can honestly tell you that since I've been going to the Survivor's Project and being in the trauma recovery empowerment group, I have definitely gotten stronger in who I am. For the first time I was validated. There were other people who understood that I had been hurt and worse, in pain, and that I get retriggered.

Ultimately, peer interactions help women connect to others and place their experiences in proper perspective. Mutual sharing is central to these interactions. Just as women find it helpful when someone listens to them, listening to others talk about their experiences aids in healing. This sharing accomplishes several things: It offers women ideas on how to deal with difficult situations and progress with their healing, and perspective on where they have been and what they can achieve. Seeing others who are not as far along in their recovery helps women see the progress they have made. Conversely, seeing what others have accomplished demonstrates that it is possible to heal and have a life that is not dictated by trauma, substance use, or mental health issues. Some women take peer relationships one step further by acting as role models. Role modeling provides an opportunity to help others and is an incentive to keep moving forward so as to not set a poor example. In addition, helping others can serve as a means of transforming the traumatic experience into something that benefits others, which helps women view their experiences in a more positive manner.

Women value common experiences within the professional realm as well. They feel that service providers who have experienced trauma or are in recovery have a greater understanding of the women's experiences, the difficulties that they face, and what helps. One woman stated,

> I've also appreciated a therapist's willingness to be there with me, kind of on the same level. The Survivor's Project has that to the extreme and that's unique and wonderful. Having the facilitators participate in the exercises right along with us is just wonderful.

Knowing that a provider shares this common experience generally strengthens the bond and sense of trust between them. It helps reduce the client therapist distinction, in turn fostering trust and a sense of safety.

DISCUSSION AND CONCLUSIONS

Women with histories of trauma and co-occurring disorders utilize a wide range of informal supports and formal treatment services in taking care of themselves and healing from trauma. Each woman's experiences are unique, as are her means of coping and recovering. Regardless of these differences, women identify several common features that they view as beneficial whether they use formal service providers or informal supports and peers. Relationships are key to women's recovery and healing. Women value individuals who listen without judging or blaming and who validate their experiences. Although service providers may serve this role, women feel that peers are crucial because of the empathy between them and ability to share stories, problems, and solutions with each other.

Women also seek out and desire activities that help them heal and recover as well as ones that provide for more complete and fulfilling lives. Activities serve multiple purposes. They may provide structure to the day by outlining what needs to be done, offer something to break up the routine or something to look forward to (i.e., a weekly support group), keep the woman busy, contribute to a sense of value (i.e., either paid or volunteer work), or offer a challenge or intellectual stimulation. Women vary in terms of the activities that they enjoy and seek out; regardless of which they choose, these activities help establish connections with others, provide personal satisfaction, and promote healing.

Women also use and value formal treatment services. It is important to understand that the criticisms the research participants voiced regarding treatment services were predominantly about barriers to services, such as cost, number of sessions and time limits, the lack of 24-hr responsiveness, and transportation and/or child care problems that limit the woman's ability to receive services. Women find individual practitioners and a variety of residential, inpatient and community-based services helpful. Harmful service elements are most often related to poor training and lack of therapeutic skills. If service providers wish to maximize the benefit to these women, the means of service delivery must reflect and be sensitive to women's experiences and needs. Outcomes for the women in their care may improve not by an increase in service delivery but via changes in how the providers interact with and treat the women in their care.

SOURCE: Vanja M. K. Stenius and Bonita M. Veysey. (2005). "It's the Little Things": Women, Trauma, and Strategies for Healing. *Journal of Interpersonal Violence, 20,* 1155-1174. © 2005 SAGE Publications.

NOTES

1. The FCWVP is funded by Substance Abuse and Mental Health Services Administration (SAMHSA) (Grant #93-230). It is part of the SAMHSA Women, Violence and Co-Occurring Disorders Study. The study was conducted in compliance with federal and Rutgers University human subjects protections (IRB# 01-166R). Please contact the authors for additional information.

2. Interviewers had either completed their doctoral degree or were near completion. One of the clinically trained interviewers was trained at the Center for Traumatic Stress.

REFERENCES

Alexander, M. J. (1996). Women with co-occurring addictive and mental disorders: An emerging profile of vulnerability. *American Journal of Orthopsychiatry, 66,* 61-70.

Alexander, M. J., & Muenzenmaier, K. (1998). Trauma, addiction and recovery: Addressing public health epidemics among women with severe mental illness. In B. Levin, A. Blanch, & A. Jennings (Eds.), *Women's mental health services: A public health perspective* (pp. 215-239). Thousand Oaks, CA: Sage.

Amaro, H., & Hardy-Fanta, C. (1995). Gender relations in addiction and recovery. *Journal of Psychoactive Drugs, 27*(4), 325-327.

Bassuk, E. L., Melnick, S., & Browne, A. (1998). Responding to the needs of low-income and homeless women who are survivors of family violence. *Journal of the American Medical Women's Association, 53,* 57-64.

Baxter, E., & Diehl, S. (1998). Emotional stages: Consumers and family members recovering from the trauma of mental illness. *Psychiatric Rehabilitation Journal, 2,* 349-355.

Blanch, A. K., & Levin, B. L. (1998). Organization and services delivery. In B. Levin, A. Blanch, & A. Jennings (Eds.), *Women's mental health services: A public health perspective* (pp. 518). Thousand Oaks, CA: Sage.

Browne, A., & Bassuk, S. (1997). Intimate violence in the lives of homeless and poor housed women: Prevalence and patterns in an ethnically diverse sample. *American Journal of Orthopsychiatry, 67,* 261-278.

Carmen, E. H., & Rieker, P. P. (1989). A psychosocial model of the victim-to-patient process: Implications for treatment. *Psychiatric Clinics of North America, 12,* 431-443.

Commonwealth Fund. (1997). *Facts on abuse and violence: The Commonwealth Fund Survey of the Health of Adolescent Girls.* New York: Louis Harris and Associates.

Commonwealth Fund. (1998). *Addressing domestic violence and its consequences: Policy report of the Commonwealth Fund Commission on Women's Health.* New York: Columbia University.

Dunn, J., Steginga, S. K., Occhipinti, S., & Wilson, K. (1999). Evaluation of a peer support program for women with breast cancer: Lessons for practitioners. *Journal of Community and Applied Social Psychology, 9*(1), 13-22.

Feldman, H. W., & Aldrich, M. R. (1990). The role of ethnography in substance abuse research and public policy: Historical precedent and future prospects. *National Institute on Drug Abuse Research Monograph Series, 98,* 12-30.

Felitti, V. J., Anda, R. F., & Nordenberg, D. (1998). Relationship of childhood abuse and household dysfunction to many of the leading causes of deaths in adults. *American Journal of Preventive Medicine, 14,* 245-258.

Glaser, B. G., & Strauss, A. L. (1967). *The discovery of grounded theory: Strategies for qualitative research.* Chicago: Aldine.

Green, B. L., Epstein, S. A., Krupnick, J. L., & Rowland, J. H. (1997). Trauma and medical illness: Assessing trauma-related disorders in medical settings. In J. P. Wilson & T. M. Keane (Eds.), *Assessing psychological trauma and PTSD* (pp. 160-191). New York: Guilford.

Gubrium, J. F., & Holstein, J. A. (1995). Biographical work and the new ethnography. In R. Josselson & A. Lieblich (Eds.), *Interpreting experience: The narrative study of lives* (pp. 45-57). Thousand Oaks, CA: Sage.

Hammersly, M., & Atkinson, P. (1997). *Ethnography: Principles in practice* (2nd ed.). New York: Routledge.

Harris, M. (1994). Modifications in service delivery and clinical treatment for women diagnosed with severe mental illness who are also the survivors of sexual abuse trauma. *Journal of Mental Health Administration, 21,* 397-406.

Harvey, M. (1996). An ecological view of psychological trauma and trauma recovery. *Journal of Traumatic Stress, 9,* 3-23.

Hedges, L. E. (2000). *Terrifying transferences: Aftershocks of childhood trauma.* Northvale, NJ: Jason Aronson.

Herman, J. L. (1992). *Trauma and recovery: The aftermath of violence—from domestic abuse to political terror.* New York: Basic Books.

Jennings, A. (1997). On being invisible in the mental health system. In B. Levin, A. Blanch, & A. Jennings (Eds.), *Women's mental health services: A public health perspective* (pp. 162-180). Thousand Oaks, CA: Sage.

Kalinowski, C., & Penney, D. (1998). Empowerment and women's mental health services. In B. Levin, A. Blanch, & A. Jennings (Eds.), *Women's mental health services: A public health perspective* (pp. 326-347). Thousand Oaks, CA: Sage.

Lipschitz, D. S., Kaplan, M. L., Sorkenn, J. B., Paedda, G. L., Chorney, P., & Asnis, G. M. (1996). Prevalence and characteristics of physical and sexual abuse among psychiatric outpatients. *Psychiatric Services, 47*(2), 189-191.

Maine Trauma Advisory Report Group. (1997). *In their own words: Trauma survivors and professionals they trust tell what hurts, what helps, and what is* needed for trauma services. Augusta, ME: Department of Mental Health, Mental Retardation and Substance Abuse Services.

Manley, J. O. (1999). Battered women and their children: A public policy response. *Affilia*, *14*(4), 439-459.

Miller, D. (1994). *Women who hurt themselves*. New York: Basic Books.

Miller, D. (1996). Challenging self-harm through transformations of the trauma story. *Sexual Addiction and Compulsivity*, *3*(3), 213-227.

Mowbray, C. T., Oysermann, D., Saunders, D., & Rueda-Riedle, A. (1998). Women with severe mental disorders: Issues and service needs. In B. Levin, A. Blanch, & A. Jennings (Eds.), *Women's mental health services: A public health perspective* (pp. 175-200). Thousand Oaks, CA: Sage.

Najavits, L. M., Weiss, R. D., & Liese, B. S. (1996). Group cognitive behavioral therapy for women with PTSD and substance abuse disorder. *Journal of Substance Abuse Treatment*, *13*(1), 13-22.

Prescott, L. (1998). *Women emerging in the wake of violence*. Culver City, CA: Prototypes Systems Change Center.

Ridgely, S., & van der Berg, P. (1997). *Women and coercion in mental health treatment: Commitment, involuntary medication, seclusion and restraint*. Tampa, FL: Louis de la Parte Mental Health Institute, Department of Mental Health Law and Policy.

Salasin, S. E., & Rich, R. F. (1993). Mental health policy for victims of violence: The case against women. In J. P. Wilson & B. Raphael (Eds.), *International handbook of traumatic stress syndromes* (pp. 947-955). New York: Plenum.

Spradley, J. P. (1979). *The ethnographic interview*. New York: Harcourt Brace Jovanovich College.

Strauss, A., & Corbin, J. (1990). *Basics of qualitative research: Grounded theory procedures and techniques*. Newbury Park, CA: Sage.

Talbot, N. L., Houghtalen, R. P., Cyrulik, S. B., Barkun, M. D., Duberstein, P. R., & Wynne, L. C. (1998). Women's safety in recovery: Group therapy for patients with a history of childhood sexual abuse. *Psychiatric Services*, *49*(2), 213-217.

van der Kolk, B. A. (1996a). The body keeps the score: Approaches to the psychobiology of posttraumatic stress disorder. In B. A. van der Kolk & A. C. McFarlan (Eds.), *Traumatic stress: The effects of overwhelming experience on mind, body and society* (pp. 303-327). New York: Guilford.

van der Kolk, B. A. (1996b). The complexity of adaptation to trauma: Self-regulation, stimulus discrimination, and characterological development. In B. A. van der Kolk & A. C. McFarlan (Eds.), *Traumatic stress: The effects of overwhelming experience on mind, body and society* (pp. 182-213). New York: Guilford.

Walker, E. A., Gelfand, A., Katon, W. J., Koss, M. P., Von Korff, M., Bernstein, D., et al. (1999). Adult health status of women with histories of childhood abuse and neglect. *American Journal of Medicine*, *107*, 332-339.

Zlotnick, C., Shea, M. T., Recupero, P., Bidadi, K., Pearlstein, T., & Brown, P. (1997). Trauma, dissociation, impulsivity, and self-mutilation among substance abuse patients. *Journal of Orthopsychiatry*, *67*(4), 650-654.

Vanja M. K. Stenius is a doctoral student at the Rutgers University School of Criminal Justice and works as a research associate at the Center for Justice and Mental Health Research at the School of Criminal Justice. Her research interests focus on sentencing policy and violence against women.

Bonita M. Veysey, Ph.D., is an assistant professor and the associate dean for the School of Criminal Justice at Rutgers University–Newark. She is also the director of the Center for Justice and Mental Health Research. Prior to her employment at Rutgers, she was a senior research associate at Policy Research Associates in Delmar, New York. During that time, she was the director of the Women's Program Core and the associate director of the National GAINS (Gathering information, Assessing what works, Interpreting/integrating the facts, Networking, Stimulating change) Center and the primary researcher in the area of mental health–criminal justice systems interactions. Her research to date has focused on behavioral health and justice issues, including police interactions with persons with mental illnesses, psychiatric practices in jails and prisons, diversion and treatment services for youth with behavioral health problems, and the effects of trauma. She consults with local adult and juvenile justice agencies to help them respond to the needs of women and youth with histories of physical and sexual abuse.

14

Family Therapy Research:
Implications for the Practicing Family Therapist

Marriage and Family Counseling

Ethics in Context

Stephen Southern

Robert L. Smith

Marvarene Oliver

Texas A&M University–Corpus Christi

Codes of ethics typically provide rules and guidelines for best practices in marriage and family counseling. An emerging model for ethical decision making emphasizes the ethics of virtues and aspirations. Exploring fundamental models of helping, as well as contemporary issues in community systems, affords context for examining the professional development of marriage and family counseling. Dialectical reasoning, professional discourse, and case study present means by which 21st-century marriage and family counselors can resolve ethical dilemmas.

Keywords: *ethics; values; virtue; vocation; helping*

Having a code of ethics and offering training in resolving ethical dilemmas are hallmarks of professionalism. Professional marriage and family counseling practice is guided by several relevant codes disseminated by the International Association of Marriage and Family Counselors (IAMFC, 2002), American Counseling Association (ACA, 1995), and the American Association for Marriage and Family Therapy (AAMFT, 2001). For some clinicians, other guidelines may apply, such as the Code of Ethics of the American Psychological Association (APA, 2002) or the code of the American Association of Sex Educators, Counselors and Therapists (AASECT, 1993). Generally, codes of ethics change over the years in response to social and professional trends.

Changes in codes of ethics reflect increasing knowledge and research evidence regarding best clinical practices. Changes are also dictated by technological advances (e.g., widespread application of computers for record keeping and professional communication). However, some changes appear to arise from liability or risk management: anticipating complaints, audits, and even litigation. As changes proliferate, the codes of ethics that apply to marriage and family counseling may be reduced to sets of specific rules or principles. Although one may argue that the ethics of principles or rules protect the public by imposing institutional constraints on professional behavior, some rules may constrain effective marriage and family counseling practice.

Marriage and family counseling has always been influenced by systems thinking and ecological approaches to defining problems and solutions. In recent years, the profession of marriage and family counseling has been affected by postmodern inquiry including constructivism and contextualism (Fergus & Reid, 2002; Steigerwald & Forrest, 2004; West, Bubenzer, & Bitter, 1998). One could argue that having an understanding of systemic dynamics and functions within various contexts is the cornerstone of marriage and family counseling. The marriage and family perspective, similar to the feminist model, profoundly affects most aspects of professional practice including client identification, problem formulation, diagnosis, informed consent, treatment planning, intervention, record keeping and release, evaluation, and follow-up. In addition, the marriage and family perspective influences the professional counselor role and function.

For example, professional role considerations regarding the exercise of power (e.g., expert, relational, coercion) would be quite relevant to the initiation of marriage and family counseling. Marriage and family counselors examine carefully the multicultural and situational contexts, as well as the problem-defining ecological factors, in determining how to join with a family to have beneficial influence. Depending on the clinician's personal practice theory, training, and values, the marriage and family counselor may choose to establish an egalitarian, hierarchical, or even "one-down" relationship. The existing IAMFC (2002) code emphasized the value of egalitarian relationships. Therefore, other approaches to intervention could be called into question if ethics were relegated to particular principles of practice.

An alternative approach to determining professional codes of conduct involves the ethics of virtue or character (Jordan & Meara, 1990; Pence, 2004, pp. 10-13). Virtue looks at the heart or intention of the professional, particularly in the role of public servant. From this perspective, a central consideration involves the implicit tension of either seeing oneself as an expert or as a community member (Sullivan, 2005, pp. 283-290). In this valuing approach, professional counselors balance achieving community recognition and respect with the duty of contributing something of value to others in society. With respect comes responsibility; with responsibility comes accountability; and with accountability comes liability. Liability is a concern, not *the* concern.

Contemporary trends in professionalism (Sullivan, 2005, pp. 35-98) confound the explication of ethical issues. Generally, there is increasing specialization, rapid expansion of the knowledge base, and technological developments. In health care, there are trends toward managed and mediated care, increased governmental regulation, and resulting limits to professional discretion. Add to this volatile mix expansion of litigation as well as scarcity and competition. Then it is easy to understand why codes of ethics turn to rules: to reduce fear and conflict.

Weber (1958) examined the Protestant ethic and the politics of capitalism. In the midst of collective conflicts of interest and competing definitions of the public good, the ethics of vocation point to the conscientious practice of one's profession. In the ethics of vocation, the professional experiences a calling to public service, having found one's place in life. This is a promising ethical perspective for professional marriage and family counseling. One's calling harkens back to the origins of the profession: helping families, promoting development, and alleviating suffering. The ethics of vocation enable marriage and family counselors to examine their roots while articulating some virtues and aspirational goals.

The struggle to pursue professional ethics reflects both rules and virtues. When one is called to be a professional helper, it is important to examine one's character and values. Then it is possible to express the conduct to which one aspires. Erosion of public confidence in the medical model as a standard for professional practice (Sullivan, 2005, pp. 55-60) actually provides opportunities to reexamine the professional bases and perspectives of marriage and family counseling.

MODELS OF HELPING

Brickman and colleagues described four general helping models that influence professional practice (Brickman, Rabinowitz, Coates, Cohn, & Kidder, 1982). These models form a foundation for understanding one's approach to marriage and family counseling. Brickman et al. (1982) described the models of helping based on combinations of attributions regarding blame and control. According to this approach, clients may be held responsible for their problems (i.e., blame), the solutions to problems (i.e., control), or both.

The classic model of helping is the medical model. In the medical model, the client is not responsible for problem or solution. Generally, external factors, such as a virus, are viewed as causes for disease states. Treatment by an expert, prototypically the physician, resolves or controls the disease state. This model emphasizes accurate diagnosis, expert treatment, technological advancement, and client compliance. There is a deterministic worldview in which the etiology and treatment of disease can be known by a well-informed expert. Psychiatry, especially with its current emphases on biological etiologies (i.e., brain science) and pharmacotherapy, is a good example of the medical model. Psychology, counseling, and other helping professions have based their professional development on the medical model.

The enlightenment model holds clients responsible for their problems but assigns responsibility for solutions to a higher authority (e.g., the "Higher Power" in Alcoholics Anonymous). Healing may be viewed as a lifelong process. Enlightenment consists in the awareness that one's thoughts and actions cause problematic behavior. Letting go of attempts at individual control reflects a solution. Helping interventions based on acceptance reflect the enlightenment perspective.

The compensatory model does not hold persons responsible for their problems. However, individuals, families, and communities are viewed as responsible for problem solving. Clients have the right to self-determination, and professional helpers are assigned roles as resource brokers and advocates. Social work and rehabilitation are good examples of the compensatory perspective.

The moral model combines responsibilities for problems and solutions, blame and control (Brickman et al., 1982). In Protestant fundamentalism, original sin is used as an explanatory construct, and salvation is the solution. Interventions involve enhancing motivation and strengthening right behavior. Guidelines for helping may be found in spiritual and authoritative texts. Christian counselors and marriage and family counselors working in religious settings may be influenced by the moral model.

There are advantages and disadvantages associated with each model. The moral model provides structure and leadership but can contribute to dependency and helplessness. The compensatory model emphasizes self-help and collaboration but can underestimate the influences of biological and social factors. The enlightenment model is solution focused but can produce true believers who are captivated by charismatic others. The medical model is scientific and technical but can reduce personal choices and the humanity of clients.

Marriage and family counselors operate from perspectives originating in each of the models. The moral model contributes motivation to problem solving. The compensatory model offers access to power. The enlightenment model produces discipline and compliance. The medical model affords the foundation for professionalism. Although professional marriage and family counseling incorporates aspects of all four models of helping, the medical model has been overemphasized in the efforts of the profession to gain respect and parity with other mental health disciplines. Our profession is chasing diseased dollars. In the process, marriage and family counseling imposes on the profession unnecessary and even iatrogenic practices such as diagnosis of an individual to receive third-party payments. There are significant ethical dilemmas to address as the profession withdraws from an incompatible medical model.

CONTEMPORARY ETHICAL QUESTIONS FOR MARRIAGE AND FAMILY COUNSELORS

As marriage and family counselors reexamine the fundamental bases of their vocation, diagnosis, an individual-oriented, medical-model practice, is an ethical issue. Other significant issues include client identification or determination and dual relationships.

In a two-part series on diagnosis in marriage and family counseling, published in *The Family Journal* (Crews & Hill, 2005; Hill & Crews, 2005), the authors addressed the clinical judgment and intention of professional counselors. In family counseling, if the family is conceptualized as having a problem, then how is one individual identified as the problem (Hill & Crews, 2005, p. 176)? Because third-party payers seldom reimburse for relational diagnoses (L. L. Christensen & Miller, 2001; Crews & Hill, 2005), diagnosing one person in family counseling may violate the systemic perspective. In addition, it places the professional counselor in an ethical double bind. How does a marriage and family counselor provide ethical, competent treatment while pursuing third-party reimbursement (Hill & Crews, 2005, p. 177)? Contemporary mental health reimbursement is tied to the medical model through diagnosis, using the *Diagnostic and Statistical Manual of Mental Disorders* (*DSM-IV-TR*; American Psychiatric Association, 2000), and managed care (J. A. Lazarus & Sharfstein, 2000, 2002; Welfel, 2001). Although there are crude indices of relational diagnoses in the *DSM-IV-TR*, as well as opportunities for sophisticated relational diagnostic systems (Ivey, Jankowski, & Scheel, 1999), the issue of diagnosis calls into question the training, perspective, and values of the marriage and family counselor. When one asks, "Who is the client?" (R. L. Smith, 1991), the essential underlying question is revealed: "What are the values and virtues of the marriage and family counselor?"

Another controversial issue in marriage and family counseling (if not all psychotherapy) is the matter of dual relationships. Although codes of ethics can and do specify the boundaries for therapeutic relationships and the risks of dual or multiple relationships, experienced and influential clinicians are questioning the rules, as well as underlying principles. Arnold Lazarus and colleagues set a firestorm of controversy by exploring how restrictive boundaries and ethics may diminish therapeutic effectiveness (T. M. Christensen, 2001; A. A. Lazarus, 1994a, 1996; A. A. Lazarus & Zur, 2003).

A. A. Lazarus (1994a) described the potential benefits of transcending traditional boundaries defining dual relationships. In a special issue of *Ethics and Behavior*, critics and supporters explored the clinical and ethical ramifications of Lazarus's arguments, especially his contention that boundary crossing for therapeutic reasons does not lead inevitably to boundary violation or sexual dual relationship (cf. Bennett, Bricklin, &

VandeCreek, 1994; Borys, 1994; L. S. Brown, 1994; Gabbard, 1994; Gottlieb, 1994; Gutheil, 1994). A. A. Lazarus (1994b), although acknowledging risks associated with boundary violations, countered critics by challenging an "illusion" (his term) of the therapist's power and the patient's fragility. Even within the basic framework of the medical model, Lazarus called into question the contemporary preoccupation with risk management. He concluded that dwelling on potential dangers and costs and attempting to follow fixed rules for clinical conduct is unsophisticated, unprofessional, and unethical (A. A. Lazarus, 1994b, 1996, 2002). Based on the outcomes of the debate over dual relationships, some professional psychologists recently integrated the rules and virtues approaches to ethics by offering some guidelines for those contemplating multiple relationships and extratherapeutic alliances (Younggren & Gottlieb, 2004).

Dual relationships and boundary issues have always presented dilemmas for marriage and family counselors. There are the fundamental ethical issues regarding how to deal with family member disclosures and secrets (cf. Fall & Lyons, 2003). Next come special considerations having to do with counselor or client characteristics as well as the setting in which professional services are rendered. Dual relationships predictably arise in professional practice in the following settings: military (Barnett & Yutrzenka, 2002), church (Llewellyn, 2002; J. A. Smith & A. H. Smith, 2001), rural community (Erickson, 2001; Weigel & Baker, 2002), client home (Cortes, 2004), and cyberspace (Jencius & Sager, 2001). Dual relationships may be indicated in professional counseling with college students (Harris, 2002), Latinos (Kertesz, 2002), and victims of violence (Walker, 2002).

Dual relationships may constitute a practice domain for marriage and family counselors. Family rituals reflect the cohesiveness of the system (Leon & Jacobvitz, 2003). Marriage and family counselors join with families to help. One of the consequences of joining the family system is to be invited to participate in meaningful family rituals, observances, and celebrations. Counselors who are helping families deal with death and grief may be asked to attend the funeral of a family member. A student who receives an award for achievement may choose to include the counselor in the event. Marriage and family counselors, especially those practicing in client homes and religious settings, could be expected to attend an important family ritual such as a wedding or baptism. Marriage and family counseling represents a nexus of important relationships, which can be facilitated and coordinated in the best interests of beneficial changes and outcomes. There may be risks associated with multiple relationships, including complaints from dissatisfied and disgruntled clients. However, there are potential benefits of expressing the counseling relationship outside the consulting room or coordinating the counseling role with other inevitable roles occurring naturally in the community.

Reflecting on the professional perspectives of marriage and family counseling helps in resolving ethical dilemmas arising in professional practice. The systemic and ecological views help counselors understand who the client is and where the counseling process can be facilitated effectively and ethically. The models of helping sharpen the awareness of the importance of counselor values and congruence. There is a dynamic interplay of the ethics of rules and the ethics of virtues. As marriage and family counseling moves away from the medical model toward novel and occasionally controversial positions, the codes of ethics afford some boundaries and guidelines. When the guidelines become overly prescriptive, rules or constraints on potentially effective practice, then the conflicts among the helping models and the ethical approaches demand attention.

Dialogue and self-disclosure are major means by which professionals can manage productively the conflicts that emerge among stakeholders (Cole, 1998; Pettifor, Sinclair, & Strong, 2005). Marriage and family counselors should embrace the ethical struggles elicited by questions and controversies. Otherwise, professionals retreat to the illusory comforts of codified rules and risk-management strategies. Marriage and family counseling in the 21st century will be fraught with conflicts and tensions that arise from the superordinate systems in which professionals operate.

CONTEMPORARY DIALECTICS IN COMMUNITY SYSTEMS

Heraclitus, the pre-Socratic philosopher, observed, "War is the father and king of all things" (cf. Kahn, 1979). He described how thoughts and actions rise and fall in contradiction until the cycles of change reveal an underlying unity. American citizens are struggling with conflicts in four community systems: politics, religion, health care, and technology. Tensions between polarized stakeholders in these systems or domains confront marriage and family counseling.

Ethics that address virtues and aspirations must arise from dialectical thinking. Otherwise, codes of ethics and the professional groups from which they arise will eventually fall prey to entropy and other closed-system characteristics. By embracing dialectical thinking and the passionate arguments of opposing parties, the profession of marriage and family counseling will remain open to new information and corrective experience.

Hegel provided the framework for dialectical reasoning (O'Neill, 1996). Dialectics include *thesis* (a cherished or conventional position), *antithesis* (an opposing, perhaps novel position), and *synthesis* (a meaningful integration of the two). Heraclitus discussed the fire-like nature of dialectics in which conflict emerged, views are consumed and extinguished, and the underlying unity of opposites appeared (Kahn, 1979). Similarly, Lao Tzu, the founder of Taoism, described in the *Tao Te Ching* (Lau, 1985) the contradictory nature of all things (e.g., yin/yang) and the means by which the wise individual comes to appreciate their essential unity. Rothenberg (1971) developed a creative problem-solving process, Janusian thinking, which incorporated dialectics.

Janus, the Roman god of gates and doors, affords an excellent perspective from which to resolve conflicts about professional positions and boundaries. Janus was depicted with two heads: one gazing on the past and one looking toward the future. He was worshipped at harvest time, birth, marriage, and other new beginnings. The gates of his temple were kept open in times of war so the god would be ready to intervene when necessary.

Rothenberg (1971) expanded on the concept of Janusian thinking, which he viewed as a key process in creativity. He recommended conceptualizing opposite viewpoints in a free response situation. By actively conceiving of the opposites, one cultivates tension or dissonance. There is movement toward a novel, even unusual synthesis that represents a potential resolution of the conflict.

Sternberg (2001) emphasized the importance of finding creative solutions to professional problems. He viewed creativity as a social context in concert with intelligence and wisdom. There exists a dialectical relationship among the three means of advancing knowledge. Intelligence is the thesis of the dialectic. Creativity is the antithesis. Wisdom shapes the old and new into a synthesis in which there can be both stability and change. Wise people balance intelligence and creativity. Perhaps a wise code of ethics would provide rules, principles, and guidelines (the structure of ethics) as well as virtues, aspirations, and risks (the process of ethics). Their admixture could produce innovative content for ethical marriage and family counseling in the 21st century.

Now it is time to address the contemporary dialectics in community systems. Some marriage and family counselors may fail to appreciate the relevance of community dialectics, claiming to not be political or religious. Most professional counselors will understand the relevance of changes in health care and technology because these domains form contexts for everyday practice. Every marriage and family counselor is affected by these systems because all professionals are afforded respect by the community and are held responsible for contributing valuable services as members of the community. In each of the systems, there are tensions between persons with polarized points of view as well as some typical issues that attract the fire of dialectical reasoning.

In politics, especially in the United States, there is the tension of social conservatism versus liberal pluralism. The last two presidential elections revealed the depths of the rifts that separate the citizens. Marriage and family counselors, like other mental health professionals, tend to be somewhat liberal. However, there are many counselors whose personal and professional experiences lead them toward conservative ideology. Underlying tensions can be quickly catalyzed by mentioning the controversial issues of gay marriage and class warfare.

In religion, there is tension between fundamentalism/orthodoxy versus revisionism/ecumenicalism. The popularity of both *The Passion of the Christ*

(Gibson, 2004) and *The Da Vinci Code* (D. Brown, 2003) exposed a split within the Christian church. Marriage and family counselors working in religious settings may experience directly the distress and upheaval associated with trying to be true to oneself and true to the institution. There are inflammatory issues related to abortion (e.g., right to life versus right to choose) and gender roles.

In health care, there is tension between biological reductionism versus nontraditional/alternative health practices. Governmental regulation and professional liability sensitized most health care providers to underlying conflicts. Familiar issues associated with the medical model, such as diagnosis and managed care, readily trigger debate. The recent controversy in *The Family Journal*, sparked by Glasser's (2004) contention that there is lack of evidence for the existence of brain pathology and widespread use of psychotropic medications, is a good example of a potentially productive dialectical process.

In technology, the last identified community system, there is a tension between technological advances and humanism. Computer technology now permits marriage and family counseling across great geographic distance. The traditional clinical concerns and values anchored in a consulting room are confronted dramatically by cybercounseling. There are basic ethical concerns with credentials and confidentiality that are confronted by the existence of cybercounseling. On the other hand, cybercounseling may redefine the therapeutic relationship. Technical advances in research (e.g., meta-analysis) provide direction for evidenced-based practice. In the future, the only accepted (and reimbursed) approach to the treatment of depression may be cognitive therapy or the combination of antidepressant medication and individual cognitive therapy. How will that affect clients and counselors who believe it is depressing to be separated from one's spouse?

Attending to dialectics in community systems fosters personal and professional development in marriage and family counselors. Professional counselors are influenced by community systems. They also have the responsibility to influence community systems of which they are a part. There are major tensions in politics, religion, health care, and technology that demand attention and invite debate. Involvement in the dialectical process can clarify professional practices and fundamental values. In turbulent times, it is helpful to have the structure of rules and conventions. Yet upheaval creates opportunities for the exercise of virtues and expression of aspirations consistent with one's calling to the vocation of marriage and family counseling. Explication of the following case demonstrates the dialectical process of ethical development in contemporary marriage and family counseling.

A CASE IN POINT

The following case explores several ethical issues arising in the context of community systems.

Michael and John, White men in their late 30s, were troubled when John was informed by a private agency that his request for adoption was being rejected. Because Michael and John were employed as professionals and enjoyed an affluent lifestyle, they were concerned about the basis for the agency's decision. Background investigations and a home study had been completed. Because they resided in a Southern state that had legislation pending to ban adoption by homosexuals, John and Michael were discrete about their relationship.

They lived together for 8 years as a committed couple. Last year, John and Michael took advantage of an opportunity to establish a civil marriage in another state, but the courts eventually overturned the union. They had been married in a religious service they shared with friends and family members. John, a sensitive, maternal person, had been talking for several years about adopting an infant. Michael supported John's efforts to arrange adoption. They looked forward to advancing the intimacy they enjoyed in a good relationship by expanding the family to include a child.

John was deeply saddened by the agency's decision. He began to have some sleep disturbance, lack of energy, tearfulness, and diminished sexual interest. Although there was no personal or family history of depression, he wondered whether he might be depressed. While they enjoyed a strong pair-bond, Michael and John began to argue over petty matters. Recently, after a long argument, Michael left in the middle of the night to stay with a friend.

John decided to seek counseling. A friend recommended that he see a well-respected licensed professional counselor who specialized in marriage and family counseling. In the intake interview, John described the recent events, including the failed adoption, sad and depressed mood, and increasing arguments with Michael. Throughout the initial evaluation, John emphasized the desire to stop arguing and strengthen the connection with Michael. He perceived that they were withdrawing from one another. He recalled how hard the coming-out process was for him given the fundamentalist religious background of his family of origin. Nevertheless, his parents and sister eventually accepted his lifestyle and relationship with Michael. John mentioned several times during the interviews with the counselor that he wondered whether his relationship might be fatally flawed as society would not accept his marriage and the agency likely rejected his application for adoption because of his sexual orientation.

The marriage and family counselor concluded from her initial interviews that John should be evaluated for depression and psychotropic medication by the psychiatrist with whom she shared an office. In addition, she shocked John when she questioned him about whether he had considered conversion therapy or sexual reorientation. During the initial visits, the counselor failed to inform John that she was an evangelical Christian. Privately, she believed that gay marriage threatened the institutions of marriage and the family. Because of some continuing education, she learned that gay individuals and couples were reported to be good parents and children raised by homosexual parents did well. However, she tacitly approved of the agency's decision to reject the adoption. The counselor told John that he should return for individual counseling after the consultation with the psychiatrist. There was no mention of couples counseling by this marriage and family counselor.

CASE ANALYSIS

Clearly, there are ethical and professional questions arising from this hypothetical case study. Given the counselor's heterosexist bias and religious fundamentalism, she was unable to hear John's concerns, resulting in potentially harmful and stigmatizing treatment recommendations. Her suggestion of conversion therapy indicated the severity of her biases and prejudices. Because conversion therapy lacks empirical support and appears to be an expression of homophobia and multicultural insensitivity (cf. Steigerwald & Janson, 2003), the counselor could be questioned for unethical conduct.

Perhaps the most revealing problem with her approach is the failure to maintain a systemic, relational perspective. She ignored the relational and cultural issues, choosing to pathologize John. In this case, she concluded that he was depressed, although his emotional state was consistent with the recent losses and stresses he experienced. She referred John to a psychiatrist—possibly because of financial motives since they share office space—applying the medical model rather than a potentially more helpful compensatory model. If she had more cultural sensitivity, she might have helped John explore at some point the precipitating issue of the failed adoption. Operating from the compensatory model, she may have discovered that there was a valid professional role of advocacy.

Assuming the mistaken marriage and family counselor could benefit from discourse regarding issues of gay clients, she could be helped by engaging in some vigorous exchanges with colleagues. Perhaps a wise colleague did call her and invited her to lunch. They talked about the situation and the colleague expressed concern about her narrow-minded approach. The marriage and family counselor perhaps redoubled her efforts to convince her peer that it is important to preserve the institutions of marriage and family. In this hypothetical case of consultation, the colleague asked the mistaken counselor to read *Gay Marriage* (Rauch, 2004), an outstanding defense of commitment in marriage based on the premise that gay marriage is good for all citizens. They discussed the ideas from the book as well as relevant cases. Eventually, they considered the promises and pitfalls of the medical and moral models in professional counseling. The marriage and family counselor decided that she would limit her work to heterosexual couples at this time. As the dialectics unfold and discussion continues, there will be opportunities for the marriage and family counselor to change her mind rather than her client's sexual orientation.

Case study, professional dialogue, and dialectical reasoning are useful means for helping marriage and family counselors return to fundamental values and perspectives of their vocational calling. To pursue aspirational ethics of virtues and character, professional counselors should review their practices as well as their models of helping. As marriage and family counselors explore new and potentially controversial models and methods, the ethics of rules and principles can guide them. Ethical marriage and family counselors will be respected by the communities they serve. Immersion in the dialectics of contemporary community systems may be helpful in preparing for ongoing professional development.

SOURCE: Stephen Southern, Robert L. Smith, and Marvarene Oliver. (2005). Marriage and Family Counseling: Ethics in Context. *The Family Journal: Counseling and Therapy for Couples and Families,* 13, 459-466. © 2005 SAGE Publications.

REFERENCES

American Association for Marriage and Family Therapy. (2001). *AAMFT code of ethics*. Washington, DC: Author.

American Association of Sex Educators, Counselors and Therapists. (1993). *Code of ethics*. Ashland, VA: Author.

American Counseling Association. (1995). *Code of ethics and standards of practice*. Alexandria, VA: Author.

American Psychiatric Association. (2000). *Diagnostic and statistical manual of mental disorders* (4th ed., text revision). Washington, DC: Author.

American Psychological Association. (2002). Ethical principles of psychologists and code of conduct. *American Psychologist, 57,* 1060-1073.

Barnett, J. E., & Yutrzenka, B. A. (2002). Nonsexual dual relationships in professional practice, with special applications to rural and military communities. In A. A. Lazarus & O. Zur (Eds.), *Dual relationships and psychotherapy* (pp. 273-286). New York: Springer.

Bennett, B. E., Bricklin, P. M., & VandeCreek, L. (1994). Response to Lazarus's "How certain boundaries and ethics diminish therapeutic effectiveness." *Ethics & Behavior, 4,* 263-266.

Borys, D. S. (1994). Maintaining therapeutic boundaries: The motive is therapeutic effectiveness, not defensive practice. *Ethics & Behavior, 4,* 267-273.

Brickman, P., Rabinowitz, V. C., Coates, D., Cohn, E., & Kidder, L. (1982). Models of helping and coping. *American Psychologist, 37,* 368-384.

Brown, D. (2003). *The Da Vinci code*. New York: Doubleday.

Brown, L. S. (1994). Concrete boundaries and the problem of literal-mindedness: A response to Lazarus. *Ethics & Behavior, 4,* 275-281.

Christensen, L. L., & Miller, R. B. (2001). Marriage and family therapists evaluate managed mental health care: A qualitative inquiry. *Journal of Marital and Family Therapy, 27,* 509-514.

Christensen, T. M. (2001). A bold perspective on counseling with couples and families: An interview with Arnold A. Lazarus. *The Family Journal: Counseling and Therapy for Couples and Families, 9,* 343-349.

Cole, E. (1998). Self-disclosure as an approach to teaching ethical decision making. *Women & Therapy, 21*, 31-39.

Cortes, L. (2004). Home-based family therapy: A misunderstanding of the role and a new challenge for therapists. *The Family Journal, 12*, 184-188.

Crews, J. A., & Hill, N. R. (2005). Diagnosis in marriage and family counseling: An ethical double bind. *The Family Journal, 13*, 63-66.

Erickson, S. H. (2001). Multiple relationships in rural counseling. *The Family Journal, 9*, 302-304.

Fall, K. A., & Lyons, C. (2003). Ethical considerations of family secret disclosure and post-session safety management. *The Family Journal, 11*, 281-285.

Fergus, K. D., & Reid, D. W. (2002). Integrating constructivist and systemic metatheory in family therapy. *Journal of Constructivist Psychology, 15*, 41-63.

Gabbard, G. O. (1994). Teetering on the precipice: A commentary on Lazarus's "How certain boundaries and ethics diminish therapeutic effectiveness." *Ethics & Behavior, 4*, 283-286.

Gibson, M. (Director). (2004). *The passion of the Christ* [Motion picture]. Los Angeles, CA: Fox Home Entertainment.

Glasser, W. (2004). A new vision for counseling. *The Family Journal, 12*, 339-341.

Gottlieb, M. C. (1994). Ethical decision making, boundaries, and treatment effectiveness: A reprise. *Ethics & Behavior, 4*, 287-293.

Gutheil, T. G. (1994). Discussion of Lazarus's "How certain boundaries and ethics diminish therapeutic effectiveness." *Ethics & Behavior, 4*, 295-298.

Harris, R. S. (2002). Dual relationships in university counseling center environments. In A. A. Lazarus & O. Zur (Eds.), *Dual relationships and psychotherapy* (pp. 337-347). New York: Springer.

Hill, N. R., & Crews, J. A. (2005). The application of an ethical lens to the issue of diagnosis in marriage and family counseling. *The Family Journal, 13*, 176-180.

International Association of Marriage and Family Counselors. (2002). *Ethical code for the International Association of Marriage and Family Counselors.* Retrieved May 5, 2004, from http://www.iamfc.com/ethical_codes.html

Ivey, D. C., Jankowski, P. J., & Scheel, M. J. (1999). Relational diagnosis: Potential advantages and drawbacks associated with a universal system for the classification of couple and family difficulties. *The Family Journal, 7*, 335-341.

Jencius, M., & Sager, D. E. (2001). The practice of marriage and family counseling in cyberspace. *The Family Journal, 9*, 295-301.

Jordan, A. E., & Meara, N. M. (1990). Ethics and the professional practice of psychologists: The role of virtues and principles. *Professional Psychology: Research and Practice, 21*, 107-114.

Kahn, C. H. (1979). *The art and thought of Heraclitus.* Cambridge, UK: Cambridge University Press.

Kertesz, R. (2002). Dual relationships in Latin America. In A. A. Lazarus & O. Zur (Eds.), *Dual relationships and psychotherapy* (pp. 329-334). New York: Springer.

Lau, D. C. (1985). *Tao te ching.* Oxford, UK: Penguin.

Lazarus, A. A. (1994a). How certain boundaries and ethics diminish therapeutic effectiveness. *Ethics & Behavior, 4*, 255-261.

Lazarus, A. A. (1994b). The illusion of the therapist's power and the patient's fragility: My rejoinder. *Ethics & Behavior, 4*, 299-306.

Lazarus, A. A. (1996). Fixed rules versus idiosyncratic needs. *Ethics & Behavior, 6*, 80-81.

Lazarus, A. A. (2002). How certain boundaries and ethics diminish therapeutic effectiveness. In A. A. Lazarus & O. Zur (Eds.), *Dual relationships and psychotherapy* (pp. 25-31). New York: Springer.

Lazarus, A. A., & Zur, O. (Eds.). (2003). *Dual relationships and psychotherapy.* New York: Springer.

Lazarus, J. A., & Sharfstein, S. S. (2000). Ethics in managed care. *Psychiatric Clinics in North America, 23,* 269-284.

Lazarus, J. A., & Sharfstein, S. S. (2002). Ethics in managed care. *Psychiatric Clinics in North America, 25,* 561-574.

Leon, K., & Jacobvitz, D. B. (2003). Relationships between adult attachment representations and family ritual quality: A prospective, longitudinal study. *Family Process, 42,* 419-432.

Llewellyn, R. (2002). Sanity and sanctity: The counselor and multiple relationships in the church. In A. A. Lazarus & O. Zur (Eds.), *Dual relationships and psychotherapy* (pp. 298-314). New York: Springer.

O'Neill, J. (Ed.). (1996). *Hegel's dialectic of desire and recognition: Text and commentary.* Albany: State University of New York Press.

Pence, G. E. (2004). *Classic cases in medical ethics: Accounts of cases that have shaped medical ethics, with philosophical, legal, and historical backgrounds* (4th ed.). New York: McGraw-Hill.

Pettifor, J. L., Sinclair, C., & Strong, T. (2005). The role of dialogue in defining ethical principles: The Canadian Code of Ethics for Psychologists. *Journal of Constructivist Psychology, 18,* 183-197.

Rauch, J. (2004). *Gay marriage: Why it is good for gays, good for straights, and good for America.* New York: Henry Holt.

Rothenberg, A. (1971). The process of Janusian thinking in creativity. *Archives of General Psychiatry, 24,* 195-205.

Smith, J. A., & Smith, A. H. (2001). Dual relationships and professional integrity: An ethical dilemma case of a family counselor as clergy. *The Family Journal, 9,* 438-443.

Smith, R. L. (1991). Ethical issues in marital and family therapy: Who is the client? *The Family Psychologist, 7,* 16.

Steigerwald, F., & Forrest, A. (2004). An examination of gender and ethics in family counseling: Part 2. A case study approach using a social constructivism model of ethical decision making. *The Family Journal, 12,* 278-281.

Steigerwald, F., & Janson, G. R. (2003). Conversion therapy: Ethical considerations in family counseling. *The Family Journal, 11,* 55-59.

Sternberg, R. J. (2001). What is the common thread of creativity? Its dialectical relation to intelligence and wisdom. *American Psychologist, 56,* 360-362.

Sullivan, W. M. (2005). *Work and integrity: The crisis and promise of professionalism in America* (2nd ed.). San Francisco: Jossey-Bass.

Walker, L. E. A. (2002). Feminist ethics, boundary crossings, dual relationships, and victims of violence. In A. A. Lazarus & O. Zur (Eds.), *Dual relationships and psychotherapy* (pp. 298-314). New York: Springer.

Weber, M. (1958). *The Protestant ethic and the spirit of capitalism.* New York: Scribner.

Weigel, D. J., & Baker, B. G. (2002). Unique issues in rural couple and family counseling. *The Family Journal, 10,* 61-69.

Welfel, E. R. (2001). Responsible interactions with managed care organizations. In E. R. Welfel & R. E. Ingersoll (Eds.), *The mental health desk reference* (pp. 496-502). Hoboken, NJ: John Wiley.

West, J. D., Bubenzer, D. L., & Bitter, J. R. (Eds.). (1998). *Social construction in couple and family counseling.* Alexandria, VA: American Counseling Association.

Younggren, J. N., & Gottlieb, M. C. (2004). Managing risk when contemplating multiple relationships. *Professional Psychology: Research and Practice, 35,* 255-260.

Stephen Southern, Ed.D., is an associate professor in the Department of Counseling and Educational Psychology at Texas A&M University–Corpus Christi. He is the chair of the International Association of Marriage and Family Counselors (IAMFC) Ethics Committee.

Robert L. Smith, Ph.D., is professor and chair of the Department of Counseling and Educational Psychology at Texas A&M University–Corpus Christi. He is the executive director of the IAMFC.

Marvarene Oliver, Ed.D., is an assistant professor in the Department of Counseling and Educational Psychology at Texas A&M University–Corpus Christi. She is the chair of the licensure board for the Texas State Board of Examiners for Marriage and Family Therapy.

About the Editors

Janice Matthews Rasheed is Professor of Social Work and the Director for the Institute for Advanced Innovative Practice, Research and Training at Loyola University Chicago's School of Social Work. Dr. Rasheed received her master's degree in social work from the University of Michigan, Ann Arbor, and her doctorate in social welfare from Columbia University in New York. She was the coprincipal investigator for a multiyear research grant funded by the John D. and Catherine T. MacArthur Foundation. She has published articles in many professional journals and is the author of chapters in books dealing with the subjects of research, program planning, African American family life, and family therapy. Dr. Rasheed published an entry on "Family Practice Interventions" in the *Encyclopedia of Social Work* (2008). She is the coauthor of two books: *Social Work Practice With African American Men: The Invisible Presence* (Sage, 1999) and *Family Therapy With Ethnic Minorities* (Sage, 2004). She has taught courses in family and couples therapy and cross-cultural practice, and research courses in the undergraduate, master's, and doctoral programs. Dr. Rasheed also conducts workshops and training in these areas of clinical practice. She is a licensed clinical social worker in Illinois and has maintained a private practice since 1979, specializing in couples and family therapy. She has served as an Approved Supervisor (in training) at the Northwestern Family Institute.

Mikal N. Rasheed is an Associate Professor and the Director of the Graduate Social Work Program at Chicago State University. He received his master's degree in social work from the University of Chicago School of Social Service Administration, and his PhD from Loyola University Chicago School of Social Work. He has published in the area of aging, and he published an entry on "Family Practice Intervention" in the *Encyclopedia of Social Work* (2008). He is the coauthor of two books: *Social Work Practice With African Men: The Invisible Presence* (Sage, 1999) and *Family Therapy With Ethnic Minorities* (Sage, 2004). He has taught courses in both graduate and undergraduate programs on men's issues in social work practice, cross-cultural practice, family and couples therapy, and ethics. Dr. Rasheed conducts workshops and training in the area of diversity and ethics. He is a licensed clinical social worker in Illinois and has maintained a private practice, in which he specializes in men's issues, practice with people of color, and couple and family therapy.

James A. Marley, PhD, is Associate Dean, Associate Professor, and Director of the PhD Program at Loyola University Chicago School of Social Work. He teaches courses on research ethics, professional ethics, and practice with people with serious mental illness. His research and writing focus on family therapy with people with severe mental illness, social work ethics, research ethics, the intersection of ethics with social work practice with people with severe mental illness, and the social-environmental influences on people with severe mental illness. He is the author of several articles related to his work with people with severe mental illness and a book on family therapy in the treatment of schizophrenia. He is currently editing a book on social work ethics and coauthoring a book on social work practice with people with severe mental illness. Dr. Marley is on the editorial board of *Clinical Social Work Journal,* a Fellow of the American Orthopsychiatric Association, a member of the Commission on Global Social Work Education for the Council on Social Work Education, and the Monitor for the National Association of Social Workers–Illinois Chapter Committee on Ethics. He frequently serves as an expert witness for the Department of Professional Regulation, Attorney General's Office, and private attorneys on cases related to social work ethics, social work malpractice and incompetence, assessment and diagnosis of mental health disorders, and wrongful death allegations. Dr. Marley received his BSW from the University of Illinois at Urbana-Champaign and his MSW and PhD from the University of Illinois at Chicago.